Metaphors of Mind

Metaphors of Mind

An Eighteenth-Century Dictionary

BRAD PASANEK

Johns Hopkins University Press *Baltimore*

Printed in the United States of America on acid-free paper
9 8 7 6 5 4 3 2 1

Johns Hopkins University Press
2715 North Charles Street
Baltimore, Maryland 21218-4363
www.press.jhu.edu

Library of Congress Cataloging-in-Publication Data

Pasanek, Brad, 1974– author.
Metaphors of mind : an eighteenth-century dictionary / Brad Pasanek.
pages cm
Includes bibliographical references and index.
ISBN 978-1-4214-1688-5 (hardcover : alk. paper)—
ISBN 978-1-4214-1689-2 (electronic)—ISBN 1-4214-1688-3
(hardcover : alk.paper)—ISBN1-4214-1689-1(electronic) 1. Metaphor—
History—18th century—Dictionaries. 2. English language—Terms and
phrases—Dictionaries. I. Title.
PE1689.P37 2015
423'.1—dc23 2014035088

A catalog record for this book is available from the British Library.

Special discounts are available for bulk purchases of this book. For more information, please contact Special Sales at 410-516-6936 or specialsales@press.jhu.edu.

Johns Hopkins University Press uses environmentally friendly book materials, including recycled text paper that is composed of at least 30 percent post-consumer waste, whenever possible.

For Megan

Contents

About This Book

THE FOLLOWING PAGES digest more than ten thousand metaphors of mind, the objects of inquiry, in a descriptive literary history. I have, in reading online, employed search technology to inspect eighteenth-century literature with an emphasis on word and trope. Conditioned by keyword searches and alphabetically ordered, my exposition configures data as a dictionary, winning interpretive insight from a mechanical method. Taking the form of an encyclopedic dictionary, this composition thematizes reading—the way we read now. As an experiment in criticism and commonplacing, the book reflects on the fate of scholarship in the age of Google Books, its pages giving shape to a database of metaphors, titled The Mind Is a Metaphor, in which the results of my reading are organized.[1] Online, the database makes my evidence available for my readers to search and sort; in this publication, the mobile metaphors report for roll call and are fixed in argument. To state these mutable relations of page and screen in epigram: this book is the text; the database, a new kind of paratext.

I have collected and categorized many more metaphors than I am able to treat here, which means this dictionary is unavoidably abridged, a part that signals a larger whole (the database), which is itself no more than a synecdoche for an indeterminately large archive of extant but unread and unrepresented texts that make up eighteenth-century literature as it survives online and in our libraries. In coming to terms with the past, the act of selection is perilous. There is too much to know. But a fragment may be complete in itself—like a life lived hitherto. So, restricted in scope, experimental in form, more than a few letters short of an alphabet, this bound volume is (nonetheless, in spite of everything) published and put forward as a companion to be referenced on new excursions into what Samuel Johnson describes in the preface to his *Dictionary* as the "boundless variety" or "boundless chaos" of language.[2]

The compendium is offered as an index of Enlightenment metaphors, a field guide to eighteenth-century figuration, and a manual of folk psychology. I assemble quotations under headings for my reader's convenience but also in order to arrange unexpected juxtapositions and reveal undercurrents in intellectual history. As an English professor, I devote specific attention to the publication of verse, fiction, and drama in the British Isles. In characterizing my subject matter, I take a hint from the philosopher Annette Baier, who nicknames David Hume's way with ideas "figurative empiricism," the sense of which phrase I extend to take in eighteenth-century metaphorical definitions of mind as a whole.[3] While writing this book, I compiled examples until the activity gave way to argument; and I have been brooding, almost from the start, on Pierre Bourdieu's assertion that "the mind is a metaphor of the world of objects which is itself but an endless circle of mutually reflecting metaphors."[4] The first part of that sentence I endorse (as metaphor), but the second I will put into question.

Given that metaphor asserts identity where there is difference (*A* is *B*), its study foregrounds the dialectics and binaries that figure importantly in the legacy of the so-called mind-body problem. On my reading, substance dualism, which dates in its modern form from Descartes, produces and is secured by what I will describe as a corresponding linguistic dualism. In a four-square fashion, dualisms of meaning (literal and figurative), and metaphysical dualisms (mind and matter) interrelate as a categorical complex. Because the metaphorical statements I collect conflate mind, body, and soul; sensation and reflection; ideas and ideology; matter and more, they are the *loci* of interest. They are the poetic assertions by which categories are instantiated and related. As literary study grounds the history of ideas in material culture, my metaphors are made to serve as indexes of thematic continuity and cultural change. Because I would display the comprehensive workings of analogies that structure conceptions of mind, matter, and meaning, cross-references among entries link and contrast metaphors typically treated in isolation in separate, specialized monographs.

My dictionary should appeal to readers interested in, variously, eighteenth-century British literature, the theory of metaphor, the history of ideas, cognitive linguistics, and the digital humanities. This preface sets the scene and issues an invitation to reading. The framing discussion in the introduction points up the eleven entries that check and challenge received ideas about the period; it also explains the methods enlisted in the compilation of these eighteenth-century metaphors for the mind. My conclusion yields theory and summarily argues that what the eighteenth century understood as "the general analogy of language" is fundamental to the history of the mind and an understanding of its metaphors.[5]

Readers eager to consult a specific entry will benefit from the following alphabetical précis. **Animals** taxonomizes beasts, birds, and insects, countering the maxim "no simile runs on all four legs" and preparing the way for a general classification of the species of figuration. **Coinage** assays eighteenth-century theories of imagination and topics in the New Economic Criticism. Examining conscience and judgment, **Court** speaks to law and literature. **Empire** dislocates center and periphery by reference to empiricism and philosophy of mind. **Fetters** narrates the ways in which the figure of the enslaved African complicates the figuration of slavery. **Impressions** considers sense data and innate ideas in the context of printing and the post. **Inhabitants** is occupied with personal identity and the personification of mental contents. Where **Metal** discovers iron and steel metaphors increasing as if in lockstep with early industrialization, **Mirror** reflects on M. H. Abrams's classic study of Romanticism and Richard Rorty's history of philosophy in light of the preceding entry. **Rooms** looks further into the metaphor of interiority. A final entry about **Writing** records the various uses and mentions of the blank slate, a metaphor associated with the philosophy of John Locke.

Acknowledgments

THIS BOOK HAS BEEN WRITTEN and rewritten over many years, and countless people have contributed to my efforts. "I've got debts," the poet says, "no honest man can pay."

Without a database, I could not have written this dictionary. So I will start with the librarians and technologists at Stanford University: Nicole Coleman, Matt Jockers, Jeremy Sabol, and Glen Worthey initiated me into the digital humanities and offered invaluable technical support when I needed it and had no way to command it. Casey Stark programmed for me at the University of Southern California. Bethany Nowviskie and Wayne Graham, at University of Virginia's Scholars' Lab, get credit for overseeing the effort that cast my metaphors online in their current form. Wayne, in particular, has been most charitable with his time and expertise. More recently I have received support from the Institute for Advanced Technology in the Humanities at the University of Virginia and must single out Worthy Martin and Douglas Ross for thanks.

The book's first readers were John Bender, Terry Castle, and Franco Moretti. I found in John Bender my coach: his way with me has been gruffly warm and relentlessly improving. Terry Castle is my spirit animal: I look for her to lead me through my most disoriented hermeneutic hallucinations. Franco Moretti's scholarship, like John Denham's Thames, is my great example and theme. I have tried to braid together formative experiences of Franco's historical methods, Brett Bourbon's analyses of literary language, and Jay Fliegelman's animating way with artifacts. In the weave is visible my *Bildung*.

At the University of Virginia I have found new mentors and coconspirators: most importantly John O'Brien, who has been for me a champion reader of drafts, a much-appreciated friend, and a model English professor. I am grateful also to Cindy Wall and Paul Hunter, Michael Suarez, David Vander Meulen, and David Whitesell, who have variously read pages, offered encouragement, and contributed insights. On multiple occasions the Davids (Whitesell and Vander Meulen) have pointed me in the right direction when I was lost in the archive. Colleagues in several periods and fields have generously read or helped me rework and reframe entries. I thank Steve Arata, Alison Booth, Rita Felski, Elizabeth Fowler, Susan Fraiman, Brie Gertler, Greg Goering, Paul Halliday, Matt Hedstrom, Walter Jost, Jerry McGann, Sophie Rosenfeld, Andy Stauffer, and Chip Tucker.

Friends new and old, near and far, have contributed helpful criticism and moral support: David Alvarez, Emily Anderson, Sarah Betzer, Danielle Bobker, Mrinalini Chakravorty, Jennifer Greeson, Jess Keiser, Aaron Kunin, James Kuzner, Crystal Lake, Tina Lupton, Laura Mandell, Felicia Martinez, Dave Moon, James Mulholland, Simone Polillo, D. Sculley, Miruna Stanica, Matt Thomas, Justin Tonra, Robin Valenza, Chad Wellmon, and Emily Wilkinson. In Sarah Tindal Kareem and Matthew Garrett I have found ideal, tireless readers and favored interlocutors. Matt's friendship and influence merits its own sentence, which I honor in an eighteenth-century narrative mode by writing it to *this* moment, Halloween morning. It's a proper day for acknowledgment because in the scrum of quotations and ventriloquizations, Matt's recommendations and responses are everywhere masking and guising dialogically.

I AM VERY GRATEFUL for opportunities to talk about the project at the University of Michigan, the University of Chicago, the Maryland Institute for Technology in the Humanities, and Wesleyan University. Research support has come from The University of Southern California, The Institute for the Future of the Book, and the University of Virginia. The benefactions of first Bob Stein and then Felicity Nussbaum kept me employed through the perilous period between graduate school and the tenure track. The librarians and staff of the British Library, the Folger Shakespeare Library, the William Andrews Clark Memorial Library, the Lewis Walpole Library, Honnold/Mudd Library Special Collections, and the University of Virginia's Albert and Shirley Small Special Collections Library have answered queries, photographed images, and helped me keep this largely digital project in touch with the printed page. Conversations with Jenny Davidson, Jonathan Kramnick, Jonathan Lamb, Felicity Nussbaum, Natalie Phillips, Sean Silver, Cliff Siskin, Blakey Vermeule, and Lisa Zunshine, have improved or refocused my drafts or spurred me on in ways that are hard to represent in the endnotes but must be acknowledged here. Teaching at the University of Virginia, I have been lucky to learn from thoughtful, impressive students: Laura All, James Ascher, Ileana Baird, Jenny Foy, and Allison Turner. Dorothy Couchman and Kelly Fleming get special notice for helping proof and correct this material. Anne Rowlenson worked closely and carefully with the manuscript for much of the summer before its submission for publication. Alexandra Grant kindly gave permission to adapt one of her *ut pictura poesis* drawings as cover art. It took the ingenuity of a poet, Alexa Selph, to index this indexical text.

Matthew McAdam and the staff at Johns Hopkins University Press have been wonderful to work with. My anonymous reader improved this book in every way, and George Roupe, who must be a principal in the Press's stable of "fixers," heroically copyedited a very woolly manuscript that was riddled with bibliographical inconsistencies. Both George and my reader have saved me from more gaffes and ill-formed references than I care to enumerate.

I am grateful to my parents for their encouragement. And I offer this book to Aunt Bev in lieu of the other one I promised her. I thank my brother for being there, ever since. Miles will, I hope, be delighted to find his name published here on this page, but Esmé is as yet too young for this line of acknowledgment to work upon her. With love, this book is dedicated to Megan.

Metaphors of Mind

Introduction
Changing the Metaphor

> It is astonishing what a different result one gets by changing the metaphor! Once call the brain an intellectual stomach, and one's ingenious conception of the classics and geometry as ploughs and harrows seems to settle nothing. But then, it is open to someone else to follow great authorities and call the mind a sheet of white paper or a mirror, in which case one's knowledge of the digestive process becomes quite irrelevant. It was doubtless an ingenious idea to call the camel the ship of the desert, but it would hardly lead one far in training that useful beast. O Aristotle! if you had the advantage of being "the freshest modern" instead of the greatest ancient, would you not have mingled your praise of metaphorical speech as a sign of high intelligence, with a lamentation that intelligence so rarely shows itself in speech without metaphor,—that we can so seldom declare what a thing is, except by saying it is something else?
>
> —George Eliot, *The Mill on the Floss*

THIS BOOK TAKES the genre of the philosophical dictionary and makes it new. It follows in form Pierre Bayle's *Historical and Critical Dictionary* or Voltaire's *Dictionnaire philosophique*, offering alphabetical order in lieu of narrative structure, mixing matters of fact and commentary. The arrangement of quotations under headwords, although of ancient custom, here exemplifies a method of research advanced by the use of keywords and search engines. I would make explicit what is by now a standard practice in the modern academy: searching and browsing online, reading in desultory fashion the page images and passages indexed and made available in large electronic text collections. By way of return and recurrence, the descriptive literary history pursued recasts our so-called digital humanities in the symbolic form, as it were, of the Enlightenment. By means of creative anachronism, I suppose my database a commonplace book and compose this monograph as a dictionary. To represent the past for my present reader, I have drawn thousands of metaphors of mind from collections of eighteenth-century literature; to register the contingency of such historical representation, eleven headwords disorder standard histories of the period. The main purpose of this dictionary is to challenge scholarly commonplaces by means of commonplacing, preparing the way for new studies of eighteenth-century writing.

I discuss the mirrors and white sheets of paper mentioned by George Eliot in this introduction's epigraph but also, and with contrasting emphases, animal spirits, milled coins, personified percepts, oak galls, and meat-roasting jacks. I make a determined effort to change the metaphors of mind we most readily associate with the eighteenth century by choosing new rubrics, multiplying examples, and comparing frequencies of usage. More than an exercise in quotation, these pages offer readings of literary works and confrontations with neoclassical and contemporary theories of metaphor. Throughout, attention has been paid to the historical, material context in which the metaphors occur. In writing about metaphor, I mingle praise with lamentation and take seriously Eliot's question: why can we so seldom say what a thing is, except by saying it is something else? *Metaphor* indicates a particular kind of problem, a problem particularly suited to the literary critic. Metaphors of the *mind* further specify a locus of concerns shared by critics, intellectual historians, and philosophers. As a critic, I have approached the concept of mind through literary analysis and intellectual history. As a student of the eighteenth century, I locate my investigations in a period, like our own, supremely interested in the mind and its metaphors.

The "astonishment" registered by Eliot's narrator is investigated at the scale of a century. What difference *does* it make when we change the metaphor? The question is not answerable in general terms but calls always for the multiplication of examples. Metaphors are routinely substituted, one for another, in disputation, with the rejection of one figure resulting in myriad new ones. When, in his *Journal of the Tour of the Western Hebrides*, James Boswell would compare different minds to different species of animals, Samuel Johnson, his fellow traveler, denies him the comparison, substituting more trenchantly mechanical metaphors instead: "One mind is a vice, and holds fast; there's a good memory. Another is a file; and he is a disputant, a controversialist. Another is a razor; and he is sarcastical." Later in the same conversation, when the vociferations of the Methodist evangelist George Whitefield are mentioned, Johnson is ready to extend and punctuate his comparison at a whack: Whitefield's is "a mind like a hammer."[1] This enumeration and changing of metaphors characterizes many eighteenth-century arguments, the dizziest passage I have encountered being a slapstick set piece from Tobias Smollett's *Adventures of an Atom*, in which a parade of twenty philosophers explain the nature of the soul collectively: "a sixth asserted it was composed of *fire*; a seventh opined it was formed of *water*; an eighth called it an *essence*; a ninth, an *idea*; a tenth stickled for *substance without extension*; an eleventh, for *extension without substance*; a twelfth cried it was an *accident*; a thirteenth called it a *reflecting mirrour*; a fourteenth, the *image reflected*; a fifteenth insisted upon its being a *tune*"—and so on, *et cetera*.[2]

With attention to such changing metaphorics, I survey the period. These entries took shape over ten years as I treated my subject in its particulars. I collected metaphors of mind while I read canonical titles, looked through more obscure works in archives, and searched online text collections. Because my study of eighteenth-century English literature took in a wide variety of printed and electronic texts—often both simultaneously—it entailed a style of extensive, discontinuous reading, which is signaled by my selection of headwords. Much of this reading, guided by keyword search, was self-conscious drudgery, almost algorithmic in its step-by-step consideration of examples. With hundreds of titles first glimpsed through a browser window, my encounters were defamiliarizing, the searches undertaken in order to find new paths through eighteenth-century literature and to define the state of the art as it might be practiced online. Though routinized, these researches were not automated and, had I world enough, and time, could have been done "by hand."[3] Whether a metaphor was discovered serendipitously with the turning of a page or turned up by more mechanical means online, the evaluation of each new passage for metaphor required of me, the constant reader, wit and judgment. Raymond Williams's *Keywords* begins with "AESTHETIC" and ends with "WORK," as if to signpost that the analysis of vocabularies—aesthetic work—involves equal parts critical taste and scholarly labor.

Metaphor is a trope of relation, and metaphors of mind figure the immaterial self in material terms: ideas are coins; the conscience, a court; the mind, a mirror; the seat of the soul in the brain, a throne. My research is abetted by the duality of metaphor, and my analysis redoubled by the import of mind-body dualism. A metaphorical sentence mixes two copresent, interacting vocabularies, giving us (as Samuel Johnson puts it) two ideas for one. Following Johnson, more recent theorists of metaphor distinguish *tenor* and *vehicle*, *frame* and *focus*, *source* and *target* in a metaphorical statement,[4] but I am wary of being too rigid in mapping the dualities of metaphor, if only because many if not most metaphors present us with more than two ideas and activate more than two conceptual domains. I read George Lakoff and Johnson (both Johnsons, Samuel and Mark) with interest, but as a literary critic, I look to the page and locate the doubleness of metaphor in an author's choice of words. In Roger M. White's supple account of metaphor's linguistic structure, to which I subscribe, a metaphorical sentence may be regarded as typically arising from the "conflation of two other, grammatically analogous, sentences."[5] This empirical emphasis on sentences purposely postpones a verdict on conceptual structures and deeper analogies. I will have more to say about White's ingenious account of metaphor and my own thinking about metaphor in what follows.

Keeping close to the keywords, I find metaphor's double-dealing syntax enables search: I pair terms (*brain* and *throne*), click through keyword-in-context search results, and collect evidence: Anne Killigrew describes how sickness "shakes the Throne of Sacred Wit, the Brain," and Matthew Prior personifies the mind as she "Sits Cock-horse on Her *Throne*, the Brain."[6] Given scope in my favored text collections (Chadwyck-Healey, Past Masters, Early English Books Online [EEBO], Eighteenth Century Collections Online [ECCO], and Google Books), a single proximity search will match hundreds or thousands of strings in which two terms appear.[7] I educe variants of what might be thought of as a single metaphor—*the brain is a throne*—to show that a metaphor does not determine the uses to which it is put. What a different result one may get—to speak with George Eliot again—even without changing the terms of a metaphor!

Metaphors of mind superimpose psychological and physical vocabularies, and so, in preparing this book, my searches collocated tens of thousands of keywords related to an entry's headword (*animal*, *cabinet*, *impression*, *mirror*, *tabula rasa*, etc.) proximate to a predetermined and invariant vocabulary for the mind-body (*mind*, *heart*, *soul*, *reason*, *passion*, *fancy*, *imagination*, *idea*, *thought*, *head*, *brain*, *breast*, and *bosom*). Why these and not other search terms? I have worked inductively: the second, set list of mind-body keywords was established in early reading and was used to locate the metaphorical terms in the first: I began with *mind*, *heart*, *soul*, and *brain* but soon added the other terms as I found them frequently recurring in metaphorical sentences. The decision to employ these thirteen terms and not a longer list—one that might include the less frequently occurring *understanding*, *spirit*, *nerves* (among other possible keywords)—is admittedly arbitrary, but my fixed list has been employed consistently so as to support generalizations about changing metaphorics. Sifting through long lists of figures of speech and false positives, I explored the language of the eighteenth century, becoming familiar with ordinary correlations and more surprising turns of phrase. The textures of my searches give form to the dictionary's content, and the quarrels between "close" or "distant" readers (discussed below) may even be mooted by the hundred-character spans or snippets I took as my first object of analysis: the *proximity* search provides a vantage on text that is neither near nor far.

Through keyword search I have built up an evidential base that is much larger than the compass of this book: searching for one metaphor, I would often find others. I might have written entries on fire metaphors or the stream of consciousness, but I have not. With regret, I did not complete entries on gardening, music, mechanisms, emotional weather, or the vehicles of thought. The dictionary threatens to expand in new editions, and the raw material for further analysis, as well as the material digested in these pages, is all available online for the interested student of metaphor to search, sort through, and recompose.

The main rubrics I came to work under are **Animals**, **Coinage**, **Court**, **Empire**, **Fetters**, **Impressions**, **Inhabitants**, **Metal**, **Mirror**, **Rooms**, and **Writing**. These categories map those constellations of metaphors that my readers will, I believe, find most interesting. *Pars pro toto*, the headings select and showcase a variety of metaphors, juxtaposing terms conventionally associated with the eighteenth century (for example, **Impressions** and **Mirror**) with more unexpected interactions of base and superstructure (literal and figurative slavery in **Fetters**, sensibility and the production of iron and steel in **Metal**). Because metaphors of "governmentality" (to borrow a portmanteau word from Michel Foucault) bulk large in the period, I devote a long entry to **Empire** metaphors. Organized by keywords and correlations, the mind's faculties are distributed throughout the book. The imagination is considered in **Coinage**; the conscience, in **Court**. Different entries develop different topics in the history of philosophy: personal identity is a problem for **Inhabitants**, while sense data are discussed under **Impressions**. By following cross-references, readers will find their way from their main interests to other entries, new interests.

In the history of modernity, the eighteenth century is a turning point, and its turnings will be taken here, almost literally, as *tropes*. But sorted by category and measured by frequency of occurrence in decade after decade, most of my metaphors do not obviously reflect the volatile history of the period. The centuries-long passage from ancient to modern is only curiously legible in pervasive neoclassical allusions that superimpose the past on the present in the period. The poetic diction characteristic of the eighteenth century—periphrastic, beholden to propriety or mock epic, a recycling of "What oft was *Thought*"—gives back the image of the mind as something familiar and thus obscures the revolutionary history of the moment.[8] Indeed, it is because this new scene of world history is presented in borrowed and time-honored language, that I investigate its conflations linguistically: tracking the traditional oppositions of ancient and modern but also its literal and figurative, material and intellectual dualities. Any metaphor of mind combines conceptual history (the mind) and material culture (the metaphor). In the eighteenth century a cultural inheritance is transferred, its values transvalued, by the workings of metaphor. The differentiation of literal and figurative is a fundamental element in what has been called "the great bifurcations" that give shape to the Enlightenment's "bipolar world."[9]

A case in a point will serve here to clarify the place of metaphor in history. In *An Essay Concerning Human Understanding*, John Locke, surely numbered among Eliot's "great authorities," calls the mind a sheet of paper: "Let us then suppose the Mind to be, as we say, white Paper" (II.i.2).[10] The supposition ranks among the best-known metaphors of mind and stands as an emblem for the Enlightenment project.[11] But the figure of the blank sheet of paper is only one among many available to readers of Locke, and Locke was hardly the first writer to use paper as a figure for the mind. What is more, the metaphor means, as I hope to show in these pages, not what we might expect. Even in situ it proves protean and provisional, as Locke mixes media and switches unsteadily between picturing a mind that is a space of storage and one that is a writing surface. Before the end of Locke's paragraph, the white paper is *furnished* (the mind, a room) with a *store* of ideas, which a *personified Fancy* (the faculty, an inhabitant) has *painted* on it, and mental observation is supposed a *fountain* (one of two fountains, in fact).

This last, the fountain, is a metaphor that M. H. Abrams claims in *The Mirror and the Lamp*, his magisterial study of Enlightenment and Romantic metaphorics, *opposes* Lockean metaphorics; that is, according to Abrams, the Lockean mind is paradigmatically a *passive* mirror or a sheet of paper, while the transcendentalism that stirs a hundred years on in Wordsworth and Coleridge is supposed to change the metaphor, remaking the Romantic mind, in contradistinction to its Enlightenment other, a lamp, a fountain, a plant, or a heterocosm (see **Mirror**).[12] But the opposition of paper to fountain, mirror to lamp, is undercut, even in paradigm instances; and as will be shown in the eleven entries below, many and manifold are the metaphors that structure eighteenth-century epistemology. I take aim at Abrams's argument without here challenging its main work with Romantic examples, instead putting its warrant—that changing metaphors of mind indicate other, broader cultural changes—sharply into question.[13]

Of course, standard readings of Locke have changed significantly since Abrams published his study in 1953, and much more has changed besides. Book history has new currency in the academy, while in publishing, the mass-culture present is understood as one of crisis—calamitously, so to say, *book-historical*. In the current moment, then, implications of Locke's metaphor, taken unmixed, newly vary as readerly attention shifts between textured paper and digital document—with associations of Locke's metaphor obscured or lost, even as others persist or are cast into high relief. Thus Alan Liu characterizes the open and exploratory, hypothesis-free, descriptive work carried out in the digital humanities as "tabula rasa interpretation" (although, in Liu's usage, Lockean connotations are so remote as to be practically absent).[14]

The medium matters, as does the moment. And so it was in the mangle of Locke's own early modern situation: the metaphor of the white sheet of paper, found in many writers before Locke, both replaced and reinforced the ancient metaphor of the scraped wax tablet (the tabula rasa). In the quarrel of the ancients and the moderns, Scholastic Aristotelians and Neoplatonists grappled with Cartesians and skeptics, and the struggle is visible in the competing, often overlapping metaphors drawn into the fray. Wax tablet, white paper—the metaphors, in specifying a medium, do not determine the meaning of inscription or impression. But historical foreshortening runs together Locke, his predecessors, his interlocutors, and his legacy, losing touch with the contemporary literary and intellectual entanglements, and with the material context. To make Locke's blank page stand for the eighteenth century is the clumsiest of reductions; it requires the razing of counterexamples and an invidious ranking of authorities, if not a misreading of Locke's prolifically metaphorical text.

In the final entry, headed **Writing**, this dictionary details the history of the blank slate metaphor as it is used by greater authorities and lesser alike, exploring the context of the hand-press period and the attendant culture of print publication. It is demonstrated that the metaphor of the blank slate is not reliably associated with Locke's philosophical project and will not reduce to a stable set of commonplaces (in this I follow and endorse William Walker's reading of the *Essay* in *Locke, Literary Criticism, and Philosophy*). Moreover, as the metaphor belongs to a contradictory set of contexts, it will not serve as an emblem of a monolithic eighteenth century. Nor will any single metaphor do. And so, in the ten entries that precede this concluding discussion, I show that a variety of metaphors of mind are as important as the tabula rasa in the history of eighteenth-century *mentalité*—if not more so.

In what follows I situate my method in the ongoing conversations about reading, metaphor, and mind. Under the rubric of reading, I look back to established scholarly models and think about what it means to read a dictionary. I introduce and defend *desultory reading*. Practiced by Grub Street hacks and perfected by the "rambling" and "idling" Samuel Johnson, it is the mode of reading of which I am "guilty."[15] I provide an account of my search protocols, further clarifying my principles of selection and contrasting the relative contributions of industry and chance. I describe in greater detail the composition of the database from out of which the entries are written, and I review the contents of the text collections from out of which that record of my reading was produced. Two sections introduce the reader to the theory of metaphor and spell out mind-body dualism's reliance on metaphor. An anatomy of the entries comes after these methodological discussions, circling back to the questions of "dictionary reading" with which I will now begin.

Dictionary Reading

My keyword-organized entries pay homage to Raymond Williams's ability to reveal social practices condensed in a single word.[16] His *Keywords: A Vocabulary of Culture and Society* is the master text providing the pattern for inquiries into clusters of words that carry us beyond definitions of their "proper" meaning. I look to Williams for an approach that unifies intellectual history and cultural studies: in figuring out the history of the mind, one continually encounters the keywords of a past culture and its allusions to contemporary politics. Class struggles are themselves recoded and internalized as psychomachia, and the eighteenth century is an especially auspicious period for analysis, as the earliest theoretical considerations of ideology (a keyword with an origin in the French Revolution) derived from its philosophy of mind.

While Williams may be numbered among the better-known readers of the dictionary (with Robert Browning, who read Johnson's *Dictionary*; William Empson, who read in the *New English Dictionary*; and, more recently, Ammon Shea, who read the *OED* through in a yearlong lexicographical stunt),[17] my earliest efforts were motivated by the program of dictionary reading that the philosopher J. L. Austin details in a methodological essay titled "A Plea for Excuses." Austin first urges us to read dictionaries from front to back, listing all the words that seem relevant to the conceptual problem or issue under consideration. Although he merrily reports, "This does not take as long as many would suppose," he allows there is another way, which is to start with "a widish selection of obviously relevant terms," consulting the dictionary under each, in order to turn up more terms "germane though not often synonymous." Looking up each of these, "bringing in more for our bag," "it will generally be found that the family circle begins to close" as the reader encounters repetitions.[18] The advantage, Austin reports, of this second approach is that evidence is grouped in convenient clusters.

Austin's dictionary reading operates at one remove from primary literature and is preparatory for further reading and research. Williams read the *OED*; Austin favored the *Little Oxford Dictionary*; I first took aim at Samuel Johnson's *Dictionary of the English Language*, the philosophic words of which W. K. Wimsatt describes as promoting "the metaphor between matter and spirit." Johnson himself hints in his preface that his arrangement of quotations in some entries might disclose a "genealogy of sentiments" or afford "a kind of intellectual history."[19] While consulting Johnson's *Dictionary* (and considering his lexicographical example: his garret reading, his marking of texts, and his employment of Scottish amanuenses who organized hundreds of slips of paper with words and quotations marked), I soon undertook a fuller-scale investigation of eighteenth-century literature.

After reading many works through and listing their metaphors in penciled endpaper indexes, I began searching online texts for more of the same, first focusing on occurrences of *mind*, *heart*, *soul*, and *brain* but soon bringing in other relevant terms. In a section that follows, this "transitory application" of keywords to books will be named and promoted as "desultory reading"—a variety of skipping and skimming associated with the dictionary—but one that takes a whole archive as its text. Sorting metaphors by family resemblance, I would often begin with a single keyword (say, tabula rasa) only to knock off with a more varied set (see, for example, the keywords listed in **Writing**). This dictionary of metaphors is, then, a writing out of my experience of reading at large in the manner Williams and Austin brought to bear upon their dictionaries—a style of reading that the eighteenth century recognized as desultory and the current moment understands as digital or "database" reading.[20] In composing a philosophical dictionary, one that dramatizes its relation to other reference works, I would emphasize the circle of hermeneutics. I take *dictionary* or *desultory* reading as both a means and an end. The work may be consulted or referenced, but it asks still more emphatically to be *read*.

Why read the dictionary? The late-Victorian scholar of the eighteenth century Austin Dobson, in a brief notice on "Dictionary Readers," confesses to sympathize with "the matter-of-fact matron who complained that, in dictionary reading, she found the story somewhat disconnected."[21] The joke centers in the phrase "dictionary reading," a curious practice: many read the dictionary, surely, but few read it through. But sustained through-reading of any book is, in general, less frequent and, in the long history of reading, less common than we might believe or admit. Certain book forms and literary periods—dictionaries, the eighteenth century—invite if not reward skipping and skimming. Samuel "Dictionary" Johnson, for one, tartly turned a question back against an interlocutor who asked if he had done more than look into a much-admired book: "No, Sir; do *you* read books *through*?"[22] Dictionaries as a genre and dictionary reading as a practice cast the question of thoroughgoing in sharpest relief; the dictionary form aspires to unabridged completeness, yet the ordinary use of lexicons is intermittent and incomplete.

The material digested in the following pages is won from reading dictionaries and anthologies, electronic texts, critical editions, rare books, archival manuscripts, articles, and scholarly monographs, from reading and keyword searching in succession, alternatingly—that is, alternately reading word by word painstakingly and hunting through a list of search results in a more desultory fashion. Austin's operations—clustering and classifying—are scholarly primitives that descend from Locke's infamous discussion of wit and judgment in the *Essay* (II.xi.2). Attention to nuances in usage is characteristic of literary critics and ordinary language philosophers, whose analytic methods insist on the close study of how (and when and where) a phrase is turned. In an inspiring case study of Johnson's *Dictionary* and Samuel Richardson's *Clarissa* as parallel texts, the eighteenth-century scholar Robin Valenza observes that, in this age of JSTOR, ECCO, and Google Books, the rhythm of research is more and more divided between modes of diligent reading and database searching.[23]

All good historical scholarship, undoubtedly, turns up family resemblances in alternating bouts of steady-on thorough reading and more discontinuous, transitory applications to archival materials, books and articles, and electronic sources. In the *London Review of Books*, Keith Thomas provides an account of his reading against the grain for incidental details. Excerpts are copied out on sheets of paper, which are cut into snippets and sorted into envelopes. His methods accumulate "a mass of casual and unpredictable references." When it is time to start writing, Thomas opens his voluminous files, tipping the contents of an envelope out onto his desktop. Shuffling his slips, he builds up a picture of a historical period.[24] The omnivorous approach is labeled the "Oxford method," in which a line of argument is contained and concealed within the many assembled references. In organizing snippets thematically, I would be recognized a probationer of the Oxford method if not an unconventional practitioner of scissors-and-paste history. Searchable full-text collections and keyboard commands (command+F, command+C) promote note taking at a new scale, and in a remarkable paragraph, Thomas surveys contemporary technology, admitting, "The sad truth is that much of what it has taken me a lifetime to build up by painful accumulation can now be achieved by a moderately diligent student in the course of a morning" (37).

Database Reading

An authority like Keith Thomas will turn over half the holdings of a library to make one book. In the present experiment, diligence has been exercised another way. My browsing has been done largely through a browser window. ProQuest's collections of eighteenth-century drama, prose, and poetry, currently mounted at Literature Online, or LION, include over twenty-five thousand texts by more than a thousand authors from the long eighteenth century (1660–1800) and were my favored quarry for quotation.[25] But because the earliest edition of LION's Chadwyck-Healey collections, in which my initial searches were conducted, did not include journalism, sermons, or many other nonfiction prose works, and because of the publisher's reliance on what is an increasingly outmoded bibliography in its initial selection of texts,[26] I have also searched competing electronic archives (EEBO and ECCO and the Text Creation Partnership [TCP] subset of titles drawn from them, Google Books, the Online Library of Liberty, and Past Masters) and, like Raymond Williams, have added texts by extramural sessions of "general and deliberate reading."[27] Also, because many full-text collections, like Chadwyck-Healey, mix and match early printings and posthumous editions, I have tried to record, or at the very least confirm, all my metaphors in their earliest available printed state. This has required the constant consultation of authoritative editions, heavy use of the online English Short Title Catalogue (ESTC), repeated searches in ECCO, and several trips to special-collections archives. Quotations in these pages, with some exceptions, are transcribed from the earliest published text available. I try always to mark an author's metaphor where it makes its debut. A different project might account for print runs, subsequent editions, collection, and quotation. Regrettably, such an ambitious bibliometric account is not feasible for me to undertake now, although I give some indication of what the multiplication of my metaphors (taking account of subsequent issues and editions) might look like in my entry on **Empire**.

A complete bibliography of the titles from which my metaphors are drawn is available online at metaphorized.net. A graphic representation of the select contents of the database from which this dictionary is written appears below. Each metaphorical sentence (which may contain multiple or mixed metaphors) is here counted only once and assigned to the decade in which it

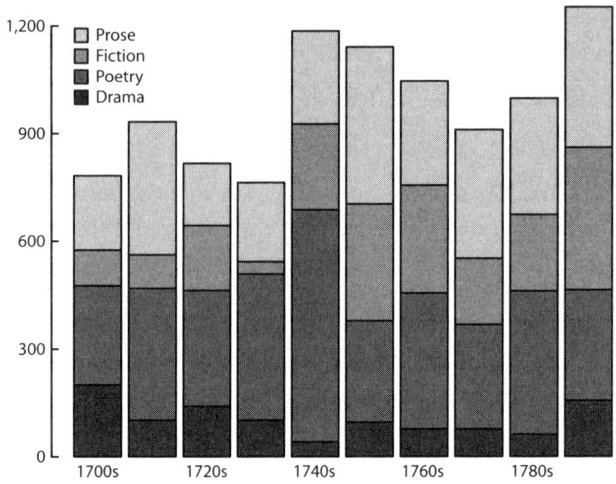

Count of metaphors collected.

first circulated. Metaphors in private letters are counted only if they were subsequently published and are dated to that printing. Again, successive editions in which an already tallied metaphor reappears are not counted a second or third time; neither are quotations of one author by another (although allusions and clever or malicious paraphrases of one author by another are cited). Important translations—Pope's translations of Homer and his Horatian imitations are paradigmatic examples—are treated as modern texts. Although I have collected thousands of metaphors from works published before and after the eighteenth century and find opportunities to quote several of them in these pages, the graphic is meant to picture the main corpus I am working from.

As shown in the graphic, the metaphors treated in these pages are drawn variously from drama, verse, fiction, and nonfiction prose. Although in a few cases I have transcribed directly from a printed or manuscript text encountered in an archive, most of my texts were selected because of their prior remediation. In order to speed collection, I worked largely from edited and encoded editions of eighteenth-century publications—whether keyed by typists or handled by anonymous workers and mechanically typed by algorithms. Even in the reading rooms of the British Library or the Folger, I am in the habit of opening up a surrogate witness in Google Books or ECCO. The distribution shown above may then say as much about the range of texts currently available online as it does about the discourse of the eighteenth century as such; that is, if nothing else, my keyword searches locate the edges of the frame through which we typically look out upon the "great unread."

Contemporary research pushes ahead. Peter de Bolla has recently published an innovative and ambitious conceptual history, titled *The Architecture of Concepts*, that exercises keyword search in ECCO in order to identify frequencies of word use in the discourse of human rights.[28] Meanwhile, a project like Visualizing English Print, 1470–1800, funded by the Mellon Foundation and based at the University of Wisconsin, seeks to survey the landscape of print culture on an entirely new scale.[29] Mine is a last-ditch John Henry effort; in the coming years new literary corpora and bespoke algorithms designed for text mining will give us new, truly panoramic views of the same period.

Departing from a limited list of canonical and recovered titles, it is hard to know how best to sample and normalize. In multiplying examples, I look for clusters and mark historical moments deserving further investigation. With a humanist audience in mind, I have kept statistical manipulations of these raw counts to a minimum. My reading and online searches, driven by keyword matching, resulted in a picture of print and a history of trope and genre that reproduce contours not too surprising: fiction rises and stalls, drama is censored after 1737, and a confluence of poets (Akenside, Thomson, and Young) contribute metaphorical masterworks at midcentury. I have not fixed my distribution by drawing from a set corpus built from an equivalent number of titles or pages for each decade. Rather, I have come at the archive the other way around and take desultory reading and keyword search as a kind of random sampling—although I recognize that no linguist or social scientist would be so sanguine in collecting and coding samples.

I focus on English-language works published in the British Isles but find occasion to mention Leibniz, Diderot, Kant, and other Continental metaphorists. I have searched, as best I was able, best-selling works in translation (translations and imitations of Horace and Juvenal, the *Arabian Nights' Entertainments*, Rousseau's *Julie*, Goethe's *Werther*, and more). I look backward to Shakespeare and Milton and forward to Keats and Austen but concentrate on original works authored and published between 1700 and 1799.[30] On average, I draw metaphors from 260 titles (poems, plays, periodical essays, fictions, sermons, and so on) from each decade of the eighteenth century. Although I have ranged more widely in my research, the analysis in these pages centers on the consideration of excerpts from 3,890 titles by 1,172 authors.[31] The steady through-reader advancing from **Animals** to **Writing**, may glimpse, in outline, a grand narrative of the Enlightenment—but he or she must find it still to be more than a little disconnected.

As yet, the available electronic archive of eighteenth-century literature remains haphazardly edited and its electronic texts, when searchable, riddled with error.[32] A researcher must guard against typos and variant spellings when searching in ProQuest's Literature Online. Optical character recognition (OCR) of the sort employed in Gale's ECCO and in the Google Books project routinely mistakes the long or medial *s* (the *ſ*) of eighteenth-century typography for an *f* and is baffled by early modern ligatures.[33] Improved text is coming: the Text Creation Partnership is transcribing hundreds of texts by hand, while initiatives overseen by Laura Mandell of 18thConnect have designed a custom OCR algorithm for the transcription of eighteenth-century texts and a tool for the crowd-sourced correction of mechanically typed text.[34] But I was impatient to press ahead. This book, authored in a moment of great change, has required the comparison and collation of texts from a variety of print and electronic sources. Which is to say, we may now begin constructing for ourselves a picture of great detail; future work with more reliable texts will help confirm or complicate it.[35]

Confronted with an uneven and treacherous online archive of remediated page images, dirty OCR, and imperfect transcriptions, I endorse keyword searching and desultory reading as a strategy for coping with the chaos. My dictionary will undoubtedly strike some matter-of-fact readers as evidence of disconnected reading as well as being, in fact, an apposite instance of and invitation to such reading. I know well that attention to keywords and commonplacing was characterized by Alexander Pope and his contemporaries as facile "Index-learning" and understand that the Scriblerian prejudice against textual scholarship and bookmaking abides.[36] Compilation, a fundamental early modern humanist activity, is near to ransacking with only satire—what Northrop Frye designated "anatomy"—or pastiche to be written beyond this farthest limit of scholarship.

I require an awareness of situational ironies: the epigraph from George Eliot is chosen not least of all for its allusion to "the freshest moderns," which is a quotation from *A Tale of a Tub*, Jonathan Swift's devastating satire of modern-day reading. Swift's Grub Street hack—a dunce, my double, my brother, his head empty but his commonplace book full—haunts the margins of these pages, one of the ghosts of scholarship past. But in underlining Enlightenment assumptions in my approach to eighteenth-century texts and declaring family resemblances, I hope to remain just this side of parody. I would that my encyclopedic descriptions prepare untimely readings useful for historicizing the present; I call upon the Smithfield muses and experiment with scholarly form because I would contrive new ideas of literary history.[37]

Desultory Reading

I introduce the Desultory Reader as an authentic eighteenth-century literary character and satiric type who makes a mock-heroic appearance in *Guardian* no. 60, contributing a fictitious and anonymous letter to the paper. He proves to be one of "a generality of Readers," among whom we must number Samuel Johnson in his father's bookshop and even Swift in the library of Sir William Temple at Moor Park, "who are pleased with wandring over a number of Books almost at the same instant."[38] The periodical essay opens in a paroxysm of contradictory commonplaces on reading before the Desultory Reader pens his miniature bildungsroman. The anonymous character locates his origins in dusting a relation's books as a young man. Obliged to take down every book, he decided to read something out of every one of them: "By frequent Exercise I became so great a Proficient in this transitory Application to Books, that I could hold open half a dozen small Authors in an Hand, grasping them with . . . dexterity . . . and feasting my curious Eye with all of them at the same Instant" (372). Sent to Oxford, the Reader progresses in his desultory practices, building his own collection, buying books by the pound, until "by frequent Conferences with an ingenious Joyner" he achieves a breakthrough, contriving "a Machine of orbicular Structure, that had its particular Receptions for a dozen Authors, and which, with the least touch of the Finger, would whirl round and present the Reader at once with a delicious View of its full Furniture. Thrice a Day did I change, not only the Books but the Languages, and had us'd my Eye to such a quick Succession of Objects, that in the most precipitate Twirl I could catch a Sentence out of each Author, as it passed fleeting by me" (373).

Like Samuel Johnson, the Reader is brought up foraging in a relative's books. And like Keith Thomas, the Reader browses the Bodleian (we discover here a possible ancestor of Thomas, or of Christopher Hill, and the origins, perhaps, of the Oxford method). Prefiguring a modern-day Internet browser, our Reader catches sentences in a contraption. He peruses unread Arabian manuscripts, and he constructs a pocket book, "each Leaf of which was a different Author," in order to gratify his "Errantry" in public places. Not until his formal education is finished does he read a complete work by a single author, settling on the Proverbs of Solomon, a miscellaneous tissue of verses that presents "as little Connexion as possible" (374).

The epigraph for *Guardian* no. 60 is taken from Pliny the Younger: *Nihil legebat quod non excerperet* (he read nothing that he did not make extracts from). Extracted from an epistle by Pliny the Younger that lists Pliny the Elder's various works and describes his uncle's working methods—waking in the night to study before the workday or lying out in the sun after a light lunch while a book was read to him "from which he made notes and extracts; he read nothing without making extracts from it" (*Epistles* 3.5)—the epigraph enacts the very process of extraction so described.[39] Both Plinys are decontextualized and reduced to a motto at the head of the paper.

Nihil legebat suggests that in making extracts our Reader reads nothing. In my own extracting of "linguistic and rhetorical" features and analysis of "small changes and slow processes," I follow the lead of Franco Moretti, whose methodology one critic labels—congenially enough—"formalism without close reading."[40] In polemical moments, Moretti seems to go farther: "We know how to read texts," he claims in the sentence most readily extracted from his descriptions of distant reading by readers piqued in new-critical consternation, "now let's learn how *not* to read them."[41] Many of Moretti's methods indeed approach, asymptotically, the zero degree of *nihil legebat*, and the literary critic Martin Mueller, with Moretti's provocations in mind, has even coined the gerund "not-reading" to describe reading at scale. How is it that an Annales school quantitative approach wins readings from literary history? How do we talk about books we have not read?

The archive is, in Margaret Cohen's memorable phrase, "the great unread." It is apt that we not-read as we come to terms with its scope.[42] My own exposition in these pages veers from distant reading to commonplacing to extreme close-up readings of individual metaphorical sentences. Metaphors retrieved from "unread" texts will illuminate a text read closely and through, and I read in these pages at a variety of scales, shifting figure and ground—taking figures as the ground against which new interpretive readings may be pursued. Much has been written recently about rival practices of extract making, intensive and extensive reading, close reading, symptomatic or suspicious reading, reparative reading, distant reading, slow reading, and surface reading. I do not see the various modes of reading as exclusive, and I hope that desultory, keyword-oriented dictionary reading will find its place among the expanding options so listed.[43]

In an exemplary essay on the extensive reading practices of the modern scholar (browsing, scanning, skimming), John Guillory observes that "scholarly books are pulled apart like the Sunday paper" and wonders if "the writing of scholarship might be retroengineered from the endpoint of [this] reading situation."[44] Sunday Styles readers may never consume the Business pages; some readers start with the Book Review, some with the Week in Review. Following Guillory's suggestion, I have engineered my dictionary to be read incompletely by a plurality of readers. For what does reading involve if not, as its Latin etymology (*legere*) emphasizes, observing, picking and choosing, selecting, collecting, and enumerating?[45] Over centuries, scholarly *reading* has narrowed to a specialized act of literary interpretation; the current proliferation of qualifying adjectives (*slow*, *suspicious*, *distant*, *surface*) may be symptomatic of a felt constriction.

Keyword searching and more advanced computational methods strain against the regime of immersive through-reading and return us to past reading practices, winning historical continuities by means of seeming anachronism. In an influential essay on books and scrolls that teases us out of present-day professional prejudices, the critic and book historian Peter Stallybrass argues that the codex, with its "capacity for random access," has long been available as a technology for achieving discontinuity.[46] And in a meditation published as part of a *PMLA* discussion of databases and archives, Stallybrass draws parallels between modern information technology and early modern note taking practices.[47]

My use of keywords and databases furthers the "athletic collation" that Michael Warner sees as required in analyses of contradiction, discrepancy, figurational pattern, redundancy, and digression, and I take hints from Margaret Cohen's recommendations concerning "reading for patterns" in the archive.[48] I find Stephen Ramsay's recently published vision of an algorithmic criticism salutary in that he understands computation as a method for enhancing, not replacing, the role of interpretation in textual analysis.[49] In a more recent monograph, Ted Underwood suggests that the introduction of computational and quantitative methods to literary history will open up "new ways of characterizing gradual change" that are not beholden to traditional taxonomies based on "authors, periods, and movements."[50]

What's old is new again. The computer, so often celebrated or reviled as a calculating, unliterary technology, returns us to literary studies past even as it renovates previous historical work. To investigate figures of speech is, of course, a long-standing rhetorical and philological enterprise that begins with the classical rhetoricians and results in the eighteenth-century rhetorical manuals of Hugh Blair and Lord Kames that collect and arrange metaphors and other tropes.[51] I summon Josephine Miles as a nearer, twentieth-century antecedent. Experimenting with the form of the monograph, I have relied on earlier and exemplary work with words. I reproduce strategies from William

Empson's *The Structure of Complex Words*, Raymond Williams's *Keywords*, and Foucault's *The Order of Things*, three texts kept ever ready to hand as models of ingenuity, engagement, and ambition. The philosopher J. L. Austin might have classed these varied efforts (although only half-seriously) as examples of "linguistic phenomenology."[52] In my own half-serious moments, I am prepared to admit connections between my research and Walter Shandy's *Tristrapaedia*.

My attempt to work at a new scale carries a principle of pastiche and the methods of montage into literary history.[53] It presents an extreme version of what Alan Liu, in a survey of new-historicist and microhistorical work, calls "detailism"—an approach that inclines toward quantity if not always achieving quantitative analysis.[54] In her introduction to Walter Benjamin's *Illuminations*, Hannah Arendt describes Benjamin's pride in arranging collections of quotations: a boasted collection of six hundred quotations "was not an accumulation of excerpts intended to facilitate the writing of the study but constituted the main work."[55] Quotations are not illustrations to be relegated to the notes but fragments rescued from their context and arranged anew according to the Will to Form expressed through a "citational poetics."[56] Accumulated examples become legible through literary montage: composition *is* explanation. This shoring of fragments against ruin belongs recognizably to eighteenth-century activities of translation and preservation, activities that are inherited and repeated in the twentieth and twenty-first centuries.[57] D'Alembert's *Avertissement* to the third volume of the *Encyclopédie* claims the work "is and should be for the most part an anthology of the best Authors [*un Ouvrage recueilli des meilleurs Auteurs*]. . . . Would that it were indeed but a collection of the best other books had to offer, with only quotation marks missing!"[58] D'Alembert and his colleagues collected only the best authors, but I am less picky. In these pages, the *best* that has been known and thought, jostles with the *rest* of what has been known and thought.

Words and Things, Metaphor and Meaning

This book defines itself as a dictionary, an alphabetical reference work and lexicographical undertaking.[59] Lexicography privileges description; and the dictionary form thematizes and celebrates *assembly*, a term of art increasingly associated with the descriptive practices of Bruno Latour and other theorists.[60] Because I am concerned with historical meanings, seventeenth- and eighteenth-century wordbooks—Samuel Johnson's *Dictionary of the English Language*, in particular—are referred to throughout these pages. I study the relation of metaphorical expressions to literal word senses. The interpretation of figurative language, in practice, turns repeatedly from words to things, from a review of intralinguistic "dictionary" knowledge to more "encyclopedic" considerations. Metaphors, in particular, involve ad hoc categorizations that direct attention from language to what language is about.[61] To misquote Locke (and Laurence Sterne), this collection of metaphors may be read as "a history-book of what passes for a man's mind."

As stated above, my dictionary claims affinity with Williams's effort in *Keywords* to limn a vocabulary but also seeks comparison with Pierre Bayle's and Voltaire's philosophical dictionaries, which are similarly driven by the description and critique of received ideas.[62] Philosophical dictionaries (like Bayle's) located critical commentary and argument under proper names, assigning errors biographically to their authors. I work analogously. Metaphor is associated, in the eighteenth century especially, with the improper use of a term. Johnson defines "METAPHOR" in his dictionary as "The application of a word to an use to which, in original import, it cannot be put." A poetic metaphor, in its marked departure from original import or first meaning, is a complexly thought thing, a tiny text to be interpreted, a vital expression that invites unlimited paraphrase.[63]

Many of the strongest metaphors are "category mistakes."[64] Error advertised as impropriety lurks in the naming of this *dictionary of metaphors*. Paul Ricoeur, among others, would seem to forbid my study at the outset: "The dictionary contains no metaphors: they exist only in discourse"; and the philosopher Max Black likewise explains, "There can be no rules for 'creatively' violating rules. And that is why there can be no *dictionary* (though there may be a thesaurus) of metaphors."[65] While traditional dictionaries mark only the most anemic metaphors among a headword's senses, I collect and analyze a range of figurative language juxtaposing vital and poetic figuration with more conventional metaphorics. Granted that the theory of metaphor belongs to pragmatics (and not semantics), changing figurative usage only becomes visible in the slow if relentless literalization of metaphorical statements by which a metaphorical use becomes established as a dictionary sense. It is the philosopher Hans Blumenberg who, in describing a "metaphorology" that operates at the boundary of semantics and conceptual history, gives a name to the systematic study of metaphors—I would encourage use of the term, only *metaphorology* is rather a mouthful.[66]

Metaphor, a trope of relation, connects two things, invites comparison between two or more domains, and mixes lexicons in order to achieve its effects. In his *Elements of Criticism* (1762), Lord Kames compactly defines metaphor as "figuring one thing to be another."[67] As noted above, Samuel Johnson maintained that the excellence of metaphorical expression is that "it gives two ideas for one."[68] In his 1936 lectures on *The Philosophy of Rhetoric*, I. A. Richards, with Johnson's remark and some of Kames's infelicities in mind, introduced the technical terms "tenor" and "vehicle"—terms that are refined by Max Black as "primary" and "secondary" subjects, which may be used to distinguish, at the sentence level, between a nonliteral "focus" and a literal "frame." In both Richards and Black, the tenor, or primary subject, is qualified by its vehicle, or secondary subject, as the two interact as a "double unit" (Richards) or an "implicative complex" (Black).[69] Richards's and Black's terminology is replaced by George Lakoff and his collaborators with a new distinction between "target" and "source" domains in a proudly self-promoting "contemporary" theory that promises to deliver new methodological clarity in its location of metaphor in the *conceptual* mappings that are supposed to underlie language and not—the contrast is sharply stated—in the *lexical* interanimations that interest Richards and Black.[70]

In the decades following the publication of Black's seminal essay, a contentious literature on the theory of metaphor appeared. Already in 1978, Wayne Booth projected—his is a stagflationary quip—that by 2039 there would be more students of metaphor than people.[71] A range of contradictory but influential accounts of metaphor are associated with work by Paul Henle, Jacques Derrida, Ted Cohen, Paul de Man, John Searle, Robert Fogelin, and other theorists cited throughout this text. My understanding of metaphor owes much to Donald Davidson's essay "What Metaphors Mean," in which the thesis that "metaphors mean what the words, in their most literal interpretation mean" is ingeniously defended.[72] Like Black or Ricoeur, Davidson locates metaphor in the domain of use and demands its effects be studied case by case. But Davidson challenges a tradition (one as old as Quintilian but preserved in Black and renewed in Fogelin) that appeals to "figurative meaning." Accounts of metaphorical meaning or figurative truth are not explanatory, argues Davidson, as they do little more than attempt to lodge a metaphor's effect *in* the metaphor. Davidson's negative argument is severe: "These ideas don't explain metaphor, metaphor explains them" (31).

Davidson's minimal way with metaphor is improved upon by Roger M. White.[73] Following Davidson, White describes metaphorical sentences as presenting a gestalt-switching double image or "duck-rabbit" in which we see one thing in terms of another.[74] But White neatly cashes out this phenomenon by means of linguistic analysis: a metaphor may be regarded as a conflation of two grammatically analogous sentences so that "He *bridles* his anger" (an example given in Samuel Johnson's definition of metaphor in the *Dictionary*) may be construed as conflating "He checks his anger" and "The rider bridles his horse."[75] White's treatment of complicated literary examples (many of which are drawn from Shakespeare) and his analytic emphasis on conjunction and shared vocabularies has come to shape importantly my own sense of how metaphor works.

Further reflections on the theory of metaphor are woven throughout the entries that follow, and my main statements on metaphor and mind are reviewed in conclusion. Here I introduce the notion of a "general Analogy of Language," to which I return in this book's conclusion. The phrase is borrowed from a central scene in the eighteenth-century philosopher George Berkeley's *Three Dialogues* in which Philonous, Berkeley's mouthpiece, is cornered by Hylas.[76] The two characters' names read almost as personifications of matter (*hyle*) and mind (*nous*), and Hylas charges Philonous, an idealist who denies the existence of material substances, with an abuse of language. He complains, "You cannot say, Objects are in your mind, as Books in your Study: or that Things are imprinted on it, as the Figure of a Seal upon Wax." Hylas, whose own insistence on a material substratum has been attacked as metaphorical, would trip up Philonous by highlighting his mental metaphorics. "In what Sense," Hylas implores, "are we to understand those Expressions?" (141).

Philonous sounds testy in his reply: "Look you, *Hylas*, when I speak of Objects as existing in the Mind or imprinted on the Senses; I would not be understood in the gross literal Sense, as when Bodies are said to exist in a place, or a Seal to make an Impression upon Wax." He excuses his own expressions as of a piece with "common Custom" and "the Rule of Language," explaining that his talk of impressions is "conformable to the general Analogy of Language," the "most part of the mental Operations being signified by words borrowed from sensible Things" (141–2). In so balking, Philonous's metaphors of mind seem ineliminable, or in Blumenberg's jargon, "absolute," unavailable for "translation into logicality." The empiricist gives sensation precedence over intellection: our ideas, derived from the world, make of the mind "a little world" governed by the general analogy of language. The inward is ordered in terms of the outward, and the mind must declare what it is by saying it is something else. Imagination preempts reason when the mind identifies itself in metaphor. As Annette Baier suggests, taking Hume as her case in point, the eighteenth-century way of ideas is in the grips of an indirect or figurative empiricism that requires the application of metaphors drawn from the sensuous impressions to describe the intellectual faculties of the mind.[77]

Paul de Man, in a famous essay on eighteenth-century metaphorics that proceeds from Locke to Kant (and that precedes Davidson's in the special issue of *Critical Inquiry* on metaphor published in 1978), pursues a deconstruction of the epistemology of metaphor that would trouble distinctions of literal and figurative, epistemology and aesthetics, history and rhetoric. Post-structuralist criticism, as exampled in de Man, traverses a two-dimensional discursive field structured by horizontal (syntagmatic) and vertical (paradigmatic) relations in order to disrupt the basic ordinal and organizing dichotomies. The total discursive structure—imagined as a kind of generalized analogy—is completely tropological, with its axes of contiguity (associated with metonymy) and substitution (associated with metaphor) readily reversed or inverted. So concepts originate as tropes, and truth is equated with metaphorical transfer; in language borrowed from Nietzsche, the truth is figured as "a mobile army of metaphors, metonyms, and anthropomorphisms—in short, a sum of human relations, which have been enhanced, transposed, and embellished poetically and rhetorically, and which after long use seem firm, canonical, and obligatory to a people."[78] The etymology of "metaphor" is insistently foregrounded in this tradition: *meta phorein*, to carry over, to translate.[79]

An earlier and related effort to read metaphor in the text of philosophy was undertaken in Jacques Derrida's "White Mythology," in which the understanding of metaphor as **Coinage** provides an outline of what Derrida calls the "problem" or paradox of metaphor: put reductively, that there is no properly philosophical, nonmetaphorical discourse within which the concept of metaphor might be analyzed without remainder. All definitions of metaphor cannot help but bring in metaphors for metaphor, or meta-metaphors, which cannot themselves be completely subordinated to philosophical analysis.[80]

No study of metaphor can simply ignore de Man's and Derrida's texts. Derrida's is especially pertinent in its criticism of historians who would taxonomize metaphors according to the ideas they express, while the conduct of metaphorology is subjected throughout "White Mythology" to what seems a bemused if wearying parody.[81] But I do not read post-structuralism here to reinscribe the problem of metaphor and render the question of "figurative meaning" undecidable. Working in the vein of Richard Rorty and other Anglo-American readers of Continental philosophy, I endeavor to write intellectual and literary history;[82] and I presume that, in reading for metaphor, to claim with Shelley, Nietzsche, and I. A. Richards that all language is vitally metaphorical amounts—perhaps surprisingly—to much the same as Davidson's prohibition of metaphorical meaning: past use necessarily informs present use without determining it. The analytic position can describe the poststructuralist one, and vice versa. Poststructuralist readings of metaphor will suit my purposes in moments in which I would effect a reorientation or gestalt switch, and in those passages my reader will find citations of deconstructive accounts of metaphor.

By choosing to concentrate on metaphors and not authors, texts, or a genre, I specify a unit of analysis favored by poststructuralist critics such as Geoffrey Hartman and de Man.[83] But in multiplying examples and focusing on small repeatable elements in literature ("devices, themes, tropes"), I show myself a student of Franco Moretti. Multiplied in my exposition and arrayed in tables, these aggregate particulars add up to something other than a reading of a text or its immediate context.[84] The metaphors treated in this compendium originated in the heyday of figurative empiricism in Great Britain, when the terms "soul" and "mind" might be used synonymously.[85] Studying dualities and metaphorical transfer by means of collocation, I stay close to the linguistic evidence and mark the difference when the metaphor is changed.

Metaphor is both deployed and understood pragmatically; it operates most powerfully at the edge of ordinary meaning: beyond alphabetization there is no a priori taxonomy for me to draw upon.[86] Metaphor marks where usual ways of making sense of sentences break down. The thousands of linguistic usages that I adduce as exemplary metaphors of mind will not be captured with a uniform theory, nor are they readily herded into entries in which their senses may be enumerated and exhausted. Indeed, it would be an abuse of the term to designate my examples all as "metaphor" except that, since Aristotle's *Poetics*, it has served as a master trope to indicate a motley collection that includes simile, metonymy, synecdoche, and allegory, all of which come in for comment in these pages.[87]

A Note on the Entries

Each entry poses my research question anew: what difference does it make when we change the metaphor? Provisional answers are offered in abecedarian order under my headwords along with a tangle of supporting claims concerning metaphor in history as well as further reflections on critical method. At the beginning of each entry, the reader will find a list of keywords, a count of metaphors, and a representative selection of quotations. Paragraphed exposition, organized in titled sections, follows this schematic apparatus. Here I provide a minimal rationale for the structure so outlined.

The headword and keywords that stand at the very top of each entry signal relations between word and concept, meaning and metaphor. The headword commands the cluster of keywords beneath it while providing a title to the surveyed pattern of interlocking senses and uses that follows. Each marks an entrance to eighteenth-century discourse: an entry. The terms are themselves a complex, a constellation pointed out among the great welkin of words. "You shall know a word," says the linguist J. R. Firth, "by the company it keeps."[88] A mental term collocates with a material one in a metaphorical statement, and my analysis explores such juxtapositions in their multiplicity. Such a cluster of words is, for Raymond Williams, a "felt structure." And Williams defines keywords as significant "binding" or "indicating" words "in certain activities and their interpretations" and "in certain forms of thought."[89] Keywords bind usage and meaning, indicating significant sites of social and intellectual interaction.

With Williams, I see keywords as binding the activity of individuals and indicating social forms, but my terms were also purposely exercised as *keywords* (literally, search terms) in online archives over a decade of proximity searching. The lists at the head of each entry memorialize these searches. Indicatively, my search terms helped me pick out metaphors of mind. As keywords, they reinforce the metaphorics of lexicography that gives form to this book. A dictionary's basic unit of analysis is lexical; a database likewise reduces discourse to an index of words, which is often termed in computer science its "dictionary."

If Williams's work with the *OED* in *Keywords* focuses almost exclusively on a *cultural semantics*, my interest in locating metaphor in primary sources requires attention to what the intellectual historian Martin Jay calls a *cultural pragmatics*.[90] The interpretation of metaphor demands attention to individual words as well as to the sentence, the compositional unit of meaning.[91] Finding a metaphor is not a matter merely of locating unusual collocations or of discovering the assignment of new senses to old terms: metaphor puts a word with an established sense to use. It requires the critic to read for an original meaning in its metaphorical setting (to hunt for a real toad in an imaginary garden).[92] It entails looking to the sentence on a first pass and then, in subsequent, deepening considerations, to those places in which that sentence can be located: the page, the more extensive scene of illocution, the historical moment of issue and its horizon. Many of my investigations come to figure context more paradoxically, seeking to sublime the logic of the literal by reading material objects—a chamber horse and a cockfighting chair in **Animals**, stamps in **Impressions**, iron gall ink in **Writing**—as if they too were metaphors.

In searching I have favored search terms that permit me to discuss both mind (and its faculties) and metaphor (and related tropes) under a single heading. I aim at substantive figures in which the mind, or one of its faculties, is made to materialize as a person, place, or thing. Some metaphors for the mind—for example, what cognitive linguists call conduit and container metaphors—are almost too prevalent to enumerate systematically by hand and were not collected in a uniform manner.[93] Other metaphors—the poet John Williams, writing as Anthony Pasquin, figures the mind as a snowball, rolling downhill through life, accumulating habits, till it reposes "at the base of the hill / A globular concrete of good and ill"—seem to appear only once or twice in the titles searched and were marked but discounted as figurative *hapax legomena*.[94] While the snowball metaphor stands as a fine emblem of my own accumulations, I could find no other place for it in this book but just here. Hundreds of other strong, poetic metaphors have been left behind to be rescued by browsers in my database.

Whereas my quotations favor poetic rather than conventional metaphor, the summaries that appear early in the body of the entries are intended to bring to attention the thousands of metaphors that could not be individually cited in these pages. Keen to follow keywords along historical trajectories, I chose search terms that guaranteed manageable yet meaningful collocations. A single proximity search might return less than ten or over one thousand results in the Chadwyck-Healey databases; I was pleased when at least one-third of these turned out to be metaphors. I aimed always to be thorough and found, after I began, that I might work through all the pairings of a single keyword with my thirteen-term fixed list in the range of full-text databases available through Stanford's Humanities Digital Information Services in a day or two before casting more widely (but less methodically) into the plenum of EEBO, ECCO, and Google. With the exception then of **Animal** and **Impression** metaphors, only those clusters I was able to collect with some exhaustiveness—exercising all the pairings in the Chadwyck Healey databases—were included in these pages.

In each entry I organize a complicated metaphorics under separate subheadings. Cross-references to an entry heading are indicated by **boldface type**; references to search terms are indicated by *italics*. At the risk of frustrating readers interested in straightforward storytelling, I use these subheadings to array clusters of metaphors and bring the uneven structure of a metaphoric field into view. Metaphors are not readily narrated, nor should they be: in classical and medieval canons of interpretation, *enarratio* typically involved the removing of metaphors and other figures (*tropoi*) from a narrative for systematic analysis. That said, where the counts and distributions signal that there is a story to tell (see especially **Empire**, **Fetters**, **Metal**, **Writing**), I tell it.

In **Empire** and **Metal**, the reader will find graphs of changing frequencies that illustrate claims about trending metaphorics: I see **Empire** metaphors as loosely correlated with British imperial fortunes, **Fetter** metaphors linked with the burgeoning of an abolitionist movement, and **Metal** metaphors increasing as if in lockstep with industrialization. (Additional graphs, corresponding to the other entries, are available at metaphorized.net.) In entries that do not make claims about large-scale semantic shifts, the exposition may appeal to a different sort of image: an illustration of a chamber horse in **Animals**; stamps and watermarks in **Coinage**, **Impressions**, and **Writing**; and a gestalt-switching puzzle picture in **Court**. These visualizations present both abstraction and phantasmagoria; my graphs and the other pictures are equally instruments of reading and new artifacts to be interpreted.

Refiguring the visualizations of digital humanities, one critic sees the stacked contours in Moretti's line-graph representations of genre history as the slopes of a (mathematically) sublime Alpine landscape.[95] My own graphs, meant to indicate objectivity and imply historical narrative, are likewise available for seeing-as. For example, they may recall the plot lines represented at the end of the sixth volume of Sterne's *Tristram Shandy*. Each plotted curve is testament to and record of my desultory path through eighteenth-century literature. The admitted weakness of my graphic visualizations is that, statistically, they are only as representative of the period as the texts and text collections I have worked with. I have exhausted only myself, not the archives. I offer pictures, not totalities.

My entries establish horizons against which much recent eighteenth-century criticism, reliant explicitly or not on search engines, has been written. As I have noted, the available eighteenth-century electronic archive is of uneven quality: clean text is hard to come by, and OCR engines are stymied by eighteenth-century typography. Worse yet, I worked on this project in a moment when the face of large-scale online text collections was continuously changing. Trends, where I have discovered them, may not generalize over larger eighteenth-century corpora. The graphs are therefore intended as summary and provocation but only receive sustained discussion in the text of the entry that follows when shifting frequencies are patent. Franco Moretti explains that the "great advantage" of abstract models is that they "renew and galvanize formal analysis."[96] My reader, provoked and galvanized, is desired to draw her own connections when entertaining the sinuous meaning of the curves and illustrations, and she is encouraged always to check statements made in these pages against the contents of the database. She is further encouraged to undertake new searches in the electronic archive.

A substantial number of citations are drawn from eighteenth-century dictionaries and wordbooks, including a 1706 edition of Edward Phillips's *New World of Words*, Nathan Bailey's 1730 *Dictionarium Britannicum*, and online and facsimile editions of Samuel Johnson's 1755 *Dictionary*.[97] Quotations from these and other unpaginated dictionaries are cited parenthetically using entry headings. Citations from philosophical works, such as John Locke's *Essay* and David Hume's *Treatise of Human Nature*, are often given by book, chapter, section, and paragraph, following the convention of a descending series of uppercase roman numerals, lowercase roman numerals, and Arabic numerals.[98] Periodical essays are referenced by issue number.[99] All other citations are collected in endnotes. In many paragraphs multiple citations have been combined in order to save space. The notes further compress bibliographic information for works published before 1800: I do not cite full titles, I compress information about publishers, and I do not record the place of publication if it is London.

The historian Perry Miller boasts in a foreword to *The New England Mind* that were he to supply a footnote for every direct quotation and indirect allusion in his monograph, he would "republish the complete bibliography of early New England," with additions and many times over. Because "the documentation would run to as many pages as the text," he consequently deposited bound volumes of his bibliography in Harvard College Library, thus shielding his more general readers from a colossal display of scholarly erudition and saving his university press the costs of preparing the supplement.[100] Because I make no such claims to exhaustiveness and, moreover, believe that my readers may well become more interested in my references than in my exposition of them, my primary evidence, the full set of metaphors of mind enumerated in these entries, is collected, along with thousands of others, in the searchable online database The Mind Is a Metaphor. Consider the complete bibliography so deposited, openly and online at http://metaphorized.net/.

1 Animals

Collocated Keywords: Animal, Beast, Bird, Cat, Dog, Fish, Horse, Insect, Monkey

Count of Metaphors in Database[1] (1700–1799): 454

He that hawks at larks and Sparrows, has no less Sport, though a much less considerable Quarry, than he that flies at nobler Game: And he is little acquainted with the Subject of this Treatise, the UNDERSTANDING, who does not know, that as it is the most elevated Faculty of the Soul, so it is employed with a greater, and more constant Delight than any of the other. Its searches after Truth, are a sort of Hawking and Hunting, wherein the very pursuit makes a great part of the Pleasure.

—John Locke, Epistle to the Reader, *Essay Concerning Human Understanding* (1690)

JOINER: Ha, ha, ha, he is shaken, my dear *Ringwood*; this Man of Depth and Inquiry; he is shaken; his Reason, like an ill-managed Horse, starts under him: What is this haughty Guide of imperious Man, this sufficient Word, *Wisdom*.

—Charles Johnson, *The Female Fortune Teller* (1726)

How, like a Worm, was I wrapt round and round
In silken thought, which reptile Fancy spun.

—Edward Young, *Night Thoughts* (1742)

When Lady *Dellwyn* finished the new furnishing her Castle, she began to be at a great Loss for Employment; she had now no Refuge from a languid, wearisome Melancholy, which is often called a Fever upon the Spirits; she had no Food from outward Objects, to employ her animal Spirits, and they therefore prey'd at home; and oppressed her own Mind.

—Sarah Fielding, *The History of the Countess of Dellwyn* (1759)

> As the bee extracts from such flowers as can supply them, the juices which are proper to be converted into honey, without losing its labour in sipping those juices which would be pernicious, or in examining those vegetables which are useless; so true genius discovers at once the ideas which are conducive to its purpose, without at all thinking of such as are unnecessary or would obstruct it.
>
> —Alexander Gerard, *An Essay on Genius* (1774)

See also **Inhabitants**

INTERESTED IN THE myriad species of figuration, I have cast my own project as a taxonomic one. Where the Linnaean taxonomist applies binomial nomenclature, a dictionary maker must arrange his or her materials according to different principles. I begin with **Animals** for alphabetical reasons (*animal*, *beast*, *creature*) and for thematic reasons besides. The two may also cooperate: an alphabetical structure provides special opportunities to redraw fundamental categorical boundaries: in illustrating the definition of the headword "METAPHOR," Johnson gives the example "He *bridles* his anger" (an example I have already cited in my introduction).[2] And at century's end Erasmus Darwin, following Hume, locates the faculty of reason under the general term "instinct."[3] Animals themselves may be ranged under headings: beast, bird, and fish; quadruped and biped; feathered or furry—the tame, the frenzied, the embalmed, the innumerables of the deep sea, those that belong to the emperor, those drawn with a fine camel-hair brush, and those that from a long way off look like flies.[4] A list both ranks and levels living creatures, as in one of Pope's better-known lines from *The Rape of the Lock*: "Men, Monkies, Lap-dogs, Parrots, perish all!"[5]

The list of search terms ranged at the head of this entry, though it includes Pope's mortal monkeys, dogs, and birds, is, like all such lists in this dictionary, necessarily incomplete. I did not and could not conduct exhaustive keyword searches online in Chadwyck-Healey's text collections (let alone in ECCO and Google Books) for every animal known to eighteenth-century natural historians: the fauna are too various; unenumerated are the innumerables. Here, as elsewhere in this book, I deliver literary history (necessarily) by means of sampling. The browsing methods employed for this entry in particular involve hunting and pecking, or, in Locke's language, "hunting and hawking." Many of the beasts were encountered in jungles of discourse in keyword searches for other metaphors or in volumes in archives and libraries. The menagerie of metaphors is surprisingly various in spite of its haphazard manner of collection, and while certain animals predominate, many are the species that are good to think on.

In this entry I explore tensions in ranking and leveling and would balance an older (early modern, humanist) tradition rooted in rhetoric with an emergent structuralist mandate to arrange and hierarchize—the latter, "Enlightenment" impulse best represented in an eighteenth-century project like Linnaeus's *Systema Naturae* (first edition published in 1735). A swarm of examples is indicated. Because the self is pictured as an ark or a zoo, any animal might come in for close treatment. And metaphorized animals abound—furry fables and feathered object lessons. In eighteenth-century literature I have discovered metaphors for the mind both wild and domestic: birds, bulls, fish, horses, monkeys, serpents, and dogs; lions and tigers; bats, bees, butterflies, spiders, and insects; harts, sheep, tortoises, oxen, pigs, cockles and oysters, wolves, and serpents.

More searching would undoubtedly uncover new animals, but their arrangement tests already my ability to rank and level. In the following pages I depart from questions of difference and identity, insisting that animal metaphors complicate easy "Cartesian" distinctions between mind and matter, as animals are used to metaphorize the mind as well as the body. Thinking is an animal activity; the faculties are one and all pictured with animals. After first making general remarks about the *anima* and animal spirits, I investigate a selection of animals high and low, reading birds as a major metaphor and moles as a minor one. I am interested also in animal behaviors and focus on horse-and-rider metaphors that hybridize the human, taking John Wesley's riding and reading as an illustration of a materialized metaphorics. In closing, I point once more out into the wilds of figuration.

The propinquity of man and beast in the Great Chain of Being was widely recognized in the long eighteenth century, but the far-reaching implications of consanguinity (biological, moral, theological implications) were slower to dawn.[6] By the end of century, radical vegetarians promoted animals' rights, even as Mary Wollstonecraft, in her *Vindication of the Rights of Woman*, bitterly wondered how "the dignity of the female soul [could] be as disputable as that of animals."[7] As Enlightenment forwards "the proper study of Mankind," culture cannot help but cull its figures from nature. The metaphors, similes, and analogies collected under this heading repeatedly contradict Dr. John Gregory—an author Wollstonecraft read carefully and critically—who lamented around midcentury that "Man has been usually considered as a Being that had no analogy to the rest of the Animal Creation."[8]

The "whole Hecatombs almost of all Animals" dissected in Thomas Willis's Oxford laboratory; the period's fascination with wild boys and "Orang-Outangs," with learned pigs and *singerie*; the translations of Aesop and composition of original fables; and a new moral (and financial) investment in the breeding and care of pets indicate that animals had become more than just ontological neighbors on the Chain of Being.[9] Indeed, in Locke's "Epistle to the Reader," quoted as an epigraph to this entry, the quarry and hunter prove one and the same.[10] Humans use animals as metaphors for other humans; metaphors make the human over as animal. Man is a beast: that is, literally animal, figuratively wild. Such statements made literally or figuratively determine the status of human resemblance to and identity with the other animals. But the sense of any such statement of identity is itself historically conditioned. Man is a wolf to man, suggests Plautus; man to man is an arrant wolf, agrees Thomas Hobbes.[11] Metaphors live and die in usage. Literary history narrates their movements, and their forms are subject to taxonomy.

Man or Beast, Duck and Rabbit

"Rational animal" is Aristotle's famous definition of man, but the adjectives "rational" and "animal" are consistently treated as antonyms in the seventeenth century and after—with rule-proving exceptions conveniently collected in Pierre Bayle's influential article "Rorarius" from his *Dictionnaire historique et critique*. "Beast" may denominate all living beings and, in its earliest usage, includes man. The "beast within" is an old metaphor, "an irrational prejudice built in to the structure of European rationalism."[12] By the eighteenth century, "beast" was often the name of a genus or order separate from fish, bird, or insect. The term belongs to an etymological gyre turning through centuries of language: the *OED* records "beast" replacing the Latin word "*animal*" which was, in turn, replaced by the English word "animal." *Anima*, the Latin root, is translated as "soul," while *animus* is often translated as "mind."[13] The complicated etymology underscores the ambiguous status of beasts in the metaphorics of mind, and the *OED* shows the adjectival use of "animal" mixed up with the attributive uses of the noun, with the medieval usage of "*animalis*" varying from "bestial" to "spiritual."

The efforts of eighteenth-century natural historians to compare and distinguish species on the basis of analogy troubled traditional distinctions between man and animal and consequently the efforts of natural philosophers and poets to mark a position on the Great Chain of Being "*Midway* from *Nothing* to the *Deity*."[14] To measure accurately that position's coordinates proved to be a project demanding endless nuance and revision. Take an example of differences split. The dualities of Aristotle's rational-animal compound are alluded to—the allusion ricochets through *Lear*—in Pope, Swift, and Arbuthnot's *Memoirs of Martinus Scriblerus*, where man is described as a "forked straddling Animal."[15] Forked, straddling: rational and animal. Locke, likewise, with the example of a dull, irrational man and an intelligent, rational parrot to hand, will not give up speciation: "the *Idea* in our Minds, of which the Sound *Man* in our Mouths is the Sign, is nothing else but of an Animal of such a certain Form" (*Essay* II.xxvii.8).[16]

But of just such a certain form are the hominoid apes newly introduced to the European imagination, and Locke, for one, is ever pretending to boggle at "Drills" (a West African species of baboon) and other animals.[17] "*Orangutan*" means "wild man of the woods," an equivalence captured in the title of Edward Tyson's *Orang-outang, sive Homo Sylvestris* (1699), a founding and influential work of comparative anatomy and primatology.[18] Carl Linnaeus did not omit to categorize man among the animals in his taxonomy (recall the list: "Men, Monkies, Lap-dogs, Parrots"). Dr. Gregory, underlining the importance of comparative work, emphasizes how "the lowest of one species and the highest of that immediately below it" are run imperceptibly together (9).

"Thin partitions Sense from Thought divide," writes Pope, imagining a half-reasoning elephant in his *Essay on Man*, "For ever sep'rate, yet for ever near." Pope borrows from Dryden, who asserts in *Absalom and Achitophel*: "Great Wits are sure to Madness near ally'd, / And thin Partitions do their Bounds divide." Like Pope and Dryden, Edward Young dramatizes the language of limits by means of enjambment: "A good Man and an Angel! These between / How thin the barrier."[19] Similes, literally and trivially true, may maintain the thinnest barrier; wit or metaphor overleaps it, imbruting the soul or exalting it. In an essay on the redoublings of literal and figurative identification by Jonathan Lamb, humanity is seen enjoying, at once, an "extraordinary proximity" to *both* gods and beasts.[20] Lamb quotes David Hume's *Natural History of Religion*: the passions that "sink men nearest to the level of beast" are "often supposed to be the only dispositions, in which we can have any immediate communication with the Deity" (Lamb, "Sympathy," 78). Figuration, Lamb argues, is itself nearly allied to transfiguration, metamorphosis.

In Nathan Bailey's 1730 *Dictionarium Britannicum*, the "ANIMAL faculty" is defined as that "by which a Man exercises Sense, Motion, and the principal Functions of the Mind"; and in the same work, "BEAST" is assigned two senses, one literal and one figurative: "a brute creature, void of reason; also metaphorically a lewd, filthy, or inhuman man or woman." The doubleness coded in Bailey's animal faculties and the oxymoronic "inhuman man" complicates those metaphors of mind collected for this book that mark the partitions between literal and figurative, not just the figures treated under this heading. Linguistic distinctions are most forcefully insisted upon when they would secure other demarcations.

The terms of a metaphorical sentence turn suddenly literal in construal. The philosopher Ted Cohen identifies a variety of figuration he names "twice-true metaphor" and gives as examples most fitting here: "People are not sheep" and "Hitler was an animal."[21] The sense of both statements is ambiguous, neither literal nor figurative until the context of the total speech act is determined. The statements switch between aspects, like the famous "duck-rabbit" image discussed by Jastrow and Wittgenstein, and the underlying duality of such manifest images is applied by Roger M. White in a theory of metaphor that serves, in this dictionary, as the orienting treatment of the figurative language.[22] Metaphorical statements are duck-rabbits; and metaphors of mind double down on duality of aspect when we would further determine if the discourse of the mind is itself literal or figurative because the mind is immaterial, a locus of the gestalt switch but not the figure itself.

The word "beast," which originally includes man, comes, in the history detailed by the *OED*, to distinguish lower animals from man. The quadruped looks to the ground. Upright man is the animal whose "upper and lower parts . . . correspond with the upper and lower in the universe itself."[23] In Shakespeare's phrase, man is "the paragon of animals," model and perfection, topmost in lower creation, a pivot point. When Joseph Addison considers "Woman as a beautiful Romantick Animal" in *Tatler* no. 116, marked again is extraordinary proximity and an insuperable barrier: not rational but *romantic*, separate but near. Woman's human distinction is maintained with an *as* in this consideration until, in what follows, it is not. She is "adorned with Furs and Feathers. . . . The Lynx shall cast its Skin at her Feet to make her a Tippet; the Peacock, Parrot, and Swan, shall pay Contributions to her Muff . . . every Part of Nature furnish out its Share towards the Embellishment of a Creature that is the most consummate Work of it."[24] Woman is but an animal dressed in animals. Not a "fair defect of Nature" but its *consummate* creature, she is naturally inferior and therefore perfectly marriageable.[25]

Crowds of Little Animals: Maggots

As paragon or consummation, Addison's image of woman collects and multiplies animals. In reductio ad absurdum, Thomas Aquinas follows Aristotle in reasoning that "If, therefore, the whole soul is in each part of the body, it follows that each part of the body is an animal."[26] The self anatomized is a zoo—and has long been figured so.[27] In book IX of the *Republic* Socrates asks his interlocutor to picture a chimera. The monster is "an image of the soul in speech," a tripartite figure that combines "a manifold and many-headed beast that has a ring of heads of tame and wild beasts" with the single image of a lion and the image of a man (588b–c).[28] In medieval allegory each sin and passion is represented by a specific emblematic animal, and fallen man is pictured as a collection of brute antagonists. John Donne compares man to "a lumpe, where all beasts kneaded bee"; it is wisdom that "makes him an Arke where all agree."[29] In his *Discourse Concerning the Mechanical Operation of the Spirit*, Jonathan Swift registers the "Opinion of choice *Virtuosi*, that the Brain is only a Crowd of little Animals."[30]

Characteristically, Swift's "crowd of little animals" is a picture drawn in darkest irony. The animals that compose the brain cling together, stinging and clawing each other, like brutish members of a Hobbist Leviathan (see **Inhabitants**). All invention, claims Swift's fictional pamphleteer, is a matter of "Morsure," or the biting by these animals of "certain capillary Nerves," just as the hoaxing pamphlet is a "bite" or a joke on the materialist, mechanical philosophy improbably outlined. Swift lets the protean image degrade before the reader's eyes: the brain is first likened to a crowd of animals, then the Leviathan, then "like Bees in a perpendicular Swarm" or "like a Carrion corrupted into Vermin, still preserving the Shape and Figure of the Mother Animal" (304). The last step down the Chain of Being punctuates the degeneration begun when man is first likened to animal: the brain is flesh, a substance that supports squirming maggots. Swift's "fall into *Matter*" is complete (322).

A pun redounds in Swift's "*Figure* of the Mother Animal," a figure that preserves both matter and metaphor in the term "MAGGOT," which is defined as "A small grub, which turns into a fly" and a "Whimsy" or "odd fancy" in Johnson's *Dictionary*. The term continues to metamorphose; materialism would literalize metaphor, while vitalism spontaneously engenders wriggling figuration. By midcentury Théophile de Bordeu's analogy of an organism as a hive of bees was influential in scientific circles.[31] Swift's swarm, with its roots in Epicurean philosophy, may have been renovated and taken seriously by Bordeu, but more obviously it migrated through Denis Diderot's dialogue *D'Alembert's Dream*, which features a polypous swarm of Swiftian bees and includes Bordeu as a character. In Diderot, Swift's bee bites are revised and softened to the continuous clingings of contiguous feet, and the body's organs are imagined as "distinct animals kept by the law of continuity in a state of general sympathy, unity, and identity."[32] Perhaps this particular animal figure—a figure of an animal made of animals, a form filled with maggots—gets its fullest treatment in Laurence Sterne's picture of the dioptrical beehive by which the soul's "maggots" may be viewed and traced "from their first engenderings to their crawling forth."[33]

Animal Spirits

For much of the eighteenth century the very foundation of thought and sensation was supposed to belong to the circulation of "animal spirits," which Ephraim Chambers defines as "a fine subtile Juice or Humour in Animal Bodies; supposed to be the great Instrument of muscular Motion, Sensation, &c."[34] While the idea of animal spirits dates to Galenic medicine, and Descartes employs these figures in his physiological accounts of thought and perception, it is the Oxford doctor Thomas Willis who influentially offers an account of the cognition and mental illness that centers on animal spirits. In his major work on the soul, *De anima brutorum* (1672)—translated by the poet Samuel Pordage in 1683 as *Two Discourses Concerning the Souls of Brutes*—Willis figures his animal spirits alternately as fiery liquids, beams of light, soldiers and watchmen, tempestuous ocean currents, and—most important under our current heading—fleet and nimble animals.[35]

Willis illustrates animal cognition by the example of a "hungry Horse" imagining a "plentiful Pasture" (36). During sensation and volition, the spirits stirred leave "Prints or Marks . . . as so many Tracts or Ways" in the brain. (Tracks and paths worn in the landscape of the brain become standard in associationist explanations of habit.) Willis's picture of the horse's animal spirits working their own hungry way through the brain parallels, of course, the description of the horse finding its way to the place of pasturage. And the descriptions are united in imagination: "the hungry Horse is carried from place to place, till he has found out the Imagined Pasture, and indeed enjoyes that good the Image of which was painted in his Brain." Literal and figurative combine, as it were, with the former supervenient upon the latter.

At Oxford, Willis moved in the same circle as Robert Boyle, Christopher Wren, Robert Hooke, and John Locke (the latter two were among Willis's students), men of science who would later found the Royal Society of London, and this circle of experimentalists or *virtuosi* is almost certainly the same that Swift aims at in his *Discourse*.[36] By the publication of Locke's *Essay* in 1690, animal spirits were a standard element in most theories of the mind.[37] Traditionally, animal spirits, which are secreted by the brain, are contrasted with "vital" spirits and "natural" spirits, which are secreted, respectively, in the heart and liver or bowels. The spirits are "animal" because of their special relationship to the soul or mind (*anima*, *animus*). In Willis's comparative neuroanatomy, man and animal are both endowed with a material, "sensitive" soul (man, divided within, has an intellectual, rational soul in addition to a corporeal, sensitive soul). Animal functions involve those *voluntary* functions of the brain, and animal spirits are an *active* part of the mechanism of nerve and muscle. The adjectival "animal" is here a modifier of distinction, marking a difference between the automatic, spontaneous processes of the body and the higher order interactions of mind and body—although, in Willis's "neurologie" (a word he coined), the animal spirits are responsible for both higher and lower processes, intentions *and* reflexes. For the Cartesian, who believes that animals are machines, animal spirits are exactly what animals lack, whereas for Willis and Locke (who both suggest that matter may think), the corporeal soul is a point of contact between man and beast. A thin barrier, it mediates between mind and matter.

In the first half of the eighteenth century, as the doctrine of animal spirits is contested, shifting paradigms result. In 1733 the physician George Cheyne, reviewing the literature of nervous distempers in his *English Malady*, observes that Thomas Willis gave the doctrine of animal spirits "all the Advantages of Eloquence and Metaphor."[38] But where Willis moves from metaphor to metaphor in his sprawling explanations, Cheyne is both more parsimonious and perhaps more coherent, complaining that "the precarious Hypothesis of Animal Spirits seems to be built" on "slender and imaginary Similitude" (74–5). From the doctrine mixed metaphors breed, and Cheyne casts his own theory by picking one metaphor and privileging it: that is, his well-known image of "a skillful Musician playing on a well-tun'd instrument," an image that may have been selected from Willis's tangle of metaphors.[39]

The mechanics of sensation remain thereafter unsettled, and as the century wears on, animal spirits appear more and more as a fiction of theory, of doubtful existence.[40] Considering the explanatory power of animal spirits, Thomas Reid invokes the Indian philosopher, a kind of stock character in eighteenth-century philosophy, who believes the world rests on a huge elephant and the elephant on a tortoise.[41] Reid observes of his philosopher, and by implication, of philosophers more generally, "His elephant was a hypothesis and our hypotheses are elephants."[42] Turned round in Reid's chiasmus, animal spirits are exposed as hypothetical elephants—fanciful, philosophical animals. Redacting scientific advances for a broad audience in his *Compendium of Natural History* (1763), John Wesley emphasizes that the existence of animal spirits has never been shown; and the physician John Aikin, brother of Anna Letitia Barbauld, likewise communicates skepticism about their existence in a natural history text prepared for the Dissenting students of Warrington academy.[43] By the end of the century, Luigi Galvani's theory of animal electricity and late eighteenth-century discussions of Franz Mesmer's animal magnetism replace serious discussion of animal spirits—although the adjective *animal* and the metaphorics persist.

With the important exception of Thomas Willis, most scientific works do not explicitly figure the animal spirits as animals (although the spirits *are* typically described as "nimble" or "fleet"). In many eighteenth-century medical texts the earlier distinctions between vital and animal spirits fall away, and nervous fluids are simply referred to as "spirits." In David Hume's *Treatise* the animal spirits are described (like so many bees?) rummaging in the cells of the brain, although the species of animal Hume would have his reader imagine is never specified (I.ii.5).[44] But metaphors cast out by science are readily adopted by literature. While Margaret Cavendish's poetry provides a great many animal-spirit metaphors, it is only in later literary works that animal spirits become more widely associated with metaphorical animals. Samuel Garth's popular poem *The Dispensary* figures animal spirits in multiple passages, mentioning Willis by name in canto VI. And in one grotesque epic simile, a personified Fury abandons the breast of an apothecary, like an insect that flies from a "Sore," leaving behind a "Brood of Maggots," or thoughts, which wriggle and roll in his breast. Richard Blackmore, royal physician and epic poet—and an antidispensarian ridiculed in Garth's poem—likewise wrote medicalized verses teeming with animal-spirit metaphors. Richard Savage versifies their circulation in "The Animalcule: A Tale," disingenuously claiming that the spirits are "of Name unknown in Song!"[45]

Literalizing the liquors of physiology, Richard Blackmore includes a set piece in *The Nature of Man* in which a climactic theory of character merges with the theory of animal spirits. The fierceness of savages who inhabit the tropical climes is attributed to the fiery animal spirits fermented in their blood. These liquorous spirits, "rais'd from Choler to the Brain," are "Like those extracted from the basest Grain"—as a result, "the Savage Beast / Reigns in their Soul and haunts their desart Breast." Blackmore's verse forces the breast-beast rhyme as his metaphors violently unite levels of explanation by bringing physiology and geography together. His figured animal spirits populate the desert wilderness of a savage breast and therefore bestialize the inhabitants of "uninhabited" desert climates. At the equator, the savage beast *reigns*, is not reined in, and in the stanza that follows the equation is confirmed as "Brute and Humane Animals" are scorched alike at latitudes where "swarthy Nations" partake of the nature of "the fierce Viper, pois'nous Rattle-Snake."[46]

Animal Diversity

The examples collected in the preceding section are indeterminate; as when the animal-spirit thesis is satirized by the Scriblerians in *The Memoirs of Martinus Scriblerus*, we learn that "a Philosopher's brain was like a great Forest, where Ideas rang'd like animals of several kinds," but we are not told what kinds (57). How should we picture these animals within? Eighteenth-century animals were divided into four genera—beasts, birds, fishes, or insects—in works such as John Ray's influential *The Wisdom of God Manifested in the Works of Creation*, which details a natural-theological pyramid of 150 beasts, 500 birds, 1,000 fishes, and innumerable insects. Thomas Boreman's popular animal picture book cites Ray and follows suit, illustrating more than three hundred "Beasts," "Birds," "Fishes," and "Serpents and Insects," while finding space for the manticora, lamia, and dragon. A 1786 edition of Boreman's *Three Hundred Animals* juxtaposes engravings of a unicorn and rhinoceros on the same page; the two animals compare such that the unicorn appears the more realistic of the two.[47]

The diversity is demonstrated in the multiplication of examples. Hume finds "some Particle of the Dove, kneaded into our Frame along with the Elements of the Wolf and Serpent."[48] In memory, a man's thoughts like "a Spaniel ranges the field, till he find a s[c]ent."[49] Sarah Fielding finds the mimicry of the imagination to be like that of a "Monkey."[50] Rumination is an animal activity. Hard reasoning puts us in a yoke like oxen; and, as will be discussed below, passions must be reined in like too-spirited horses. Hester Chapone likens her "vagrant soul" to "a wanton lamb . . . / Many long years from her Shepherd stray'd." In a John Hopkins poem, thoughts like "Silver Fishes shine." Edward Young likens the mind to a spider that spins "curious Webs / Of subtle Thought." Coleridge compares thinking to a small "water-insect on the surface of rivulets" making its way by "alternate pulses of active and passive motion."[51] Boswell finds some minds to be like "the cameleon," which, having no color of its own, takes its color from its company.[52] The passions are figured as various beasts that consume each other: Pope's ruling passion "Like Aaron's Serpent, swallows up the rest" (*Essay* 29).

Many figurative identifications break through thin partitions, joining inside and outside, top and bottom, lady and lapdog. The literary historian Laura Brown calls the latter, the lady and her lapdog, "an especially resonant figure," arguing animal metonymy (lap/dog) shows pets to be "simultaneously within and outside the realm of the human, or—from another perspective—places the woman both within and outside the realm of the animal."[53] Metaphor exposes and then elides categorical boundaries: the rogue is a dog; the fool, a puppy.[54] Under the headword "PINEAL" in Johnson's *Dictionary*, a Scriblerian attestation collapses differences: "Courtiers and spaniels exactly resemble one another in the *pineal* gland." The verses inscribed by Pope on the collar of the dog presented to Frederick, Prince of Wales, ask, self-importantly, "I am his Highness' dog at *Kew*; / Pray tell me, sir, whose dog are you?"[55] Even "his Highness," the prince and son of the king (who himself never ascended to the throne), might be bitten by such a question.

Birds and the Flight of Fancy

Winged thoughts and feelings buzz and flutter in the head and breast, and several pages could be devoted to birds, particularly to the commonplace metaphors that evoke flights of fancy. Having birds in the brain is a metaphor that might be traced from Plato's picture of the mind as an aviary (in the *Theaetetus*) to the mental life described by William James as made up of "flights and perchings."[56] The imagery of reasoning as flight recurs in the verses of Edward Young's *Night Thoughts* that would ascend, beyond the bounds of sensation, to the contemplation of divinity. In sentimental drama and comedies, the heart springs and flutters in the breast. Boswell, featured in this entry for all his animal metaphors, advises the gloomy "Hypochondriack" to stock well the park of his mind with gay and airy bird ideas. In verses written by John and Charles Wesley, the unredeemed heart is "A Cage of Birds, and Beasts unclean, / . . . a dire abode / Of Dragons."[57] The image of the unclean birdcage, which recurs in Wesleyan hymns, may have originated in a hymn written by John Cennick, a charismatic preacher who turned away from Whitefield to embrace Moravian fellowship. The scriptural origins of the devotional birdcage image are likely Revelation 18:2.

In Psalms, the soul is "as a bird" escaped from "the snare of fowlers" (124:7), and allusions to the simile are to be found throughout eighteenth-century literature. In a parenthesis in a long letter on libertinage that takes as trope "a bird new-caught," Samuel Richardson's Lovelace observes, "a bird is all soul," a formula he repurposes for Clarissa herself and which—in its scriptural associations—ironically figures and foreshadows Clarissa's eventual escape.[58] While the figure from Psalms is found far and wide, more secular uses of traps, springes, and snares are also available. Hobbes, for example, figures poor reasoning in terms of birds and birdlime. The seeker after truth who does not work from precise definitions becomes "entangled in words, as a bird in lime twiggs," and those who rely on other authorities, on discovering their errors, "know not which way to cleere themselves; but spend time in fluttering over their bookes; as birds that entring by the chimney, and finding themselves inclosed in a chamber, flutter at the false light of a glasse window" (15). John Wolcot, in a satiric ode penned under his nom de plume, Peter Pindar, figures fat as the "Birdlime of the Brain" that "holds Ideas by the legs and wings."[59] Hannah More clips the wings of would-be (fledgling?) teenage girl poets in the epilogue to a didactic pastoral drama: "Fancy no more on airy wings shall rise, / We now must scold the maids, and make the pies."[60]

Moles (and Other Insects)

Trading sky for earth and investigating a habitat below ground, I might choose the blind and burrowing mole or "mouldwarp" as an especially curious specimen. The lowly mole may seem an unlikely candidate for the mind's mascot, except I have encountered eight remarkable instances of the mole metaphor of mind in eighteenth-century literature. The mole is a limit case in the Age of Enlightenment but also an illustration that just about any animal will suffice for metaphorizing.[61] Well beneath the mole on the Chain of Being are cockles, oysters, and mussels, all useful for figuring the lowest limits of sensation. Locke, for one, wonders how far above "the condition of a Cockle, or an Oyster," is the man in whom "decrepid old Age" has blotted out memory (*Essay* II.ix.14).[62]

The mole makes an unanticipated appearance in the fourth volume of Samuel Richardson's *Pamela* when Pamela transcribes the following lines from John Dryden's *All for Love* into a letter addressed to her dearest Mr. B.:

> And yet the Soul, shut up in her dark Room,
> Viewing so clear *abroad*, at *home* sees nothing:
> But like a Mole in Earth, busy and blind,
> Works all her Folly up, and casts it outward
> To the World's open View—[63]

The mind is a mole, locked in, a creature incapable of introspection. We are hypocrites, and "at home" the mind is only "busy and blind." Dryden's use of the mole metaphor is representative of an earlier period's pessimism. But in the context of *Pamela* the mole connects with John Locke's famous "*dark room*" of the mind (*Essay* II.xi.17) so that Dryden's lines become a buried precedent for the Lockean metaphor (see **Rooms**). Or at least Richardson yokes the two authors together: Pamela quotes Dryden in her discussion of Locke's thoughts on home education, exposing a subterranean metaphorics of moles and dark rooms (*camera obscura*) and connecting one of the great dramatists of the Restoration period to one of its great philosophers. The mole is an ironic emblem for Pamela herself, who shuts herself up in a closet to write her letters and who, in the context of Locke's pedagogy, may fail to recognize that the manipulation by tutor and governess of her pretty little Miss Goodwin "at home" is of a piece with her manipulative governance by Mr. B. and his family. Pamela's letters are cast outward, exposing both her insight and her folly to our view. Indeed the tensions between home and abroad define the central drama of the earlier volumes: Pamela quickly comes to view ideological structures clearly "abroad" but is ever blind to her own feelings. Or, again, perhaps more obscurely, Richardson is having a laugh at the philosopher who would claim with some false humility, as Locke does in his "Epistle to the Reader," to be a mere "Under-Labourer . . . clearing the Ground a little, and removing some Rubbish, that lies in the way to knowledge" (*Essay* p. 10). Throughout the century, philosophers are caricatured as moles poring on their clods in Augustan profundity.[64]

The mole resurfaces in Oliver Goldsmith's *The Vicar of Wakefield*, another novel that scrutinizes eighteenth-century notions of hierarchy. The vicar's son, Moses, revises moral sense philosophy in making the point that we are not to judge the feelings of others by what we would feel in their place. Moses claims that a poor "man's mind seems fitted to its station" and argues by animal analogy, "However dark the habitation of the mole to our eyes, yet the animal finds the apartment sufficiently lightsome."[65] Moles often appear in such moments of perspective adjustment as mountain and molehill are measured, and each creature is fit to its station in the Great Chain of Being. Lilliputian tricks of perspective involve animals (like flies or mites in cheese) in order to effect micro-mega adjustments. Samuel Bishop, headmaster of Merchant Taylors School, observes in an interlude written in imitation of Shakespeare and intended to be staged in compliment to the royal family that "Little minds / Do judge of great things, like the purblind gnat, / That deems a fly, a monster."[66]

But Moses's pedantic equation of the laboring classes with burrowing insectivorous mammals proves appalling. In eighteenth-century poetic diction, moles are "poor," "low," "busy," and "laborious" (we imagine a mole-ish multitude), and Moses's apologetic for poverty is heavily ironized by Goldsmith. The mole-man in question, the impoverished Mr. Burchell, is a wealthy man in disguise. It is the Primrose family who are blind to his actual station, for he is, in fact, Sir William Thornhill, uncle of their landlord, Squire Thornhill. In the expanding irony of the narrative, the entire Primrose family is plunged into far worse straits than Mr. Burchell's, so that Moses has ample opportunity to judge the feelings of Burchell from his own newly lowered station.

Predation and Parasites

Anthony Ashley Cooper, Earl of Shaftesbury, warns that if both body and mind are not exercised, "the Spirits, unimploy'd abroad, help to consume the Parts within; and Nature, as it were, preys upon her-self."[67] During a long confinement owing to illness or nervous complaint, animals within will turn predator, with the metaphorics of predation prevailing especially in the novel of sensibility. In Sarah Fielding's *History of the Countess of Dellwyn* (the metaphor is cited above in epigraph), for example, Lady Dellwyn while suffering from melancholy has "no Food from outward Objects, to employ her animal Spirits, and they therefore prey'd at home; and oppressed her own Mind" (1:92). Alternately, James Boswell, recovering from gonorrhea, finds his "animal spirits were necessarily *tamed* and [his] relish for pleasure and amusement and whim evaporated."[68]

Many beasts prey upon the mind, and they sting or rend, tear and growl. In the early Irish novel *Vertue Rewarded* (1693), Plutarch's story of a young Spartan boy, who catches a fox and keeps it hidden under his gown "till it tore out his Bowels," is related as an illustration of the modesty of English ladies, who closely hide their passion even as it "gnaws the fiercer."[69] There are carrion creatures of the conscience, and sorrow and remorse also gnaw at the soul. Yet conscience (or reflection) is identified by Joseph Butler, among many other authors, as the instinct or principle of action "which Brutes have not." And in *Tom Jones* Henry Fielding likewise writes, "This active Principle may perhaps be said to constitute the most essential Barrier between us, and our Neighbours the Brutes."[70] It is surprising, then, that conscience is so often figured *as* an animal—as in the case of Lovelace's "troublesome bosom-visiter" that flies out the window (*Clarissa* 4:172) or the burrowing "mole" in John Keats's "Sonnet to Sleep" (ll. 11–2).

In echoes of Mark 9:48, conscience is a worm that will not die. This last is a verse that Pope puts to satiric use in his epistle to John Moore, the quack who hawked a "Worm-Powder" in gruesome advertisements that detailed the size and shape of the worms "brought away" by purgation. The poem's thesis—that "All Humankind are Worms"—brings classification to wormy characters, closing with the Statesmen whose conscience "gnaws them Night and Day" and the Courtiers, who might be made to void this same "Worm [that] never dies" by the workings of Moore's medicinal powder. [71]

The worm trope turns more seriously in other texts, and conscience stings like an insect or serpent. Passion tears into the rotten mind, as in Gray's ode on Eton College, like a vulture. After a visit from the libertine Belcour, a "scorpion" is fixed in the heart of the seduced and abandoned Charlotte Temple, the title character in Susanna Rowson's best-selling American novel; its "venom embittered every future hour of her life." Edward Ward pictures a suicide who "Conquer'd those Vipers in his Conscience bred, / And with himself, shot all the stinging Fantoms dead."[72] Brute behavior escapes the domestications of conscience, drives us out into a wilderness where hawking and hunting turn to self-murder. Self-discipline discloses secret animality.[73]

Horses

If conscience is an animal that punishes us when we do wrong, other beasts are used to figure the proper *husbandry* or *management* (a ready pun on *manège*, an eighteenth-century term for horsemanship, is available) of self.[74] And even as riding manuals emphasize the rationality of horses,[75] the passions, as figured in moral and devotional works, must be yoked and tamed—although fancy and imagination, under appropriate conditions, may be given freer rein.

The evangelical clergyman James Hervey marvels at the soul's sway over the body: "Ten thousand Reins are put into her Hands; yet she manages all, conducts all."[76] The poet John Wolcot satirically figures passions in a "martingale" (i.e., the arrangement of straps that prevent a horse from rearing or throwing back its head). As horses are put in trammels (another mechanical device of straps and shackles) to learn to pace and amble, so wit may be trained in a metaphorical harness. Samuel Butler caricatures the logician exercising a syllogism in mood and figure as one who "has been broke / To ride and pace his Reason by the Book," and poets find their invention or muse trammeled variously by rules, rhyme, and meter (see also **Fetters**).[77] Keats's early poetry is filled with "trammels," and his critics are perhaps anticipated in the favored figure: the early imaginative verse is too wild and must be broken, his work denigrated as the offerings of a "stable boy."

Animals have long been especially useful for picturing a self turned upside down: so Swift writes in *A Tale of a Tub* that "a Man's Fancy gets *astride* on his Reason" (171) and in *Gulliver's Travels* imagines a society of rational horses that keep his narrator, Lemuel Gulliver, as a pet. Swift's inversion of horse and rider takes a page from the logic manuals of the later seventeenth century and activates popular world-upside-down woodcuts and broadside imagery of animals driving their owners to market and charivari traditions of "riding the stang" or "Skimmington riding."[78] In *Tristram Shandy*, Laurence

Sterne memorably translates a popular political metaphor into animal terms: a man who "gives himself up to the government of a ruling passion" allows "in other words . . . his Hobby-Horse" to grow "head-strong."[79] Horse-and-rider metaphors are also found in more urbane, less satirical situations. James Boswell, feeling himself grow too fond of Lord Eglinton, decides to remain more aloof; he writes in his London journal, "I pulled the reins hard" (53).

The technical vocabulary of horsemanship and farriery finds its way into metapoetic discussions of versifying and more prosaic composition. An allegorical traveler in a Margaret Cavendish poem rides through "The several Countries in the Brain" on a "*Strong imagination*" that is abstractly saddled, girt, and bridled in states of mind.[80] In dedicatory verses by Charles Cotton written for Thomas Flatman's *Poems*, a poet's fancy is likened to "a rough, but ready *Horse*, / Whose mouth is govern'd more by *skil* than *force*," with the simile turned to encomium when Cotton compares Flatman's fancy to Pegasus. Fancy's "airy horse," a piece of poetic diction from Isaac Watts's *Horae Lyricae*, reappears eighty-five years on in Nathaniel Cotton's (no relation to Charles) *Visions in Verse*.[81] Alexander Gerard writing on genius compares imagination to a "horse of high mettle ranging at liberty" that requires "the management of sound judgment."[82] In the satirical fragments on pedantry posthumously published in 1759, Samuel Butler warns that "constant overstraining of the mind / Distorts the Brain, as Horses break their Wind." While Edward Gibbon claims to have used his reading in Locke as a bridle, he applied Bayle as a spur.[83]

Fancy, repeatedly figured as a horse, is in a variety of poems "spurred," "coursing," "on full stretch," or "checked." In Pope's *Essay on Criticism*, for example, the Muse's winged steed, "like a gen'rous Horse, / Shows most true Mettle when you *check* his Course."[84] The couplet might serve as an epigraph to an anecdote: Pope, riding to Oxford in 1716 was overtaken on the way, in Windsor Forest, by his bookseller Bernard Lintot and a young "printer's devil" (an apprentice). Pope notices Lintot is uncomfortable in the saddle of his borrowed stallion, and the company alights to rest. Lintot, businessman-like, produces a copy of Horace and encourages Pope to turn an ode, "till we mount again"; but Pope demurs, preferring to ride on, and puts off the "courteous *stationer*" (emphasis added) and the attempt to harness his talents by explaining, "motion is an aid to my fancy, a round trot very much awakens my spirits." Puns compound after Lintot asks, an hour on, how "far" Pope has gone in his translation. When Pope replies innocently, "seven miles," Lintot "lugg'd the reins" and "stopt short," his frustration providing a punch line: "I thought you had done seven stanzas."[85]

The locus classicus of horse-and-rider metaphors is, of course, Plato's *Phaedrus*, in which the soul is "likened to the union of powers in a team of winged steeds and their winged charioteer."[86] The poet John Byrom would almost overstrain the classical conceit in a poem on human nature that figures the passions as strong horses that draw the "Body Coach of Flesh and Blood," while "subtle Reason," reins in hand, sits on the box. Byrom replaces Plato's chariot with a coach and associates the revised image with modern materialist philosophy. Those philosophers who praise reason seem to suppose "That Passions, Reason, and Machine, is all" and thus forget the inhabitant of the coach. Byrom's insistence on interiority is not available in the classical figure, and the difference between a coach and a chariot seems important. To the materialist, "the Windows are drawn up" and the careening coach empty. We are to recall, perhaps, Pope's verse in which "Coaches Coaches drive."[87]

Like Byrom, Isaac Bickerstaff, the Irish librettist, is updating Plato's famous picture in his comic opera *Love in the City* by replacing ancient chariots with modern hackney coaches—pointing up, with a wink, the classic if not *hackneyed* quality of the metaphor: "Man in this world, Sir, may be compared to a hackney-coach upon a stand; continually subject to be drawn by his unruly appetites, on one foolish jaunt or another; but you will say, if his appetites are horses, which as it were drag him along, reason is the coachman to rule those horses."[88] Developing the metaphor, Bickerstaff avers that coachman Reason may get drunk and lose control of the horses. Such intoxication is one key scenario in which the brute elements of man might overthrow his reason, and the literary historian J. B. Bamborough notes, "The different stages of drunkenness were sometimes classified according to the different beasts which they resembled."[89] In contradistinction, the animal capable of enjoying a drink shows itself to be something more than a beast.[90] The examples, as usual, are often complicated, and the reader is reminded that animal spirits, the basis of nervous sensation, are themselves described by physicians as a kind of liquor. In one Restoration comedy, drink is celebrated by a libertine character as "the very thing that distinguishes the Life of Man from that of Beast!"—but then the distinction is ironically undercut when drink is further said to be "the onely Spur of Wit and Reason."[91] Poetical intoxication, more figurative than literal, may be cause for letting slip the reins. But Hugh Blair complains that Edward Young, in his *Night Thoughts* (a poem swarming with animal metaphors), has given his imagination "too loose reins" so that the "Metaphors are frequently too bold, and frequently too far pursued; the reader is . . . kept constantly on the stretch to comprehend, and keep pace with the author."[92]

Reading and Riding: John Wesley

By way of conclusion, while keeping to horse-and-rider metaphorics, I turn to John Wesley's reading habits. Wesley, one of the great evangelicals of the eighteenth century, was an itinerant preacher who traveled over 250,000 miles—many of those miles on horseback—on a London-Bristol-Newcastle circuit evangelizing the laboring classes.[93] Wesley's *Journals* offer a detailed account of his horsemanship as he rides from one town to the next, the relentless narrative punctuated by falls and accidents, which appear almost as comic relief. A dedicated reader, Wesley would prop up a book on his saddle. His habit is recorded in a journal entry (April 21, 1770):

> Nearly thirty years ago I was thinking, "How is it that no horse ever stumbles while I am reading?" (History, poetry, and philosophy I commonly read on horseback, having other employment at other times.) No account can possibly be given but this: Because then I throw the reins on his neck. I then set myself to observe; and I aver, that in riding above a hundred thousand miles, I scarcely ever remember any horse (except, two, that would fall head over heels anyway) to fall or make a considerable stumble while I rode *with a slack rein*. To fancy, therefore, that a *tight rein* prevents stumbling is a capital blunder. I have repeated the trial more frequently than most men in the kingdom can do. A slack rein will prevent stumbling if anything will. But in some horses nothing can.[94]

The reveries of reading, so often pictured as the fancy or imagination moving through mental spaces, are here almost literalized. With half of his time on horseback spent reading, Wesley is a Desultory Reader *par excellence* and in both of the senses forecasted in this book's introduction. He is a virtuoso rider-reader (a *desultor*) but is also one of the most active extractor-redactors of the eighteenth century, tirelessly abridging and editing books for his flock. Reading, like riding (rummaging, ruminating, foraging), is an animal activity. Wesley avoids the nervous illnesses Cheyne assigns to the studious, sedentary lifestyle by reading and riding at the same time. His dreaming by the book appears no less poignant when we learn that, as a lover of animals, Wesley refused to wear spurs. Horse-and-rider metaphorics complicate the biography of the Methodist. Indeed, the thematic of the horse carries us deep

Chamber horse, from Thomas Sheraton's *Appendix to the Cabinet-Maker and Upholsterer's Drawing-Book* (1796). Albert and Shirley Small Special Collections Library, University of Virginia.

into Wesley's private life and the interior of his home. The term "furniture" is ambiguously applicable to horses—to their harness and housings—as well as to homes and houses (see **Rooms**). And in Wesley's London townhouse, two pieces of furniture serve as indoor horses: a so-called Chamber-Horse (a sprung exercise machine, a kind of Enlightenment home gym) and a horsey chair given to Wesley as a gift and on which Wesley sat backward, reading in a riding posture.[95] Wesley is almost never not riding.

Early in the eighteenth century, in works like Francis Fuller's popular 1705 treatise *Medicina gymnastica*, exercise comes to be preferred over emetics and bleedings in the cure of several distempers.[96] Fuller, like Locke, is keen to promote riding, an activity I cannot now but read as an emblem of the mind astride its own passions, exercised by them and seemingly exercising its mastery, an emblem that satirically twists and turns into Sterne's hobbyhorse. Wesley, fully Methodized, never not riding, is a grave gentleman getting on at a sober pace, like *Tristram Shandy*'s Parson Yorick, who spends his time "as he [rides] slowly along,—to as much account as in his study" (1:13). It is Cheyne who recommends light reading as a "hobby-horse" in the *English Malady* and prescribes the "Chamber-Horse" for his novelist friend and patient, Samuel Richardson.[97] So in his *Primitive Physick* Wesley follows Cheyne and other physicians like Fuller in recommending riding as exercise (xxi).[98] Riding strengthens the nerves (and digestion) and is more suitable for those nervous sensibilities too weak to exercise by walking. It is exercise that will protect us from our animal spirits, which would prey on us, exercise by which we may get astride them.

Under this first rubric I have only just begun to treat of the available language of predator and prey[99] and have not considered the frisking senses of animality in a neologism like Derrida's *animot* (a term that conflates the French plural *animaux* and the singular *mot*, while recollecting older senses of the Latin *anima*).[100] There are countless animals to be differentiated, named, and numbered; the variety is prodigal, and my methods are not exhaustive. Worse yet, tropes are always on the move—as another theorist of metaphor writes—"more like quicksilver than like flowers or butterflies which one can at least hope to pin down and insert in a neat taxonomy."[101] Figurative language will not be domesticated, and the work of taxonomy is never adequate to the endless forms and phrasings that have been, and are being, evolved.

In this initial survey of the mind's metaphors I have tried to prepare the reader for the treatment of figuration in entries that follow by taking taxonomy as both object of inquiry and thematic. This is the primary entry, a primal scene. Under other headwords we will find again that our metaphors turn against us and that distinctions will not hold. Here also I contribute historical background for readers interested in the field of animal studies. Where one might expect to mark distance between man and beast with metaphors of mind, he or she will find the mind repeatedly figured *as* an animal. The thin partitions between human and nonhuman animals will not be maintained by metaphor, which repeatedly collapses distinctions between mind and matter, turns the soul inside out, and puts passion to pettishness.

As my main concerns are literary critical, I have taken the tangled topology of the Great Chain of Being as "the great commonplace" by which the collected figures are linked (the chain trope is revisited in **Fetters**), ranked, or leveled.[102] Figuration discovers resemblance—at least similarity is at the heart of traditional accounts of metaphor in which metaphor is understood as a kind of compressed simile. Resemblance is also an important element in satire, a mode in which comparison works more literally. Eighteenth-century satire inherits the "ambiguous tortured genealogy" of goatish satyrs and satyr plays,[103] and it is not easy to say who or what (a satyr?) speaks in the Earl of Rochester's "A Satyr Against Mankind." The paradoxical poem, continuously reprinted and debated in the eighteenth century, poses its questions—"Which is the basest Creature, Man, or Beast?"—only to disturb commonplaces.[104] Terms of insult drawn "from the animal world" constrain invective because, as Northrop Frye observes, "most of the unpleasant qualities of the animal are human projections."[105] To speak with Gulliver, who is repeatedly interrogated by the Houyhnhnms but forced finally to confess when found in the fulsome embrace of a brute: "I could no longer deny, that I was a real *Yahoo*."[106] Metaphor declares what something is by saying that it is something else (what it is not). But on a chain of being there is a vanishing difference between similitude and identity.

2 Coinage

Collocated Keywords: Coin, Counterfeit, Fund, Guinea, Medal, Mint

Count of Metaphors in Database[1] (1700–1799): 123

[Locke] will allow no idea innate but such as a man brings coined in his mind like a shilling.

—William King, enclosed in a letter from William Molyneux to Locke (1692)

This Work, I say, shall not only contain various Impressions of my Mind, (as in *Louis the Fourteenth* his Cabinet you have seen the growing Medals of his Person from Infancy to Old Age,) but shall likewise include with them the *Theatrical History of my Own Time.*

—Colley Cibber, *An Apology for the Life of Mr. Colley Cibber* (1740)

ELFRIDA: Do you too fear? Alas!
I flatter'd my poor soul that all its Fears
Were Grief's distemper'd coinage, that my Love
Rais'd causeless apprehensions, and at length
Edgar would quite forgive.

—William Mason, *Elfrida: A Dramatic Poem* (1752)

But yet so difficult is the intellectual commerce, so narrow the intellectual fund, that the wisest men are frequently obliged to employ their money like counters, and their counters like money, in one case, however, without loss, in the other without fraud. We may be said to do the first, that is, to employ our money like counters, when we employ ideas of one kind to mark and suggest ideas of another. We employ, as it were, in this case, good and current money of one species, to compute and fix the sum payable in another: and thus guineas may stand in the place of shillings, or shillings serve to represent guineas. This happens whenever we make use of figures.

—Henry St. John, Viscount Bolingbroke, *Letters or Essays Addressed to Alexander Pope* (1754)

> The pleasure of a train of ideas, is the most remarkable in a reverie; especially where the imagination interposes, and is active in coining new ideas, which is done with wonderful facility.
>
> —Henry Home, Lord Kames, *Elements of Criticism* (1762)

> Ideas, dealt about, like current coin,
> By motion, smooth'd, assimilate—and shine;
> Thro' circulation still increasing store,
> New generations rising, more and more—
> But cloister'd, close, in such sequester'd shades,
> Each strong impression, clear inscription, fades;
> While all their features, fine; complexions, pure,
> Neglected rust—nor long their dates endure—
>
> —James Woodhouse, *The Life and Lucubrations of Crispinus Scriblerus* (1814, written 1795)

See also **Impressions** and **Metal**

MINDS AND BRAINS ARE figured as both treasure-houses and as mints, places in which knowledge is stored and in which it is produced. In the first and last two epigraphs above, ideas are themselves likened to coins, minted and circulated, tested and tried. As substance stamped, coins prove useful for picturing minds or souls, and the stamping of coins with the bust of an emperor or with the profile of a king or hero advances associations of character and currency. The scriptural tradition further informs figuration by way of the parable of the talents (Matthew 25:14–30, Luke 19:11–27). Generally in question is the origin and assessment of intellectual and moral worth. Honor, conceived as it is in Hobbes and his inheritors, is a value placed on each man by others in a marketplace of opinions; and across the eighteenth century, "sterling virtue" is measured against "fancy's coinage."[2] To be sure, the figure of the coin complicates ideologies of valuation, as coinage is believed by many of the writers discussed below to be a medium or standard of valuation and not itself a commodity or object of market relations.

Edward Phillips defines "Coin" as "any sort of stamped Money" ("Coin"); Samuel Johnson, as "Money stamped with a legal impression" (*Dictionary* "COIN"). While I investigate impressions and stamping in one entry (see **Impression**) and the differences between mettle and **Metal** in another, I am concerned under the present heading with coinage per se and attend to the interaction of a legal impression and the metal so stamped—with both intrinsic and extrinsic valuations, substance and form, self and shape, what passes in circulation and what is worn away in the process. As listed, these distinctions map variously to the basic dualities that inform this study: mind and body, figurative and literal. The coinage of words or ideas figures but elides systematic relations to material foundations as a source of value.[3] Coinage here as elsewhere provides an important metaphor for metaphor as well as mind: "In order to signify the metaphorical process, the paradigms of money, silver and gold are imposed with remarkable insistence."[4] By means of exchange, metaphors of money and money as metaphor will be seen to work symmetrically in this entry: metaphors, not typically reversible, trade tenor for vehicle, passing between source and target domains.[5]

Clipped coins, tokens, bills of exchange, banknotes, and lottery tickets all circulated in eighteenth-century England's cash nexus. The multiple coinages—the different objects that all passed as markers of value—aggravate valuation. In an environment of debased currency transactions, exchanges of commodity for coin were moments of drama and conflict, and a "tale" is both a story and a sum or number reckoned. To tell out coins is not to weigh them but to count them out. To tell or test one's own mettle is to embark in narrative.[6] Counterfeit words and counterfeit actions are subject to much scrutiny in literature, and the reader is taught to recognize villains such as Iago, Maskwell, Lothario, Blifil, Lovelace, Sir Clement Willoughby, Young Thornhill, and Wickham.

More than in any other entry, my concerns here are meta-metaphorical. In a *thesaurus* or "treasury" of words, an account of economic metaphors may even be requisite. Departing from classical and scriptural examples, this entry broadly treats metaphors for ideas, for wit, and for the counterfeits and coinings of the imagination, character, credit, honor, and inner worth. The political history examined proceeds from the recoinage of 1696 to the Restriction Act of 1797. By way of conclusion and contrast, I look briefly at the figuration of gems and jewels, which provide alternate metaphors of value.

From the Mint

Monetary metaphors date from the origin of critical thinking when, in the writings of Heraclitus and Plato, "philosophy confronts the economics of thought itself."[7] "The Latines," observes Thomas Hobbes in *Leviathan*, "called Accounts of mony *Rationes*, and accounting, *Ratiocinatio*," and thence "they extended the word *Ratio*, to the faculty of Reckoning in all other things."[8] But philosophy newly and importantly confronts economics in the long eighteenth century; and the major philosophers of mind—Locke, Berkeley, and Hume—each writes on economic subjects. Ancient figures return and compound with neoclassical interest. At the end of the century, Maria Edgeworth draws on a tradition in empiricism when she complains, "Words without correspondent ideas are worse than useless, they are counterfeit coin," while "words, which really represent ideas" are "of sterling value" and "increase our wealth by keeping it in continual circulation; both the principal and interest increase together."[9]

One of the earliest figures of coinage is located in Epictetus's *Discourses.* Characterizing the nature of true property, Epictetus describes those few things that truly belong to a man as "his personal Qualifications as a Man, the Impressions which he brought into the World stampt upon his Mind: such as we seek in Money; and, if we find them, allow it to be good; if not, throw it away."[10] Qualifications connote "talents," an ancient measure of weight or a sum of money. Samuel Johnson, recognizing a common figurative usage, indicates a second sense of the term "TALENT" as "Faculty; power; gift of nature. A metaphor borrowed from the talents mentioned in the holy writ." Surveying the Christian homiletic tradition, the literary critic Deidre Lynch confirms, "Preachers had long seen in the piece of metal a symbol for the person."[11] A coin is stamped on the obverse with a face, and personified coins narrate several important it-narratives.[12] These personifications present busts without bodies—signifiers of pure personal identity that survive exchange and may be minted anew.

Coin metaphors of mind may be used to figure early ductility and durability, two salient features shared by coins and selves. While coins are not particularly malleable, they will take an impress: a warm blank is struck with a hammer or pressed in a coin press.[13] Those who would make further impressions must "countermark" the coin or melt the coin down and start over. Seventeenth- and eighteenth-century theorists of money point out that precious metals are useful, durable, rare, and divisible and can be stamped so that the value of the circulating piece is certified.[14] In his *Discourse of Coin and Coinage*, published posthumously in 1675, Rice Vaughan writes almost metaphorically of the precious metals that are "fit to *conceive*" a form or impression of "exceeding long indurance against the Injuries of time or accident" (5, emphasis added).

This endurance is given narrative form in *Tatler* no. 246, when Joseph Addison relates the adventures of a shilling who is born Peruvian, "naturalized and put into the *British* Mode," bent and beaten flat again, melted down and treated to a sex change (he changes Queen Elizabeth's stamp for King William's). In **Metal**, "imperishable" metals will be associated with religious matters: precious metals are typically described as incorruptible, immutable, or of long durance. Like an immortal soul, worn out by the world, the old coin may be recalled to the mint to be fired and refined, melted and reminted at full weight.

This metaphor of being new minted—born again, as it were—appears twice in Henry Brooke's Methodistical novel, *The Fool of Quality*. On almost all eighteenth-century British coinage, along with an impression of a monarch's head appears the inscription "DEI GRATIA" or "DG." As an indication of divine right, the "DEI GRATIA" may by read as an assurance that a king's position (and his coinage) is secured "by the grace of God." In devotional explications of Matthew 22:21 ("render unto Caesar"), the soul is a coin stamped with God's image (the *imago Dei*), to be rendered unto him. Wesleyan hymns are filled with prayers that God stamp his image in the singer's heart, breast, or soul. Debased coinage is imagined in these devotional entreaties to be called in and new stamped as to fineness (see **Impressions**). But the metaphor is not uniquely Methodist. Wesley's sharpest Calvinist critic employs the metaphor: the unregenerate elect are like bullion, passed through "the mint of effectual calling" and "stamped" into "current coin."[15] A shilling survives the furnace and emerges in a new, fine dress.

In pursuit of self-knowledge, Antony Ashley Cooper, third Earl of Shaftesbury searches the "Mint and Foundery of *Imagination*," while in Bernard Mandeville's dialogues "the Mind of Man" is figured as a "general Mint."[16] Oliver Goldsmith (his surname not without meaning), in an epitaph for William Burke, describes "honest William, whose heart was a mint/While the owner ne'er knew half the good that was in't."[17] When in *The Progress of Error* William Cowper writes, "The mind and conduct mutually imprint/And stamp their image in each other's mint," the lines of the couplet may act "mutually," as the metaphor of the mint is construed first in terms of the *mind*, on which it puns if not rhymes, and then in terms of *conduct*, which may also pun (albeit very obscurely) on "conduct-money."[18]

Whereas the Epictetan metaphor cited above implies that mental markings predate experience, Lockeans will be pleased to know that disks of metal that have not yet been stamped are called "blanks." Indeed, early in the *Essay*, Locke compares claims of the innatist to those of a man who says he has £100 sterling in his pocket yet denies "that he hath there either Penny, Shilling, Crown, or any other Coin, out of which the sum is to be made up" (I.iv.19). Locke's ideas, as William King observes, are like coined shillings. The innate idea, implies Locke, must be some kind of coin that will not spend, an impossible, private currency. Shaftesbury and Mandeville, as heirs of Locke and antagonists with opposed theories of mankind's inherent generosity, both employ the mint metaphor, although they would cash it out in different contexts.[19]

When Charles II mechanized the production of coin in the London Mint in 1666, molten metal was rolled out into fillets, and coins were cut from the fillet on a fly press.[20] These punched-out blanks were revolved between engraved steel bars that marked the edge of each blank before it was placed in a coining press. The revolved blank was circumscribed with language, with the poetic inscription "*Decus Et Tutamen*" (an ornament and a safeguard) appearing on the edges of some of the earliest British milled coins. The motto, intended to prevent the clipping of the coinage, furthered associations of poetic diction and coins.[21] Teams of five laborers operated the press at the mint; four moved the arms of the press, and the fifth placed the blank between the dies. The structural analogies of presswork no doubt further enforce the association of coining and printing (see **Impressions**).

On Sundays, reports Pope in his *Epistle to Arbuthnot*, "The Man of Ryme" walks forth "from the *Mint*"—that is, from the privileged district in Southwark that (until 1723) was a sanctuary for debtors.[22] The debtor character, who cannot be arrested on Sunday, presumably applies to the Twickenham poet for advice, contributions, or support. When another admirer wishes for these three things in one go—"Friendship, and a Prologue, and ten Pound"—the "ands" dilate the overfriendly impertinence of the line, conjoining unlike but convertible objects: personal relations, poetry, and pounds sterling. Pope's verses—which absurdly portray acts of dunning in reverse (the debtor, like the other applicants, importunes Pope) and almost figure this "Man of Ryme" *as* coinage (he issues, after all, "from the *Mint*")—ironically condense the complex of associations involving poetic imagination and the coining of metaphor in verse to be explored below.

Restoration and Recoinage

In 1662, after the Restoration, older hammered coins, which had become clipped and worn, were demonetized, withdrawn from circulation, and replaced by new milled coins. The calling in of the coinage that took place after the Glorious Revolution further encodes and veils a program of dynastic change (same metal, new stamp). Coins minted in 1689 represented two heads on one coin, the dual sovereigns, William and Mary.[23] In a revolutionary design, he covers her, suggesting legal coverture but also that Mary, the Stuart daughter of James II, is the foundation of succession (find her undercover, figure

Milled coins: obverses and reverses from Charles II to William III, detail from Thomas Snelling, *A View of the Silver Coin and Coinage of England* (1762), plate 17.

above): William is the stamp, Mary the metal. In the 1696 recoinage, after the death of Mary in 1694, worn coins with Charles's and James's faces on them were replaced with William's own coinage. The light, worn, clipped Stuart coinage would no longer pass, and the new "King Williams" returned the nation's currency to its former Elizabethan standard. The adventures of Addison's shilling thus include the convulsive political history of the past century, the Civil War, Restoration, and Revolution. Circulation circles back on itself, closes a circuit. The English nation and its history is continuous, tracing a succession from Elizabeth to William, and this continuity is troped by John Locke and Charles Montagu during the recoinage debates of 1695 in terms of identity—*silver* is *silver*.[24] Revolution implies a circle, is pictured with a coin.

It was Charles Montagu (1661–1715), Earl of Halifax, who forced the 1695 recoinage debate in the House of Commons—a debate that may be the proximate cause of much early eighteenth-century monetary metaphorics.[25] A master Whig politician, Montagu was made lord of the Treasury and chancellor of the Exchequer in 1691. Montagu, who helped found the national debt along with the Bank of England, was much involved with the Treasury and was instrumental in the issue of the first Exchequer bills. Observing that the ill state of England's coinage was to the nation's prejudice on the foreign exchange, Montagu—alongside Somers, Locke, and Newton—warned that the foreign trade would ultimately bring English gold out onto the market, where it would be drained away by foreign countries.[26]

Montagu's political and economic thinking motivate the metaphors of mind in the much-reprinted poem "The Man of Honour," in which honor is described as "The richest *Treasure* of a generous Breast, / That gives the Stamp and Standard to the rest." In the lines that follow, money's coding of social relations is made explicit as Montagu describes how

> Men, like our Money, come the most in Play,
> For being base, and of a coarse Allay.
> The richest Medals, and the purest Gold,
> Of native Value, and exactest Mould,
> By Worth conceal'd, in private Closets shine,
> For vulgar Use too precious, and too fine;
> Whilst Tin and Copper with new stamping bright,
> Coin of base Metal, counterfeit and light,
> Do all the Bus'ness of the Nation's Turn,
> Rais'd in Contempt, us'd and employ'd in Scorn.[27]

Montagu's metaphorics personify Gresham's law and have the lower metals circulating most. The limning of private and public occurs at the historical moment in which the private debt of the king is redefined as the public debt of the nation. The metaphors challenge our notion of how politicians might participate in the public sphere: here the most valuable and exact currencies are those that retire and shine in "private Closets"; lighter currencies are more subject to corruption and counterfeiting and are "Rais'd" (note the pun on class hierarchy and coining standards) only "in Contempt."[28] The verses complicate mercantilist theories of circulation, which maintain that currency circulating *within* a country is beneficial to that country.[29]

Beyond the economic consequences of changing the amount of silver in the coin of the realm is a subtext of worth and value that extends to persons. Money is a social relation; an individual carries his social power in his pocket.[30] Samuel Cobb's first publication commemorates Queen Mary II's "mighty Soul, stamp'd of Heav'n's noblest Coin" and finds it "More Pure than Gold, more Precious and Divine"; conversely, in his satire *The Medal*, Dryden compares the first Earl of Shaftesbury to the modern medal struck by his Whig supporters in commemoration of his acquittal on high treason: "So like the

Man" is the medal, "so golden to the sight, / So base the within, so counterfeit and light."[31] To mint medals, Dryden insists, is to counterfeit coinage, an act of high treason that therefore *cannot* memorialize Shaftesbury's acquittal.

A person whose sole property is found in himself enters into circulation, where others approve or reject his character. In a 1720 poem prompted by the bursting of the South Sea Bubble, Jonathan Swift imagines a banker's soul "*Weigh'd in the Ballance, and found light.*"[32] In *Walpoliana*, an anecdote headed "A PRETTY METAPHOR" relates how a young lady marrying the man she loves leaves many friends in London to retire to the country. The metaphor comes in a summary quip: "She has turned one and twenty shillings into a guinea."[33] The metaphor gains in interest when we try to decide if the exchange is an even one. Twenty-one silver shillings, which may be worn from circulation, may not add up to the value of the golden guinea.

Base Metal or Sterling Honor

Montagu disdains the base coinage. The tin coins produced under William and Mary easily corroded and were widely counterfeited; they were withdrawn from circulation in 1792. Brass was the alloy used to counterfeit gold coins, and it is brass and copper that are used to produce the cheaper currencies. Copper pence were counterfeited throughout the eighteenth century. While the guinea was thought to be a gentlemanly coin, copper and brass were supposed adulterate, sordid, and base: when the metals are used to figure "lower" social orders, the metaphor attaches low and base associations to the laboring classes. In 1684 tin halfpence and farthings were inscribed on their edges with the inscription *Nummorum Famulus*, "the servant of the coinage."[34] And in Montagu's verse the base coins *serve* the more aristocratic coins. At the end of the eighteenth century, the satirist John Wolcot, writing under his pseudonym Peter Pindar, protests the same association:

> Yet are there some who think (but what a shame!)
> Poor people's souls like pence of Birmingham,
> Adulterated brass—base stuff—abhorr'd—
> That never can pass current with the LORD;
> And think because of wealth they boast a store,
> With ev'ry freedom they may treat the *poor*.[35]

Wolcot's "pence of Birmingham" alludes to and reverses "Bromingham" or "Brummagem," traditional Tory nicknames for Whigs: after 1680 "bromingham" connotes both a false groat struck at Birmingham and a counterfeit Protestant.[36] But Wolcot's is also a topical allusion to the more recent coinage projects undertaken by Matthew Boulton and James Watt at their mint, in Birmingham. The party politics of the 1680 Exclusion Bill are thus reworked in new industrial terms. Boulton had been experimenting with coinage since 1772. In 1786 he minted copper coins for the East India Company. In 1797 he was contracted by the Royal Mint to produce "cartwheel" twopences and pennies. Boulton's coins are one of many privately produced coins that circulated in the eighteenth century. In addition to contracted coinage, private companies produced copper, tin, and brass tokens independent of the Royal Mint.[37] This token coinage passed when coin of the realm was in short supply, but it was not officially recognized as money of account.

Montagu might be happy to see tokens and base metals "Do all the Bus'ness of the Nation's Turn," but merchants would rather be paid in full-weight sterling. Silver is the metal of exchange and commerce, and British accounts are kept in pounds sterling.[38] The Great Recoinage puts gold and silver on "good equilibrium," and yet, before the Recoinage Act and through much of the eighteenth century, gold plate is preferred to "light silver" coin as a more secure value.[39] In part, silver circulates more because it is the less precious metal. Not as soft as gold, it is exchanged with less wear; and when it is abraded and worn, it becomes so with less loss of value.

"Sterling" indicates English coin, but it also, for obvious jingoist reasons, indicates that the sterling heart or soul is genuine. Johnson illustrates one definition of "STERLING" with Swift's ironical pronouncement (in *Polite Conversation*) that the witty discourse is "all genuine, sterling, and authentick." Swift's irony is easy to surface, as the baseness of England's currency was a fact of eighteenth-century exchange. Twice in the period the currency was found to weigh only about half of what it should. When in 1695 the officers of the Exchequer weighed £57,000 of coin, it was found to weigh a little less than half of what it should, and in 1777 a sampling of the currency from London goldsmiths was found to weigh only a little more that half of what it should.[40] Still, the coinage passed, like Swift's well-worn clichés of polite conversation, all genuine, sterling, and authentic.

Yorick's Polished Shillings

The preceding should pay out in the reading of a passage from Sterne's *Sentimental Journey* that is much cited in contemporary literary criticism.[41] While traveling abroad Yorick is asked if he finds France to be a polished nation and answers in the affirmative. In contrast to the smooth and polished French, Yorick compares the English to "antient medals, kept more apart." These medals, "passing but few peoples hands, preserve their first sharpnesses which the fine hand of nature has given them—they are not so pleasant to feel—but in return, the legend is so visible, that at the first look you see whose image and superscription they bear."[42] In illustrating his "hypothesis" that the French are polished to an excess, Yorick produces a few coins from his pocket. The illustration of social relations is an ambiguous one: the coins are both *English* and *polished*; the ancient medals are no longer coins at all. The context of the Recoinage Act is clearly referred to when the coins are identified as "king William's shillings."[43] That these once-new coins have been worn "smooth as glass" is a clear indication that a new recoinage must be at hand. That the coins are meant to stand for the refined French is teasing, as the coinage is undoubtedly light. It has been brought abroad where it hopes to pass, like Yorick, by tale.

"Polish" is a polysemous term in the eighteenth century and refers to both manners and artificial gloss; "polite" is also a word used by Newton in his *Opticks* to describe glass and reflective surfaces. Sterne's is then an execrable play on words, involving a kind of (Irish) bull, or pun: *English*, *French*, and *Polish*. And in Yorick's illustration, polishing would seem even to threaten personal identity because the face or "character" on the coin may be worn away completely. But that silver *is* silver, and Addison's narrator-shilling from the *Tatler* somehow survives the furnace. Likewise, Chrysal, the it-narrator of Charles Johnstone's *Adventures of a Guinea*, maintains his identity when melted down (in the early chapters Chrysal changes from a crucifix to a doubloon before finally taking the shape of a guinea).

It is a main contention of this book that metaphors are alterable and adaptable and that they need not determine the uses to which they are put. Notice how James Woodhouse rewrites Sterne's metaphors in those verses given as the last of this entry's epigraphs: coins ("ideas") are polished, smoothed, and shine in circulation, yes—"*But* cloister'd, close, in such sequester'd shades, / Each strong impression, clear inscription, fades" (ll. 887–8, emphasis added). In the next couplet, Woodhouse asserts, "features, fine; complexions, pure, / Neglected rust—nor long their dates endure."[44] Here we might also compare Montagu's circulation metaphors, which line up more with Sterne's than Woodhouse's: Montagu sees the richest shining brightest in private closets. Taking Sterne and Woodhouse as exemplars, there are then at least two ways of being effaced: by circulation or by being "kept more apart." The metaphor, like so many others in this study, is reversible.

Sterne and Woodhouse may have Shaftesbury in mind, who claims in *Sensus Communis*, that "All Politeness is owing to Liberty," explaining, "We polish one another, and rub off our Corners and rough Sides by a sort of *amicable Collision*. To restrain this, is inevitably to bring a Rust upon Mens Understandings."[45] The British are proud of their rural simplicity and their eccentricities, but dullness is no asset. Montesquieu, one of the more influential promoters of *la doux commerce* in the period, dissects the expression: gentleness is *douceur*; commerce and politeness are *moeurs douces*; commerce polishes and softens (*adoucit*).[46]

Faculties, endowments, wit, and all manner of mental powers will rust if neglected. Here the mind may be as much like one of Boulton's minting machines as a coin. Akenside describes "Passion's fierce illapse" and the "daily impulse," which "polishes anew / By that collision all the fine machine: / Else rust would arise."[47] Coinage is polished by the world of exchange and circulation, and travel knocks off the rust of inexperience. Of course, Woodhouse's and Sterne's oppositions of rust and polish yield to dialectic, and rust is also, perhaps surprisingly, a preservative. In *Dialogues Upon the Usefulness of Ancient Medals*, Joseph Addison's spokesman Philander describes "two or three" sorts of rust "which are extremely beautiful in the eye of an Antiquary, and preserve a coin better than the best artificial varnish."[48] Philander also describes how other crusts of dross are easily removed by the medalist and how this process of cleansing coin may fix, in the memory, stamped impressions that may otherwise be forgotten. "Money," asserts Foucault, "is a material memory."[49] In fact, claims Addison, "The intrinsic value of an old coin does not consist in its metal but its erudition" (13).

Intrinsic and Extrinsic

Throughout the eighteenth century, political economists compare and contrast intrinsic and extrinsic value. At issue is where value comes from—who, if anyone, has the power to assign it. Either value belongs necessarily to the coin, or it is something assayed after fact. The contrast may be drawn in philosophical jargon (a priori and a posteriori), as in the opening of the ninth and final volume of *Tristram Shandy*, where we find another complicating coin metaphor. Here Sterne seems to allude to Epictetus in a dedication to William Pitt the Elder: "Honours, like impressions upon coin, may give an ideal and local value to a bit of base metal; but Gold and Silver will pass all the world over without any other recommendation than their own weight."[50] In so dedicating his volume, Sterne displays "Honours" as local and extrinsic, assignable by authors to great men. Or again: that Sterne's noun is plural suggests not coinage but the many medals worn by a decorated hero. Pitt had been elevated and made Earl of Chatham and Viscount Pitt in 1766, but only because in forming the government he assigned himself the office of Lord Privy Seal, which *required* his installment in the House of Lords. For all that, Sterne's opinion of the man remains "neither better or worse" than it had been when he dedicated the first two volumes to Mr. ***, now Lord *******.[51]

Contrast the equally convoluted assertion in the verses from Montagu discussed above. "Honour" for Montagu is *internal*, a treasure of the breast: it is an inward worth that gives the stamp and standard. Like silver, the medium of exchange, honor should not vary with respect to itself—it is the stamp of a sovereign self. The theme is a favorite of eighteenth-century moral writers and an especial favorite of Mandeville's. But honor in Mandeville's philosophical system is purely extrinsic. Overturning Montagu's metaphor, he describes how ambitious men of honor are bought with "the Aerial Coyn of Praise" (*Fable* 38)—with dedications and other forms of fanciful coinage. Mandeville observes, "the meanest Wretch puts an inestimable value upon himself" (37). For Mandeville, who follows Hobbes here as elsewhere, honor is supposed to devolve from above: "when we say the Sovereign is the Fountain of Honour, it signifies that he has the Power, by Titles or Ceremonies, or both together, to stamp a Mark upon whom he pleases, that shall be as current as his Coin, and procure the Owner the good Opinion of every Body, whether he deserves it or not" (50). Honor derives from structures of power; because it is the king whose face is stamped on the coinage, it is the king's prerogative to raise or debase the currency. With King William, the sovereign's private debts are made public. Mandeville's slogan circles back on itself: private vices, public virtues.

Opposing the arguments of Hobbes and Mandeville are the discussions of inner or inward worth of moral sense theorists. The Scottish writer on education, David Fordyce, for one, in his *Elements of Moral Philosophy*, articulates the relation of extrinsic and intrinsic worth by picturing the mind as a kind of mint. In Fordyce the imagination is a middle faculty between sense and reason. It is a "Storehouse" in which imagery is "treasured up" and where the raw materials of sensation are worked upon and transmuted into something more valuable.[52] Fordyce explains the interaction of moral qualities and the materials of sensation in metallurgical terms: "The *sensible* Beauty, or Good, is refined from its Dross by partaking of the *Moral*, and the *Moral* receives a Stamp, a visible Character and Currency from the *Sensible*" (236). This is pretty image making on Fordyce's part and unites a number of metaphors of mind in one coherent picture. The imagination, which is often figured as a place in which metal and medals are worked (see **Metal**), here becomes a kind of mint. It is in the imagination that coinage is milled.[53]

New from the mint, coins establish boundaries with mercantilists preferring coin to circulate *in* the realm.[54] On Addison's view, ancient coins educated those through whose hands they passed, defining the communities in which they originally circulated and enriching their current collector.[55] That coins are themselves understood to be like ideas—metaphors or memes, I might add—"dealt about, like current coin," is evidenced by the lines from James Woodhouse quoted as an epigraph to this entry. But there are also economies within, both physiological and psychological, and ideas are treasured up in the mind or brain. In Fielding's *Amelia*, after Dr. Harrison protests he knows not how to get or keep a shilling in his pocket, he is congratulated instead on a "Mind" that "is a Treasury of all ancient and modern Learning."[56] Bernard Mandeville has recourse to an elaborate analogy on the "abstruse Oeconomy" of the brain in his dialogues in the second volume of *The Fable of the Bees*. In the fourth dialogue, Cleomenes demurs, answering his interlocutor Horatio, who would know where the soul lodges. Cleomenes notes that even "the most consummate Anatomist" knows not where the soul is seated and can only figure the brain as "the capacious Exchequer of human Knowledge, in which the faithful Senses deposite the vast Treasure of Images" (2:178–9).

Fancy's Coinage

Coinage metaphors organize a symbolic economy in the period that increasingly exchanges ideas of money as metaphor and metaphors of money.[57] As ideas are themselves figured with coins, so the term *specie* (or *species*) is found in both philosophical and financial lexicons.[58] And Johnson records multiple senses of "SPECIES" as "appearance to the senses," "Representation to the mind," and "Circulating money." Locke contributes a pamphlet to recoinage debates and appeals repeatedly to gold, cash, and coinage for examples in his other writings. Literary criticism uncovers a common structure of signification in Locke's economic, epistemological, and moral writings, with John O'Brien arguing that Locke's "*Idea*" "becomes the central term in the *Essay*'s symbolic economy"—the *Idea*, as a circulating term or token, belongs to "a homology between the economy of *Ideas* and the economy of money."[59]

Hamlet's mother tells her son that the apparition of the ghost of King Hamlet is "the very coynage of your Braine."[60] Shakespeare's expression enters eighteenth-century ordinary language, and "coinage" suggests coin that is fictitious or false. Dryden in particular is taken with coin metaphors, using them repeatedly to mark poetic affectation and specious sentiments. We have already encountered his punning on "Bromingham" and his satire of

Shaftesbury, *The Medal*. In fact, the *OED* cites Dryden's *Juvenal* as the earliest attestation for "coinage" in the figurative sense of "The (deliberate) formation of a new word." In his *Discourse Concerning the Original and Progress of Satire*, we find him complaining of "Clipt Poetry and false Coin."[61] In his dedication to *Aeneis*, he nearly despairs at translating Virgil's Latin figures into "inferior" English: "Words are not so easily Coyn'd as Money. . . . *Virgil* call'd upon me in every line for some new word: and I paid so long that I was almost Banckrupt." The immediate context of the translation is the recoinage; so when Dryden publishes in 1697, he pretends to be happy he has no more Virgil to translate: "I had certainly been reduc'd to pay the Publick in hammer'd Money, for want of Mill'd; that is, in the same old Words which I had used before."[62] Where, in the same year, the nation had completed a project of replacing hammered with new milled money, Dryden seems to have completed just the opposite in his translation. In his 1699 *Satyr Against Wit*, Dryden's enemy Sir Richard Blackmore imagines a demonetization of Restoration wit: "If once the Muses Chequer would deny / To take false Wit, 'twould lose its currency."[63]

Multiplying instances of the phrase "fancy's coinage" in eighteenth-century literature indicate that the expression is close to being an established piece of poetic diction. The fancy or imagination, as in Fordyce and elsewhere, is repeatedly figured as a mint. Here again ideas are figured as a kind of coinage, but more often than not these coins—especially when assigned to the fancy—prove counterfeit. In Richard Ames's satire on women *The Folly of Love*, Satan is described plotting his ruination of Paradise: "New-minted Mischeifs rumble in his brain, / Each false Stamp'd Coin is melted down again" until his "refin'd Fancy fix'd on *Woman*." The title character of William Mason's *Elfrida* exclaims (the passage is among this entry's epigraphs) "I flatter'd my poor soul that all its Fears / Were Grief's distemper'd coinage." And William Walsh dismisses "all the tender Words an amorous Fancy coins" as unreliable tokens of love.[64] In a letter, Elizabeth Montagu complains to Gilbert West that Bishop Berkeley, too retired from "commerce with mankind," has worked the rich ore of his imagination into "bright but useless medals," which otherwise might "have been stamp'd into current coin."[65]

False Coin and Forgery

In 1777 the "Macaroni Parson" William Dodd passed a forged bill of exchange, allegedly drawn by the Earl of Chesterfield. At the time, Dodd was a popular preacher, probably best known for his *The Beauties of Shakespeare* (1752), a treasury of quotations. His earliest literary efforts are derivative of earlier eighteenth-century works: a stage farce on Sir Roger de Coverley and *A New Book of the Dunciad* (1750). Catering his sermons to aristocratic audiences, Dodd kept a carriage and dressed fashionably. Ultimately, extravagant spending and waning literary success made Dodd prey to his creditors. Arrested four days after cashing out the forged bill for £4,200, he confessed to the crime and was convicted of capital forgery.[66] A public campaign attempted to obtain mercy for Dodd through petitions, and Samuel Johnson wrote prayers and speeches that were published—one detects something like situational irony here—under Dodd's name.[67] Friends prepared to bribe the turnkeys, and Boswell records Johnson's belief that some of them prepared a counterfeit image of Dodd in wax, "which was to have been left in his place" and was even "carried into the prison" (748). But all to no avail. Dodd was hanged at Tyburn in 1777.[68]

Two coining metaphors feature relevantly in Dodd's last work, *Thoughts in Prison*. The first appears in a passage that registers disbelief at his imprisonment: "A prisoner in—Impossible!—I sleep: / 'Tis fancy's coinage; 'tis a dream's delusion." The second comes after he imagines, like young Hamlet, that his father's ghost visits him in his cell. Dodd dismisses the specter: "'Twas but a coinage vain / Of the distemper'd fancy! Gone, 'tis gone."[69] The preacher and poet who counterfeited another's promise to pay writes of his own fancy's false coinage—or is the coin here Shakespeare's? Indeed, Dodd has collected Gertrude's famous exchange with Hamlet in his *Beauties*: "This is the very coinage of your brain: / This bodiless creation extasy / Is very cunning in" (III.iv).[70] The cunning may be deep and the standard remote. Dodd cites *King John* in his preface to the *Beauties*, acknowledging that the act of prefacing Shakespeare is "wasteful and ridiculous excess" of "gild[ing] refined gold" (IV.ii). Where is the value added when another's coin is claimed as one's own? A treasury locates value in the act of collection and arrangement. Dodd must make appeal to the medieval tradition of the thesaurus or *treasure* book. Shakespeare's words were for Dodd a treasure-house; his *Beauties of Shakespeare* remained continuously in print until the twentieth century.

Lord Kames follows Addison's *Spectator* no. 62 in defining false wit as a resemblance "in words only, not in sense."[71] Twice in the third volume of *Elements of Criticism*, figures in which figurative and proper sense fail to connect are termed "false coin," and Kames may, in fact, have Queen Gertrude in mind when he identifies "phantom similes," in this context, as "mere witticisms" (III.xix.42–3). Dodd's associations are worn coinage.

Dodd was executed in the modern copyright regime, dated to the *Donaldson v. Becket* decision (1774), and wrote in a moment in which originality was newly valued and conventional forms of imitation were newly interrogated.[72] In this later part of century, as signaled with the publication of Edward Young's *Conjectures on Original Composition*, we get repeated calls for raising the standard of composition. Not surprisingly, Young draws on monetary metaphor in preferring an original to an imitation: "Thoughts, when become too common, should lose their Currency; and we should send new metal to the Mint, that is, new meaning to the Press."[73]

In the next twenty years counterfeiting continued to escalate as gold became increasingly scarce and was hoarded. The French Revolutionary Wars drained the supply of gold, and in 1799 the production of gold guineas came to an end. In 1797 a period of restriction began during which, for the first time in the history of the Bank of England, its notes could not be converted into cash. It is only two years later that Wordsworth pens his preface to *Lyrical Ballads*. Like Blackmore, complaining of the coinage of a previous literary period, Wordsworth would demonetize poetic diction. The poetry of the eighteenth century will, no more, pass current. Thomas Gray's description of the sun's "golden fire" is, pointedly, *not* one of the lines in the "Sonnet to Richard West" to which Wordsworth assigns "any value." He is likewise, in the 1802 appendix, suspicious of a stanza of Cowper's that tropes "Religion" as a "heavenly word" in which resides "treasure untold," treasure "More precious than silver or gold."[74] Wordsworth complains of artificial devices that would *raise* poetry above prose.

Modern Values

A good-hearted person has "a heart of gold," and yet guineas or shillings seem not the right currencies to value a person. So William Blake affirms that "The countless gold of a merry heart" can never be brought "to the mart" nor hoarded in a "treasury." A person is not to be confused with a commodity; and yet a British gentleman is described as a man of so many pounds a year, and in 1776 that gentleman might have visited a market in Kingston, Jamaica, and purchased a slave—an "animate instrument" or "ensouled article of property," in Aristotle's phrase—for £37 14s. 3d. (see **Fetters**).[75] Thomas Piketty estimates, in the recent best seller *Capital*, that between £30 and £500 a year is required to qualify as a fictional character in a Jane Austen novel.[76]

Again, Hobbes writes: "The *Value*, or WORTH of a man, is as all other things, his Price; that is to say, so much as would be given for the use of his Power."[77] Saxons accorded a man his *weregeld*, a "blood money" compensation based on his rank in society; the life insurance companies that schemed and boomed in London in the first decades of the eighteenth century proposed other means of pricing persons: a life in eighteenth-century England was valued at £50,000 at the beginning of the century, £1,000,000 at the height of the insurance boom, before falling to £200,000 in 1750 and later rising to £600,000.[78]

Investigating and complicating the root metaphor of "possessive individualism," recent scholarship remains engrossed with the seventeenth- and eighteenth-century realizations that other people assign us our value.[79] Hobbes observes of reputation, perhaps satirically, "as in other things, so in men, not the seller, but the buyer determines the Price." Market relations seem here ratified: "let a man, as most men do, rate themselves at the highest Value they can; yet their true Value is no more than it is esteemed by others" (*Leviathan* 42). In a "Modern Glossary" published in the fourth number of Fielding's *Covent-Garden Journal*, "Worth" is defined as "Power. Rank. Wealth"; "Wisdom," as the art of "acquiring all three." After the late seventeenth century, honor, credit, and worth—concepts with aristocratic and feudal associations—are increasingly informed by market relations (as in Montagu's "Man of Honor") and increasingly conflated in terms of creditworthiness.[80]

"The most trifling Actions that affect a Man's Credit, are to be regarded," or so Benjamin Franklin famously advises the young tradesman: "The Sound of your Hammer at Five in the morning, or Nine at Night, heard by a Creditor, makes him easy Six Months longer; but if he sees you at a Billiard Table, or hears your Voice at a Tavern, when you should be at Work, he sends for his Money the next Day."[81] The community is to determine the value of all things. But the satirical Hobbist or Mandevillean is right to stress that one is prone to overvalue himself—to value himself beyond value. We cannot be relied upon to assess our own worth. But is, then, a person's value imaginary, consensual, or both? In Franklin, it is performative—in at least two senses—the hammer at work rings out and the creditor can hear his money working. In a single writer's revision we may find both obverse and reverse: currency has "chiefly a fictitious value" in the 1770 printing of Hume's essay "Of Interest," while in earlier versions money's value is described as arising "from the agreement and convention of men."[82]

Invaluable Worth

Given that coins dramatize the separability of intrinsic and extrinsic valuations, coin metaphors may not finally be the most suitable means for representing inestimable, inward worth. Precious metals may or may not be "intrinsically valuable" in the eighteenth century (this is certainly up for debate in Locke, Hume, and Smith), and the stamp, in any case, that attests to a coin's value is necessarily extrinsic. For a believer, the Kingdom and Treasury of Heaven alone can secure a soul's currency. It is a "pearl of great price," a "treasure hidden in a field," that is purchased with one's life (Matthew 13:44–5). But here a different metaphor may be called for, and jewel or gem metaphors may well be preferred to the coinage metaphors featured thus far. These metaphorical jewels and gems of a breast's treasury—what Lady Mary Lee Chudleigh calls the "true, substantial Wealth" that "is lodg'd within"[83]—have no way of circulating and therefore are not worn out in transactions. The gem is a token of love; we should not ask its price. Divine grace is free, unpurchasable, unbought. In *The Vicar of Wakefield* Oliver Goldsmith poses the rhetorical question "is there upon earth a gem so precious as the human soul?"[84]

The moral sense theory that influences Kantian ethics understands the rational self as valuable in itself—as an "end in itself." In the *Groundwork of the Metaphysics of Morals*, Kant compares the will ("valued incomparably") to a jewel, explaining that even if a good will lacked the capacity to carry out its purpose and "should yet achieve nothing and only the good will were left . . . then, like a jewel, it would shine by itself, as something that has its full worth in itself."[85] The will's incomparable value is necessarily intrinsic and not assigned by another.[86] Like a jewel, the good will is supposed to have worth in itself. In Kant's incomparable comparison we find a crystallization of self-ownership in a hard, gem-like emblem of possessive individualism. Compare further the "Gem" pictured in a famous stanza of Thomas Gray's famous churchyard *Elegy*: it is submarine and "of purest Ray serene."[87] In contrast, coins are explicitly valued and shine not by themselves but in circulation. In what sort of unfathomable cavern are we to imagine Kant's good will crazily shining? The coinage of the Kingdom of Heaven, as a treasure laid up, cannot pass in a secular economy and self-valorize.[88] What, then, is the coin of the realm in Kant's Kingdom of Ends? We seem in the tightening grip of a picture (a nightmare of rational misers, grasping with invisible hands)—confounded by parables of the market and buried talents. The discourse of value is obviously not one the literary critic can give up if he will continue to sort, select, and privilege metaphors. Perhaps the metaphor is one best exchanged—but for what?

3 Court

Collocated Keywords: Attorney, Court, Judge, Law, Testimony, Verdict, Witness

Count of Metaphors in Database[1] (1700–1799): 182

A thousand little Nerves She sends
Quite to our Toes, and Fingers Ends;
And These in Gratitude again
Return their Spirits to the Brain;
In which their Figure being printed
(As just before, I think, I hinted)
Alma inform'd can try the Case,
As She had been upon the Place.

Thus, while the Judge gives diff'rent Journeys
To Country Counsel, and Attornies;
He on the Bench in quiet sits,
Deciding, as They bring the Writs.

—Matthew Prior, *Alma: Or, The Progress of the Mind* (1718)

By reason's standard, then, you judge amiss
Of those whose legislator is *caprice.*

—Elizabeth Griffith, *The Platonic Wife* (1765)

God and reason made the law, and have placed conscience within you to determine;—not like an *Asiatic* Cadi, according to the ebbs and flows of his own passions,—but like a *British* judge in this land of liberty and good sense, who makes no new law, but faithfully declares that law which he knows already written.

—Laurence Sterne, *Tristram Shandy* (1760–7)

And he who teaches men to think, though nobly,
Doth raise within their minds a busy judge
To scan his actions.

—Joanna Baillie, *Basil: A Tragedy* (1798)

See also **Empire** and **Inhabitants**

While judgment may be associated with matters of theology and aesthetics, the most intricately realized metaphors collected under this heading are found in texts that picture an allegorical "court of conscience" in which the "testimony" of the senses is heard, "suits" are brought by the passions, and "verdicts" rendered by a presiding psychological faculty, often personified as a chief justice or chancellor. A metaphorics of judgment, which my contemporary reader might associate with the head, is repeatedly located in the bosom or breast in the long eighteenth century. Particularly in sentimental and devotional contexts, this court and its "judge within" is so located. The metaphorical court is not necessarily self-legislating or *sui juris*: philosophers and theologians claim to discover innate, metaphysical laws of nature structuring the self a priori. Laws may become legible by the light of reason or the light of nature or may be "already written" and said to resemble—as in the epigraph from Sterne above—British common law. These pictures of the mind or soul as a court remain juridical, even as philosophers and theologians quote chapter and verse (e.g., Romans 2:15—"Which shew the work of the law written in their hearts, their conscience also bearing witness") or make higher, apocalyptic appeals to final judgment. As the historian E. P. Thompson observes, "The eighteenth century was indeed a great century for constitutional theorists, judges, and lawyers," claiming further that the rhetoric of the period is "saturated with the notion of law."[2]

After Sir Edward Coke's struggles with King James I and his removal from office in 1616, judges, legal theorists, and legal commentators increasingly described the law as an autonomous, independent, neutral realm of activity. At the end of the seventeenth century, James II's meddling with the courts helped precipitate the revolutionary events of 1688, while the resulting declarations of the Convention Parliament of 1689 reinforced distinctions between the executive and judicial powers of government.[3] Eighteenth-century legal theory circumscribes conscience and gives up certain private or subjective aspects of judgment, or at least pretends to; the period is one that legal historians associate with the increase of statutes, the empowering of juries, and the rise of evidence in legal reasoning.[4] This separation of the public practice of law from the practical philosophy of private conscience is secured by new disciplinary relations between law and literature—or so I suggest—and the relations themselves are structured by discriminations between literal and figurative that complicate the law's supposed autonomy. Juridical metaphors both connect and hold apart literary critical and legal judgment.

In the following pages, judicial metaphors of mind are situated in the context of legal and literary history. I try to locate the "court of conscience," a phrase that moves between literary and legal contexts and troubles easy discriminations between the literal and figurative, but I will adjourn, repeatedly, to read specific passages from Restoration and eighteenth-century literature. Eighteenth-century law insists on precedent and procedure at the same moment its literary criticism turns away from classical precedents to valorizations of novelty and natural genius. I take judge and literary critic, looking in opposite directions, to stand as figural opposites, each defined by the other. In the closing paragraphs of this entry, I offer an image and emblem of judgment that enacts the play between objective and subjective judgment.

The increase in the frequency of judicial metaphors at midcentury (in the 1750s and 1760s) is of particular interest. These metaphors belong to a set of authors, and in this case sustained keyword searching connects a cluster of authors reworking the same figure—what Arthur Murphy, writing in the *Gray's-Inn Journal*, calls the "mental Court of Judicature."[5] I pay particular attention to these shared metaphors in the works of Henry Fielding, Laurence Sterne, Adam Smith, and Charles Churchill, examining each text in light of the others. William Blackstone, whose monumental *Commentaries on the Laws of England* was published in four volumes from 1765 to 1769 is cited throughout.[6] Hobbes is likewise a point of reference, as his impatience with common law serves as a useful counterpoint to more chauvinistic celebrations of English law and liberty.

The Courts

As attested in Johnson's *Dictionary*, a "COURT" is originally the "place where the prince resides" and therefore the "hall or chamber where justice is administered"—but more than a location, the court is also those persons collected in that location: those who are "assembled for the administration of justice." While I have tried to sift my metaphors and number only the juridical sort in this entry, in truth, different senses of the word overlap in political history and etymology. Originally the sovereign himself dispensed justice and presided over his court, and William Blackstone notes that in the contemplation of the law, "the king is supposed in contemplation of law to be always present," and where he is not actually present, he is "represented by his judges" (*Commentaries* 3:24). The importance of the sovereign is clear from the architecture and geography of justice: throughout the eighteenth century the four central courts of law were located in and around Westminster Hall—the Royal Courts of Law moved to central London, north of the Inns of Court, only in 1882.

The early pamphlets of the English Civil War would expose and negate metaphors of royal prerogative, warning that the king would figure his will as supreme law and institute his breast as the highest court.[7] A celebrated quip by the sixteenth-century humanist and MP John Selden questions appeals for equity as arbitrary and "roguish": taking the chancellor's conscience as a standard is like making "the standard for the measure we call a foot a chancellor's foot."[8] After detailing the means by which precedents are recorded, William Blackstone asserts that "it is not in the breast of any subsequent judge to alter or vary" them "according to his own private sentiments" or "his own private judgment" (1:69). If the law is to be located in a breast or bosom, the Anglican theologian Richard Hooker would have us acknowledge that "her seate is the bosome of God."[9]

The English subject is answerable to revealed law, the law of nature, the law of nations, and civil law.[10] In his religious poem *Redemption* (1722), Sir Richard Blackmore favors juridical metaphors, many of which rehearse jurisdictional distinctions. Describing revelation brought to "reason's bar," the poet warns that reason's is the "wrong court of appeals." Why? "For reason, reason's self being judge . . . can't decide the cause."[11] The doubled, divided senses of the term *reason*—"For reason" (that is, for the reason) and "reason's self"—undermine a judgment that would decide its own *cause*, another double entendre coordinating the matter pleaded in court as well as more extensive ideas of causation. From within the space of reasons, reason must recognize its own limits. For Blackmore and the moderate Anglican tradition from which he draws his distinctions, the spiritual falls outside reason's jurisdiction; the structures of revealed and natural law are made visible in the earlier assertion of scripture's "high unerring bar," at which "revelation's light" decides "the cause" (192).[12]

Blackmore's opposition of reason and revelation dramatizes divisions in the English ecclesiastical courts and the courts of equity, secular divisions that shadow divinity and suggest eschatological structures of final justice. As in Blackmore's verse, many distinctions, in both poetry and law, work by positing incommensurable structures—conflicting courts, a literal and a figurative, an earthly and a divine, a private, internal court and a public or political one. This entry in a dictionary of metaphors revisits the narratives of legal history that would divide literal from figurative structures of justice and assign them to separate spheres: the former, secularized, disenchanted, rationalized, walled off behind precedent and procedure; the latter, a realm of rhetoric, culture, and literature, ostensibly outside self-consistent autonomous legal practice.

But metaphor bridges—both separates and connects—the disciplines of law and literature. And the public-private dichotomy, like the literal-figurative dichotomy, is unstable, complicated by imagery wrested as evidence from historical and material contexts. For example, I read Blackmore's phrase "revelation's light" as a synecdoche for the mirrored reflectors placed above the bar in courts like the Old Bailey. These mirrors cast light on the faces of the accused so that their verbal testimony could be evaluated together with their facial expressions. Context is illuminating, and illumination is contextualizing.

Law of Reason

Pieces of language move across conceptual and disciplinary gaps, complicating the law's claim to autonomy—and, at the same time, complicating the tenor and vehicle of juridical metaphorics. A writer may divide reason from higher, divine law; or the two terms may be brought together, as in the phrase "the law of reason." Throughout the middle ages, scholastics figured the body of Roman law known as Justinian's Code as *ratio scripta*, or "written reason."[13] For Sir Edward Coke, the law is "artificial reason." As it is conditioned by centuries of experience and supposed superior to the reasoning of any individual, the common law is frequently described as "the perfection of reason."[14] Identifying common law and natural law in his *Commentaries*, William Blackstone describes an unwritten constitution (*lex non scripta*) as a paradoxical object: revered in terms borrowed from metaphorics of mind, it is "immemorial" and antique, if not innate to the English body politic.[15] The metaphors toggle between an unspecific legal history and specified legal actor: because the written constitution is an expression of the popular will and a record of custom, the judge or lawyer who claims to apply *unwritten* principles or equity may be accused of substituting his own judgment for the law, his private reason for *ratio scripta*, thus making his breast the court in which the motion is decided.[16]

In the Stoic tradition *ratio* or reason is a law implanted by God in mind and nature.[17] Neoclassical, geometrical reasoning observes ratio, proportion, and propriety, balancing political powers as well as the mental faculties. Throughout the period here surveyed, reason equates with law, and Christian apologists develop allusions to the Pauline gentiles who are "a law to themselves" (Romans 2:14). So Locke writes in the *Second Treatise*: "The State of Nature has a Law of Nature to govern it" and reason "*is that Law*" (II.ii.6, emphasis added). Joseph Butler claims that every man is naturally a law to himself and to follow our conscience is to follow the law of our nature, while the poet Charles Churchill affirms that "Reason to herself alone is law."[18] But because laws do not apply themselves, the metaphor of self-legislation in ethics may even, as in the writings of Kant, prove more literal than it first appears.[19] Likewise, self-legislation becomes more than metaphor in those revolutionary writings of the late eighteenth century that appeal to man's equality and make declaration of the self-evident rights of life, liberty, and property.

Early in the *Second Treatise* (II.iii.20), Locke alludes to the story of Jephthah and the Ammonites (Judges 11), which exemplifies two parties plunged into a state of war, both holding that they act in accord with the law of nature. Where there is no common court of appeal, no superior jurisdiction, "Who shall judge?" asks Locke (II.iii.20, II.xiv.168). The question is variously posed and answered throughout the eighteenth century. An appeal to a higher power or to more fundamental law is preceded by its own judgment of wrongdoing, so that in Locke's state of nature, men must be their own judges (II.ii.13). God is almost beside the point when those who have triumphed over their Ammonite neighbors read God's divine will or judgment into the aftermath of war. Still, Christianity promotes God as the first and final judge, and so understood, Jephthah's appeal to a higher power is an appeal before God's tribunal.

Samuel Johnson's first definition of "JUDGE" is "One who is invested with authority to determine any cause or question, real or personal," but he cites religious material from Genesis, Psalms, and Milton by way of illustration. (As is often the case, the priority of tenor or vehicle, source or target, proves hard to establish.) The lexicographer would show his piety, and yet Johnson's definition is underdetermined by its attestations. James Thomson identifies God as the "sole perfect Judge" in his 1737 poem to the memory of Lord Talbot, "Late Chancellor of *Great Britain*."[20] In early modernity, church haunts state: if the divine judge is the sole perfect judge, the judge within seems an image or reflection of divinity, not jurisprudence.[21] And when God is figured as a judge, details are purposefully left unspecified. The Final Judgment of mankind is eschatological abstraction of the grandest juridical sort, and nothing in legal history seems to supply any new content to the prophesized occasion. Legal history may well be beside the point, as both men's actions and intentions are to be fully and finally scrutinized at this judgment. Apocalypse brings all trials to an end.

Court of Conscience

The defining example of literal-figurative dualism in this context is the expression "court of conscience." A history of secularization enforces the boundary between internal and external (accusations made *in foro conscientiae* will not be heard *in foro legis*), but metaphor turns many expressions inside out. Hobbes, for example, works from public to private, from the outward to the inward in *Leviathan*, in which "the Law is the publique Conscience" and private conscience is logically dependent on and figurative of public acts of knowledge (II.xxix.7). The individual's internalization of public judgment—*conscience* is knowing together, intersubjectively and therefore publically—as private conscience or self-knowledge is necessarily parasitic on the structure of public reasoning: "Afterwards, men made use of the same word *metaphorically* for the knowledge of their own secret facts and secret thoughts" (I.vii.4, emphasis added). Individual conscience, a category mistake, belongs to metaphor.[22]

Compare Hobbes with the twentieth-century philosopher and externalist Gilbert Ryle, who writes, "The sorts of things I can find out about myself are the same as the sorts of things I can find out about other people, and the methods of finding them out are much the same."[23] Hobbes has us reimagine the proverbial equation of conscience with "a thousand witnesses," warning against the rhetoric of vainglorious men who swear vehemently by their own conscience, as if it were "*unlawfull*, to change or speak against them" (emphasis added).[24] Self and other must both be cross-examined; the king cannot adjudicate of his own case. Blackstone may have Hobbes in mind, and is close to Blackmore on "reason's self," when he writes that "it is unreasonable that any man should determine his own quarrel" (1:91). *Con-science* implies at least two knowers. In Ryle even self-consciousness is overtly juridical: a "more or less efficient handling of a less or more honest and intelligent witness" (195). The chiasmus of "less or more," "more or less" provides space for the self to look upon itself and alerts us to manipulations of a boundary by which a self brings testimony forward as self-evidence.

Whereas modern legal practice separates conscience from secular law, medieval theory finds conscience rooted in both factual knowledge and moral apperception.[25] Modern legal developments would set aside morality as long as it does not impinge (through considerations of intent) on criminal cases. But between the medieval and modern moments, in the early modern period here surveyed, conscience moves under secular jurisdiction—where it is partially conceived in common law terms—before being more clearly separated from legal practice.[26] The legacy of the seventeenth century, a period in which the English Civil War stands out as a great case and crisis of conscience, is a clearer separation of law and conscience in the political philosophy and legal theory written by Hobbes, Locke, and later thinkers. In Reinhart Koselleck's formula, conscience is neutralized by politics.[27]

Casuistical thinking moves first into pulpit "Morning Exercise" sermons and newspapers, such as John Dunton's *Athenian Mercury*, and onward into the novel.[28] In Aaron Hill's periodical the *Prompter*, stage proceedings are morally circumscribed: leaving aside "such Vices as are *cognizable* by Course of Law, and *punitively terminable* at *Tyburn*," drama exercises "Poetical Justice," which "extends only to such as the Law cannot lay hold of, such as are to be tried in *Foro Conscientiae*, where the Delinquent, being strongly touched by a Resemblance of Himself, may amend."[29] The definition of private conscience by Hobbes and others as a sphere of figuration may even empower a new kind of judge, the literary critic, to preside over it. Addison and Steele's Mr. Spectator informs us that his pregnant mother, at the end of her first trimester, "dreamt that she was brought to Bed of a Judge."[30]

Chancery and the Lord High Chancellor

The common law courts and the court of chancery are also often described as being at odds, and in certain instances of conflict the law may be set aside in favor of "conscience." That is, in the early modern moment, the court of conscience has legal reality.[31] A persistent concern that the "subjective" criterion of conscience is an uncertain ground for the law may be read into the longer course of legal commentary that would circumscribe conscience.[32] The Chancery is an ancient court, presided over by the lord chancellor, who is appointed by the king himself and is the custodian of the king's Great Seal (See *Seal* under **Impressions**).[33] In his *Commentaries on the Laws of England*, William Blackstone notes of the chancellor, "Being formerly usually an ecclesiastic, (for none else were then capable of an office so conversant in writings) and presiding over the royal chapel, he became keeper of the king's conscience" (3:47). In a notebook owned by the actor and dramatist Charles Macklin, I find some comic dialogue improvised under the character name Sir Constantine Conscience: "A king has no Conscience—no—no—why so—What is become of it? Why the Chancellor keeps it for him—and who keeps the Chancellor's?—His Strong Box.—to be Sure."[34]

That the Chancery is a "court of conscience" may complicate Hobbes's etymological interpretation of conscience and his figuring of private conscience as parasitic on the model of the court. It is not clear which is prior in etymology: the private or the public, the metaphor of mind or the court itself. Hobbes's etymology notwithstanding, courts of conscience trouble the distinction between literal and figurative, putting a putative metaphor of mind in an obscure relationship with the court of law. Compare the political metaphor of the cabinet and the privy counselors who are the king's most intimate advisors (see **Rooms**). In Blackstone's description of a confessor figure who both keeps the king's *conscience* and presides over the king's *court*, separating the literal elements from the figurative is not fully possible. And it will be seen in what follows that this magisterial figure, the lord chancellor, further complicates our distinctions by coming to personify conscience itself.

It is a thesis of this book that figurative and literal distinctions are often difficult to maintain and that the pursuit of etymology rarely settles anything. A literary critic must produce the metaphor and worry the individual case. With the semantics of "conscience," the historical court and the location of some inmost self appear mutually informing. In the seventeenth century particularly, the term "conscience" is under scrutiny in legal and theological discourses, both of which apply the court of conscience metaphor. In fact, historians characterize the seventeenth century as the "Age of Conscience."[35] Court metaphors for the mind multiply in the writings of William Perkins, Joseph Hall, and Jeremy Taylor. When conscience proved variable and offensive to the rigorous procedures of the law, Blackstone credits Sir Heneage Finch, later Lord Nottingham, as the first lord chancellor to begin building "a system of jurisprudence and jurisdiction upon wide and rational foundations" (3:55). Nottingham, who takes office in 1675, is the first in a line of lord chancellors whose commentaries on conscience make it more compatible with the prosecution of equity on the basis of precedents, elevating the keeping of contracts—even contracts that take advantage of another—above complaints of good conscience.

In *Cook v. Fountain* (1676), Lord Chancellor Nottingham describes a "twofold conscience," which employs a distinction between "*conscientia politica et civilis, et conscientia naturalis et interna*"—that is, between civic, political conscience and an inward, natural conscience.[36] As in Hobbes, Nottingham's distinction divides the public man from the private, separating he who governs and is governable through law from the interior man, whose conscience is beyond the command of law. Both forms of conscience (*civilis* and *interna*) are described as ruled and regular, but a chancellor should only exercise a politic and civil judgment that is tied to precedents. It is better for a secret trust or agreement made in private to miscarry "than that men should lose their estates by the mere fancy and imagination of a Chancellor."[37]

Nottingham's distinction survives to be travestied in the stage satire *The Man of the World* (a play much concerned with conscience), when Sir Pertinax MacSycophant, a corrupt Scottish MP modeled on Shylock, explains how every man has "twa consciencees, a releegious, and a poleetical conscience"; the first is to be left to the clergy, while the second more usefully excuses bribery, corruption, and false oaths "in a Chancery suit" on the grounds of business as usual.[38] The anti-Scottish context of the play, which premiered in Dublin in 1764 under the title *The Trueborn Scotchman*, is examined below.

The seventeenth century—as an age of conscience—discomfits eighteenth-century England, at midcentury, in both the 1745 Jacobite rebellion and the popular unrest that followed John Wilkes's arrest in April 1763 on a general warrant for the publication of seditious and treasonable material. As Chancery had been used as a metaphor for personal conscience in the previous century,[39] Henry Fielding appropriates both the court of conscience metaphor and the office of the lord chancellor in the novel *Tom Jones* (set in 1745, with the Jacobite rising serving as a background), fusing Nottingham's two consciences by means of a topical comparison. In a well-known passage from book IV, Fielding brings forward this figure of the lord chancellor in order to personify Tom Jones's internal "Somewhat":

> Mr. *Jones* had Somewhat about him, which, though I think Writers are not thoroughly agreed in its Name, doth certainly inhabit some human Breasts; whose Use is not so properly to distinguish Right from Wrong, as to prompt and incite them to the former, and to restrain and with-hold them from the latter. . . . To give a higher Idea of the Principle I mean, as well as one more familiar to the present Age; it may be considered as sitting on its Throne in the Mind, like the Lord High Chancellor of this Kingdom in his Court; where it presides, governs, directs, judges, acquits and condemns according to Merit and Justice; with a Knowledge which nothing escapes, a Penetration which nothing can deceive, and an Integrity which nothing can corrupt. (II.iv.6)[40]

That Fielding does not denominate that something that Tom has in him suggests that public language will not pick out private parts. Because something more "familiar" is needed to give a higher idea of the principle, Fielding points in panegyric to the "present Age" and identifies his internal "Somewhat" with the contemporary lord high chancellor of England, Philip Yorke, first Earl of Hardwicke, who presided over the treason trials of Scottish peers involved in the Jacobite uprising of 1745.[41] The private, unnamed Somewhat borrows the name of a real, very public person, one who "became renowned for his immense conscientiousness in his desire to do justice."[42] But the designation "Somewhat" is also reminiscent of the ineffable aesthetic judgment *je ne sais quoi*, and Fielding complicates or mixes his juridical metaphor by bringing in another "familiar" reference to the fictitious Trunkmaker described in *Spectator* no. 235. The Trunkmaker, more critic than judge, sits in the upper gallery of a playhouse and bangs his oak staff in approbation whenever he sees something in the play that pleases him. By the middle of the eighteenth century, "judgment" has developed two related senses, one juridical and one literary critical, a distinction underscored in *Tom Jones* when Fielding describes the operation of judicial authority *in foro literario.*

The chancellor is the king's first minister and is second only to the king, advising the monarch in matters of conscience. Conscience is supposed to minister to the sovereign self, making the chancellor an appropriate personification of Tom's—or anyone's—internal Somewhat. So Joseph Butler, in his *Fifteen Sermons*, describes "a superior Principle of Reflection or Conscience in every Man, which distinguishes between the internal Principles of his Heart, as well as his external Actions [which] *magisterially* exerts itself," approving, condemning, and passing "a higher and more effectual sentence."[43] In the eighteenth century the chancellor was first recognized as the "head of law."[44] The lord chancellor presides over the House of Lords, participates in the cabinet, and heads the judiciary—in short, he combines executive, legislative, and judiciary functions. The lord high chancellor also presides over impeachment trials in the House of Lords, and the chancellor's ability to determine cases outside of the law made him as omnipotent as Fielding describes. Still, the Somewhat is not identical with Tom, nor is he located in Tom's head.[45] A separation of powers obtains within, dividing the self into judge and judged of, preventing Tom from playing both parts.

The chancellor is a particularly active figure and not merely a figure of deliberation. We are to imagine the prickings or proddings of the Somewhat. In his *Letters*, for example, Ignatius Sancho identifies "Conscience" as "the high chancellor of the human breast" and describes its "still small voice" pricking the Duchess of Kingston, who, charged with bigamy, was the talk of London in 1775 before being tried and found guilty at Westminster in 1776.[46] But where Sancho seems already to have convicted the Duchess, Fielding's sketch of conscience, as well as Butler's, may be more readily categorized as an example of motivation theory in which conscience does not so much distinguish right from wrong or deliberate or reflect on moral considerations as it prompts and incites.[47] The blurring of executive, judicial, legislative, and constitutional functions in the office of the chancellor permits Fielding to sketch a picture of conscience that is fully active. Fielding is closest to the theory of conscience presented in Joseph Butler's *Fifteen Sermons*.[48] Although Fielding does not explicitly equate the Somewhat with Tom's conscience, it is a "Principle" in both Butler and Fielding—or, in the philosophical terminology shared by Shaftesbury, Francis Hutcheson, Butler, and Adam Smith, a "moral sense."

Testimony

While often personified as a judge, conscience is also figured as a kind of testimony or, as in an entry from George William Lemon's 1783 etymological dictionary that would seem to overturn Hobbes, "the internal witness of our own minds" ("CON-SCIENCE"). Indeed, testimony is repeatedly assigned to the conscience, as in Phillips's *Dictionary*, where "Conscience" is defined as "the Testimony or Witness of one's own Mind, the inward Knowledge of a thing; a Scruple." In an early eighteenth-century court of law, testimony is delivered by a defendant and heard by the judge; it is not to be addressed to the jury.[49] And after the introduction of defense counsel in the 1730s, active testimony by defendants began to slip away altogether.[50] If not a prevalent metaphor in eighteenth-century verse, it figures importantly in gothic fictions like Charles Brockden Brown's *Wieland*.

The metaphor of testimony is available early on in seventeenth-century moral philosophy—the metaphor appears in William Perkins, Jeremy Taylor, and the natural law theorist Richard Cumberland's *De Legibus Naturae* (V, §xlv).[51] To produce soliloquial, self-incriminations Shaftesbury recommends erecting within oneself "as cruel a Court as the *Inquisition*" in order to discipline the self and secure personal identity.[52] Metaphorics of judgment much occupy Shaftesbury, before becoming a fixture of Scottish moral sense philosophy. Francis Hutcheson, for one, describes "the Testimony of our own Hearts" in his *Essay on Nature and Conduct of the Passions and Affections*.[53] David Fordyce also favors the metaphor of testimony in his discussion of virtue, characterizing virtue in terms of the judgment of conscience: "the Mind gives its Sanction or Testimony" to "good Dispositions" and "all Actions which flow from such Dispositions" (*Elements of Moral Philosophy* 101). And Fordyce brings in an issue of logical regression and intrinsic value—one already raised in **Coinage**—when he writes, "if Virtue is something that deserves our Esteem and Love, then it must exist before *Conscience* is exerted, or gives its Testimony. *Therefore* to say that the Testimony of Conscience is necessary to the *Being* or *Form* of a virtuous Action, is, in plain Terms, to affirm, that *Virtue* is not *Virtue*, till it is reflected on and approved as Virtue" (104–5). The testimony of conscience cannot be solely responsible, "necessary to the *Being* or *Form*," of the virtuous action. Fordyce argues that virtue is prior to our esteem for it; the "Office" of conscience (like the Trunkmaker's) is to observe and applaud virtue. Our esteem displays our agency and self-consciousness, and reason guides our affections.[54] Testimony may discover virtue, but virtue is something more basic than those proceedings that discover it. It is, for the innatist, the law supposed already written in the heart—like the law that the common lawyer imagines written and recorded, a chain of precedents pointing backward to custom and time immemorial.

The Exercise and Abuse of Judgment

The turbulent politics of the late seventeenth and early eighteenth century and "the great change in property by the extension of trade" afforded an opportunity to reform the law, or so claims Blackstone (3:55). Property and trust at this early modern moment is part of the longer history reconciling conscience and precedent. The formula inherited from medieval canon lawyers is *Iudex secundum allegata non secundum conscientiam iudicat*—i.e., the judge judges according to the evidence presented, not according to his conscience.[55] The sixteenth-century common lawyer Christopher St. German writes, "The lorde Chauncellor must ordre his conscyence after the rewles and groundes of the lawe of the realme"; and Nottingham follows him, citing the same formula but in a new historical moment.[56] Conceptions of conscience outrun the older formulas and are newly figured from Hobbes to Fielding. While Hardwicke was much celebrated for his "Integrity" and his purging of the office of the corruption of bribery,[57] he is also renowned for more solidly establishing equity law in rational precedents, following Lord Nottingham's earlier attempts. To choose Hardwicke as a figure of conscience is not without legal historical ironies.

Indeed, the eighteenth-century legal history complicates court metaphors, as Hardwicke's office marked a shift in legal practice away from the exercise of "conscience" (in the sense of private, subjective conscience) and toward a reliance on precedent. Judge and critic—chancellor and Trunkmaker—are paired but Janus-faced. The law revalues legal precedent at the very moment literary practice turns away from "neoclassical" rewritings, translations, and the imitation of ancient precedents.[58] Fielding's novel is both modern and mock heroic. In a series of *Spectator* papers on *Paradise Lost*, Addison finds new ways to prefer Milton's modern, Christian epic to its ancient precedents; in other numbers of the periodical essay, Shakespeare's flouting of dramatic unities is defended against the inflexible unities of French theory. Fielding revisits Addison's critical writings and no doubt borrows from Lewis Theobald's periodical the *Censor* in his own periodical essays published under the masthead of the *Covent-Garden Journal*, particularly in his "Court of Censorial Enquiry," a section in which authors are tried for literary crimes.[59] Aesthetic judgment in the eighteenth century relaxes its rigor, newly praises "original genius," and finds room for the novelty of the novel in its canons of taste. The Augustan gives way to Sensibility, in part, by observing legalistic distinctions between law and evidence, that is, between inherited rules and classical forms to be applied, on the one hand, and the facts of modern life to be represented, on the other.

Even as Hardwicke read deeply in the law, his decisions became well-cited precedents. In his *Dialogue Between a Phylosopher and a Student*, Hobbes surveys the common law and puts the matter in terms that should be, by now, familiar: "the Lawyers themselves seek not for their Judgments in their own Breasts, but in the precedents of former Judges, as the Antient Judges sought the same, not in their own Reason, but in the Laws of the Empire."[60] As usual, Hobbes emphasizes the externality of judgment, but here he worries about the increase in suits and the abuse of the law. Precedents recede into the past, and each precedent must itself be chosen by a judge who, in choosing, must consult, of course, his own judgment.

Another relation of conscience to legal precedent is visible in the passage from Sterne's sermon the "Abuses of Conscience," an epigraph appearing at the head of this entry.[61] In Sterne, conscience is seen, like a "*British* judge," fully conforming to English statutory law. Statute, the strongest form of law, is explicitly written and may abrogate precedent.[62] And in Sterne's practice—in the experimental novel *Tristram Shandy*—almost every law governing composition is tested, flouted, broken, and overturned. Or so a traditional reading of *Shandy* might have it; but, as is now better recognized, reflexive innovation was widespread at midcentury.[63] And as amply documented in the Florida edition of *Tristram Shandy*, Sterne's particular genius relies on the tradition of learned wit, even as it folds precedent into the unprecedented. In short, Sterne turns common law metaphorics inside out. His own writing is installed as new precedent, reprinted in collections like *The Beauties of Sterne* and called upon in new contexts—his metaphor for conscience cited by Godwin in *Political Justice* (1:167), for example.

Then again, Sterne's metaphor is also inside out because subjective and private conscience, marked by the ebb and flow of passion, is orientalized by the mention of an "*Asiatic* Cadi." And the metaphor is inside out in yet another way that involves Sterne and his own pseudonymous writing. As discussed below, Sterne divides himself so he can accuse conscience of corruption. At issue in Sterne—and in the culture of the 1760s at large—is the power of the judge in the face of established law and the prerogative of the critic to overturn the standard of taste. (Must all judgments be grounded in law, or does "conscience" permit a judge to set aside the tradition?) Natural lawyers claim that the law must depend on moral criteria; positivists argue that law is determined only by institutional arrangements. In the *Republic*, Plato argues that the city should be ruled by a wise and unfettered ruler and not by law; Aristotle believed the laws to be wiser than rulers (1248a and 82a–b).[64]

Hobbes, likely responding to Coke's opinions on the supremacy of the law, emphasizes the problem of the judge's judge.[65] The judge of the king is assigned by the king: "A King perhaps will not sit to determine of Causes of Treason against his Person, lest he should seem to make himself Judge in his own Cause; but that it shall be Judged by Judges of his own making, can never be avoided, which is also one as if he were Judge himself."[66] While the Leviathan is necessarily unified and absolute, eighteenth-century political philosophy imagines new schemes for separating and balancing power. The sovereign self is likewise newly divisible in eighteenth-century philosophy of mind. Tom Jones should seem separable from the internal Somewhat that prompts and restrains his conduct. Faculty psychology separates reason from understanding and both from judgment. Kant gives each faculty its own critique.

Impartial Spectator: The Judge Judged Of

Adam Smith's *The Theory of Moral Sentiments* reads almost as a belated response to Hobbes's objections and Coke's opinions. In a discussion of the foundation of self-judgment and the sense of duty, Smith observes himself. And it is apt that the passage first appears in a draft revision of the first edition, first published in the second edition:

> When I endeavour to examine my own conduct, when I endeavour to pass sentence upon it, and either to approve or condemn it, it is evident that, in all such cases, I divide myself, as it were, into two persons, and that I, the examiner and judge, represent a different character from that other I, the person whose conduct is examined and judged of. . . . The first is the judge; the second the person judged of. But that the judge should in every respect, be the same with the person judged of, is as impossible, as that the cause should, in every respect, be the same with the effect.[67]

In Smith's theory of judgment, a self-conscious person is host to two moral persons: a judge and a person judged (I leave aside what must be wordplay involving the legal sense of "cause"). Smith personifies the judging part of this divided self alternately as the "impartial spectator," "the man within the breast," "the great inmate," and "the awful and respectable judge" (the personifications multiply in later editions of *The Theory*). Revising his own argument, he describes the man of perfect self-command who is able to adopt the sentiments of the impartial spectator so perfectly that he stands toward himself as a stranger.

Thus far I have been following a history of distinctions by which questions of judgment typically divide internal from external. But in Smith's moral philosophy, the internal is reliably divided against itself in self-evidence (the division, I have suggested, is enacted in the textual history of *The Theory*). Such self-consciousness necessitates division and a separation of powers that Hobbes's philosophy of absolutism cannot abide. Or, to bring in the metaphor Smith employs in the first edition of *The Theory*, it is "a bold surgeon, they say, whose hand does not tremble when he performs an operation upon his own person" (263).

This impartial spectator may be modeled as an impartial judge, but the analogy should not mislead us. Smith's best modern commentator, Charles Griswold, explains, "Smith insists that moralists err when they take [moral] rules as the 'ultimate foundations' for morality, as though moral judgment were simply analogous to juridical reasoning that consists of applying law-like rules to specific cases, through a process of subsumption." For Smith, "The impartial spectator remains the ultimate court of appeal as to the soundness of the rule or maxim."[68] Smith himself shapes the disanalogy, and Griswold cites Smith's *Theory of Moral Sentiments* to confirm the point: "original judgments of mankind with regard to right and wrong" are *not* "formed like the decisions of a court of judicatory."[69]

The separation of public and private, external and internal concludes in disanalogy, separating the judge and his juridical concerns from the literary critic and his aesthetic and moral concerns. But the separation is also a doubling: judge and critic are doppelgangers; both are impartial spectators, but they are assigned to different disciplines. The metaphors matter in the contexts where the practice of law is separated from the practical philosophy of conscience. Adam Smith effects a division of labor along modern disciplinary lines. It should also be emphasized that Smith first tried out his arguments in lectures on rhetoric, moral philosophy, and jurisprudence. His audience was largely composed of students of law.

Smith publishes his *Theory of Moral Sentiments* in 1759. In that same year Sterne's metaphor of the Asiatic Cadi and British judge discussed above appear in an interpolated sermon on conscience in volume 2, chapter 17, of *Tris-*

tram Shandy.[70] The sermon, first delivered by Sterne at the opening of the summer court assizes in York in 1750, had been published separately the same year, nineteen years before the publication of *Shandy.*[71] But this provenance may be further complicated: Sterne's sermon draws on an earlier sermon by Swift on the same topic. It was after the success of *Tristram Shandy* that Sterne brought out a collection of his sermons, including the previously published sermon on conscience, under the new pen name "Parson Yorick." Yorick is, of course, both a character in *Tristram Shandy* and Sterne's pseudonymous alter ego (not to mention the court jester in *Hamlet*, "a man of infinite jest"). I set out this publication history in detail because the relation of the sermon to the novel as a whole recalls the structure of a text divided against itself in the posture of Adam Smith's impartial spectation. By means of a text within a text, Sterne estranges his own writing from itself.

The sermon, which falls out of a book in Tristram's father's library, derailing the narrative, warns against the failures of a dishonest or negligent conscience. Not all quiet consciences are good ones; the "sacred COURT" of conscience may be host to corruptions. A merry-go-round of faculty psychology follows. Wit takes a bribe, Interest stands not "unconcerned whilst the cause was hearing," passion gets into the "judgment-seat" and pronounces the "sentence in the stead of reason" (112). Conscience tries to get itself "safely entrenched behind the Letter of the Law" and fortify itself with the "**Cases** and **Reports**" of casuistry (121). But the sermon concludes with a clear pronouncement of disanalogy: "your conscience is not a law" (149). The lines that follow, which expand the negation, are the same quoted above and at the head of this entry: conscience is to determine, like a British judge, "who makes no new law, but faithfully declares that law which he knows already written" (149). The declared law, like the sermon, is a text "already written," plagiarized or published pseudonymously, and produced *mise en abyme.* A frontispiece to the first volume of the novel, by William Hogarth, depicts Corporal Trim reading the sermon aloud to three other characters. This engraving actualizes impartial spectation for the reader who, holding and reading Sterne's novel, identifies himself with the image of Trim, holding and reading Sterne's sermon on conscience.[72]

Charles Churchill and the Lord Chief Justice

Following Fielding, Smith, and Sterne, Charles Churchill works up a more acidly satirical treatment of the judge in his elaborate and sprawling, sometimes Shandean, sometimes Duncical poem titled *The Ghost.* Churchill takes as incident the investigations of the Cock Lane Ghost in 1762 by Samuel

Johnson (among others) and uses it as an occasion for miscellaneous political and philosophical satire. Empiricism's reliance on the "testimony" of the senses is crazily cross-examined in related juridical metaphors in book IV:

> Within the brain's most secret cells,
> A certain *Lord Chief Justice* dwells
> Of sov'reign pow'r, whom One and All,
> With common Voice, We REASON call;
> Tho', for the purposes of Satire,
> A name in Truth is no great Matter,
> JEFFERIES or MANSFIELD, which You will,
> It means a *Lord Chief Justice* still.[73]

Churchill personifies Reason in an earlier poem as the "LORD-CHEIF-JUSTICE in the COURT OF MAN," and in a later poem "*Judge* REASON"[74] appears; but in this passage from *The Ghost*, Churchill's ironic satire turns personal, naming William Murray, first Earl of Mansfield and lord chief justice, as a target. Churchill, a friend and ally of John Wilkes, published book IV of his poem in November 1763, at the height of Wilkes's troubles with Parliament, and anticipated Wilkes's case would be tried before Mansfield.

In producing a portrait of a lord chief justice in *The Ghost*, Churchill reverses the honorific allusions and associations employed by Fielding in *Tom Jones*. Oblique references to Mansfield—who was involved in the Cock Lane affair investigations as well as libel hearings concerning the *North Briton*, the periodical Churchill edited for John Wilkes—appear throughout the poem.[75] In effect, Mansfield, who is here, there, and nowhere, haunts the verses as Churchill himself deadpans without libeling. In the lines quoted above, Mansfield is linked with the George Jeffreys, the justice who presided over the "Bloody" Assizes of 1685, as both share a title and the pronoun *It*.[76] At the end of the poem a "Figure . . . Whom Justice would, but dare not, name" appears. Described at length (ll. 1797–1908) as an antitype, this allegorical figure of false justice is and is not Mansfield (who is then ironically named again in the final line of the poem). Churchill judges the judge who would obviate the role of juries in libel decisions and locates the law's "real pow'r" in "*one corrupted rotten breast*."[77] And he does so without naming him in any way that would bring new charges of libel upon himself.

Churchill's radical energies are exercised ironically when the poet describes those philosophers who imagine a court of wit or wisdom over which the "upright Justicer" Reason presides and to which "The Senses all must homage pay":

He on their merits holds debate,
Examines, Cross-examines, Weighs
Their right to censure or to praise;
Nor doth his equal voice depend
On narrow Views of foe and friend,
Nor can or flattery or force
Divert him from his steady course;
The Channel of Enquiry's clear,
No *sham Examination*'s here.[78]

Elements of the scene parallel those explored in the entry **Empire**, and as Churchill switches between the two senses of "court" set out in the opening pages of this entry, the scene of justice gives way to one of revolution. The "five Senses" are imagined, "in alliance," defying Reason and throwing off the yoke and bondage; a new "mimic formal Court" is set up in which Reason presides as mere "Puppet King" (*The Ghost. Book IV* 135). Stanzas follow in which mental and political metaphors swerve between *reason* and *treason* (a repeated rhyme in *The Ghost*). The riot of metaphors is safer than the near libelous teasings of Justice in the person of its Lord Chief. Churchill calls for freedom of opinion and frolics of fancy: "Let Those, who rigid Judgment own, / Submissive bow at Judgment's throne" (139).

Perhaps surprisingly, Justice Mansfield came to support John Wilkes and his allies in their attempt to end the use of general warrants against printers by endorsing the 1765 judgment in *Entick v. Carrington*.[79] In 1768 he reversed the decree of outlawry against Wilkes on a legal technicality. Wilkes is able to defy king and Parliament by using the law courts and rallying the mob.[80] The public sphere pushes back against the state where it is weakest. In their attempts to conduct and guide public opinion, Churchill and Wilkes were not ultimately successful, but a new answer to the question of who shall judge was offered in their publications.

The Head of a Judge

By way of summary argument, I repeat that "judgment" is an eighteenth-century keyword. There is no single context in which to locate decisively its use (although the midcentury decade between 1755 and 1765 demands further investigation). Judgment is an indispensable human activity, and judgments are produced in art, ethics, science, and politics—in all the activities of ordinary life.[81] The second book of Akenside's *Pleasures of Imagination* ends, in many editions, with a paean to "The native judgment of the human soul."[82] Kant, for one, insists on the primacy of judgment in human thought and composes his *Critique of Judgment* in order to reconcile the operations of reason and understanding—the laws of reason and the judgments of understanding.[83] Owing to this ubiquity of judgment, a number of the examples I have collected may be only weakly metaphorical. So in Thomas Shadwell's play *The Libertine*, when freethinking Don John, the libertine, makes an argument against free will, it is not clear if we should understand him as speaking literally or figuratively:

> All objects are ready form'd and plac'd
> To our hands; and these the Senses to the Mind convey,
> And as those represent them, this must judge.[84]

What sort of representation is described? And what kind of judgment rendered? The senses would seem to be personified as counsel and the mind as judge, with the scene so taking a juridical aspect. But the taxonomist of metaphor must consult his own judgment, as it were, in deciding if the personification is "ready form'd" or an interpretive overlay. The term "convey" troubles the reading, suggesting a conveyance of property that may not cohere well (*these*, *those*, *this*) with a juxtaposition of lawyerly hands and a presiding personification of mind. Perhaps the weak metaphorics are to the point, as understanding and judgment are previously likened to a scale or balance by the libertine character who speaks the lines, so that the connotations of justice hang in suspense.

In the last decade of the eighteenth century, Parliament suspended habeas corpus, and several vocal supporters of the French Revolution were put on trial.[85] A mezzotint printed on March 16, 1795, purports to be a sketch of a frozen fountain in the Temple, the area of central London home to the Inns of Court and the Royal Courts of justice. The print, titled *Head of a Judge*, is captioned "A Representation of the Ice, in the Fountain of Garden Court in the Temple, on Monday the 26th of Jany 1795 which remained in nearly the same shape for several Days." On closer inspection the fountain of ice shows itself to be a gestalt-switching "duck-rabbit" of the sort first discussed by Joseph Jastrow and featured in Ludwig Wittgenstein's discussion of "seeing as" in his *Philosophical Investigations*. An empty wig looks out of the page, the law frozen and evacuated of subjectivity. But on a second look, a face may be made out in profile. A pictorial metaphor, the image exhibits a dual aspect and simultaneously presents tenor and vehicle.[86] We see one thing (a frozen fountain) as another (the head of a judge).

The face has been identified as Alexander Wedderburn's, first Earl of Rosslyn's. Wedderburn, made Baron Loughborough, served as lord chancellor from

A frozen head. *Head of a Judge* (1795). Courtesy of the Lewis Walpole Library.

1793 to 1801.[87] Stiff and pompous, he was famous for his "cold, detached public manner."[88] Hilary term had just begun on January 21, and London was experiencing one of its coldest winters ever. The sedition trials of 1794 had been recently heard, and Warren Hastings's trial was drawing to conclusion. Confounding inside and out, the frozen head of the judge presides over a courtyard, one of many such cloistered courts and passages in the Temple. The empty wig—formal, frozen, monumental—is undercut by the caption's sardonic insistence that the representation "remained in nearly the same shape for several days." Switching back and forth before our eyes, the mezzotint pictures the subjective free play of imagination and understanding described in Kant's *Critique of Judgment*. I exhibit the image as a final emblem of the distinction-driven history of conscience traced in this entry. If it is not too late, let it be entered in the record.

A statistical account of metaphor is most imperiled at the moment of collection, in the judgment or decision that fixes free play as form and counts one, another, and third. Still, I multiply examples and insist on a high-water mark of juridical metaphors that coincides with Smith's, Sterne's, and Churchill's publications, with the publication of Blackstone's *Commentaries*, with Wilkite radicalism and the political instability that precedes the American Revolution. I recognize that my attempt to account for the movement of metaphors through history by collecting examples is caught up, peculiarly in this entry, with the very metaphorics of judgment and precedent I hope to describe.[89] Collecting and citing precedents, I take upon myself the role of the literary critic passing judgment on both the literary and legal history I hope to record. But I am vexed by judgment because many a metaphor, like Shadwell's, comes alive only under the right kind of attention and scrutiny—only when placed under the appropriate rubric, brought to the correct court—where its juxtaposition with the preceding metaphors serves to secure my interpretation of it.

4 Empire

Collocated Keywords: Conquest, Empire, Emporium, Frontier, Imperium, Invasion, Seat, Throne

Count of Metaphors in Database[1] (1700–1799): 1,846

MRS. MARWOOD
We may affect Endearments to each other, profess eternal Friendships, and seem to doat like Lovers; but 'tis not in our Natures long to persevere. Love will resume his Empire in our Breasts, and every Heart, or soon or late, receive and readmit him as its lawful Tyrant.

—William Congreve, *The Way of the World*, II.i (1700)

We are a little kingdom; But the Man
That chains his Rebel Will to Reason's Throne,
Forms it a large one, ATWOOD, whilst his Mind
Makes Heaven its Council, from the Rolls above
Draws his own Statutes, and with Joy obeys.

—Isaac Watts, *Horae Lyricae* (1706)

I told him, I once thought my self a kind of a Monarch in my old Station, of which I had given him an Account, but that I thought he was not a Monarch only, but a great Conqueror; for that he that has got a Victory over his own exorbitant Desires, and has the absolute Dominion over himself, whose Reason entirely governs his Will, is certainly greater than he that conquers a City.

—Daniel Defoe, *The Farther Adventures of Robinson Crusoe* (1719)

I know her imprudent, I believe her virtuous: a great flow of spirits has been ever hurrying her into indiscretions; but allow me to say, my Lord, it is particularly hard to fix the character by our conduct, at a time of life when we are not competent judges of our own actions; and when the hurry and

> vivacity of youth carries us to commit a thousand follies and indiscretions, for which we blush when the empire of reason begins.
>
> —Frances Moore Brooke, *The History of Emily Montague* (1769)

> In this style, argue tyrants of every denomination, from the weak king to the weak father of a family; they are all eager to crush reason; yet always assert that they usurp its throne only to be useful.
>
> —Mary Wollstonecraft, *A Vindication of the Rights of Woman* (1792)

See also **Fetters, Impressions,** and **Inhabitants**

THE EIGHTEENTH CENTURY associates world empires with instability, if not corruption, decline, and fall; and in its literature, hearts, minds, and souls are all, variously, figured as empires that may be invaded, conquered, gained, or lost. **Empire** metaphors are a subset of the government and war metaphors that bulk large in the database: figures of rule and subjection, conquest, empire, and thrones are among the most frequently encountered in my searches and are given graphic representation below. The wavering lines below picture the frequency of these metaphors and inform my recounting of the rise and fall of British imperial fortunes. But that picture is bifurcated in two competing graphs. In the first, a dotted line shows the *frequency* of empire metaphors declining at the end of the century (calculated as a ratio of all the metaphors collected). In the second, the steady accumulation of government metaphors can be seen multiplying in reprintings and revised editions. The upwardly trending line figures the resonance of self-command and ideological expansion, while the frequency of metaphors as they first appear may more closely follow a history of events in which the fate of the British empire seems more uncertain and the metaphorics more obviously embattled. I include the two graphs to illustrate both ways of measuring metaphors. Taken together they trouble the easy correlation of metaphor and military action.

The nineteenth-century term "imperialism," connoting monolithic and arbitrary expansion, is not yet in use in the period, and the metaphors in this entry picture a territory with changing and permeable boundaries that may well be overrun and find itself beholden to foreign rule. Contested borders are exemplified by the contested synonymies of *mind*, *heart*, and *soul*; and, as will be demonstrated, metaphors of empire often emphasize embodiment in their mappings of center and periphery. The inward and outward orientations of empiricism are complicated by the semantics of empire. *Ex*pansion is *in*vasive: empire sets out barriers and then overreaches them; it requires an outside even as it brings the foreign home.[2]

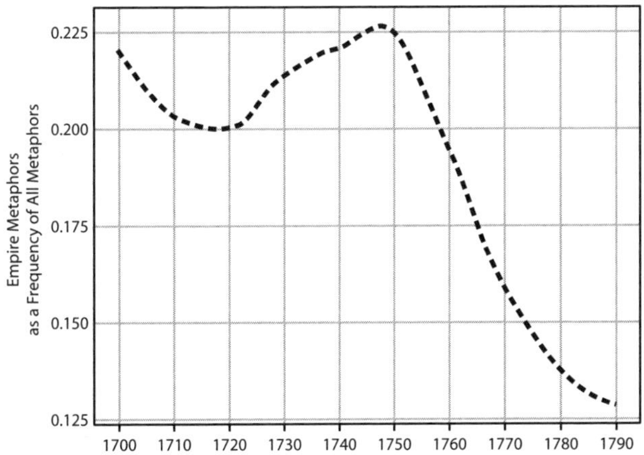

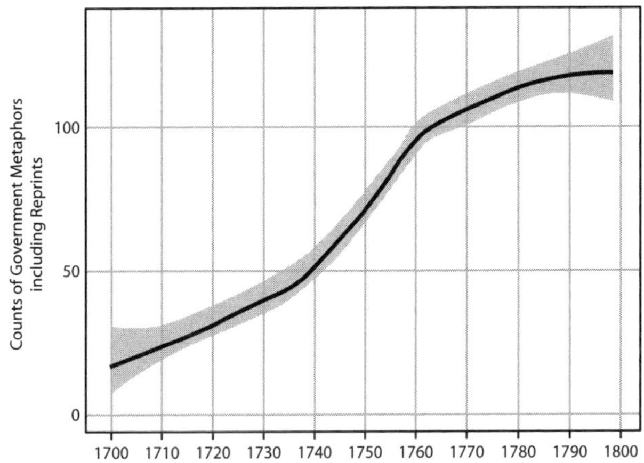

Two competing graphs. In the first, frequencies are plotted by decade: compared to all other metaphors collected for this study, the **Empire** metaphors described in this entry decrease as a percentage of the total. In the second, raw counts of a large subset of these same metaphors accumulate year after year in reprintings. In the first graph, the majority of the metaphors were located by keyword searching. In the second, these same metaphors have been located and relocated, shown multiplied in the print culture (reprintings were checked in the ESTC and confirmed by spot-checking in ECCO). The first graph represents metaphors of rule and subjection, imperial conquest, and invasion; the second, a governmental subset of the same. The first line falls off; the second climbs up. The question of how to count metaphors is here posed in the face of what Kathleen Woodward calls "statistical panic." A smoothing function has been applied to both graphs; the second displays confidence intervals.

Imperial desires repeatedly figure the heart or the breast as a metaphorical or metonymical locus of action. Congreve's Mrs. Marwood (cited first in the epigraphs above) finds temporary freedom in feigning and dissembling but recognizes "Love" as a "lawful Tyrant," who "will resume his Empire" in her breast. Turning points in novelistic and dramatic narratives—in history—are repeatedly marked by the gaining and resuming of a figurative empire. Rakes and ladies, like generals and emperors, number their conquests. Action moves between the heart and the head. Eliza Haywood's novel *Betsy Thoughtless* miniaturizes narrative as maxim: "While the blood runs high, and desire is rampant for possession, prudence is of little force; but when the one begins to flag, the other resumes its empire over the mind, and never rests till it finds means to retrieve what it has lost."[3] Haywood's clauses display struggle at the grammatical level, and the reader runs back over the plot, numbering the forces, their flags and flaggings.

By contrast, the epigraphs from Defoe and Brooke anticipate a more stable and mature "empire of reason," a *Pax Romana* of the Stoic who has learned like Marcus Aurelius in Edward Gibbon's *Decline and Fall of the Roman Empire* to "submit his body to his mind, his passions to his reason; to consider virtue as the only good, vice as the only evil, all things external as things indifferent."[4] The emperor considers empire indifferently, prepared to withdraw entirely into the self and command the passions: the Stoic defines his own state as an *imperium in imperio* (a sovereign state within a state). Expansion seems even to require episodes of withdrawal and consolidation. As Congreve's and Haywood's metaphors suggest, the baser desires and higher powers of reason and prudence alternately and ceaselessly assume and reassume empire over the mind or heart. Trajan and the Antonines are preceded by the "dark unrelenting Tiberius, the furious Caligula, the feeble Claudius, the profligate and cruel Nero," in Gibbon's history of the Roman Empire; they are succeeded by the worthless, violent Commodus (1:128).

Empires are then gained and regained, won, lost, and won again in narratives of successive deterritorialization and reterritorialization. In instance after instance, the multitudinous meanings of the trio *heart*, *mind*, *soul* are unified, if only temporarily, by a metaphorics of empire. After first considering the ambiguous semantics of my headword, I treat empire in the context of the theater, the varieties of conquest, the advance of commerce, and eighteenth-century oppositions of head and heart. Psychomachia informs narratives of imperial empiricism and stoic self-command. I conclude with Mary Wollstonecraft's use of empire metaphors in the final decade of the period.

"Command over Any Thing"

Empires are large and composite in character and have poorly defined frontiers.[5] Poorly defined as such, the term "empire" covers diverse semantic regions: it denotes both power exercised and the territory over which the power is exercised.[6] The word has a wide extension. And although Caligula wished that the people of Rome had one neck that he might behead them all with one blow, neither imperial power nor the populations over which it is exercised is ever so unified. Before the seventeenth century, "empire" indicated the exercise of sovereignty *within* England, but by the first decades of the eighteenth century the term is inflected by British naval prominence on the seas, its conceptual extension proving expansive and multiple.[7]

In the eighteenth century the majority of the world's population lived in one of several great empires: under the Ottomans, the Romanovs, the Habsburgs, in Qing China, Mughal India, Tokugawa Japan, Safayi Iran, or Java. According to the second numbered definition in Samuel Johnson's *Dictionary*, an empire is "The region over which dominion is extended," with different regions loosely associated with different empires. Johnson cites William Temple to illustrate the term's more contemporary usage: "A nation extended over vast tracts of land, and numbers of people, arrives in time at the ancient name of kingdom, or modern of empire" ("EMPIRE").[8] Perhaps surprisingly, in Temple's usage "empire" is a *modern* and "kingdom" an ancient name for the nation. But then the term "empire" poorly translates the ancient term *imperium*, a key concept inherited from the Romans.[9]

"Empire" is now a shibboleth in today's academy, and the concept exercises texts as different as Hardt and Negri's *Empire* and Niall Ferguson's *Empire*.[10] Imperialism has been identified as the highest form or last stage of capitalism; Adorno and Horkheimer figure imperialism as "reason in its most terrible form."[11] I use the word to collect a number of imperial metaphors of mind and will not propose a new theory of empire. As in recent studies by Srinivas Aravamudan and Lynn Festa, it is the tropes and metaphors of empire that most interest me.[12] Close-reading seventeenth- and eighteenth-century anthems of empire, the critic Suvir Kaul convincingly locates the structure of British anxieties in loose, baggy, repetitious verse: the eighteenth-century poetry of empire is shapeless; mixing genres, it struggles to resolve ideological contradictions at the level of form.[13] As are Kaul's, my concerns are formal and political, but I will look first to the basic figurative units of imperial ideology and would locate the incongruities of inwardness and the exercise of authority over others at the sentence level. Nationalist and imperial projects are legible, in miniature, in the contradictory eighteenth-century metaphorics of the mind.

Seen from the inside, the limit of an empire is a frontier, the border of a settled or inhabited region. But such frontiers are unsettled "contact zones" where disparate cultures face one another.[14] The English knew themselves to be twice conquered historically: first by the Romans and then by the Normans. As the English secured new borders in Ireland and Scotland, they became vulnerable, in their composite British identity, to invasion from without and Jacobite rebellions from within. Even as the line of royal succession was settled, the British were ruled by a Dutch king and then a series of Hanoverian kings. Centered on foreign-born monarchs, the British "Empire of the Seas" confuses inward and outward, the national and international.

Written in the wake of Jacobite rebellion and in a moment of new Scotch-English tensions, John Home's popular 1757 tragedy *Douglas* brings Highland sensibilities to the London stage in the character of Lady Randolph, who laments that the sister kingdoms, Scottish and English, war over an "ideal line,/By fancy drawn" and then later complains that "fear and melancholy still divide/The empire of my breast with hope and joy."[15] Metaphors of conquest consolidate the united kingdoms of the body, soul, heart, and mind, but they complicate our ability to limn the frontiers of our faculties. The mind patrols the body's borders as it pretends to consider all things external as things indifferent.

Johnson's third and last definition of "EMPIRE" is simply "Command over any thing." Empires are obtained violently and consolidated under military occupation. It is this characteristic belligerence that I will use to draw distinctions between metaphors of empire and those of nation. The distinctions, it should go without saying, are convenient but artificial: national governments employ force to subjugate individuals; empires develop administrations in order to manage territory. In Gibbon new territories are acquired by "violence and rapine"; in Burke, by "fraud or force . . . or a mixture of both."[16] For my purposes, I mark command of territory as a salient feature of the collected empire metaphors: "Wheresoever the Roman conquers, he inhabits," observes Seneca;[17] but inhabitation, governmentality and other technologies of administration must be treated under separate heads (compare **Court** and **Fetters** for reciprocal relations of law and violence and **Inhabitants** for the subjection of a population). As the keywords listed at the head of this entry indicate, I am most interested for now in the seat of empire, the example of ancient Rome, conquest, invasion, frontiers, and unsettled territories.

The Seat of the Soul

At the center of the self or soul is a seat of consciousness or life, often a throne. In one passage translated and located under the heading "Reason" in Henry Baker's *Medulla Poetarum Romanorum*, the soul's seat is located and its empire is newly measured in pentameter couplets:

> So, from the narrow Limits of the Heart,
> The active Soul does vig'rous Life impart
> To all the Limbs: it's Sway the Members own,
> And wide it's Empire spreads around it's Throne.[18]

As in the selections from Watts and Wollstonecraft above, the metaphorical thrones I have encountered belong, more often than not, to a personification of royal reason: the metaphor circulates through poetic diction in eighteenth-century literature, and I have collected over seventy examples in which a writer mentions "Reason's throne" or the "throne of Reason." As with the metaphors considered in **Inhabitants** that picture the self as a society, personification is closely related to throne metaphors. Reason rules the realm of the mind, or, as in Watts's poem, the "royal mind" itself is personified. Moreover, and more surprisingly, reason, or the royal ruling part of the mind, is typically gendered as female, personified as a queen.[19]

Reason may be dethroned, her throne shaken or usurped by a "rebel will," by custom, by (ruling) passions, by wine, by an idea, by a sensation, by love or a lover. Any mental particle personified may become a cunning contender for or pretender to the throne. Reason may also willingly give up the throne, abdicating responsibility: George Crabbe explains that "Reason, through anguish," may "her throne forsake." Eliza Haywood warns that "Lethargy of Thought" or "Stupefaction" may overwhelm the "Throne of Reason." Perhaps, as Mary Barber writes, Reason is only a "Weak Viceroy" and its throne easily usurped.[20] Because the throne is only a fancy chair, it is easy to imagine a succession of powers sitting upon it, its permanence being no guarantee of political stability. "Through ev'ry Age some Tyrant Passion reigns," writes Anne Finch, "Now *Love* prevails, and now *Ambition* gains / Reason's lost Throne, and sov'reign Rule maintains."[21]

Informing a metaphorics of usurpation and abdication is the parlous political history of royal succession at home, in England, which plays as counterpoint to the wars of trade and expansion abroad: from the execution of Charles I to the investiture of Oliver Cromwell as Lord Protector, the Restoration of Charles II, the "abdication" of James II, and the settlement of the

Hanoverian line. Beneath this succession, so to speak, was Westminster Abbey's Coronation Chair, a high-backed oak armchair, its legs decorated with four gilded lions. Royalty must be seated. After 1688, in the exiled court at Saint-Germain-en-Laye, the king and his court "over the water" negotiated formal precedence by means of armchairs and taborets.[22]

Famously, David Hume opens part 4 of the first book of his *Treatise* with Queen Reason apparently "in possession of the throne." As Hume provides no further *reason* or first principle for reason's monarchy, he prepares the scene for rebellion. But the skeptic, necessarily making use of rational arguments, produces "a patent under her hand and seal" that diminishes the force of both reason and skepticism (I.iv.1).[23] Doubts and reasons cancel each other, leaving behind the empty throne. Seventeenth-century French moralists did much to show how the passions might lord over weaker reason, and the impassioned political revolutions of the seventeenth and eighteenth centuries may well have done even more to disturb the ground on which reason's throne rests. That said, the metaphor of the throne, ever residual, abides: in the first Senate of the United States, John Adams suggested that President George Washington might sit on some kind of throne when he addressed congress.[24]

Materialists take special pains to locate and embody thought, and in the new science it is the brain that is widely recognized as "the seat of thought." In Chambers's *Cyclopaedia*, the "SENSORY, or *Sensorium Commune*" is the "Seat of the *Common Sense*," or that part of the brain where the nerves terminate and "where the sensible Soul is supposed more immediately to reside."[25] Cartesians point with even more precision within the body's machinery to the *conarion*, or pineal gland (the "*seat of imagination and 'common' sense*"), centrally located in the brain.[26] In these texts scientific materialism deadens metaphor, trading it for metonym. Or rather, dualism and certain post-Cartesian varieties of materialism specify a literal sense of embodiment that may be denoted by the phrase "seat of thought." When in Vanbrugh's comedy *Aesop*, Hortentia, an "affected learned lady" describes the soul as "that awful Throne of Thought, That sacred Seat of Contemplation," I suspect we are to understand her as having garbled her Descartes, confusing the soul with its seat (I.i).[27] Hortentia's throne seems to be empty; more often the soul is seated upon the throne than identified with it. But the metonym wields literal as well as poetic power: in Louis XIV's court anyone who passed his throne, even if it was unoccupied, was required to bow before it.

In the *Memoirs of Martinus Scriblerus* the Scriblerians satirize the absurdity of locating the seat of thought with too much precision. Scriblerus searches the brain, the heart, the stomach to find or "confine that sovereign Lady," resolving at last on the *glandula pinealis*. He then dissects an assortment of pineal glands to support his hypothesis that the character of the seat correlates with the character of the soul and "that in factious and restless-spirited people he should find it sharp and pointed, allowing no room for the soul to repose herself; that in quiet Tempers it was flat, smooth, and soft, affording the Soul as it were an easy cushion."[28] In their satire ad absurdum, the Scriblerians warn that the search for the immaterial soul leads directly to the questioning of its existence.[29]

Locke metonymizes the brain as the "the mind's Presence-room" and envisions tastes and smells admitted and conveyed by the nerves for an audience with the understanding (see **Rooms**).[30] In the physician and poet Richard Blackmore's epic poem *Eliza*, the soul is described as being "high seated in her Throne the Brain."[31] In Locke's and Blackmore's metaphors, as in Watts's, the body at large is figured as a kingdom or court, and the extended analogy or allegory may be easily sketched in: different organs stand as different regions of a kingdom, nerves and veins are like passages or avenues, and animal spirits and fluids function as ministers of the court (see **Animals**).[32] John Arbuthnot, in a 1714 letter to Swift, summarizes the work of the German physicians Helmont and Dolaeus, both of whom describe the sensitive soul as a first minister to the queenly rational soul and detail a bureaucracy of "Genii" and "Princes" that serve below in the heart, stomach, and reproductive organs.[33]

The throne metaphor implies a larger empire open to invasion by sensations or disease. The motley princes and ministers that Arbuthnot describes remind us that there may be departments, kingdoms, and colonies within an individual: the eighteenth-century self is eminently divisible, and my search terms (*mind*, *heart*, *soul*, *reason*, *passion*) emphasize the overlapping realms and acts of union. Reason's is not the only throne; others are found in the heart or bosom. Samuel Richardson's Miss Byron, for example, writes of Sir Charles Grandison, "I seem sometimes to feel, as if my gratitude had raised a throne for him in my heart."[34] Charlotte Smith pictures a more dominating relation in the closing couplet of one of her elegiac sonnets: "For thou to me canst sov'reign bliss impart, / Thy mind my empire—and my throne thy heart."[35] As further explained in **Inhabitants**, political metaphors divide and multiply the self. The singular throne in philosophical discussions of identity readily becomes a trope of difference in verse and prose fiction. Two thrones in one body may well lead to internal struggles between the head and the heart.

Throne metaphors fill the Wesleys' best-selling hymns and outnumber throne metaphors by any other single author in my collection of metaphors.[36]

The relation between Methodism and the Royalist politics—between heart-religion and reason's throne—is strongly correlated. And the Wesleys continually bulk large in my collection of metaphors. Influential but understudied metaphorists of mind, the Wesleys, along with Sir Richard Blackmore, Thomas Amory, Anna Seward, and James Woodhouse compete with canonical writers such as Samuel Richardson and Laurence Sterne in their introduction of metaphors of mind to literature. The research I undertake displaces certain well-known writers and seats others in their place. Such is the main work of new literary history.

Imperial Fortunes

The imagination of an imperial consciousness is required by the imperial project. The ambitious may have a mind "formed" or "designed" for empire or may be "born for empire"—born to sway the rod of empire or hold its reins. Thoughts of empire "fire" the mind or soul. Juxtapositions of physical and figurative empires locate the self in a wider geopolitical landscape, often retranslating geopolitical concerns in terms of romance, fixing the imperial in the imperious heart. On the stage, histrionic tyrants swear they would trade their empire for the heart of some woman. The poet John Smith writes of Cleopatra that she "justly cou'd a Nobler Empire boast / In *Caesar*'s Heart, than *Ptolomy* had lost."[37] Repeatedly, an interior or spiritual empire is measured against an external expanse. The comparison of literal and figurative empires often includes an allusion to scripture. Jesus quizzes his disciples after rebuking Peter: "For what is a man profited, if he shall gain the whole world, and lose his own soul?" (Matthew 16:26, but see also Mark 8:36 and Luke 9:25).

In one popular translation of Horace's Ode II.ii, the man who restrains his own cravings will gain a nobler empire than that which joins "distant *Spain* and *Lybia's Land*"; and in the translation of another Horatian ode (IV.ix), the wealthy and powerful are described as less truly happy than those that ably "Govern that little empire, Man; / Bridle their passions and direct their will."[38] These sentiments exploit the structure of rule and subjection. Figures of self-governance are central to the cluster of metaphors cross-referenced in this entry. As noted, the intertexts, Roman and Stoic, may be one origin of the metaphors of self-rule and self-command. The Horatian examples along with earlier pro-Stuart Virgilian productions by Sir John Denham, John Boys, and John Ogilby explicitly translate imperial Rome in Royalist terms and promote the model of Roman poetry—and patronage. Pope's *Imitations of Horace* (1733–8), like the series of translations and imitations by Jonson, Dryden, and Thomson, do much to encourage comparisons of Augustan Rome and "Augustan" England.[39]

Dated from the founding of Jamestown in 1607, the first British empire is secured in the early eighteenth century. With the Treaty of Utrecht in 1713, Britain secured a presence in Gibraltar, Minorca, and the Caribbean and gained the right to trade slaves with Spanish colonies. Fifty years later, the resolution of the Seven Years' War added Indian and Canadian territories, Martinique, Manila, and Havana to Britain's colonial possessions. While my keyword searches indicate a slight increase in the circulation of empire metaphors in the 1720s and the 1760s and a subsequent decrease during the years of the American Revolution (whose outcome many contemporaries believed to herald the decline and fall of British imperialism), I am not willing to make overmuch of these—how to say it?—"primitive accumulations" of metaphors. The earliest imperial and commercial ventures are looting expeditions; later plantations require colonial governance and monopoly protections. Only after the eighteenth century ends is the continued expansion of the British empire assured; English imperial ascendancy should be dated to a later period.

This is not to discount predictions of expansion, like those in Poet Laureate Henry James Pye's jingoist and martial poem *Naucratia; Or, Naval Dominion*, in which "Law and Reason's empire to the skies, / On the firm base of British freedom, rise."[40] The associations are conventional. Published after Britain's naval victories of 1797 (also after mutinies that same year), Pye figures a British empire of freedom ruling over the waves, an empire based in law and reason, not violence. In Pye's verse history of navigation, commerce spreads "her peaceful empire" even before naval power is turned to military purposes (14). Like many earlier eighteenth-century "Augustan" writers, the poet repeatedly rejects ancient imperial and militaristic topics, associating them with Spanish and French conquests and substituting in their place commercial themes.[41] Such preferences for trade over war ignore the ways in which the jealousy of trade results in war and the "distinguishing of commerce from conquest . . . mystifies their connivance."[42]

Ideology and Theater

In the longer span of the eighteenth and nineteenth centuries, nation and empire come to define one another by contrasting center and periphery, capital and colony.[43] Many of the verbs associated with throne metaphors are also associated with metaphors of empire in general: empires, like thrones, may be erected and fixed in minds and hearts and souls.[44] Both entities invite and endure vicissitudes: reason may quit her empire as easily as her throne, and both thrones and empires may be usurped. (It is a quirk of psychology—of identity—that while one regime replaces another and territories change hands, there remains something, a throne or an expanse of territory, that remains.) Lovers hope to "fix" an empire in the heart of their beloveds. A successful monarch must likewise fix his or her empire in a people's hearts, or so advise the poets who issue this conventional piece of wisdom in their epistles to royalty.[45] In Montesquieu's *Lettres Persanes* (1721), after the young Persian nobleman Rica arrives in Paris, he marvels at the king of France, who seems a kind of magician who "exercises his empire even over the minds of his subjects."[46] The metaphor of an empire fixed or founded in a people's heart or mind epitomizes an ideological distinction increasingly promoted by the freeborn English patriot: willing British subjects are ruled by love; slaves, Turks, Spaniards, and Frenchmen, by fear and cruelty.

Any empire over the minds of men is, almost by definition, ideological; its advance and administration, cultural. Where Richard Blackmore imagines, in a moment of deep Whig suspicion, how a Catholic Rome set out to "found a wider Empire o'er the Mind" in order to "recompence" its loss of former imperial power and prestige, Hester Chapone describes how Mahomet founded a "new empire" by extending "his usurped dominions equally over the minds and properties of men."[47] In his third letter on a regicide peace, Burke warns of the Jacobin attempts to "form an universal empire, by producing an universal revolution."[48] Empires other than geopolitical are often measured as counterconquests: both Pope's *Essay on Criticism* and his four-book *Dunciad* close with an image of restoration, the latter a dark inversion of *translatio studii*: "Lo! Thy dread Empire, CHAOS! is restor'd" so that "Universal Darkness buries All."[49] With greater optimism William Hayley celebrates Gibbon's achievements, balancing the decline and fall chronicled with the expansion of historical scholarship by the chronicler:

> Learning ne'er saw, in all her numerous race,
> A son more worthy of her fond embrace:
> Thy mind expanded to her empire's bound;
> There every Science a firm station found.[50]

Empire metaphors prove especially prevalent in dramatic contexts, most explicitly in Restoration heroic romances and siege dramas (in which Tamerlane, Caesar, Antony and Cleopatra, and other imperial heroes appear); later imperial and commercial concerns and references begin to center on the characters of the merchant or sea captain. In addition to the plays' main texts, dramatic paratexts figure the power of performance in imperial terms. In prologues and epilogues (forms posted at the boundary or "frontier" of a dramatic presentation), actors and actresses seek to gain empire over the hearts of theatergoers. These metadramatic verses mark debuts and retirements and describe audiences in the thrall of celebrity. For example, a manuscript poem addressed to David Garrick on his retirement from acting opens "by way of simile" in order to compare the conquests of Alexander (who "made the Globe his own") with Garrick ("King of the Stage!"), who modernized the dramaturgy of Shakespeare's Globe Theater.[51] The eighteenth-century repertory is an important "instrument of empire" that carries away an audience to global, colonial locations by enacting scenes before elaborately painted canvas backgrounds.[52]

Perhaps the bourgeois dramas and comedies that emerge in the early eighteenth century sublimate empire, locating it not in any salient dramatic content but in the performance of the actor and in the very experience of theater.[53] (I believe that such dislocations and manipulations of publicity are what distinguished bourgeois drama from earlier stage offerings.) In *A Poem To the Memory of Mrs. Oldfield*, the poet (possibly Richard Savage) writes of the actress Mrs. Oldfield, "She gain'd despotick Empire o'er the Heart"; and Anna Seward, seven decades on, may be echoing these lines (while reversing the gender positions) as she praises the "young Roscius" (the boy actor William Henry West Betty): "Genius her proudest miracle began; / Gave thee despotic empire o'er the heart."[54] In his "Prologue for the First Appearance of Mrs. Simpson," Samuel Jackson Pratt puffs Simpson's debut at the Orchard Street Theater in Bath, asking the audience, now that Sarah Siddons has left for Drury Lane, "who may claim *her* empire in *your hearts*?"[55]

Theatrical empire is exercised over an unruly multitude of theatergoers, and the command performance unites pit, boxes, and galleries, different regions of the playhouse associated with different classes. The audience is reminded in the epilogue to Richard Cumberland's *The Brothers* how "This Night we'd fix her [the Muse of Comedy's] Empire in your Hearts."[56] Contrasting tragedy and comedy in his *Essay on Acting*, Garrick writes, "the *first* fixes her Empire on the *Passions*," while the second "holds her Rule over the less enobled Qualities and Districts of human Nature, which are call'd the *Humours*." And in "Prologue Written for Mr Penn," Seward theorizes how a dramatist such as Rowe or Otway works upon the actor and theatergoer so that "Memory hints no more / The woes unreal; but, with forfeit power, / Resigns her empire o'er the yielding soul."[57]

Empiricism, Imperium, Emporium

The logic of empire outlined above is neoclassical, commercial, significantly theatrical; it radiates outward, looks westward. In so characterizing my figuration, I outline a metaphorics that complements and complicates what C. B. Macpherson memorably termed the politics of "possessive individualism."[58] An empire grows by winning and holding foreign territory. All empire begins in conquest, although the figuring of invasion and conquest more often than not brings the metaphor of empire home, foregrounding vulnerability in the way the eighteenth-century theory of ideas pictures sensations pouring in upon the passive subject. Stoic self-command would delineate borders and boundaries, regions internal and external, which in turn exacerbate anxiety about self-propriety and its appropriations.

Indeed, conceptions of the self as emperor-proprietor are complicated by the theory of an empiricism that pictures the mind as a bare enclosure first colonized from without. Eighteenth-century ideas are adventitious; the period's feelings, impersonal and conventional.[59] So Lord Kames writes, repeating a commonplace of Enlightenment psychology, "Our first perceptions are of external objects."[60] The mind's borders are permeable; the mind, not simply acquisitive or reliably autonomous but easily overrun and dislocated. The expansion of Rome, before modern schemes of political representation, meant "the admission of the greater part of the inhabitants of Italy to the privileges of Roman citizens," an inclusiveness that "completely ruined the Roman republic."[61] We can't help but have our impressions and are therefore at their mercy. Ideas pour across the sensorium, populate the mind, constitute experience, and complicate identity. The mind is a nation of foreigners not easily subjugated.

Self and society are concepts introduced here but treated more thoroughly under the rubric **Inhabitants**. In the *Second Treatise*, after his treatment of the social contract, Locke asks,

> If man in the state of nature be so free, as has been said; if he be absolute lord of his own person and possessions, equal to the greatest, and subject to no body, why will he part with his freedom? why will he give up this *empire*, and subject himself to the *dominion* and control of any other power? To which it is obvious to answer, that though in the state of nature he hath such a right, yet the enjoyment of it is very uncertain, and constantly exposed to the *invasion* of others. (II.ix.123, emphasis added)[62]

The sense of "invasion" active in Locke's political philosophy—that our rights, like our property, may be invaded—is continuous with, if not dependent upon, his philosophy of mind.[63] Invasion, or its threat, is what precedes government and precedes knowledge (it is, so to speak, a priori). In his *Essay*, Locke observes that our "first Years are usually imploy'd and diverted in looking abroad" (II.i.8). The understanding is "meerly passive" in that "the Objects of our Senses, do, many of them, obtrude their particular *Ideas* upon our minds, whether we will or no," and the mind is "forced to receive the Impressions" (II.i.25). Occupied by its own ideas, the mind has little freedom of action beyond surveying, accommodating, and rearranging them. Writing of the association of ideas in his *Conduct of the Understanding*, Locke notes that many men have not the vigor of mind "to contest the Empire of Habit."[64] Locke's simple, adventitious ideas are invaders, imposing laws of association—although in the paragraph following the foregoing citations Locke chooses other, perhaps less insidious, figures of speech and describes in mixed metaphor how "*the understanding can* no more refuse to have, nor alter, when [ideas] are imprinted, nor blot them out, and make new ones in it self, than a mirror can refuse, alter or obliterate the Images of *Ideas*, which the Objects set before it, do therein produce" (II.i.25).[65] The mixed metaphors of printing and mirroring point ambivalently to **Mirror** and **Writing** metaphors.

Metaphors of conquest and invasion occupy eighteenth-century literature. Fear, cares, grief, and anguish invade heart, mind, and soul; ideas, images, and fancies invade the mind. The blind Scottish poet Thomas Blacklock writes, "When painful truths invade the mind, / Ev'n wisdom wishes to be blind."[66] In *The Pleasures of Imagination,* Mark Akenside describes how the rearguard forces of ambition, revenge, lust, and rapine steal into the mind "under shapes / Of honour, safety, pleasure, ease or pomp" and grasp the "empire of the soul."[67] Surveying the skeptical conclusions of eighteenth-century philosophy, James Beattie complains that "Reason invades the rights of Common Sense, and presumes to arraign that authority by which she herself acts."[68] In book VII of the second part of his epic *King Arthur*, the poet Richard Blackmore depicts a gruesome death in heroic couplets, mixing literal and figurative senses of invasion when a dart pierces a knight's skull and reaches "the inmost Marrow of the Brain / . . . / . . . where the Soul upon her Throne abides, / And from our Sight conceal'd her Empire guides." Here, striking the knight between the eyes, the dart does the soul's "high Seat invade" and spread "the Courts of Life with horrid Shade."[69]

Shaftesbury, in his *Soliloquy, or Advice to an Author*, figures self-knowledge in terms of psychomachia and *self*-conquest, including an exhortation to his reader to "assemble the best Forces of his Wit and Judgment" and "make a formal descent on the Territorys of *the Heart*: resolving to decline no Combat, nor hearken to any Terms till he had pierc'd into its inmost Provinces and reach'd the Seat of Empire."[70] The metaphor returns in the opening of Hume's *Treatise*, but the ambitions are amplified from self-knowledge to the scientific conquest: the ambitious David Hume, only twenty-eight years old when his *Treatise* was published, would march directly into "the capital or center" of the sciences, "to human nature itself."[71] But the bravado is quickly turned inside out, ironized and undercut in narration: first in the following pages of the introduction and then more completely in the closing sections of the first book of the *Treatise*. Shortly after Hume's initial call for invasion we find ourselves at "The utmost extent of human reason," transferred from center to periphery, finding it impossible to "make any farther progress" (8). Hume's thought is ever on the move, and yet he finds "we never really advance a step beyond ourselves" (I.ii.6). After marking the farthest boundaries, Hume's skeptical project comes to confine enquiry within the bounds of common life.[72]

Imperium is, originally, a term for military command; later, the state of martial law imposed by the victorious general (*imperator*) and his legions. In early modern England the term "empire" primarily connotes *internal* sovereignty, but it continues to collect expansive and colonial connotations.[73] When the Cambridge Platonist Henry More introduces the idea of "the inward *Imperium* of our Minde" in his influential *Immortality of the Soul* (1659), he asserts the priority and plastic powers of mind over matter. The metaphor recurs in More's writing (as well as in Ralph Cudworth's, who likewise asserts the mind's "natural imperium" over matter).[74] In contrast to these signal seventeenth-century uses of the metaphor for mind, metaphors of empire more typically picture struggles within rather than asserting the serene superiority of mind. The relation of inward and outward are complicated by military history and colonial endeavor, and More's immediate context is the English Civil Wars, which, of course, irrevocably complicated conceptions of *imperium*. But insofar as More successfully avoided fatal controversy in his studious retirement during the Interregnum and extended his influence after the Restoration, his scholarly practice exemplifies rational autonomy and private conscience as an *imperium in imperio*.

At the end of the eighteenth century, in *A Postscript to the New Bath Guide*, John Williams, writing under the pen name Anthony Pasquin, puns on mental and martial as he describes how Custom "wars with Wit for empire o'er the mind; / Fights to the last unknowing how to yield, / And inch by inch disputes the mental field."[75] Eighteenth-century philosophy discovers the limits of intellectual command, reversing More's easy figuration of "inward imperium" in a variety of metaphors of reconquest, restoration, and revolution. Self-command is in question when Francis Hutcheson writes of the "empire of sensuality" and when Hume, in his *Abstract* to the *Treatise*, writes of the "empire of the imagination"; when Smith, in *The Theory of Moral Sentiments*, imagines the "empire of fortune"; or when Godwin, in the second edition of his *Memoirs* of Wollstonecraft, describes the "empire of feeling," which governs the "delicate" female frame.[76]

As various powers compete for empire over the mind, a core self may be identified as that part of a person that survives invasion and struggles to maintain autonomy through the exercise of philosophy, laboring in thought, reordering given experience—reconquering it in Shaftesbury's metaphor—in the face of contingency, custom, and habit. Those who describe the mind in these terms recast and personify the mind itself as sovereign, secure in the seat of empire, able to weather the divisions and disruptions of faction, maintain its state, survive inconstancy and corruption, and put down rebellion.

In a midcentury dialogue on animal economy intended for young ladies, Benjamin Martin describes the brain as the "Capital Organ of all Sensation," the "Seat or Residence of the MIND or SOUL" and "the Grand *Emporium* of all Intelligence."[77] The picture of an empire, if not an emporium, speaks to the contrasts drawn between a homogenous core nation-state and an expansive heterogeneous empire, or, in the classical case of Rome, the historical distinction between the republic and the empire that succeeded it.[78] For Locke, foreign materials keep reason employed in abstraction and generalization, and Martin tropes these mental activities more explicitly as manufacturing and fabrication; both cite the axiom *nothing can exist in the mind that was not first in the senses*. Although "empire" and "empiricism" are not related etymologically, the terms are brought closest by the medical discourse, appropriated by Martin, in which the brain figures as a commercial space, a capital or market town at the center of a sprawling empire. In the *Dictionarium Britannicum* Nathan Bailey, unexpectedly, defines "Emporium" as the "common sensory of the brain," a medical sense also recorded in the *Encyclopedia Britannica*. In John Quincy's *Lexicon Physico-Medicum*, which ran through eleven editions in the period, the metaphor is likewise acknowledged: "*Emporium*, a market-town; but metaphorically applied to the brain, which is the seat of all rational and sensitive transaction."

"A Kind of Additional Empire"

The Enlightenment would establish the extent to which a mind may operate autonomously, uncolonized or beyond transaction, untroubled by imperial passions, unmolested by invasion, unregulated by foreign rule, and free from tutelage, corruption, or Locke's "empire of habit." To borrow a Kantian metaphor, such an autonomous, spontaneous self would be "self-legislating." In the discourse of empiricist associationism, it is largely incumbent on British authors to turn their metaphors of mind around, recasting invasion as acquisition and replacing metaphors of legislation with those of commerce. Thus Joseph Addison rewrites Locke, first admitting in a much-discussed passage from his essays on the "Pleasures of the Imagination" that for a spectator, "It is but opening the Eye, and the Scene enters," but then revising the invasive prospect in terms of property: "It gives him indeed, a kind of Property in every thing he sees, and makes the most rude uncultivated Parts of Nature administer to his Pleasure."[79] The disinterested spectator is passive but imperious. Ostensibly preferring the prospect to the possession, the spectator is promoted as neither subject nor object of conquest but a site of transaction. Addison's vocabulary—manifestly expansionist—politicizes the self's pleasures in terms of property (a fictitious, imaginary "kind of Property") and brings colonial concerns of *administration* into focus. Addison writes in *Spectator* no. 69 (on the Royal Exchange), "Trade, without enlarging the *British* Territories, has given us a kind of additional Empire."[80]

Addison would allay traditional worries that a trading empire overextends a virtuous, self-sufficient republic, bringing corruption upon it. Thus, trade's empire is only "a kind of additional Empire." In Adam Smith's analysis of England's monopoly trade with the American colonies, England first took a "fictitious possession of the country" by means of the discovery and mapping of the North American coast but has come to exercise its dominion in the jealous and narrow interest of shopkeepers.[81] The revolutions and crises of finance—symptoms of an expanding and volatile trading empire crisscrossing the Atlantic—replace property in land with the increasing circulation of mobile, fictitious paper properties valued on the Royal Exchange and in the backrooms of coffeehouses in terms of passion, opinion, and interest.

The ascent of moneyed interests and the political ambivalences of classical virtue and commercial credit described in the work of J. G. A. Pocock seem to turn empire inside out when considered in the context of the metaphors for the mind treated here.[82] Figuring the self in terms of empire depends on reciprocal inversions: expansion and depopulation, virtue and corruption. As with the metaphor of the emporium, the locus of transactions and the focus of inversion trouble the boundaries of the self. In the poetry of Oliver Goldsmith, "trade's proud empire hastes to swift decay," forcing emigration upon sturdy English villagers, depopulating the English countryside as the British empire expands.[83] Foreign commerce precipitates national decline by accumulating wealth and land in the hands of a few rich men—who, like the worst emperors of Rome, become slaves to luxury. Contrasting Italy's imperial past and its impoverished present in *The Traveller*, Goldsmith deploys an epic simile that compares the peasant living among the decayed ruins "where Caesars once bore sway," to a personified "nobler aim" that "Now sinks at last or feebly mans the soul" of the effeminate modern Italian—a stereotyped castrato interested only in fashion and frippery.[84] The simile of the soul's empire contrasts martial virtue and effeminate vice in the figures of Caesar and the peasant, the glorious domes of the past and the empty, depopulated ruins of the present.

Foreign peoples, ideas, and luxury goods pour in upon the subject of empire—into the brain's emporium as into the Royal Exchange (itself described by Addison in *Spectator* no. 69 as "a kind of Emporium for the whole World").[85] Early eighteenth-century inheritors of civic humanism struggle to reconcile two political goods: the patriot's love of liberty (*libertas*) and national imperial pursuits (*imperium*). Robinson Crusoe, archetypal colonist, paranoid builder of walls and fences, describes his time on his island as "my Reign, or my Captivity, which you please."[86] Reign and captivity, the westward course of empire brings both ambivalently, and in senses both literal and figurative. Lecturing in 1791, James Wilson characterizes the expansion or the Roman Empire in reversible terms: "it may be said, not that the Romans extended themselves over the whole globe, but that the inhabitants of the globe poured themselves upon the Romans." For Wilson, "This is the most secure method of enlarging an empire."[87] In *The True-Born Englishman*, Defoe reveals the truth of the "uncertain and unev'n" English race, derived from bastard generations of raiders and invaders: a "*Roman-Saxon-Danish-Norman* English." On the aptly named "'Change," Addison's Spectator trades in these identities and more: "Sometimes I am lost in a Crowd of *Jews*; and sometimes make one in a Groupe of *Dutch-men*. I am a *Dane*, *Swede* or *French-man* at different times."[88]

An empire is imagined through reciprocal relations: center and periphery, self and other, colonizer and colonized. New conquest is followed by old corruptions: the expansion of the slave trade, the growth and deployment of professional standing armies, the influx of luxury goods all undermine civic virtue and result in the mixture, loss of identity, decline and decay familiar to eighteenth-century readers of Tacitus, Polybius, Machiavelli, Harrington, Montesquieu, Goldsmith, and Gibbon. Luxury imports enervate a nation, leaving a people effeminate and unable to defend itself from foreign invasion: "It is the Pride of *Equipage*, the Pride of *Title*, the Pride of *Fortune*, or the Pride of *Dress*, that have assumed the Empire over our Souls."[89] The importation of French fashion by frivolous aristocracy is doubly insidious as it corrupts martial spirit at home and weakens English trade abroad. In his final epic poem, Blackmore describes King Alfred's travels to Sicily and pictures the natives of Messina "sunk in Riot." Having "resign'd / Celestial Reason's Empire of the Mind," they forget to plant and sow; commerce, public business, and learning thereby decline.[90]

Where Pocock reads political philosophy and its neighboring discourses for virtue and corruption, I detail a related ambivalence located in eighteenth-century philosophy of mind: ideas may be figured as acquisitions (a kind of property) but also as invaders. Luxuriating in experience proves enervating. Does the individual maintain empire over his ideas, or do they exert empire over him? Does he own them or do they own him?[91] In a paragraph written to be inserted in the text of the *Treatise* (presumably in press), Hume tries to measure "the empire of the will over our mind," which he finds uncertain: "We have command over our mind to a certain degree, but beyond that lose all empire over it: and it is evidently impossible to fix any precise bounds to our authority, where we consult not experience."[92]

Romans, Stoics

Informing the foregoing discussion is the classical figure of the Stoic, the severe man who fully conquers or governs his own passions and exercises command over his own mind. Stoicism would reinforce the self's boundaries.[93] Self-denying, inward-looking Stoicism personifies anti-imperialism and opposition in the character of Cato the Younger. In the eighteenth century, "the master plot of the republican hero" was brought to the stage by Addison's popular tragedy *Cato* (1713) and restaged and remade by later writers on both sides of the Atlantic.[94] When the virtuous republic reaches beyond its circumscribed and invincible boundaries and embraces an empire of external things, confusion and corruption result. The Stoic Roman emperor Marcus Aurelius Antoninus (like his Stoic predecessors) urges the cultivation of the faculty that forms opinions; because the formation of opinion, like all other intellectual operations, is within our power, external things can have no power in causing opinions (VI.52).[95] "Nature hath not so blended the soul with the body, as that it cannot circumscribe itself, and execute its own office by itself": so Francis Hutcheson renders the Aurelian description of autonomy in a popular eighteenth-century translation of the *Meditations* (VII.67). The soul free from passions is a "strong fort" to which one may always retreat or retire (VIII.48). It is significant that the action of Addison's *Cato: A Tragedy* unfolds *inside* the besieged palace in Utica and concludes when Cato "opens to himself a passage" through suicide (IV.ii.17). Falling on his sword, Cato escapes unconquered and master of himself even as Caesar's "troops beset [the] gates, / And bar each avenue" and his "fleets / "O'erspread the sea and stop up every port" (V.ii.14–7). Cato's corpse is figured finally as a "fence" against Caesar (V.iv.105).[96]

As Stoic thought pervades eighteenth-century literature, the figure of the Stoic comes to feature in the writing of political economists and moral sense theorists: in Mandeville, Hume, and Smith, analysis of a Stoic sentimentality usefully divides human nature along lines of sensibility and self-denial, exposing pleasure-seeking hypocrisy and the paradoxes of sympathy and apathy. The impossible assertions of autonomy and the heroic postures of self-denial are gleefully undermined in Mandeville's remark in *The Fable of the Bees*, which takes aim at the "haughty Pretences" of both Christian and modern philosophical versions of Stoicism. Moral philosophy, then, revises the Stoic along sentimental lines in response to Mandeville's mordant analysis of contradiction.[97] Adam Smith's impartial spectator negotiates self and other. Hume's Stoic is both sage and patriot; Aurelius, both emperor and philosopher.

Stoicism and "reason of state" appear (speciously) complementary: a ruler's absolutist policy looks not unlike the subject's exercise of power over his passions; every ruler—every individual—is an emperor in his own kingdom.[98] Looking inward need not lead to parochialism; rather, in the original Stoic writings, it is the source of cosmopolitanism. The Roman soul would bring the uncivilized world "under the restraint of laws" (*Cato*, I.iv). The eighteenth century would bring the laws of nation and the laws of nature into accord. Nature is overmastered by a culture that itself derives from natural law. If the circle doesn't close, there remains at least the gesture of circumscription.

A year after the Stuart Restoration, Thomas Ross, a former member of Charles II's exiled court at Bruges, published the first English translation of Silius Italicus's *Punica*, an epic account of the Second Punic War. Framed by dedicatory epistles and poetry to Charles and his family, the poem asserts Virgilian values of empire and divine right and reads as a Royalist response to the English Civil Wars—although the historical allegory is very loose, as

Ross recommends both victorious Scipio and vanquished Hannibal to Charles's notice.[99]

In the first book of Ross's continuation of the Latin poem, Syphax, defeated and sent to Scipio as a prisoner, makes a final speech before his death:

> *Rome* shall finde,
> I still retain the Empire of my Minde,
> That stands above her reach, where I alone
> Will rule, and scorn to live, but on a Throne.[100]

The North African king vaunts that the mind is an unconquerable territory; similar sentiments are rehearsed by a parade of eighteenth-century Catonic characters—many of them Africans, Indians, and slaves. The sovereign mind is supposed to exert empire over its passions but finds itself in a state of "mutual siege."[101] In dialectical reversals of rule and subjection, the self is perpetually changing, ever reterritorialized. Further reversals feature in the black-and-white binaries of abolitionist poetry, where the trader of slaves falls slave to his passions (in William Cowper's "The Negro's Complaint," the traders are "Slaves of gold"), and the suffering slave's stoicism, as in Hannah More's poem *Slavery*, is a sign of a "high unbroken haughtiness of heart; / That self-same stuff which erst proud empires sway'd" (see **Fetters**).[102]

These assertions of an "empire of mind" recall Henry More's figures of "inward imperium" and any number of English Civil War survivors (the Puritan William Prynne, for one, was nicknamed "the Cato of his Age"). Many assertions of sovereignty are explicitly Stoic or neo-Stoic in flavor and contradict the figures of empiricism and empire treated above and seem to belie the way of ideas and inflexible laws of association rehearsed in Enlightenment philosophy. So, in *Don Sebastian* (I.i), Dryden's title character asserts that "Souls know no Conquerors," and Blackmore asks with rhetorical point if arms can conquer reason and triumph over the "awful Judge within," or if kings can "the Empire of the Soul invade?" Godwin, in his rationalist optimism, believes the powers of the mind to be progressive and reasons that "If mind be now in a great degree the ruler of the system, why should it be incapable of extending its empire?"[103]

But the majority of eighteenth-century metaphors undercut such pictures of autonomy, and the century is filled with ruling passions and fatally compromised sentimental exchanges. When, in Richardson's *Clarissa*, a reformed Lovelace cites the line from Dryden quoted above, he does so to dispute and revise the metaphorics of private conscience, complaining, "the poet says not truth; for CONSCIENCE is the conqueror of souls: at least it is the conqueror of mine."[104] Henry Fielding is quick to point out the limits of reason's mental tyranny: "Reason, however we flatter ourselves, hath not such despotic Empire in our Minds, that it can, with imperial Voice, hush all our Sorrow in a Moment." And in a moralizing reading aimed at the title character of Shakespeare's *Coriolanus*, Elizabeth Griffith marks the limits of self-command and shows "the strained principles of stoical pride, whose throne is only in the mind" give way—in act V, scene 3, of the play—to "great Nature, whose more sovereign seat of empire is *in the heart*."[105]

Romantic Conquests

Love of country and command of passion, if not conceptually at odds, look reciprocally inverse: complicating the character of a Cato, dislocating conflicted subjects of civil war, and fracturing imperial drama along tragic and comic-romantic lines. Addison's *Cato* itself opens with two brothers discussing romantic conquests. Amatory and sentimental modes do work that epic and romance cannot. In the early eighteenth century, it is seduction plots that gather a great preponderance of empire metaphors: in these fictions conquest is figurative—not empire but a "kind of empire," not the epic but the mock epic. Still later in the period, sentimentality becomes "the effective mode in the context of empire."[106] In Restoration dramas and amatory fictions, then, ladies of fashion pride themselves on their conquests; their rake counterparts, too, figure themselves as conquerors. It may be enough to capture the heart or some other capital city of the self in order to annex territory to an expanding empire. Women conquer affections and enslave their lovers, whereas a rake's empire usually involves the winning of sexual favors; in much literature the conquest is forced.

But love's empire, though often figured as complete and absolute, is not permanent. Women, ever figured as tyrants in love, soon find themselves the basest of slaves in marriage. In her much reprinted "Advice to a Young Lady Lately Married," Esther Lewis advises a wife to fix her empire in her husband's heart in the "early days of wedded life."[107] As affection and female power wane together, maintenance figures importantly. Eliza Haywood writes in *Idalia* that "once a Woman has disposed of every Thing in her Power to give, it must be Softness only, and fond Compliance with her Lover's Will, that can maintain her Empire o'er his Heart."[108]

Literature translates empire into narrative. Characters struggle to conquer the hearts and then minds of other characters. Indeed, the heart is a primary target of conquest, a base of operations. As in love, so in war. Conquest of the heart is often "absolute" (the adjective is especially favored by the amatory novelists and is easily associated with a Royalist poetics). And while the conquest of hearts may occasionally be construed in more positive terms (with a conqueror finding herself at the center of a large group of true friends), fashionable ladies, in the violent language of Restoration theater, more typically surround themselves with their conquests and figure them as slaves. Libertines brag of their sexual conquests, and here the conquest is physical—language descends from metaphor to metonym as rhetoric prepares the way for rape.[109] The euphemisms tend toward violent literalization: a woman's virtue is conquered, her innocence surrendered, her body invaded.[110] Rousseau's description of Sophie in *Emile* differentiates male force and female resistance: women, claims Rousseau, feign resistance to procure sex.[111]

Sarah Fielding quotes Rochefoucauld: "It is difficult to conquer the Passions, but it is impossible to satisfy them."[112] One may struggle to conquer his or her passions, desires, inclinations, and ambitions. We conquer our own passions or conquer another's heart. Haywood pairs these possibilities: "subdue your self, as you have conquer'd me! be satisfied with vanquishing my Soul, fix there your Throne, but leave my Honour free!"[113] It is a plea of virtue in distress: conquer the soul, not the body. The conquest begs the conqueror to conquer himself—so often "his" is the right pronoun for the conqueror in these early eighteenth-century novels—to conquer his own energies, to turn and point the force of his advances inward. Mr. B. summarizes the fairy-tale plot of *Pamela*: "I could not conquer my Love; so I conquer'd a Pride, which every one thought unconquerable."[114] The figuration of conquest is especially prevalent in Restoration dramas and amatory novels from the early part of the century (see again the first graph at the beginning of this entry). And so it is hearts that are fortified in the long eighteenth century more than egos, because it is hearts that are most typically figured as conquerable. The heart, understood as both material and immaterial, is capable of being conquered twice over. The self-conqueror gains control of himself; conquest of the female heart is thinly disguised euphemism for sexual violence.

Henry Fielding's fiction famously crosses sex with violence in mock-epic narrative passages, with one of the best-known examples being the tavern scene in *Tom Jones* that details "a Battle of an amorous Kind" between Tom Jones and Mrs. Waters. Fielding describes how by carelessly letting a handkerchief drop from her neck, Mrs. Waters "unmasked the Royal Battery." The heart of Tom Jones is "entirely taken," and "the fair Conqueror" is able to enjoy "the usual Fruits of her Victory."[115] Cruel and satirical eighteenth-century fiction has much fun inverting the *Pamela* plot (itself more prankish and comic than we may recognize), and here Fielding elaborates a parody of conquest:

a female conquest of the male body. Similar scenes are found in *Joseph Andrews*, and in *Tristram Shandy* the "skirmishes" between Widow Wadman and Toby Shandy function similarly. The cruel fun may be ultimately had at the expense of the female characters, as the scenes stage eighteenth-century "rape jokes" and libertine thought problems as narrative set pieces. What could it mean, *literally*, for a woman to conquer a man or for a man, *figuratively*, to conquer a woman?[116] High imperial metaphorics descend to metonym and euphemism in satire and comedy.

The libertine problem is carefully staged in *Clarissa*, a novel that collects all of the senses of "conquest" discussed in the paragraphs above. Lovelace claims to be ruled by three "imperial" passions that sway him by turns: "Love, Revenge, Ambition, or a desire of conquest"; and Clarissa claims repeatedly that she cannot "conquer [her] aversion to Mr. Solmes" (2:121).[117] Throughout, Lovelace plans his triumph over Clarissa: "when completed, [it] will be so glorious a one, that I shall never be able to keep up to it. All my future attempts must be poor to this. I shall be as unhappy after a while, from my reflections upon this conquest, as Don John of Austria was, in his, on the renowned victory of Lepanto, when he found, that none of his future atchievements could keep pace with his early glory" (3:352). And yet in a denial of any metaphorical similarity between territories internal and external, Richardson continually emphasizes that interior empires are ultimately not conquerable and cannot be invaded. Lovelace despairs of conquering Clarissa's will: "There is no triumph in *force*! No conquest over the will!" (4:169). And until her demise, Clarissa's will—like Hannibal's mind—remains inviolate. So Clarissa claims, "My will is unviolated. The evil (respecting *myself*, and not my *friends*) is merely personal" (7:50–1). Alternately, Lovelace, by the novel's end, claims to be conquered by his own conscience and disavows Dryden's Restoration metaphor of conquest. Richardson would prove that the properly fortified empire of self is unconquerable and pairs Clarissa and Lovelace in an epitome and repudiation of amatory literature.

Wollstonecraft's *A Vindication of the Rights of Woman* collects and analyzes these and related figures of empire. Her whole text might be described as a brilliant exploration of the metaphors of sexual and mental politics—one of the earliest examples of *Metapherngeschichte* and one of the more insightful.[118] On Wollstonecraft's account, tyranny over women and the tyranny of woman, two aspects of what Anna Laetitia Barbauld terms "beauty's empire," produce a dialectic of rule and subjection, adoration and scorn, that characterizes courtship and marriage. In Wollstonecraft's diagnosis, artificial weakness and beauty's empire produce in women a propensity to tyrannize. She repudiates Barbauld's claim—variations of which she locates in Rousseau and Madame de Stael—that woman's "BEST" and "SWEETEST empire is—to PLEASE."[119] Wollstonecraft's radical politics expose the despotic and tyrannical connotations of *empire*: the woman who exercises her imperious sexuality is "not a more irrational monster than some of the Roman emperors, who were depraved by lawless power" (89).

Drawing from the patriotic political tradition concerned with liberty, luxury, and effeminacy, Wollstonecraft employs and dissects metaphors of empire; but then her rhetoric itself often prepares a new nineteenth-century colonial imagination of empire. Wollstonecraft invokes and associates multiple images of empire, tyranny, and slavery but verges on racism in her defense of the rights of woman.[120] In contradistinction to the Roman Empire, Wollstonecraft imagines the Muslim empire as unequivocally tyrannical. Male domination of women is therefore described by Wollstonecraft as a "Mahometan strain" that would deprive women of their souls, and Wollstonecraft despises the arts of the "seraglio" (33, 55). Women glory in their "illicit sway" like "Turkish bashaws" and are depraved like Sybarites (80, 89). From a husband's demands, it follows that "from their infancy women should be shut up like Eastern princes" (96). As the eighteenth century comes to a close, metaphors of empire that had carried connotations of ancient Rome seem to give way to new empire metaphors: Turks, Asians, Indians, and Africans crowd out Stoic Romans.

5 Fetters

Collocated Keywords: Bond, Chain, Fetter, Iron, Shackle

Count of Metaphors in Database[1] (1700–1799): 329

Now how should he possibly do this, unless he is absolutely free, and undisturbed by tormenting Passions, which bind him, as it were, and if I may use that expression, chain him fast to himself.

—John Dennis, *A Large Account of the Taste in Poetry* (1702)

You see, my Lord, said he with a Sigh, that I have put it out of her Power to triumph over my Weakness, for I confess my Heart still wears her Chains; but e'er my Eyes or Tongue betray to her the shameful Bondage, these Hands should tear them out.

—Eliza Haywood, *Love in Excess* (1719)

Poor *Mind*, who heard all with extreme Moderation,
Thought it now Time to speak, and make her Allegation.
'Tis I that, methinks, have most Cause to complain,
Who am cramped and confin'd like a Slave in a Chain.

—Elizabeth Carter, *A Dialogue* (1741)

Thus a lively *Imagination* and unperceived *Self-Love*, fetter the Heart in certain *ideal* Bonds of their own creating: Till at length some turbulent and furious Passion arising in its Strength, breaks these fantastic Shackles which Fancy had imposed, and leaps to its Prey like a *Tyger* chained by *Cobwebs*.

—John Brown, *Essays on Characteristics* (1751)

ZAMEO
(*Embraces* William's *knees*) Fetters are needless where the affections are rivetted by beneficent actions. Thou hast left me free, and I am thy slave for

> ever; with my arms in bonds, I could have escaped, but thou fetterest my heart—I will never forsake thee!
>
> —Translation of August Von Kotzebue's *The Negro Slaves* (1796)

See also **Animals**, **Empire**, and **Metal**

Because slavery is my theme under this heading, devices of bondage—the fetters, chains, clogs, irons, and grislier instruments of torture—will figure as metonyms and metaphors of mind and then materialize as props. In other entries a chain of associations competes with a historical narrative in structuring the exposition, but under this headword the figuration makes history (the history of abolition). Radical arguments *for* revolution and *against* slavery in the last three decades of the eighteenth century take the distinction between literal and figurative forms of bondage as a rallying point. When liberty and property are at issue, semantics and synonymy feature in public debate. Both proslavery and abolitionist writers are careful to underline their literal claims.

As David Brion Davis observes repeatedly in *The Problem of Slavery in Western Culture*, the long history of slavery revisits basic inherent contradictions, generating dualisms physical and metaphysical. In Davis's words, the duality of the slave (a person-thing) lent itself to explorations of "religious, philosophical, and political dualisms, and was thus implicitly connected with some of the greatest problems in the history of human thought."[2] Slavery metaphors are indeed ubiquitous. They inform hundreds of sermons, notably those that take John 8:34 as a text; they pervade libertine discussions of free will, appear in amatory fiction and poetry, in the context of empiricist associationism, in political theory and revolutionary pamphlets, and in abolitionist writing. (The entry will treat these various discourses in roughly the foregoing order.) Fetter metaphors will serve here, as other metaphors serve throughout this study, to expose distinctions between literal and figurative. Surveying an intellectual history that includes classical and neoclassical examples, I find that before the rise of antislavery and antiabolitionist discourses, most thinking about slavery was figurative, with metaphors of slavery far outnumbering literal references to enslaved persons.[3] The entry concludes with a close reading of an abolitionist poem by the Hannah More as a case in point.

Liberty and Property: Personal Things

A trope of relation, a metaphor of mind links mind and matter. The mental is identified or compared with the material; the mind, with a thing. This characterization of metaphors for the mind brings them near the legal-economic relation of slavery, which identifies the enslaved person, in the language of one eighteenth-century apologist for slavery, as "merely a commodity, or *chose* in merchandize." Manacled man, made an object of purchase and sale and so "transferrable like any other goods or chattels," would be completely reduced to mindlessness but that the literal marks a limit for metaphor. In the language of Edward Long (the Jamaican planter quoted twice above), that limit is made evident syntactically. Long's assertions and comparisons mirror the structure of simile: "*As* our trade esteemed Negroe labourers merely commodity or *chose* in merchandize, *so* the parliament of Great Britain has uniformly adhered to the same idea" (emphasis added). Enslaved Africans are esteemed objects—things, the French word pluralized is *choses*—and deemed "transferrable *like* any another goods or chattels," so that a planter's "right of property" is "*as* that of any other British merchant over the goods in his warehouse" (emphasis added).[4]

With man's labor merchandized and alienated, slavery itself stands as the limit case of dependence, in which "a man's condition most closely approximates the status of a thing."[5] When Long asserts that African slaves are property in the hands of their owners and may be sold in the same manner as other "personal things," the reader suspects a dreadful pun.[6] The slave, both a person and a thing, makes paradoxical those twin values of the eighteenth century: liberty and property. Liberal democratic institutions accommodate plantation slavery, and an expanding "free" market includes and is propelled by the African slave trade. On my reading, the abolitionist sentiments that flourished in the last two decades of the century do not unravel the contradictions at the core of the Enlightenment project but do go some way toward drawing new distinctions between literal and figurative slavery.[7]

Defining Slavery

"To chain," in Johnson's *Dictionary*, is "to bring into slavery." As Enlightenment teleology imagines a "vast chain of being," metaphors come to link poetic descriptions of love, philosophical discussions of the will, and political theory and rhetoric. The metaphor works persistently through discourse; and Johnson employs it in self-description: "the writer of dictionaries" is "the slave of science." In the mechanical philosophy associated variously with Descartes, Boyle, and Newton, iron necessity governs the material world, fettering possibility in chains of cause and effect. Associationism pictures thought structured in chains of ideas, and in his *Encyclopedia*, Hegel labels empiricism "a doctrine of bondage."[8] Phillips's *New World of Words* defines "captivate" as "take captive, to inslave"; the word is "altogether apply'd to the Affections of the Mind." Still older traditions figure the soul as a slave to sin: Martin Luther, following Paul (Romans 6:17–8, 6:22), figures sin as "bondage of will" but also belief in terms of slavery.[9] From within and from out of literary history, the figure of the enslaved African was bodied forth as, in the 1760s and 1770s, the first black writers in English began to write about slavery finding new uses for older religious and philosophical metaphors. African figures are consistently overdetermined by representations as revolutionary art and literature asserts liberty and declares independence.[10] In the final decades of the eighteenth century the frequency of figuration sharply increases, even as the movement for the abolition of the slave trade altered the terms of debate by emphasizing literal slavery.

The definitive discussion of slavery is found in book I of Aristotle's *Politics*, where the slave is a kind of metaphor, "a living possession"—literally, an *ensouled* article of property.[11] Aristotle's further analogies would seem to yoke the immaterial to the material and compactly present the duality of slavery: "For the body is the soul's tool born with it, a slave is as it were a member or tool of his master, a tool is a sort of inanimate slave."[12] According to Aristotle, in rule and subjection we observe a duality that originates in the very constitution of the universe: in any compound entity there is a ruling principle, and by implication an element that serves that principle. So, in the *Politics*, Aristotle has us imagine the pilot of a ship who has in his rudder a *lifeless* (and in his lookout man, a *living*) instrument. Aristotle's more modern readers may imagine the eighteenth-century slave ship crossing the Atlantic and locate the human cargo somewhere between; the slave trader turned abolitionist John Newton, for one, describes living and lifeless Africans chained together below decks during the Middle Passage.[13]

Stoic and early Christian writers deconstruct or recompose Aristotle's compound: the body may be bound, chained, fettered, shackled, but the mind remains free and independent. In *Of Benefits*, Seneca insists that while the slave's body is subjected to the master, the mind remains independent (III. xx).[14] The late eighteenth-century evangelical poet William Cowper updates Seneca and puts the sentiment in the mouth of an enslaved African in the poem "The Negro's Complaint": "But though slave they have enrolled me / Minds are never to be sold."[15] As the master-slave dialectic turns, slaver is enslaved; and in Cowper's poem, the slave trader is a "slave of gold." More elaborately, John Newton describes himself, in his autobiographical *Thoughts Upon the African Slave Trade*, "bound, in conscience," to confess himself an "active instrument" (note the Aristotelian phrase) in the slave trade; Newton, captured and held captive in Africa for over a year, thus figures his situation: "I was in effect, though without a name, Captive and Slave myself."[16]

The Merchandise of Men

In 1652, Gerrard Winstanley published his final and best-known statement of principle, a pamphlet titled *The Law of Freedom*. In it Winstanley asserts, "the inward bondages of the mind . . . are all occasioned by the outward bondage that one sort of people lay upon another."[17] Writing in the revolutionary English republic, Winstanley appeals to Oliver Cromwell to advance the revolution or risk laying "the foundation of greater slavery." In an earlier Digger pamphlet that Winstanley helped author, the laws of England set down since the Norman Conquest are described as so many "Cords, Bands, Manacles, and Yokes"; and, in Winstanley's less radical, leveling contemporary John Lilburne's words, the Rump Parliament threatened to forge "New Chains."[18] Until outward political structures change, inward, ostensibly freeborn rights are not secure. Andrew Marvell memorably politicizes dualism and complicates Puritan politics in his "Dialogue Between the Soul and Body" when he alternately voices the complaints of "A Soul inslav'd . . . hung up, as 'twere, in Chains / Of Nerves, and Arteries, and Veins," and then the counter plaints of the body, in "bonds," made to labor restlessly by its "Tyrannic" possessor.[19]

Outward-bound religious sectarians, many of them slave owners and revolutionaries both, colonized America and the West Indies. These colonists established tobacco and sugar plantations that employed slaves and indentured servants even as Winstanley's Diggers set up their own utopian "plantation" outside London on Saint George's Hill. To this revolutionary decade, in which the foundations of slavery in the West Indies were laid, some of the earliest antislavery writings in English may also be dated.[20] The complexion of English Civil War servitude, however, is often perplexing: thousands of Royalist prisoners of war were sold by the Commonwealth and Protectorate as "white chattel" in Barbados and Virginia—some to labor in African Guinea.[21] "I hope it is not the effect of our war," stated Parliamentarian John Lenthall, "to make merchandise of men."[22] With the Restoration, the world turned downside up again, and radicals and Roundheads were sold into servitude in Barbados and other slave colonies. John Bunyan's allegorical figures (the man in an iron cage in the House of Interpreter, Christian and Faithful caged and made a spectacle of in Vanity Fair) in *Pilgrim's Progress* are standard emblems in the patristic tradition—which figures the body as a cage; the soul, a slave, caged and exhibited in the marketplace—but they may also be read more literally. Bunyan himself wrote from prison, having been arrested for preaching illegally.[23]

The African slave trade, dating from the fifteenth century and long controlled by the Portuguese, Spanish, and Dutch, was not yet fully institutionalized in early seventeenth-century England or its colonies. But in the decades following the Restoration, new forms of bondage were codified in laws that more strongly distinguished indentured servitude and African slavery—substituting "black ivory" for white chattel.[24] Slavery and the African slave trade became objects of legislation, and the newly formed Royal Adventurers to Africa—re-formed in 1672 as the Royal African Company—was chartered with monopoly rights over the merchandising of men to the colonies. Trading from the African coast, the company branded many enslaved Africans with the letters "DY," the initials of James, the Duke of York, a main investor along with Charles II and Prince Rupert. In 1713, following the negotiation of the Treaty of Utrecht, the *asiento* or permission to supply slaves to Spanish colonies in the Americas was given to the British. In the eighteenth century the slave trade expanded rapidly, with well more than 6 million captives taken from Africa in the Atlantic trade and more than 2.5 million transported by British slave traders.

At the close of the period here surveyed (a moment in which the revolutionary millenarian ideas associated with the English Civil Wars began to circulate again), William Blake sowed his poetry with metaphors that repeatedly elide the difference between inward and outward slavery. Blake thus makes slavery—a trade increasingly literalized in abolitionist writing—newly mythic, figurative, and universal. In Blake's "London," "mind-forg'd manacles" are heard "In every cry of every Man, / In every Infants cry of fear, / In every voice, in every ban."[25] Blake's manacles are forged by ideology, audible everywhere. Through bans, cries, sighs, and curses, the vocabulary of slavery pervades the long century that separates and connects Winstanley and Blake. In civil war pamphlets and abolitionist tracts, slaveries inward and outward, figurative and literal, are rehearsed. And in the pamphlets and poetry of Blake's contemporaries, theological, commercial, and political forms of slavery are purposefully conflated. The final decade finds new metaphors in every genre, on every page, with a congeries in drama that is discussed below.

Synonymy and Semantics

While many conflate slaveries, other writers study subtler semantic differences or despair at the proliferating senses of slavery. In *De Cive*, Hobbes explores diversity of signification in *slave*, *servant*, *serf*, and *esclave*, his etymology preparing the way for later proslavery discussions of villeinage. Terminological considerations animate much of the argument in and surrounding the landmark cases *Somerset v. Stewart* (1772) and *Knight v. Wedderburn* (1778). In the former case, the decision was often interpreted to imply that the state of slavery was not recognized in England (and supported elsewhere in the empire only by positive law).[26] In the latter case, discussed by Johnson and Boswell, the colliers and salters in Scotland were described as enduring greater servitude than enslaved Africans. Transported convicts and pressed sailors were widely understood to suffer varieties of unfreedom. A comedy like Thomas Bellamy's *The Benevolent Planters* mixes apologetics for slavery with insipid abolitionist sentiment, concluding in epigram: "SLAVERY IS BUT A NAME."[27]

Names for black slavery and white servitude are increasingly juxtaposed and defined one against the other in the early decades of industrial revolution. London chimney sweeps were even imagined as "Africans of our own growth."[28] John Wesley's 1774 *Thoughts on Slavery* opens with the problem of definition by citing Francis Hargrave, the junior counsel who volunteered his legal services in the Somerset case of 1772: "The variety of forms in which Slavery appears, makes it almost impossible to convey a just notion of it by way of Definition."[29] The *Encyclopedia Britannica*, at the end of the century, likewise observes that "SLAVERY is a word, of which, though generally understood, it is not easy to give a proper definition."[30] But the term is defined explicitly in the opening of Justinian's *Digest* of Roman law: "Slavery is an institution of the *jus gentium* [law of nations], whereby someone is against nature made subject to the ownership of another."[31] In the very codification of slavery is a tension or contradiction: treating a person as a thing is contrary to nature and paradoxical.[32] Later usage of men and language further confounds the relation between law and nature. Beatitudinous theological writing imagines yet deeper reversals, and accommodations of paradox result in a long tradition of literary ambiguities.

In the final decades of the eighteenth century, abolitionist poetry codes tension in complicated antitheses and reversals. The heroic couplet, a favored form for juxtapositions of great and small, finds a new sociopolitical use in verses that pair, balance, and reverse master and slave, black and white, fettered and free. A well-known couplet composed by the "Negro Servant" Phillis Wheatley ambiguously opposes interjection and appositive: "Remember, *Christians*, *Negroes*, black as *Cain*, / May be refin'd, and join the angelic train."[33] Relocating savagery with the "Christian" trader of slaves, Samuel Jackson Pratt likewise quizzes and puzzles his reader in *Humanity* (1788): "Beat not your hearts the miscreant arms to bind, / Of the proud Christian with a savage mind?" The implied reader, presumed sympathetic to abolition, is invited to fix the savagely minded traders in bondage "till they humanize."[34]

As liberty is defined as slavery's antonym in classical political definitions, the American loyalist pamphleteer James Chalmers embraces paradox when he writes to rebut Thomas Paine's *Common Sense* in 1776. Chalmers's pamphlet, titled *Plain Truth*, ends with a sententious line, a small-capital summary of the perils of rebelling against the English constitution and its system of liberty: "INDEPENDENCE and SLAVERY are SYNONYMOUS TERMS."[35] Chalmers argues that an independent America must fall prey to France or Spain, and yet Chalmers's dialectical punch line seems to voice the same impossible insights explored in Orlando Patterson's *Slavery and Social Death*: that slave owners are parasitically dependent on their slaves, that what the manumitted slave gains is not what the master gives him, and that freedom historically follows from slavery because, without profits and class contrasts provided by slavery, there could be no freedmen.[36]

His own common sense outraged, Samuel Johnson asks in a pamphlet published a year before Paine's and Chalmers's, "how is it we hear the loudest yelps for liberty among the drivers of slaves?"[37] Chalmers's, Johnson's, and other Loyalist punch lines show civil and natural law at cross-purposes and remind readers that since ancient Greece, conceptions of slavery and liberty developed in the same polis. Chalmers's assertion means differently, again, if construed in an Aristotelian context in which the slave, as a member of the household, labors so that the master may develop his powers of thought and virtue. Indeed, the Aristotelian house-holding philosopher *requires* "natural" slavery to afford him the leisure to theorize his politics.

Royal Slaves, Ruling Passions

Early modern readers encountered ancient philosophical accounts of slavery newly translated.[38] These neoclassical readings appear at the same time British slave traders began to emerge as the leading suppliers of Africans in the colonial markets. From Aristotle, Justinian, and scripture, the eighteenth century took philosophical, legal, and doctrinal defenses and apologetics for slavery. The conjunction of classical traditions and modern trade is legible in the faces of characters such as Aphra Behn's Oroonoko, the enslaved African described with Roman features and ebony complexion, attributed greatness of soul (Aristotle's *megalopsychia* or Cicero's *magnificentia or magnanimitas*) but enrolled as slave.[39] In Hume, magnanimity or "GREATNESS of MIND" is instanced by the "Disdain of Slavery."[40] The noble slave's character brings together—to borrow vocabulary from postcolonial theory, it *creolizes*, *hybridizes*—high and low, ancient and modern, European and African.[41] Given Behn's historical context, her noble African may figure the Royalist slaves mentioned above or the enslaved Africans branded with the Duke of York's initials. "Royal African" and "noble slave" are themselves hybrid, oxymoronic terms that dramatize the contradictions of freedom and slavery born in the English Civil Wars and their uneasy aftermath. Perhaps contradiction may be traced to the root: the 1797 *Encyclopedia Britannica* asserts that the Sclavonian etymon for "slave" in "its original sense . . . was of the same import with *noble, illustrious*."[42]

In *The Order of Things*, Foucault illustrates his analytic of finitude—"in which man appears in his ambiguous position as an object of knowledge and as a subject that knows"—with the figure of the "enslaved sovereign."[43] The analytic plays historically in the French Revolution when the royal family was confined to the Tuilleries Palace in 1791. Burke performs moral outrage in his *Letter to A Member of the National Assembly*, complaining of the imprisonment of the king, while intemperate politicians are unable "to put moral chains on their own appetites"; and in the more famous phrase that follows, Burke summarizes revolutionary paradox, reversing inward and outward: these men of intemperate minds cannot be free because, "Their passions forge their fetters" (68–9).

Varied images of a defeated ruler chained and put into clogs recur with regularity in the figuring of psychomachia. Reversing the terms in a description of sublime autonomy, Edward Young pictures a slave in the sixth part of *Night-Thoughts* who "forgets his chain / And, thron'd in thought, his absent sceptre waves." (ll. 611–2). In the context of Alexander Pope's ruling passions, reason is but a "weak Queen."[44] The poet and physician Nathaniel Cotton exercises metaphysical wit or mixed metaphor in the following lines from *Visions in Verse*:

> Know too, the joys of sense controul,
> And clog the motions of the soul;
> Forbid her pinions to aspire,
> Damp and impair her native fire:
> And sure as Sense (that tyrant!) reigns,
> She holds the empress, SOUL, in chains.[45]

An empress chained figures the entanglements of the British imperial project, so that the preceding entry (**Empire**) is obviously linked to this entry (**Fetters**), which follows alphabetically. Locke, for one, updated a long tradition of understanding slavery in terms of war: the slave is a captive of a just war, and slavery is, in the *Second Treatise*, "the State of War continued, between a lawful Conqueror, and a Captive" (II.iv.24). Ideology maintains slave and captive as synonymous terms even as it becomes clearer that African slaves are not prisoners of war but victims of kidnapping. Historically, the British empire outlasts the British slave trade. Boswell, satirizing the efforts of abolition, asserts by way of non sequitur, "T'abolish negro slavery . . . would be vain / Since Love's strong empire must remain."[46]

Although he would take substantial credit for the moral theory, ruling passions were commonplace long before Alexander Pope memorably versified them in the *Essay on Man* and his moral epistles. If Pope's metaphors are among the most influential figures of governmentality in the period, Hume's pronouncement that "Reason is, and ought only to be, the slave of the passions, and can never pretend to any other office than to serve and obey them" may be the most philosophically fretful.[47] It is in the later eighteenth century that Humean arguments revalue sentiment in terms of motivation, as when the plantation owner Belcour, in the comedy *The West Indian*, admits, "My passions are my masters, they take me where they will; and oftentimes they leave to reason and to virtue nothing but my wishes and my sighs" (I.v).[48] More than half the governmental metaphors I have collected explicitly concern the rule and subjection among a hierarchy of competing psychological faculties and figure ruling passions or the rule of reason. More narrowly, in the examples digested under the current heading, subjection is troped in terms of slavery.

Slaves to Sin

Moral sentimentalists like Hutcheson, Hume, and Smith would revise older metaphorics that descend from Greek sources to shape Christian texts. In Plato's *Republic*, Cephalus (citing Sophocles) complains of "many mad masters" that ruled him in his youth (329d). Reading eighteenth-century novels in their religious context, Martin Battestin identifies the Neoplatonic writings of Boethius as locus classicus and emphasizes the homiletic importance of John 8:34, a verse in which Christ asserts before the Pharisees that all who sin are slaves of sin.[49] John Tillotson, the archbishop of Canterbury, preached several sermons on the slavery of sin, warning that "a wicked Man is a Slave to as many Masters as he hath Passions and Vices."[50]

Augustine may provide the earliest theological rationale for slavery by making original sin the prime cause of slavery.[51] His argument structures centuries of theological debate: the postlapsarian soul is bound to sin or vice. And this slavery is inescapable because the slave to sin cannot escape himself: "An evil conscience flees not from itself; it has no place to go to; it follows itself."[52] In a catechism written by Cotton Mather for the conversion of enslaved Africans, the catechized slave is asked, "*What is the Misery of our present Condition?*" and is to respond, "My Heart is full of Sin; My Life is full of Sin; I am under the wrath of God for Sin; I am a Slave to Sin and Satan."[53] The plural pronoun of "our present Condition" should include catechized and catechizer, but it is the slave who is made to say, "I am a slave." Catechized, the slave is newly mastered by Christ. Admittedly, Mather's insistence on conversion is unusual. Before the end of the eighteenth century, few missionaries visited the Caribbean sugar islands to preach deliverance to captive slaves, although Morgan Godwyn's advocacy in Virginia and Barbados and the Society for the Propagation of the Gospel in Foreign Parts (SPG), which later took up Godwyn's charge, are notable in early making the case for evangelizing and therefore ameliorating slavery.[54]

Before a 1784 sermon delivered to the annual meeting of the SPG by Beilby Porter, then bishop of Chester, few mainstream Anglican voices urged baptism or conversion for enslaved Africans, and many slaveholding colonists worried that baptism would lead to manumission.[55] It is the religious awakening of North America at midcentury and colonial revolt that brings new awareness to both black and white, and new slavery metaphors are found throughout evangelical writings and revolutionary pamphlets. So John Marrant, although born to free black parents, recognizes himself as "a slave to every vice suited to my nature and years" after hearing Whitefield preach.[56] Egalitarian impulses of Christianity redraw distinctions between complexion and spiritual colorings, asserting identity and maintaining difference. Considered from a wider vantage, evangelicalism interacts importantly with the culture of sensibility, and the first stirrings of abolitionist writing interact with universalizing declarations of the American revolutionaries.

Free Will

The controversies of predestination, free will, and grace shadow secular philosophical discussion of the antinomies of free will and determinism in a period in which, to speak with Rousseau, man is "born free" and is everywhere "in chains."[57] Traditional metaphorical and spiritual senses of slavery, rooted in Greek thought and Christian doctrine, are revised in Hobbes's and Locke's modern philosophy of action.[58] For a philosopher like Thomas Hobbes, only imprisonment or physical bondage corresponds meaningfully to the phrase "loss of liberty," as, for Hobbes, liberty in its proper and literal sense is always corporal liberty. The body may be free or confined, but the will is not to be so described. To extend the meaning of "liberty" to the subjects of monarchy or tyranny is an abuse of language.[59] Only in the historical context of slavery would the concept of freedom require such analysis and critique. It is the enslaved who must illustrate that being free refers to the absence of impediment.[60] An abuse of metaphysical terminology is literalized as physical abuse when relocated in the social relations that structured the system of chattel slavery.

In his *Essay* Locke's compatibilist discussion of liberty and necessity hews closely to Hobbes's: "*Liberty*, which is but a power, belongs only to Agents, and cannot be an attribute or modification of the *Will*" (II.xxi.14). Locke's too is a problem of proper definition (II.xxi.6); abuse of language personifies the will as a freely acting because internal agent (see **Inhabitants**). Again emphasized is linguistic analysis that separates literal compulsion from figured freedom. (Tradition and folk psychology, deeper than reasoning, seem undisturbed by the seeming incompatibility of determinism and free will and are ready to multiply figurative agents.)[61] In a discussion of "the pursuit of happiness,"[62] Locke locates real freedom in forbearance and examination, working the perhaps by now expected antitheses: "The stronger *ties* we have to an unalterable pursuit of happiness . . . the more are we *free*" (II.xii.51, emphasis added); the less able we are to suspend the prosecution of desire, "the nearer we are to Misery and Slavery" (II.xxi.30); once our will is determined, "a Chain of Consequences linked one to another" follows (II.xxi.52).

Chains of Thought

In the majority of the metaphors treated thus far, the mind or soul is not itself identified *as* a chain or iron or fetter; it is rather *fettered* by something else—by the body, the passions, custom, ignorance. So the "silver cord" of Ecclesiastes 12:6 is understood to tie soul to body. Berkeley writes in *Three Dialogues*, "We are chained to a Body, that is to say, our Perceptions are connected with corporeal Motions." And Richard Blackmore avers, God "only can'st the wond'rous Links descry/That Minds unbody'd to a Body tye."[63] In a recurrent analogy, found throughout the century, the body is to the soul as a clog tied to a leg—that is, the body is as a "clog" or "a piece of wood, fastened on the legs of beasts to prevent them from running astray" (Bailey, "CLOG"; see **Animals**). Bondage characterizes a phenomenology of embodiment. In Cowper's poem *Charity*, the slave "feels his body's bondage in his mind."[64]

The mind, captured by these metaphorics, looks to be another link, itself part of the chain of association. Consciousness is located in the physical world in eighteenth-century philosophy, and Locke is only one of the first of many post-Newtonian philosophers to figure ideas as motions in the mind (*Essay* II.xxi.12). From impressions or simple ideas we build complex and abstract concatenations, which are themselves linked in mental discourse. Discursive thought is relentlessly figured as a "chain of reasoning" or a "chain of ideas" in the eighteenth century. In a popular late eighteenth-century poem inspired by Akenside's influential *Pleasures of the Imagination*, Samuel Rogers figures association in distinctly Humean terms: "Our thoughts are link'd by many a hidden chain."[65] From motives to volition and from volition to action, the mind's actions belong to the great chain of cause and effect. So the compatibilist, like Hobbes, finds liberty and necessity consistent insofar as every desire proceeds from some cause, which proceeds from another cause, "in a continuall chaine, (whose first link is in the hand of God the first of all causes)" (*Leviathan* 108).

Book IV of *The Dunciad* opens with an explicit scene of disciplinary bondage (IV.21–35). Learning, personified as "*Science*," is located beneath the footstool that rests before the Throne of Dulness; there it "groans in Chains," while *Morality* is strangled in a cord, and the *Muses* are held in tenfold bonds. Only "mad *Mathesis*" proves "too mad for mere material chains to bind" but is kept, all the same, circumscribed by her attempts to square the circle. The first address to Dulness that follows repeats the theme as it describes the education of youth by schoolmasters who "double chain on chain," "confine the thought," and "hang one jingling Padlock on the mind."[66]

Figuring "*Logic*" as similarly "gagg'd and bound" (IV.23), Pope may recall Locke's description of the mind "intangled perhaps, and as it were manacled in the Chain of Syllogisms" (*Essay* IV.xvii.5). Because it is not easy to hold a complete chain of reasoning in mind, reasoning itself is both abetted and undermined by the joining of ideas in association. Locke's approach to logical tangles, forwarded everywhere in the *Essay*, is to investigate particular ideas, "subjecting each Link in the Chain, to the immediate view" (IV.xvii.4). But self-reflexive thought may struggle only to find itself more tightly tangled in its chain of its interlinked ideas—Locke's repetitive discourse repeatedly circles back on itself. And so in Sarah Fielding's *The History of the Countess of Dellwyn* the title character wrongly believes herself unfree and is "bound in the most whimsical Chain, made only by her own Imagination." Lady Dellwyn is compared to Don Quixote; her thralldom, like his, is as "full as difficult to be broken as the strongest real Bonds."[67] More darkly still, Samuel Johnson describes the poet William Collins languishing "under that depression of mind which enchains the faculties without destroying them, and leaves reason the knowledge of right without the power of pursuing it."[68]

A chain of consequences is determined by succession and contiguity. Effect follows cause. The constant conjunctions of resemblance, contiguity, and causation (mistaken as "necessary connexions") are, for David Hume, the "links that bind the parts of the universe together."[69] But the metaphor of the chain works invisibly in Hume: we perceive no "tie" joining cause and effect beyond the "chain of thought, which a man supports even in the loosest *reverie*" (ibid. 32). Chaining belongs to mental or verbal discourse; all objects of thought remain separable in imagination. See the figure of the prisoner from Hobbes and Locke reappear only to be executed in a chilling set piece in Hume's *Treatise*. Interlinked natural and moral evidence forms a single "chain of argument," as the prisoner finds the walls and bars of his prison as inflexible as the nature of his jailer and executioner. Hume renders the prisoner's execution in free indirect discourse and bare narration simultaneously: the prisoner's mind, while he stands on the scaffold, "runs along a certain train of ideas: the refusal of the soldiers to consent to his escape; the action of the executioner; the separation of the head and body, bleeding, convulsive motions, and death" (*Treatise* II.iii.1). The terminal clause follows the chain of ideas and causes, which had been inseparable, to the last: "Here is a connected chain of natural causes and voluntary actions; but the mind feels no difference betwixt them in passing from one link to another."[70] The chain of reasoning remains unbroken—even after head is struck from body.

Another prisoner imagined in a widely anthologized set piece from Laurence Sterne's *Sentimental Journey* makes an appearance at the end of this entry, but a different prisoner serves now to break us out of philosophical concern. Jack Sheppard, a hero of eighteenth-century broadsheets and penny newspapers, was the eighteenth century's most famous escape artist and figure of freedom.[71] First arrested in 1724, he escaped soon after, wearing his irons. In his second escape he filed them off. Arrested a fourth time he was put in leg irons, chained to the metal staples in the floor of his cell. When he showed his jailers how he could pick the locks, he was then bound more tightly and handcuffed. After his final arrest he was loaded with three hundred pounds of irons. A sermon based on Sheppard's exploits reenacts his energetic bids for freedom: "Let me exhort ye then to open the *locks* of your *hearts* with the *nail* of *repentance*: burst asunder the *fetters* of your *beloved lusts*, mount the *chimney* of *hope*, take from hence the *bar* of *good resolution*, break through the *stone-wall* of *despair*, and all the *strong holds* in the *dark entry* of the *valley of the shadow of death*."[72]

Adamantine or Silken

In eighteenth-century poetic diction, chains and fetters are *iron*, *arbitrary*, *ignoble*, *adamantine*, *galling*. The weight of the fetters is materially meaningful. Obligations seem so many ties, bonds, and bands, but chains and fetters are, as abolitionists insist, wounding, literally excoriating. The abolitionist MP William Wilberforce reports that several white male convicts transported to New South Wales died en route because "the person whose province it was to provide necessaries for the voyage, had, by mistake, purchased such fetters as were used on board Slave ships, instead of the common fetters for convicts."[73] The severity of servitude correlates with the style and material of the fetters. When Macheath is sentenced to Newgate in *The Beggar's Opera* (act II, scene v), Lockit offers to sell him genteel and handsome fetters that "the nicest Man in *England* might not be ashamed to wear."[74]

Nicer still, affect and imagination figure in soft, amorous entanglements. Belinda's curling ringlets in *The Rape of the Lock* are mock-heroic instruments of slavery: "mighty Hearts are held in slender Chains"; while in his *Essay on Man*, Pope universalizes "the Chain of Love / Combining all below, and all above" (III, l. 7). Frances Brooke has a suitor in the *History of Emily Montague* describe the "soft chains of affection."[75] The literary critic Jay Fliegelman well describes new rhetorical and antirationalist investments in "soft compulsion" and mesmeric manipulation.[76] The later eighteenth century comes to celebrate the pleasures of aesthetic reverie: what Mark Akenside influentially describes in the 1744 edition of *The Pleasures of Imagination* as "The silken fetters of delicious ease" (II, l. 562). Phillis Wheatley, perhaps borrowing from Akenside but with all the difference of scene and situation, pictures reverie as a "soft captivity," in which "silken fetters" bind the mind, while, paradoxically, "th' unbounded soul" is set free.[77]

As the eighteenth century progresses, women seem more fettered than free in the complicating negotiations of property relations and sexual propriety. As seen in Sarah Fielding's descriptions of Lady Dellwyn's depression, women—slaves to feeling—are figured as particularly prone to debilitating nervous disorder. Many heroines would break free: Frances Burney, in a sentimental scene pervaded with the language of bewildered agency, lost liberty, and enchainment, figures her eponymous Camilla liberated, in a crisis of emotion, from "the shackles of reminiscence." In Burney, as in other authors, it is family ties that bind. So in her novel *Mary*, Wollstonecraft describes a family of women all "shackled with a set of notions concerning propriety."[78] Wollstonecraft and other protofeminists identify the ways in which home education only promotes female slavishness.[79] The young woman who comes out is, according to one 1797 conduct book, "Emancipated from the shackles of instructions."[80] But in her *Vindication*, Wollstonecraft complains that woman's degraded reason is employed "rather to burnish than to snap her chains."[81]

The softest but most binding chains belong to the slumbering of sense and the sleep of reason, as in Blackmore's *Alfred*, "downy Chains that softly bind/Our slumb'ring Sense" (99). Sleep fetters the mind, as does Bacchus, binding thought in "torpid chains" or "lethargic fetters." The connotations involve ideological slumberings as well. Joseph Mitchell, the Scottish poet famously dependent on Robert Walpole's patronage, figures "Slumber's silky Chain" binding "bold Thought" in his amusing call to supineness titled "Charms of Indolence."[82] Such drowsings of a subject population are satirized in Pope's *Dunciad*, particularly in the closing stanzas of book IV (the opening lines of which are discussed above), in which the contagious yawn of Dullness covers England in a sleep.

The Great Chain of Being

Attached to the throne of Jupiter, the Great Chain of Being links the lowest clod to God. In his *Disquisitions on Several Subjects*, Soame Jenyns writes, "Man is that link of the chain of universal existence, by which spiritual and corporeal beings are united."[83] In a different disquisition Jenyns overturns the favored liberal principles of the eighteenth century, describing the course of terrestrial existence in terms of imprisonment, slavery, and tyranny. For the first nine months of life man is "confined in a dark and sultry prison"; by "Habeas Corpus" he is delivered into new swaddling bondage, tyrannized by nurse and schoolmaster, only to end this slavery by becoming the "involuntary subject of some civil government; to whose authority he must submit" (143–4). Like Jenyns, a wide variety of eighteenth-century writers imagine all-comprehending systems of enchainment. The Great Chain of Being unites social ranks and classes: "Rich and Poor are equally links of nature's chain, and mutually support each other."[84] The Jamaican proslavery writer Gilbert Francklyn surveys contemporary varieties of servitude, to conclude that slavery is "a *genus* of the state of man, of which the different kinds of servitude are distinct species."[85]

Samuel Jackson Pratt invokes the figure to undermine natural hierarchy and warn against revolution:

The polish'd links that form the social chain,
For ages still to ages may remain,
Nor snapt by rage, nor undermin'd by art,
If well the rivets join in every part;
But if those links that would the peasant bind,
Gall his chaf'd body, and corrode his mind,
The poor man's iron, and the rich man's gold,
Say, who the future changes may unfold?[86]

Here the figured "social chain" chafes the poor man's body. Bimetallic, it links poor to rich, iron to gold. The abstract institutional arrangements are metallically coded and materialize as so many links, rivets, and chains. In Roger L'Estrange's popular redaction of Seneca, all are slaves to fortune, "some only in loose and Golden Chains, others in straight ones, and coarser."[87] But Pratt's use of the metaphor mixes tenor and vehicle with interest, as if to recognize the maintenance of hierarchy requires both abstract relations and more material measures. In Pratt's verse, the body is chafed by abstract social relations; and the mind is corroded, as if metallic and not mental (see **Metal**).

Chains of love in earlier amatory poetry give way to softer chains of sympathy in later poems that celebrate friendship and sensibility. In the poetry of the period some of these chains are associated with bracelets and chains of flowers. The chain of flowers or the jeweled chain might itself become a figure of bondage (as in William Jones's *Sacontalá*). But, as mentioned above, not all chains bear negative connotations: friendship, in particular, is a relation in which two minds may be bound together in "equal chains." Matrimony amicably chains two hearts together; tender chains of love bind two wedded minds. Sympathy, likewise, is increasingly figured in terms of bondage. In the later eighteenth century these metaphors complicate mental politics as sensibility is figured in terms of slavery and is mobilized, by early abolitionist writers, to get men and women of feeling to identify with the suffering of enslaved Africans.

The melodramatic plot that overlays legal and amatory bondage in prose romances and in stage productions proved particularly popular in the closing decades of the eighteenth century. While in Restoration dramas captivity may be both more farcical and violent—a wife's love is "like a chain," firmly uniting hearts, "whereon the least stroak given, is by both sensibly felt" (*The Wary Widdow*, V.v)—matrimony is the "gentle Chain" in sentimental contexts that unites constant hearts (in Lillo's *Silvia*).[88] Late eighteenth-century dramatic texts abound with references to slavery, with chains and fetters appearing in speeches as metaphors and on stage as props in several melodramas that represent "fond links" of love and family feeling broken by circumstance.[89] In all, I mark more than forty eighteenth-century dramatic characters who declare their hearts to be in chains (the majority of them appearing in plays from the last two decades of the century). In these histrionic speeches, lovers at first struggle to break or burst the chains of love—and then they submit to them.

Literal Slavery

Slavery was treated widely in the eighteenth century, first as figure and then, by century's end, more literally in the pamphlets of the abolitionist movement. Surveying the decades, we see libertine arguments inherited and curiously renovated by evangelical abolitionists. The increasingly vehement assertion of liberty across the period, which flares out in the 1760s, culminates in the American Revolution and retracts in response to the French Revolution. While the Society for the Abolition of the Slave Trade forms in 1787, its agitations do not result, until 1807, in the passage of Wilberforce's Bill for the Abolition of the Slave Trade. As the abolitionist cause spreads, an increasing number of set pieces depict African bodies as sites of both violence and Stoic composure, with the quiet pains of Coromantins, for example, serving as conflicted signs of suffering, sympathy, and heroism.[90] The horrors of the Middle Passage test the discourse of sensibility in which the abolitionist imagines and asks others to imagine the suffering of the enslaved.[91] In his *Narrative of a Five Years' Expedition Against the Revolted Negroes of Surinam*, Captain John Stedman describes one "Object" of compassion, a beautiful "Samboe Girl," tied naked to a tree and whipped so severely that "she was from her neck to her ancles literally dyed over with blood."[92]

Stedman's "literally" is a problematic adjective, as is the pun that lurks in "died": are we to imagine the blood shed has newly darkened the complexion of a mixed-race ("samboe") body, or does "literal" here mean something like its opposite? The semantics of slaveries figurative and literal were unsettled and unsettling in the age of "revolted" slaves and New World rebellions, and liberal voices of reform thus require while failing to provide new semantic clarity. When Wilberforce first spoke in the House of Commons in support of abolition on May 13, 1789, he asserted that "the Slave Trade" had degraded Africans, "*enslaved their minds*, blackened their character, and sunk them so low in the scale of beings" (emphasis in original).[93] The enslavement, blackening, and degradation is, perhaps surprisingly, marked by Wilberforce as socioeconomic construction, the result of a trade that would justify its treatment of enslaved people, after the fact, by the racism that is its consequence.[94] When social relations are written onto mind, character, and the order of things, the figure of slavery proves ambiguous.

Abolitionists of the 1780s report "facts" and "evidence," and speakers in Parliament refer repeatedly to reports, testimony, and statistics. Thomas Clarkson collected handcuffs, leg shackles, and thumbscrews while researching his *Summary View of the Slave Trade*. During the abolition debates in the House of Commons, the distinction between personal and political slavery is repeatedly drawn. "What means Slavery?" asks the MP Charles James Fox in the debate. "A Slave is one whom another man commands at his pleasure: who belongs not to himself . . . this is *personal* slavery. Political slavery is but a metaphor."[95] In the last decade of the century, after the outbreak of the French Revolution enervates the abolitionist cause, even Jacobin writers like Wollstonecraft are more careful to specify their meaning: "When, therefore, I call women slaves, I mean in a political and civil sense."[96]

"This Is Not Said Figuratively"

The polemical, devotional verses of Hannah More's *Slavery: A Poem* (1788) collect and confound the oxymoronic commonplaces of white savagery, royal slavery, and stoic feeling explored above. At its heart is a curious, urgent footnote, analyzed here by way of conclusion. The popular poem, which castigates slave traders while celebrating Cook's imperial exploits, would balance literal and figurative slavery in couplet form. An early stanza invokes Southerne's 1696 staging of *Oroonoko* (the play remained popular in repertoire throughout the eighteenth century) only to distinguish "fictitious ills" from "living anguish, and substantial woe." The contrast is then tortured as an imagined slave is. When she looks to "Afric's" shore, More claims to see by "more than Fancy's mirror."[97] Her rhetoric is throughout antirhetorical: "Rhetoric or verse may point the feeling line, / They do not whet sensation, but define" (12). The Stoic Zeno's assertion that there is no ill in pain is dismissed, as is the proslavery assertion that Africans do not feel affliction as Europeans do.

At the poem's emotional center, its high noon, the figurative sun of Liberty, the image with which More opens, is replaced by "the fierce Sun" (a literal sun?) darting "vertical his beams" (12). Thirst and hunger "mix their wild extremes" and "the sharp iron wounds [the slave's] inmost soul" (12–13). An asterisk punctuates More's impassioned page between "iron" and "wounds."

Below, in a linked note, we read, "This is not said figuratively" (13n). That iron wounds the soul, I should suppose, must be said figuratively, with More's effort to literalize suffering requiring both the figure of a slave and a metaphor of mind. In fact, More, a native of Bristol, Britain's second-busiest slave port, retails her own eyewitness account of the chains fitted "to every separate limb" and "instruments for wrenching open the jaws."

The paradoxes of slavery link wide and wild extremes. In her footnote, More's insistence that she speaks not figuratively evokes Sterne's *Sentimental Journey*: "I saw the iron enter his soul"; and both share an allusion to the imprisonment of Joseph in irons in Psalm 105:8, a verse that commentators note should be read "literally."[98] In what sense can iron *enter* or *wound* a soul, literally? In an earlier stanza More has already questioned the materialist who believes that matter can govern spirit or the mind be degraded by the form to which it is joined. But the trope turns typological, the iron recalling the nails with which Jesus was crucified. In a line from the final stanza quoted with approval by the *Monthly Review*, More's poem steers to conclusion through the capitalized personifications of "LIBERTY" and "OPPRESSION" as "The chain untouch'd, drops off; the fetter falls" (20).[99] In these closing lines the traditional dualities of body and soul are restored. From "two-fold bands" of literal and figurative bondage, the "dusky myriads" must be twice emancipated. In this duplicitous language, the patriot More suggests **Empire** will bring both faith and freedom to enslaved Africans, effecting reform without struggle. But today, these hundreds of years on, what emancipations from the manacles of segregation and chains of discrimination have been brought by such evangelism alone?

6 Impressions

Collocated Keywords: Engraving, Impression, Imprint, Seal, Signet, Stamp, Wax

Count of Metaphors in Database[1] (1700–1799): 744

For to return again to visible Objects, to help us to apprehend this matter. If the Organs, or Faculties of Perception, like Wax over-hardned with Cold, will not receive the Impression of the Seal, from the usual impulse wont to imprint it; or, like Wax of a temper too soft, will not hold it well, when well imprinted; or else supposing the Wax of a temper fit, but the Seal not applied with a sufficient force, to make a clear Impression: In any of these cases, the print left by the Seal will be obscure.

—Locke, *Essay Concerning Human Understanding*, II.xix.3 (1690)

THEN *as to Correction*, the Heart being hardned, as before, by Opinion and Practice, and especially in a Belief that *he ought not to be corrected*, the Rod of Correction has a different Effect; for as *the Blow* of a Stripe makes an Impression on the Heart of a Child, as stamping a Seal does upon the soft Wax, the Reproof even of Words on the same Heart when grown up, and made hard, is like striking upon Steel, which instead of making an Impression *on the Metal*, darts back sparks of Fire in your Face.

—Defoe, *The Family Instructor* (1715)

SOPH.
(*Dashing the Pen away.*)
I won't, I will not write any more of his plaguy conveyances and law-gibberish!—Was ever poor girl so used as I am by this wicked old Attorney! Cruel Mama!—to make such a wretch her executor, and condemn me to the guardianship of one, who will never suffer me to be united to the man I esteem, whilst it's his interest to keep my fortune in his hands.—Here—won't even hire a clerk, but claps a pen in my hand, and ties me

like a seal to his ugly parchment, while my heart can receive no impression, but the idea of my beloved Aircourt—

—John O'Keeffe, *The Toy; or, The Lie of the Day* (1788)

No picture, be it ever so well painted, can vie with the memory in that exactness, with which she presents, early in absence, the image of that form and face, whose lineaments are dear to us. Therefore, actual pictures of beloved friends would not be so eagerly coveted, but that we render this darling, internal image indistinct, by recalling it too frequently; as that strength of line, which gives sharpness and spirit to a copper-plate, becomes injured after a certain number of impressions have been taken off. By repeated use, the plate, if not retouched, will produce only a dim and shadowy mass, in which the features and countenance cannot be very distinctly discerned.

—Anna Seward, *Epistle to William Hayley, Esq.* (1810)

See also **Coinage** and **Writing**

To HAVE AN IMPRESSION is for things to strike you as being a certain way. If the vitality of a metaphor—the force with which it strikes a reader or auditor—correlates inversely with the frequency of its usage in the language at large, then metaphors of impression (of being struck) are already worn out and etiolated in much ordinary eighteenth-century discourse. At the beginning of the century, in the sixth edition of Phillips's *New World of Words*, the term "To Impress" is defined, without comment on its figurative or literal status, as "to print, stamp, or make an Impression upon the Mind, or upon the Natural Faculties of the Body"; and an almost identical definition is found in Bailey's *Dictionarium Britannicum*. But consider all the ways things, including words, might *strike* somebody. Samuel Johnson, for example, made an indelible impression on Boswell in 1763 after the two men came out of church in Harwich and stood together for a while talking of Bishop Berkeley's "ingenious sophistry." The famous moment is recorded in *The Life of Johnson*, where, after Boswell claims he finds Berkeley's arguments for idealism to be irrefutable, Johnson responds with violence. Boswell declares, "I never shall forget the alacrity with which Johnson answered, striking his foot with mighty force against a large stone, till he rebounded from it, 'I refute it *thus*.'"[2]

To rebut is to rebound: Johnson's performance presses the stone into service, making it over as an agent or correspondent, from which Johnson, the kicker, rebounds. The large man kicking the large stone should impress the reader as it seems to have impressed Boswell: the stone kicks back.[3] The point is perhaps doubled or driven deeper when we remember that Johnson's outbursts in the *Life* are particularly aimed against "blockheads," on whom one cannot make an impression. Hoping his pamphlet *Taxation No Tyranny* would have stirred more controversy, Johnson famously quipped: "Attack is the reaction; I never think I have hit hard, unless it rebounds." In a word, Johnson's "mode of speaking" is characterized by Boswell as "impressive."[4]

In the case of impressions, questions of metaphoricity are vexed by distinctions drawn between mind and body. When we bump up against things—nightstand, thigh—and find they leave marks on us, we might say an impression has been made, *literally*. But in what sense are some impressions literal and others figurative? Are sense impressions left in the brain *literal* impressions, and impressions left in the mind *figurative*? This traditional distinction between literal and figurative senses of the term depends upon an analogy of external sensation and internal reflection. It raises (again, in the context of this book) the possibility that the drawing of distinctions between the literal and figurative is vexed work from which one can expect, in the application of an emphasis on *literally*, only stubbings and consequent soreness. In fact, as Thomas Reid will be seen to argue, usage suggests that the distinction so maintained is itself no simple dichotomy.[5] Repeatedly, when one analyzes metaphors of mind, the sorting out of literal senses from figurative senses becomes a game of arrogating functions to either the mind or the body. Distinctions that govern the senses of words for sensation have all the flavor of dualism, because the most traditional distinctions can only be drawn comfortably by a substance-dualist, whether witting or unwitting.

The senses of "IMPRESSION" enumerated by the curb-kicking Samuel Johnson are as follows: 1. "The act of pressing one body upon another"; 2. "Mark made by pressure; stamp"; 3. "Image fixed in the mind"; 4. "Operation; influence"; 5. "Edition; number printed at once; one course of printing"; and 6. "Effect of an attack." It is the first three senses given by Johnson that will most concern us in this entry; the fifth carries us forward to **Writing**. The sixth recalls Johnson's quip "Attack is the reaction." It then may be a surprise to find the first sense—not the third—illustrated with this excerpt from Locke: "Sensation is such an *impression* or motion, made in some part of the body, as produces some perception in the understanding" (from *Essay*, II.i.23).[6] But as is usual in the *Dictionary*, the first sense, founded in the physical, prepares for those that follow.[7] We imagine Johnson rebounding, pressed by the stone, producing a coeval understanding in Boswell. (Later in book II, Locke is more explicit that "*Bodies* produce *Ideas* in us" by "*impulse*, the only way which we can conceive Bodies operate in" [II.viii.11].)

Impressions give rise to perceptions; but impressions are, in another *sense* (my terminology compounds), perceptions as such. And so Johnson's third sense of the term is illustrated with politically inflected citations from Atterbury and Swift that feature impressions made directly in or on the mind. His fourth sense collects more motley examples, the last of which, from Cheyne, brings us back to refutations of idealism: "There is a real knowledge of material things, when the thing itself, and the real action and *impression* thereof on our senses is perceived." The competing definitions and examples hold open the distance between impression and perception. In the first and third senses of the headword "IMPRESSION," this distance is perhaps attributable to the parallax of the third- and first-person perspectives, a distance not quite closed by the examples adduced. The clever lexicographer, making sense of sensation, presents the mind-body problem in miniature: bodies press one "upon another," but impressions are also made or fixed in one's mind.

Although "Impression" is not one of my thirteen search terms, it might well have been but that there are too many appearances of the term "impression" to chase down, evaluate, and taxonomize without automating the collection process.[8] As I would work by hand and meticulously consider my metaphors case by case, I restricted the scope of my searches to collocations (of heart, mind, soul, etc.) and the keywords at the head of this entry. As elsewhere, I move inductively from my examples to make interpretive claims, and this entry will pressure some commonplaces in the theory of metaphor as it surveys the philosophy of impressions. Two main concerns of my project conspicuously overlap as eighteenth-century philosophers explicitly consider their own figurative language. As I proceed, I will focus on some general comments by Reid as well as specific passages in Descartes and Berkeley.

Even if the metaphor of impression is not a particularly vital figure of speech, there is a set of models by which the imagery of impression might be poetically elaborated. Under three headings, then, metaphors of impression are contextualized (*Stamp*, *Wax*, *Seal*). Beyond the sealing wax and signet rings of letter writing and the inked stamps used by the eighteenth-century London post office, further discussions of impression may be found under the heading **Coinage** and **Empire**. Focusing here on impression metaphors as such, I postpone a more summary consideration of print culture to **Writing**. Under that rubric, I discuss the remediation of the wax tablets by means of print and paper analogues and shift emphasis from impression to inscription.

First Impressions, Innate Stamps

Any number of objects make impressions: words, reasons, conspicuous wealth, sublime natural scenes—even kisses, which may imprint and be imprinted by the lips as well as more immaterial parts of the self. In John Cleland's *Fanny Hill*, for example, the narrator, reunited with her Charles, describes "giving and taking, with a gust inexpressible, a kiss of welcome, that my heart rising to my lips, stamp'd with its warmest impression."[9] The kiss, itself a kind of stamp, is stamped by Fanny's heart. Stephen Duck describes how one "Alexis keeps/The dear Impression of her Lips" in his mind.[10] These impressions are particularly interesting cases of what Johnson denotes "the act of pressing one body upon another." Such interacting sensoria are much relished by Laurence Sterne's Sentimental Traveller, Yorick, and a few more amorous metaphors will be discussed in the fourth section of this entry. Cleland, for one, revisits his impression metaphor in a euphemism that shortly follows Fanny's stamped kiss: Charles's "instrument of pleasure" is "the great-seal of love" (2:242).

A thought may itself make an impression, or an impression may strike one's thoughts. Fixed, struck, or stamped, impressions are variously made on and in the brain, the mind, the heart, the soul, the memory, the understanding, the imagination, and the passions. While the majority of impressions are made in the mind, late-century works of sensibility—Charlotte Smith's novels and Ann Radcliffe's gothic romances—frequently fix the locus of impressions in the heart. Sensibility multiplies sensorial pressure points: in the epistolary novel *Julia de Roubigné* by Henry Mackenzie, assorted pressures are summed as Julia's mother's last words "press upon" her mind "with the sacredness of a parent's dying instructions," while grief "presses" on her bosom and the "impression" her absent childhood friend Savillon made on her heart continues to gain in strength.[11] William Shenstone writes of the coldness of a beloved in anapests that capture the nervous pit-a-pat of sensibility: "And the more I with study my Fancy refin'd,/The deeper Impression she made on my mind."[12] As in the examples so far given, an impression may be deep or it may lay strong; conversely, an impression may be mild or light. Some impressions are lively, others dull. Like a shadow flying "over fields of corn," experiences insensible or unremembered, may "scarce leave an impression with us."[13] Still other impressions, where left behind, may prove to be false. So-called first impressions—the original title of Jane Austen's *Pride and Prejudice*—have a privileged status in the organization and processing of later impressions.

The word "stamp" was put to a wide variety of uses in the eighteenth century. Johnson's *Dictionary* ranges the stamping of feet, the pounding of mortars, the fixing of marks, and the minting of coins under the headword "STAMP." Above I cited Johnson's definition of an "impression" as a "Mark made by pressure; stamp." An ambiguity I will treat below doubles several of these activities: a "stamp" is an instrument by which a hollow impression is made, but it is *also* the mark or impression made upon any material soft enough to be so marked or impressed. A stamp is a "picture cut in wood or metal" or a mark "set upon things that pay customs to the government." It is "a character or reputation, good or bad, fixed upon anything." And it is "authority" or "currency" or "value." Most abstractly, a stamp is a "form." The term's multiplicity qualifies it for use in a variety of metaphors, all of which are adaptable to different discourses and theories of the self. Sense organs are stamped like wax tablets, the Lord may melt us down like wax or metal and seal our salvation, our hearts may be stamped like coinage, and innate principles or the law of nature may be stamped on our souls. Both words and images are stamped on hearts, minds, and souls.

The mind is figured throughout the long eighteenth century as both that which stamps and that which is stamped. The impression and that which impresses are related formally. As Johnson's myriad collection of definitions evidences, the instrument that stamps may be confused with the mark that is made by that instrument, promoting a doubling of entities and terms in analysis. Do we perceive ideas or those things outside of us that produce ideas in us?[14] Which is to ask, which sort of stamp are we directly acquainted with, the impression or the hollow instrument? Berkeley and Hume both remark that the "vulgar" don't distinguish between external bodies and perceptions; rather it is the materialist or skeptic who creates and then doubts "double existences" who hopes and despairs of locating the stamp's stamp.[15]

Stamping metaphors of mind are useful for linking entities and sense impressions or correlating perceptions and that which provokes those perceptions. For Locke, the relation between ideas and the entities that produce ideas is *not* one of resemblance except in one special case. Locke distinguishes between the primary qualities of "*Solidity*, *Extension*, *Figure*, and *Mobility*," which are "utterly inseparable from the Body" (*Essay* II.viii.9), and the secondary qualities of "Colours, Sounds, Tastes, *etc.*," "which in truth are nothing in the Objects themselves, but Powers to produce various Sensations in us by their *primary Qualities*" (II.viii.10). Primary qualities are *like that which produces them*; secondary qualities are not (II.viii.15).[16] Locke splits a difference between stamping and that which is stamped, and his distinction comes to animate much eighteenth-century philosophical controversy. This use of the metaphor of stamping to explain the process by which we acquire the simple ideas of sensation is consistent with his strategy of correcting the "established Opinion amongst some Men, That there are in the Understanding certain *innate Principles*; some primary Notions, Κοιναὶ ἔννοιαι, Characters, as it were stamped upon the Mind of Man, which the Soul receives in its very first Being" (I.ii.1). Locke's own position is that all our ideas derive from "Experience"—that sense perception and reflection alone stamp and furnish us with impressions.

I discuss Locke's quarrel with the innatists at some length in another entry (see **Writing**). The attempt to replace one metaphor with another is a fixture of disputation and is documented throughout this encyclopedic survey of the eighteenth century. It is important to note that Locke's refinement of the so-called tabula rasa metaphor does not ultimately displace innatist figures of speech in eighteenth-century discourse, in part because it denies one metaphor and replaces it with another, related metaphor. The original, stamped characters differ from the later impressions made largely through associations with different technologies of impression. Throughout the eighteenth century, writers continue to claim that savages, infants, and other (putatively) blank slates show the stamp of moral sense—if not harbor full blown innate principles. And so metaphors of stamping persist in the language of the moral sense theorists, in spite of Lockean descriptions of the mind as a piece of "white Paper, void of all Characters" (*Essay* II.i.2).

If we turn to the material culture for clarification, we find that two metaphors of impression may coexist. Taking an eighteenth-century half-sheet newspaper as analogue, the mind may be *stamped* with innate principles as well as *imprinted* by experience. The Stamp Acts passed by Parliament in eighteenth-century Britain supply content to the metaphorics of impression.[17] The earliest newspaper stamp tax was passed under Queen Anne, and the stamp taxes raised revenue by taxing printed material: legal documents, newspapers, pamphlets, and advertisements. The eponymous stamp, a red mark placed on a blank sheet of paper, indicated that the stamp tax had been paid. And because sheets of paper were stamped *before* anything was printed on them, Locke's "white Paper" may be pictured as already marked with a red stamp.[18] The blank slate metaphor may be vitiated by print culture or even prove reversible. Metaphors of mind prove meaningful in their *materiality*, so a phenomenology of metaphor should include discussions of physical objects.

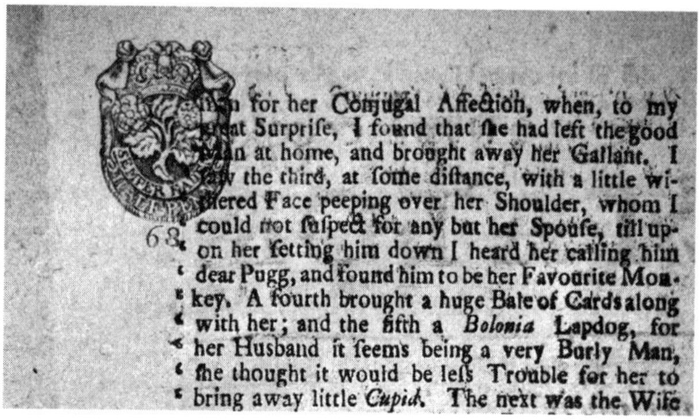
n for her Conjugal Affection, when, to my
at Surpriſe, I found that ſhe had left the good
n at home, and brought away her Gallant. I
the third, at ſome diſtance, with a little wi-
ered Face peeping over her Shoulder, whom I
could not ſuſpect for any but her Spouſe, till up-
on her ſetting him down I heard her calling him
' dear Pugg, and found him to be her Favourite Mon-
' key. A fourth brought a huge Bale of Cards along
' with her; and the fifth a *Bolonia* Lapdog, for
' her Husband it ſeems being a very Burly Man,
' ſhe thought it would be leſs Trouble for her to
' bring away little *Cupid*. The next was the Wife

Newsprint superimposed on stamped paper, from *Spectator* no. 499. Albert and Shirley Small Special Collections Library, University of Virginia.

That the stamps include the Latin motto "*Semper Eadem*" (always the same) qualifies them for figuration in critical discussions of the "Conservation of Character" and philosophical conceptions of personal identity.[19] Moreover, the use of the stamps in taxation may recommend them to the moral sense theorists who would employ a stamp as a metaphor for conscience. A tax is a "duty," and many stamps incorporate the word "DUTY" in their design. The crowns invariably included in the design further associate original duty with both royalty and divinity: a tax obligation reinforces the idea of moral obligation, and both are connected with ideas of divine right. This picture of a duty stamped originally on the mind by God appears in *Elements of Moral Philosophy*, where the moral sense philosopher David Fordyce writes, "these Terms, *Obligation*, *Duty*, *Ought*, and the like" are "a fair genuine Stamp of his Hand, who impressed every vital and original Energy on the Mind."[20]

Fordyce deploys the blank slate metaphor twice in his *Dialogues Concerning Education*. A character named Constant, "a violent *Republican*" and "severe, recluse Scholar," references those "Philosophers, of no small Note," who compare the Mind to "a kind of *Tabula rasa*, or . . . Piece of blank Paper." Constant emphasizes that the untaught, undisciplined mind lies "the most open to Impressions from without."[21] In the second reference, a character named Philander denies the resemblance of the mind to a "Leaf of white Paper"; the mind is instead like "a Seed, which contains all the Stamina of the future Plant" (1:116).[22] Blank slate metaphors are often followed by seed metaphors; the infant mind is a white page or unplanted soil.[23] Fordyce adjusts the metaphorics by making the mind a seed and not the ground in which the seed is planted; the mind is then not passive, blank, or fallow. In part, Fordyce's association of seeds and paper involves the two senses of the word "leaf" (see *Paper* in **Writing**).

The Idea of Impression

Perhaps it is David Hume who helped to fix the headword's enduring philosophical sense by distinguishing between impressions and ideas. Early in the *Treatise* he explains, "Those perceptions, which enter with most force and violence, we may name *impressions*; and, under this name, I comprehend all our sensations, passions, and emotions, as they make their first appearance in the soul" (I.i.1).[24] Ideas are reflections or copies of impressions, therefore fainter and less vivid. Hume requires that every idea have an impression source, although concerning our *idea* of impressions—the original impression of an impression, its copying, and so forth—Hume is not finally informative.[25] Hume's distinctions, meant to restore "idea" to its original import by correcting Locke's perversion of the term, would explode metaphor and set aside skepticism with regard to the senses.[26] He excludes discussion of the literal, physical basis of sensation, leaving such matters to the anatomist and natural philosopher: "By the term of *impression*, I wou'd not be understood to express the manner, in which our lively perceptions are produc'd in the soul, but merely the perceptions themselves" (*Treatise* I.i.1, 7n).

Hume's term is an avowed coinage, and as Jonathan Lamb keenly observes in a discussion of Hume's and Hartley's language, "The reciprocal play of ideas and impressions always bear analogy to the reciprocal play of figurative and literal language."[27] Hume can keep neither the manner of impression nor Lockean metaphors of ideation from contaminating his discussion—and, in truth, he is usually happy to mix his metaphors and can well tolerate philosophical fictions. He is patently aware he employs the word "in a Sense somewhat different from the usual."[28] Still, metaphor will creep in. Hume's impressions that enter with "force and violence" recall Johnson's definition of "IMPRESSION" as "Effect of an attack" (again, see *Conquest* in **Empire**). Hume's "copy theory" reinscribes the mechanical metaphors by which impressions are produced (see **Mirror** and **Writing**).[29] He is quick to personify ideas and picture interiority (see **Inhabitants** and **Rooms**).

Hume's metaphors did not go unremarked. Thomas Reid, for one, investigates "idea" and "impression" as terms of art in the opening of *Essays on the Intellectual Powers of Man* (1785). In these pages, as elsewhere, Reid appeals to ordinary language to bring out Hume's abuses of the term against its "proper" meaning. He protests that in Hume's philosophy the term "impression" is ambiguously used to signify "an operation of the mind" and "the object of operation" (29). Unconcerned by the deeper ambiguities of figures stamped and figures figured, Reid identifies the "literal" sense of the challenged term: "When a figure is stamped upon a body by pressure, that figure is called an *impression*, as the impression of a seal on wax, of printings-types, or of a copperplate, on paper" (30–1). Common usage extends and authorizes this meaning, by identifying cause and effect, the seal with its impression, the printing-types with the printed letters, the copperplate with the published engraving. Usage carries the term "still farther from its literal meaning," to include impressions on the mind, as Reid knows and uneasily allows.

A Literal Limit: "A Body Meet a Body"

Bodies press on bodies, one upon another. What is there for us to tell about these bodies? Shadows in the corn, coming through the rye: "The thing's a body's ain." The difference between Chambers's matter-of-fact discussions of "SENSATION" and "IMPRESSION" in the *Cyclopaedia* and his longer, Lockean article on "IDEA" is a case in miniature.[30] By the eighteenth century, mechanistic explanations of sensation are largely unobjectionable. Varieties of physicalist explanation had already taken hold in the philosophy of the seventeenth century, so that Descartes, Boyle, Newton, and many others explain sensation as the result of causal interactions between minute entities. In the early eighteenth century these explanations are carried to a wider readership in the poetry of Blackmore, the journalism of Addison, the medical writing of Cheyne, and the satire of the Scriblerians. However, any fully materialist position remains heterodox or libertine, and the continuing cry raised against Hobbes, Locke, Mettrie, D'Holbach, and Priestley—all of whom held different positions about the ability of matter to think—are instructive.[31]

Accounts of sensation in natural philosophy mobilize impressions, which are carried from the sense organs to the brain, often conveyed there by animal spirits.[32] Explanations of sensation by Cartesians, Hobbesians, Newtonians, Lockeans, and associationists hypothesize all manner of particles, tracings, corpuscles, vibrations, or nerve plumbing (through which spirits or liquors flow). Impressions are literal in so far as they are physical. But figurative language finds purchase in the articulation of analogy, and many anatomists prove positively picturesque in their descriptions of the animal spirits whose footsteps follow well-worn routes or come to trace new tracks in the brain's landscape.[33] Further figuration results when these philosophers describe the interactions of these impressions with ideas and other mental representations. While many of the scientific theories of sensation ignore strict differences between body and soul at the level of sensation, moments of real interest appear when a writer turns to his descriptions and tries to mark clearly a distinction between the mental and the physical.[34] Here metaphor marks the difference even as it asserts similitude.

The philosopher who grounds knowledge in sensation seeks a certain foundation of distinct, determinate ideas on which to build.[35] But the strict empiricist, who derives all thought from previous sensations, may be forced to deny that we can have a sensible impression of an impression—or, to express the difficulty in Hume's favored terms, it may not be possible to trace the *idea* of an *impression* to a source.[36] The strictest empiricist must go without certain abstractions (e.g., the elements of geometry) and is haunted by insensible mental entities: unconscious processes, psychological faculties, the mind as such. He or she hopes to correlate things "without" with some sort of impression within, left by way of impulse or surface irritation. This correlation may require comparison but the impress is ever superficial, only pressing inward: the thing without *resembles* the thought within, as that which makes an impression leaves a mark by which it is recognizable. (I wake from a dream with lines from my pillow pressed into my face; I leave my keyboard-reverie with the edge of the desk cut into my wrists.) An impress is set in sealing wax by a stamp, an embossed design on a sheet of paper, a manufacturer's stamp on a bar of metal or a jug of liquor; the engraver makes impressions with his copper plate, coins are struck and stamped with faces and figures, a footprint is left behind in sand and mud. These impressions are sensible but not in themselves sense impressions.

In an essay titled "Of Memory and Imagination" from his popular *Dissertations Moral and Critical* (1783), James Beattie simply denies that impressions are made in the brain, because thoughts do not occupy space and cannot therefore be laid up "in certain cells or repositories."[37] Entertaining the possibility that impressions must "so far resemble those made on sand by the foot, or on wax by the seal, as to have a certain shape, length, breadth, and deepness" (11–2), Beattie finds himself at a loss to determine the size or weight of a sound, a thought, or feeling, the figure of a toothache. Beattie, like Reid (and Hume), wields Berkeley's tautological, thus irrefutable, axiom—"an idea can be like nothing but an idea." Between mental impressions and the objects of impression resemblance fails; without shape or figure, an impression must be merely physical or merely figurative. Absurdity is pursued through similitude in Beattie's mocking embrace of materialist models: "supposing impressions to be made on the brain, I would ask *how* the mind perceives them. . . . Does the human soul go up to the *pia mater*, as a housewife does to her garret?" (12).[38] Consciousness, influentially described as having a "what is it like" character, it seems, can be nothing like an impression.[39] With the resemblance denied and the metaphor literalized, explanation fails to locate qualia. Perception terminates in the immediacies of redness, smoothness, or sweetness; it can go no farther than the aromatic pains or visual discomforts at the limit of the manifold pleasures of imagination.

Beattie's huswifery is meant to impugn that line of philosophy, from Hobbes through Hartley, that gives "figure" (the term is now exceedingly slippery) to impressions and follows them, as they are carried or conveyed from the surface of the body to a sensorium, where they are granted audience with the intellect. The brain is the site of interaction, a sensorium or an emporium, a theater, a closet, or a royal presence chamber—or garret (see **Rooms**). Mark how metaphor prepares the way for mind-body dualism, converting surface irritations into ideas: following George Puttenham's description of metaphor as "the figure of *transport*" in the 1589 *Arte of English Poesie* (149), it is a favored etymological detail that the Greek *phora*, our root word for metaphor, includes the notion of movement or, in Paul Ricoeur's words, "change with respect to location."[40] A metaphor is exhumed in this etymology of "metaphor"; metaphor is a carrying over—but of what? In the classical tradition metaphor pertains to the noun: meaning is transported from noun to noun, or a name is carried over from one entity to another. In the context of impressions, at the moment of crossing over from impression to sensation or from body to mind, theories of metaphysical dualism and metaphorical meaning cooperate in the bridging of two substances and two kinds of meaning.[41] Just how the transport is arranged from the world of matter into the space of meaning is necessarily left unspecified or deferred while the two spurious dichotomies take in each other's washing.[42] The distinction between mind and matter (A and B) is preserved by the metaphor of mind (A is B) even as the metaphor seems to discard the difference in its identification of mind *with* matter. One dichotomy locates a point of departure and a destination (the surface of the skin and the seat of consciousness); the other transfers meaning across the gap. It is one of the purposes of this dictionary to show how linguistic dualism reinforced mind-body dualism in the eighteenth century—and continues to do so today.

Many philosophers who claim we directly perceive sense data or ideas and not material objects seem obliged to personify some part of the mind or brain that observes or entertains impressions, locating the mind's eye in a space it shares with its own impressions or mental representations. The scene in which a wax tablet or a table book or a still-warm pool of wax is stamped or impressed by a stylus or seal implies a looker on. Some presiding consciousness is suggested by sense impressions, some eye or I that would read the characters written in the wax or identify the image left by the seal or signet.[43] Richard Rorty writes of impressions in general: "If the metaphor is unpacked . . . it becomes obvious that imprinting is of less interest than the observation of the imprint—all the knowing gets done, so to speak, by the Eye which observes the imprinted tablet, rather than the tablet itself."[44] The metaphor opens on a vertiginous regress: are we to imagine the relation of the presiding ego to its impressed sense data in terms more immediate, or does the spectator within also come equipped with its own wax-tablet sense organs? (See **Inhabitants.**)

General Analogy

In an early work of Descartes, not available in its original Latin until the eighteenth century,[45] an attempt is made to describe in detail how the intellect receives "figures or ideas" from the common sense and the corporeal imagination. Titled *Regulae ad Directionem Ingenii*, the work applies a traditional analogy of impression to four different faculties: sense perception, memory, imagination, and intellect. The analogy first appears in Descartes's description of physical sense perception: "sense-perception occurs in the same way in which wax takes on an impression from a seal" (40). Because the so-called external senses are part of the body, all sense perception is a matter of passive impression. But in stating this claim, Descartes emphasizes that he is not speaking figuratively: "It should not be thought that I have a mere analogy in mind here: we must think of the external shape of the body as really changed by the object in exactly the same way as the surface of the wax is altered by the seal" (40). The analogy is collapsed, introduced only to be denied.[46]

Descartes continues with his comparison in the paragraphs that follow, disclosing how "the 'common' sense functions like a seal, fashioning in the phantasy or imagination as if in wax" (41). The analogy, transported, is internal to the workings of perception; the stamp is here within, newly located with faculties that bind disparate external sensations. Although Descartes makes no comment, we are, presumably, to understand the analogy still to be no mere analogy. Finally, Descartes describes how the spiritual or cognitive power, which receives ideas from the common sense, applies itself to those ideas already in the memory, or transmits ideas to the body: "In all these functions the cognitive power is sometimes passive, sometimes active; sometimes resembling the seal, sometimes the wax" (42). For a second time Descartes qualifies his analogy: "But this should be understood merely as an analogy, for nothing quite like this power is to be found in corporeal things" (42).

In these passages the Cartesian interactions of mind and body depend upon a dualist theory of figurative language. The analogy requires physical things (seals, sealing wax) even as it denies that the mind works in corporeal ways. Sense impressions made in the body are not figurative because the body is changed in "exactly the same way as the surface of the wax is altered by the seal" (40). But comparisons of mind and body must be figurative—must be understood as confounding "mere analogy"—because nothing in the physical realm truly answers the mental. But then what is the mind like? And how are we to imagine impressions made upon a substance that lacks solidity and extension? How are we to imagine a substance that is without extension playing the part of the seal or stamp? What sort of substance is simple, immaterial, and unextended? What is that like? Notice the purported incommensurability between metaphorical and literal meanings, on one hand, and mental and physical substances, on the other.[47] The two distinctions, stated thus, are both poisoned, and one would do well to give them up. That said, it matters how one collapses the distinction. Is all meaning metaphorical? All substance ideal? There are several monisms from among which one may thoughtfully make a selection.

For example, compare George Berkeley, the eighteenth century's most famous idealist, who is also an early and interesting philosopher of language.[48] Berkeley would seem to have Descartes in mind in his *Three Dialogues* when his characters Philonous and Hylas discuss the propriety of the sealing wax metaphor. In fact, Hylas challenges Philonous, hoping to catch him out in his use of metaphors (I treat this same quotation in a different light in this book's conclusion): "You cannot say . . . that Things are imprinted on [your mind], as the Figure of a Seal upon Wax."[49] Philonous's response is telling: "Look you, Hylas, when I speak of Objects, as existing in the Mind, or imprinted on the Senses; I would not be understood in the gross, literal Sense, as when Bodies are said to exist in a place, or a Seal to make an Impression upon wax." The *as-when* syntax of epic simile is denied: Philonous's "meaning is only that the Mind comprehends or perceives them [its objects]; and that it is affected from without, or by some Being distinct from itself" (141–2).

The implications of the exchange, in which Berkeley gives Descartes's analogy a linguistic turn, will be reconsidered in the concluding essay of the book. I want here to emphasize that both Berkeley and Descartes make points about rhetoric as they detail a philosophy of mind. The limits of the literal are negotiated. Descartes is insistent that corporeal things are not like minds—"for nothing quite like this power is to be found in corporeal things." Hylas, who is associated with various Cartesian and Lockean positions, would make distinctions between the figurative and the literal pictures of the mind; Philonous, Berkeley's mouthpiece, sweeps the distinction away. For Berkeley, of course, no strong material-immaterial distinction can be made. Mind-body dualism and figurative-literal dualisms will not structure one another.

The Character of Sealing Wax

The tradition of using wax to figure the soul and its powers reaches back to ancient Greece. A locus classicus is Plato's *Theaetetus*. Socrates has his interlocutor imagine that the mind contains a block of wax: "Let us . . . say that whenever we wish to remember something we see or hear or conceive in our own minds, we hold this wax under the perceptions or ideas and imprint them on it as we might stamp the impression of a seal ring. Whatever is so imprinted we remember and know so long as the image remains; whatever is rubbed out or has not succeeded in leaving an impression we have forgotten and do not know."[50] Differences in individual abilities to remember may be attributed to larger or smaller, cleaner or muddier, harder or softer blocks of wax. Men with "a good thick slab of wax, smooth and kneaded to the right consistency" will be quick to learn and will have good memories (194b–d).

The metaphor appears in other ancient authors. Plato cites the *Iliad* in his discussion of the wax "tables of the heart" (194b–d). In *On the Soul* Aristotle clarifies his own doctrine of the soul thus: "It is not necessary to ask whether the soul and its body are one, just as we do not ask about wax and its shape" (412b6-7).[51] Epictetus suggests the wax tablets on which a student might figure and learn to write when he warns that "like Wax before the sun" whatever a student inscribes on his mind in school may be melted away (III.xvi).[52] He advises, "IMMEDIATELY prescribe some Character and Form [of Behaviour] to yourself, which you may preserve, both alone, and in Company" (the injunction is favored by Shaftesbury). The etymology of "character," from the Greek *kharasso*, is active in the original (*kharaktēra kai tupon*), suggesting sharpening, branding, stamping, or engraving.[53]

Character is associated with early or original stampings; impressions, more readily with sensation. As discussed in the next section, the metaphor also has a specific place in conversion narratives. Stamps made by God or Nature are one thing; more worrisome are those impressed by nursemaids, the beau monde, unreliable associates, or frivolous novels. If we do not stamp ourselves, we will be stamped from without. If we do not fix our purposes early and carefully refresh our impressions, we may well lose all distinction and stamp, reverting to the unmolded waxy stuff we began as.

A limit case and a vision of eternal mutability is set out in John Dryden's translation of book XV of Ovid's *Metamorphoses*. The transmigratory soul, changing bodies, is as wax: "The Soul is still the same, the Figure only lost: / . . . / This Face assumes, and that Impression leaves."[54] But Dryden's lines (the whole poem, it being a translation) show that despite the malleable "Figure," the soul's substance remains, continuity being enacted when the already quoted clause, "The Soul is still the same," returns four lines later as "the Wax is still the same." In Dryden—as in Locke, the *Spectator* papers, and elsewhere—philosophical debates over personal identity are shadowed by an interest in Pythagorean theories, and in the several contexts wax is a favored image.[55]

Minds that are stamped must be *softer* than that which stamps them. The logic of the metaphor gainsays certain forms of idealism and promises that the exterior world—or better, the stamp—is more real, more certain, and more enduring than the individual surface that is stamped.[56] But waxen softness is also troped as moral and intellectual weakness.[57] James Harris uses wax and water to contrast sense and imagination: "As the Wax would not be adequate to its business of Signature, had it not a Power to *retain*, as well as to *receive*; the same holds of the SOUL, with respect to *Sense* and *Imagination*. . . . Had it Sense without Imagination, it would not be as Wax, but as Water, where tho' all Impressions may be instantly made, yet as soon as made they are as instantly lost" (356–7).[58]

A waxy self may prove too ductile, changeable, weak, watery—in a word, womanly.[59] In *The Rape of Lucrece* Shakespeare divides the sexes: "men have marble, women waxen mindes" (ll. 1240).[60] The beloved is typically figured as deeply impressed at the first sight of her lover, and Eliza Haywood gives a specific explanation of the pernicious softening effects of amatory novels—a woman's genre—describing how "Books were, as it were, Preparatives to Love, and by their softning Influence, melted the Soul, and made it fit for Amorous Impressions."[61] Haywood's use of "impression" is no doubt double entendre: one body presses upon another in narration rendering the reader glib and lubricious. This language of sensibility makes fluid the sexual politics of the seduction plot, as *Clarissa*'s Lovelace complains of the female heart that it is "at one time *adamant*, at another *wax*" but is himself reduced to a kind of softness in the end, finding that in remorse and penitence, "my mind is made such wax, as to be fit to take what impression [Clarissa] pleases to give it."[62]

It matters when we are stamped and how deeply: a mind "heedless" or "otherwise employed" will not set "the stamp deep into it self" (Locke, *Essay*

II.x.4); and eighteenth-century pedagogical theories liken the mind to a block of wax that hardens with age. Because the young waxen mind is pliant and plastic, it should be impressed early with virtuous principles: Locke's influential treatise *Some Thoughts Concerning Education* is designed "for a Gentleman's Son, who being then very little, I considered only as white Paper, or Wax, to be moulded and fashioned as one pleases." Dryden, too, describes the pliancy of "tender Age," how like "Wax it yield[s] to the forming hand."[63] Swift registers this metaphor of impression as a commonplace in his *Tritical Essay*: "The mind of man is at first (if you will pardon the Expression) like a Tabula rasa, or like Wax, which, while it is Soft, is capable of any Impression, till time has hardened it."[64] In her continuation, Pamela engages Locke's *Some Thoughts Concerning Education* and differs with the revered philosopher, although she does not upset his metaphorics. She believes that a parent should be "no less careful to shun the Practice of such fond Fathers and Mothers, as are wont to indulge their Children in bad Habits, and give them their Head, at a time when, like Wax, their tender Minds may be moulded into what Shape they please."[65]

The metaphor is much favored by poets, such as Samuel Wesley the Younger in "A Letter from a Guardian to a Young Lady":

> When Fancy's mimick Pow'r is warm and strong,
> Engraving deeply, and retaining long,
> What Age can scarcely learn and hardly hold.
> The Signet thus cast in the best-wrought Mould,
> Imprints no Likeness when the Wax is cold.[66]

In *The Progress of Error* Cowper asserts that in "our earliest years" the mind is "impressible and soft, with ease / Imbibes and copies what she hears and sees." Ann Yearsley writes of the infant soul that must be lifted to Jehovah's throne because "the ductile mind, / Pliant as wax, shall wear the mould you give."[67]

Devotional Writing: Stamps and Seals

Psalm 22 is an important source for metaphors of softening and melting hearts. Sir James Chamberlayne, Charles Darby, Sir Richard Blackmore, the Wesleys, Thomas Parnell, James Merrick, Christopher Smart, and John Hookham Frere all compose translations of the psalm in the long eighteenth century. The King James Bible gives the relevant verse as "I am poured out like water, and all my bones are out of joint: my heart is like wax; it is melted in the midst of my bowels" (Psalm 22:14). Hearts melt, flow, and dissolve throughout eighteenth-century literature echoing the psalmist's verse. In

John Sheffield's *Tragedy of Marcus Brutus*, Brutus admits that his heart melts "like wax before your hottest Anger" (IV.iii).[68] The Wesleys especially favor the metaphor. John and Charles Wesley pray: "Stamp us with the Stamp Divine, / Seal our Souls for ever Thine."[69] Isaac Watts complicates the image by asking, "Is then my Heart to all the World beside / Softer than melting Wax or Summer Snow, / But to myself, harder than Adamant?"[70] In religious literature these melted hearts ask to be stamped with God's image or seal. Devotional pleading to be stamped suggests different readings of the metaphors as coinage, documents, and letters, and other materials are associated with these actions. Further variation brings us to the metaphorics of **Writing**: in a hymn based on Isaiah 51 John and Charles Wesley claim righteous souls "shew / The Law engraven on [their] Hearts."[71]

A seal is "any act of confirmation," and Johnson lists other uses of the term as a verb ("SEAL"). A seal prevents a letter from being read or tampered with or identifies a document as authentic. Johnson cites lines from Shakespeare's *As You Like It* as an example of "To fasten with a seal": "He that brings this love to thee, / Little knows this love in me; / And by him seal my mind" (IV.iii.57–9). To seal is also "To confirm, to ratify, to settle"; "To shut, to close"; "To mark with a stamp"; and "To fix a seal." These uses of the word lend themselves to metaphorical applications beyond the narrower and philosophical exploration of sense perception discussed just above.

Specifically, many of these verb forms feature prominently in metaphors of the heart and soul. Typical is the passage from John and Charles Wesley's *Short Hymns* (a versification of Job 23:16):

> TROUBLED by th' Almighty I
> From the fiery furnace cry,
> Melted down at last I am,
> Soft as wax before the flame:
> Now the form Divine impress,
> True, substantial holiness;
> *Jesus*, thou that image art,
> Seal Thy name upon my heart.[72]

The Wesleys invoke the psalmist's description of the heart like wax that melts in the bowels, and they connect those verses with the command in the Song of Songs to "Set me as a seal upon thine heart, as a seal upon thine arm" (Song of Solomon 8:6). The reciter of the hymn prays for God to seal his name upon his or her heart—stamp and seal the heart so that God's seal will "confirm," "ratify," or "settle" his heart's status as saved.[73] In other hymns

God is asked to seal his image on the heart. Watts writes in *Horae Lyricae*, "But let thine Image ever dwell / Stampt as a Seal upon my Heart,"[74] and the lines are recycled in various seventeenth- and eighteenth-century paraphrases of the Song of Songs in which hearts are sealed "thine"; "names" and "images" are sealed or stamped on the heart (and sometimes on the arm); and pardon or forgiveness is sealed on the heart, soul, or conscience. A clear majority of seal metaphors (two-thirds of the metaphors collected) are found in the devotional poetry of the Wesleys, Isaac Watts, and others; indeed, more than half of such metaphors can be attributed to the Wesley brothers' hymns.[75] A typical Wesleyan refrain pleads, "Seal my soul forever thine."

Formal Concerns and Material Culture

According to Thomas Reid, it is Aristotle who first taught that as "the impression of a seal upon wax has the form of the seal, but nothing of the matter of it," so our sensations are "impressions upon the mind, which bear the image, likeness, or form of the external thing perceived without the matter of it."[76] Formal and material concerns divide this dictionary of figures, organizing its historical concerns. So, while the picturing of sense perception as a wax block has a long history, at the end of the seventeenth century sealing-wax stamps were more widely employed in sealing and posting letters than ever before. Devices of correspondence encourage poets and philosophers to rework and remediate metaphors of impression as a metaphor of ancient vintage interacts with modern technologies and institutions.[77] Wax, stamps, and seals figure importantly beyond this history of inscription and impression. The political events of the seventeenth century may, for example, be given in miniature as an it-narrative of the Great Seal of England's adventures: Charles I's seal was captured and defaced, new seals were ordered by Parliament, and Charles II, on his return brought a new royal seal with him; James II threw his own Great Seal into the Thames before fleeing England so that William could not command it, and so on.

Bringing wax and stamping together, a "SEAL" is defined by Johnson as "A stamp engraved with a particular impression, which is fixed upon the wax that closes letters, or affixed as testimony" ("SEAL"). And it is under that definition that Johnson cites the passage from Locke's *Essay* that appears as the first epigraph to this entry—Johnson's citations of Locke repeatedly surprise. Johnson defines the active verb "seal" as "to mark with a stamp" ("SEAL"). Again, the stamp is either the mark or the object that leaves the mark. A mark may be left on the mind. Stamps, seals, and signet rings impress the warm, waxen mind, but the mind is itself directly identified with the seal. Letters

Penny Post stamp, first made public in William Dockwra's flyer, *The Practical Method of the Penny-Post* (1681)

were sealed with paste wafers or wax seals. A received letter that was not sealed with a distinct impression was suspect and may have been read or otherwise tampered with. The identity of a letter writer was certified by his or her personal seal stamped in the wax that closed the letter.

Across the early modern moment, the use of private or "privy" seals descends the ranks, so that from the sixteenth century many members of the middling classes employ a *sigillum secreti* in business. Seals were early used by lower gentry who had the right to bear arms and also by merchants, as trade and exchange required individual identification: any property holder might require a seal. Early widespread use belongs importantly to the seventeenth century only to survive in the metaphors and memory of the eighteenth. With the rise of the courts and the increasing complications of property rights, personal seals are replaced in transaction by official notary seals kept by solicitors.[78]

And increasingly, as more letters were carried by the modern post, personal authentication marks on the outsides of letters were joined by impersonal stamps and institutional markings. Writers increasingly used glue wafers, not stamped wax, to seal informal letters. In London, circular postmark "stamps" were first employed by the Restoration postmaster Henry Bishop.[79] The original Penny Post employed triangular stamps that indicated to which district a letter was to be mailed and heart-shaped stamps that indicated when the letter was marked for delivery.[80] After the Duke of York took over the Penny Post in 1682, these heart-shaped stamps indicated that a letter was transferred from the General Post Office to the London Penny Post. Biblical metaphors of a heart stamped and sealed—exploited by the devotional writers cited above—must have interacted curiously with the modern technologies of the postal system.

Stamp and seal, from John Lewis, *A Dissertation on the Antiquity and Use of Seals in England* (1740). The William Andrews Clark Memorial Library, University of California, Los Angeles.

The widespread belief in eighteenth-century Britain that the post office was opening and reading private mail contributes to an analogy of the self as a letter looked over by a great postal clerk in the sky.[81] The powerful abilities of the post office to sort letters is not unlike the sorting of individuals who are "delivered" on the Day of Judgment or are damned to hell. Consider the practice of "franking," a special privilege accorded members of Parliament for the free delivery of a letter; the sender wrote "FREE" or "FRANK" on the letter.[82] The poet John Wolcot invokes the practice in the satirical line about Romish priests and the practice of indulgences: "The parson frank'd their souls to kingdom-come!"[83]

Sealing is intended as a final act: the letter leaves its author, a will and testament is authenticated. In a sigillographic dissertation published in 1740 we read of the great anxiety generated by the surviving seal of a deceased person: "therefore as soon as any one shall depart this Life, his Seal which he used to put up in a little Box or Purse, where it might be safely kept, and that Box, &c. sealed with the Seals of three honest Persons, that so the Seal of the Testator may be carried safe to the Judge the first Opportunity: And, that when the Heirs or Executor shall have brought the Seal to him, he shall immediately deface it, or delete the Image and Form of the Seal, and return the Materials of it to the Executors, &c."[84] The seal's security is triply sealed before its form is deleted.

Seals and signets were often buried with their owners. The eighteenth-century image shown here is reproduced from the dissertation just quoted, where the image is described ambiguously as both "an Impression and a Representation of a Seal" (7). The duplicitous picture is readily confounded with what it represents: Jonathan Lamb, writing in a related context, describes such icons as "a pleonasm of 'thing' and thing."[85] The figure figured works by double principle to switch between idea and impression. Or rather, it is a true impression and therefore an uncanny representation of a deceased person's seal. Retrieved from the grave, it is made visible by engraving; pressed into the print medium, it is a memento mori or lasting impression of an earlier instance of figural practice.

7 Inhabitants

COLLOCATED KEYWORDS: Council, Crowd, Guest, Haunt, Stranger, Tenant

COUNT OF METAPHORS IN DATABASE[1] (1700–1799): 754

My Braine, Ille proue the Female to my Soule,
My Soule, the Father: and these two beget
A generation of still breeding Thoughts
And these same Thoughts, people this Little World.

—Shakespeare, *Richard II* (First Folio, 1623)

The ready Phantomes at her [the soul's] Nod advance,
And form the busie Intellectual Dance:
While her fair Scenes to vary, or supply,
She singles out fit Images, that lye
In Memory's Records, which faithful hold
Objects immense in secret Marks inroll'd,
The sleeping Forms at her Command awake,
And now return, and now their Cells forsake;
On active Fancy's crowded Theater,
As she directs, they rise or disappear.

—Richard Blackmore, *Creation* (1712)

And whereas it is objected that here are *two Wills*, and therefore *two* different *Persons*, we answer, if Multiplicity of Wills implied multiplicity of Persons, there are few Husbands but what are guilty of *Polygamy*, there being in the same Woman great and notorious diversity of Wills: A Point which we shall not need to insist upon before any marri'd person, much less of your Honour's Experience.

—Arbuthnot and Pope, *The Memoirs of Martinus Scriblerus* (1741)

> [D]ive deep into thy bosom; learn the depth, extent, biass, and full fort of thy mind; contract full intimacy with the Stranger within thee.
>
> —Edward Young, *Conjectures on Original Composition* (1759)

> The same force of association which makes us perceive the connexion of all ideas with the subject, leads us soon to perceive also the various degrees of that connexion. By means of it, these ideas, like a well-disciplined army, fall, of their own accord, into rank and order, and divide themselves into different classes according to their different relations.
>
> —Alexander Gerard, *An Essay on Genius* (1774)

> Deadly ideas crowded upon their imaginations, and inspired a terror which scarcely allowed them to breathe.
>
> —Ann Radcliffe, *A Sicilian Romance* (1790)

See also **Court** and **Empire**

Under this heading I look at how the "Little World" of the mind named above in Richard II's soliloquy comes to be "peopled" and what happens when these people begin interacting.[2] While in several entries I investigate how minds and souls are figured by things or with places, in this I focus on how the mind and its contents are *personified*.[3] The critic Blakey Vermeule, for one, emphasizes the importance of personification in this historical context: "We might say that giving meaning to the human face (prosopopoeia) is the eighteenth century's most common trope and that persons are its most common unit of interest."[4] The eighteenth-century self is often pictured as busy, populated. It is a city, a kingdom, or a little world teeming with people. In its projection of agency, poetic prosopopoeia works outwardly but also inwardly, peopling, personating, personifying, and "personizing," to borrow a term from the poet James Thomson. In poetic contexts particularly (Thomson's *The Seasons* is a much-studied example), the category of person is not restricted to human persons but compasses material entities and immaterial abstractions. The disturbing countermovements of personification may not secure a distinction between human persons and nonhuman things when both are invested with feeling and agency.[5]

Following Locke and Descartes, the person is newly described as a "thinking intelligent Being" that can know itself as a "thinking thing" in different times and places.[6] A person *is* a thinking thing; a thinking intelligent being *has* a mind or soul. The personification of minds, souls, and selves would seem circular or recursive, but the transfer of attributes from the whole (the person) to the part (the mind or its ideas) accords with the traditional descriptions of metaphor that derive from Aristotle's *Poetics*, in which figurative focus shifts from species to species, between genus and species, or on the grounds of analogy. We might see the personifications collected here as a special variety of metaphor of mind, one especially prevalent in the period.[7] The "persistent personification of person-ingredients" that Annette Baier associates with Hume's philosophy holds for the eighteenth century at large.[8] Because thoroughgoing empiricists believe it impossible to form an image of the impassioned mind in the abstract, independent of a person, such abstractions are frequently personified in imaginative writing.[9] But this personification of persons can result in something more than individual: division may even occasion the divine.[10] As reported in Nathan Bailey's *Dictionarium Britannicum*, "the poets have personified all the passions, vertues, and vices, by making divinities of them" ("Personifying").

My discussion focuses on lurkers within, those tenants or guests of the soul, mind, and breast, whether divine or mundane. I am census-taking: counting the objects of thought (percepts, ideas, beliefs, desires, and intentions) as they are variously personified. I hope to better understand a number of things: how someone can be of two—or more—minds, how one comes to change her mind, how one can come to be someone other than himself, how identity might fail us, how one can listen to his or her own better judgment or better self, how the heart could have reasons that reason does not know. Our idioms suggest that a person is not strictly identifiable with his or her own mind, which, on inspection, reveals an ensemble of social relations. Host to various intentions, a mind not yet made up must sort through different versions of its self, negotiating a settlement acceptable to both the parts and the whole and consistent with personal identity. Personal identity is troubled by the plurality and diversity of experience; attempts to locate the ground of cognition *within* curiously import the communities from *without*.[11] Every idea is readily personified; every percept, a person. After an initial discussion of divine personifications, I detail a more mundane self that seems to have internalized a modern, urban phenomenon—the sensation of being surrounded at all times by complete strangers.[12] By way of concluding, I set aside historicization and look to contemporary theoretical models of a populated self.

Peopling and Personizing

The eighteenth-century mind is imagined as a court of reason in which opinions, judgment, and the passions may bring suit (**Court**). It is a peculiarly British system of government, in which reason presides or rules over an unruly parliament of passions (**Empire**). But it is also a society, a debating club, or a place of war. In the medical writings of Thomas Willis and others, the animal spirits are personified as soldiers, watchmen, ministers, and messengers. Personified ideas "throng" and "crowd" in the mind. A train of impressions makes its way through the mind. The mind is torn and distracted by contending passions. Imagination may be at cuffs with the senses; those same senses may offer erroneous reports to the understanding. Adela Pinch summarizes, "Passions often act *like* persons: the form of personhood is assumed by many mental entities."[13] Minds were bustling, noisy, conflicted, populated places during the age of faculty psychology.[14] So it is that introspection and meditation—activities that are meant to be lonely, personal, and private—discover the surprisingly populated structure of the mind.

The frontispiece to Hobbes's *Leviathan* depicts an "artificial man" whose body is composed of persons who are all oriented toward a crowned head. The face is not unlike that of Charles I, but we cannot make out the individual faces of the persons. This is a picture that comes quite close to the prosopopoetic picture I am working with in this entry. But there is an important difference. Where Hobbes's frontispiece shows how the body politic is composed quite literally of the bodies of the contractually united, so that the sovereign is able to represent or—the Latin etymology is important here—*personate* them, the picture investigated here is an upside down, inside out version of Hobbes's frontispiece. Turning the Leviathan on his head, I reverse Hobbes's analysis of sovereignty in the terms of an artificial soul. Political associations structure metaphors of mind: sensations are so many ministers who appear before the sovereign soul, passions are so many unruly citizens, and each faculty may step into some civic or social role.[15] Within are strangers, crowds, tribes, judges, monarchs, ghosts, generals, governors, children, and families.

Intent on describing the inner self, eighteenth-century philosophers, poets, and doctors analyze and divide the self by imagining a human agent in terms of its agencies. Locke warns that talk of "*Faculties*," in particular, "has misled many into a confused Notion of so many distinct Agents in us, which had their several Provinces and Authorities, and did command, obey, and perform several Actions, as so many distinct Beings" (*Essay* II.xxi.6). But even as Locke censures such personification, he is credited by Henry Jones for opening "wide the Senses' various Doors/Thro' which the thronging Thoughts their Passage find,/In social Tribes, and stock the peopled Mind."[16] By the end of the century, in his *Zoonomia*, Erasmus Darwin repeatedly describes "trains" and "tribes" of ideas, evacuating from the Lockean legacy most but not all of its residual personification that characterizes the association of ideas. Psychological allegories build departments and install faculties. The distinctions quickly establish hierarchies in the society of mind. In Richard Savage's *Wanderer*, man's fabric is likened to "a well-form'd State" with "first-rank'd" thoughts and "*Plebeian*" passions.[17] A politics follows. Taken together, the governmental metaphors of mind that picture populated personhood (ruling passions, the sovereign soul, the mind that inhabits the body, the personified ideas that inhabit the mind) far outnumber the metaphors collected in each of the other categories.

To invoke Hobbes again—this time his *Elements of Law*—"Man's nature is the sum of his natural faculties and powers" (I.i.1).[18] On this view, a person is eminently divisible: a sum of parts, a collection of faculties and powers, or a bundle of impressions. Although the part-whole scheme invoked by Hobbes may be construed teleologically or mechanically, it is most readily available for personification. If the self is the unit of analysis, it implies a larger system of selves; the unit that tries to apprehend itself sees the system writ large. Only Hobbes's materialism keeps pervasive personification at bay. The body is composed of bodies. There is no personification here, only "personation."[19]

A more proper personification of the *mind* is available in Joseph Butler's *Fifteen Sermons*. In his first sermon Butler would seem to start from Hobbesian premises treating the relations between the several parts of the body and the "Relation which each particular Person in Society has to other particular Persons, and to the whole Society."[20] Butler and Hobbes, two philosophers who agree about very little else, both apprise themselves of the same picture, but Butler transfers the analogy from the external to the internal: "it is the inward Frame of Man considered as a *System* or *Constitution*: Whose several Parts are united" (46n). Each part of man is delegated a constitutional role: conscience, the supreme and ruling principle, is "our proper Governour" or magistrate (see **Court**), and the appetites, passions, and affections are figured as upstart subordinates in the political economy of man (42, 45).

The Association of Ideas and Strangers Within

In the eighteenth century, the self is increasingly made over in the form of a society. Locke's discussion of the association of ideas in the fourth edition of the *Essay* depends on an unusual pun: ideas that "are not at all kin, come to be so united in some Mens Minds, that 'tis very hard to separate them, they always keep company, and the one no sooner at any time comes into the

Understanding but its *Associate* appears with it" (II.xxxiii.5, emphasis added). Familiar bonds of kinship are supplanted with other forms of association: in one relentlessly historical reading, the feudal, familiar order gives way to new social structures. Locke's associations are sociopolitical and anticipate the eighteenth-century rage of party. This gang of impressions—"the whole gang always inseparable shew themselves together"—might also suggest a press-gang or impressment (see **Impressions**).[21] The poet Mark Akenside articulates a political imaginary in his versification of association. When the mind recalls "one partner," its "confederates rise." In consciousness the personifications are united and "One movement governs the consenting throng."[22]

Who are these persons within if not the self's selves? The slogan cited as the third epigraph to this entry—"dive deep into thy bosom; learn the depth, extent, biass, and full fort of thy mind; contract full intimacy with the Stranger within thee"—is taken from Edward Young's *Conjectures on Original Composition*, a landmark work usually cited in surveys of eighteenth-century literary theory.[23] I am not so much concerned here with Young's views on composition but his decomposition or division of the self, his image—or perhaps metaphor—of a stranger within. My target is the stranger as such: his place in eighteenth-century British literature, his role in eighteenth-century figurative language, and his residence in the mind. Young is but one source of the image, albeit an important one.

Domestic and foreign cross paradoxically in these figures: a popular piece of poetic diction figures each newly felt passion as "a stranger to the breast," and the stock expression "stranger at home" repeatedly appears in seventeenth- and early eighteenth-century sermons on conscience and self-knowledge by moderate Calvinists and Anglicans. Later in the century it features in evangelical writing. Katherine Philips opens her poem "The Soul" with a lament that the noblest part of man "Traverses Heav'n, finds out the depth of Art, / Yet is so ignorant at home?"[24] In a meditation on self-knowledge collected in his juvenilia, Isaac Watts finds the soul "so unhappy a Stranger at home."[25] While Anna Letitia Barbauld describes "the self-collected soul" that "Turns inward and beholds a stranger there," William Godwin asserts that the "mind may be aptly described under the denomination of 'the stranger at home'" in *Thoughts on Man*.[26]

Young encourages the poet to "contract full intimacy with the Stranger within thee."[27] Young's use of the stranger within first appears in his *Night Thoughts*, in which he writes, "At home a Stranger, / Thought wanders up and down, surpiz'd, amaz'd."[28] Seventeen years later, in the *Conjectures*, the command "contract full intimacy with the Stranger within" is set up in parallel with the Delphic injunction to "Know Thyself" and a quotation from Martial's *Epigrams*, which describes a bad neighbor as "Nil tam prope, proculque nobis" (there is nothing so close, and yet so far from us).[29] Nothing so close and so far as that bad neighbor; nothing so far or so close as that self to be known. There is some debate in the literary critical treatments of Young about who this stranger within might be. It is, for example, not settled if the self is its own neighbor, if Young's project owes more to religious devotion or narcissism. The stranger reads as both a divine presence and as a reflected self; Robert Miles has recently seen the figure as therefore mediating self and soul, immanence and transcendence.[30]

Young would seem to draw from Shaftesbury, who, in *Soliloquy, or Advice to an Author*, treats his readers to a fresh translation of the Delphic inscription.[31] "RECOGNIZE YOUR SELF," writes Shaftesbury, and he explains, which is as much to say, "*Divide your self*, or *Be* Two."[32] Shaftesbury prescribes a regimen of soliloquy to writers as a way of purging froth and crudities and making contact with that "a *Demon*, *Genius*, *Angel* or *Guardian-Spirit*" within (16). In Shaftesbury the stranger within proves multiplicitous. For Shaftesbury the self is divisible, and the practice of soliloquy serves in the apostrophization of the mind's "truant" fancies, which must be raised in their "proper *Shapes* and *Personages*" (35). In a passage that certainly informs Butler's rewriting of Hobbes, Shaftesbury goes so far as to imagine a whole parliament and party system. "Like modern Politicians," those party hacks of "Appetite" affect a "mysterious Manner" and speak in "Nods and Winks" (36–7). They must be called out as "*Sophisters* and *Impostors*, who have not the least to do with the party of REASON and *good Sense*" (37).

Personifying Parts of Persons

Young and Shaftesbury complicate relations between the individual and the crowd. Their topic is "personal identity," but their figuration suggests that the mind is really many minds and that identity is best understood with tropes of plurality. Locke's influential chapter on identity and diversity was written in 1693.[33] Personal identity—the persistence of a unitary self through time—was, from Locke's *Essay* forward, a going concern in eighteenth-century philosophy. Throughout the period, philosophical arguments against multiplicity and materialism employ divisible selves in arguments reductio ad absurdum—that is, in arguments in which the patent absurdity of divisibility is meant to secure identity in consciousness.[34] So Abraham Tucker writes in *The Light of Nature Pursued*, "if composition prevailed . . . every Self must contain a number of little Selves, every Mind many little Minds."[35] But the multiplicity of experience proves hard to assign to a single, unifying figure, and ubiquitous personifications of mental contents undermine the claim to absurdity.

Recognized now as a locus classicus, Hume's skeptical arguments in the *Treatise* enact identity in crisis. Hume instructs us that the "self or the person is not any one impression, but that to which our several impressions and ideas are suppos'd to have a reference" (*Treatise* I.iv.6). We have no *one* impression of ourselves. Hume complains that when he enters into himself he is never able to "catch" himself. The attempted encounter fails. The self, Hume reasons, is not a simple, indivisible substance but a plurality, a bundle of perceptions. Take note of two metaphors employed by Hume in this discussion: twice in the section on personal identity the mind is figured as a group of people. The bundled self becomes a bundle of selves. First, Hume asserts that the mind is a kind of theater, "where several perceptions successively make their appearance; pass, re-pass, glide away, and mingle in an infinite variety of postures and situations" (I.iv.6).[36] Next, following Hobbes, Shaftesbury, and Butler, Hume resurrects Plato's picture of the soul from the *Republic* and puts it to new use, comparing the soul to a republic or commonwealth "in which the several members are united by the reciprocal ties of government and subordination" (I.iv.6). In these two figures the unity of a self is not essential—that is, the self is not an immaterial, eternal substance that survives change. The self's identity to itself over time is owing to the manner of its organization. The self's organization persists, not any particular substance.[37]

Minds were especially noisy, conflicted, populated places during the age of faculty psychology. So it is that introspection and meditation—activities that are meant to be lonely, personal, and private—discover the populated structure of the mind. Introspection of the Humean variety, where the introspector tries to spy out a self, seems especially prone to make over any mental particle in the image of a person. When I consult the metaphors of mind used to imagine the self's interior by eighteenth-century writers, I find pervasive personifications of the mental contents. In particular, that new fixture of empiricist philosophy, the idea, is readily personified. Sensations are so many ministers who appear before the sovereign soul, passions are so many unruly citizens, and each faculty may step into some civic or social role.

Within are strangers of all stripes, and there is not space to count all the noses: stage actors, servants, crowds, throngs, "modern politicians," judges and lawyers, savage tribes, generals, messengers, ghost-memories, and close-knit families. "Wit, Understanding, Memory, and Will" inhabit "The pallace of the soul" (Billingsley). Reason is "the Steward of your Soul, / And Ruler of your Senses" (Dryden); conscience is a drummer "that can beat an allarm when he pleases, and so loud as no other Noise can drown it" (Defoe). Memory is "the Nurse and Guardian" of wit (Pilkington); fancy, an "Inward Limner or Painter" (Cudworth).[38] Setting lower faculties against the higher functions of reasoning, desire divides the self and multiplies agents: "Love is a generous Volunteer; Lust a Mercenary Slave" (Charles Johnson). Because Pamela's *heart* is a "busy Fool," Pamela knows not always her own self (Richardson).[39] Passions, in particular, complicate accounts of activity and passivity and seem to produce persons even as they are themselves personified. Ambiguously, from an internal perspective, an unendorsed passion feels external to the thinker, even as it contributes to the economy of decision making. Thus personified the self is disintegrated.

These and other personifications are common in the philosophical poetry of the time and are particularly favored in the allegorical versifications of Lockean philosophy written by Sir Richard Blackmore early in the eighteenth century.[40] The impassioned poet personifies passions. In eighteenth-century theories of poetry, as Adela Pinch explains, "passion prompts personification, turning feelings themselves into persons."[41] Later eighteenth-century poets settle into abstracted personifications: Reason guides, Glory blushes, Conscience congratulates, and Virtue yields in Samuel Johnson's satire *The Vanity of Human Wishes*. Ambition, Memory, Knowledge, and Pride haunt Thomas Gray's "Country Churchyard."[42] While fully articulated pictures of the mind as a government (see **Empire**), a courtroom (see **Court**), or a battlefield (see *Conquest* in **Empire**) are all deserving of further analysis, but a complete roll call is not possible in these pages. I will focus more narrowly in what follows on the common denominator of strangers and crowds.

In Populous Cities Pent

In an age of faculty psychology minds are busy, populated places. John Moore, observing the multitudes sauntering at Saint Mark's Place in Venice, finds his "ideas are broken, bruised, and dislocated in the crowd."[43] London—even more than Venice or Amsterdam or Paris—is a busy, populous place. In *Evelina* the eponymous ingenue arrives in London and walks the Mall in Saint James Park. She is astounded by the crowds and writes that she has never seen "so many people assembled together before . . . all the world seemed there."[44] According to the seventeenth-century statistician Gregory King, two-thirds of all English townsfolk were living in London by 1680.[45] The population of England doubled in the eighteenth century. The metaphors of mind surveyed here would seem to register the Malthusian crush. Ideas throng and crowd the mind like so many pleasure seekers in Saint Mark's Place or Saint James Park.

In Smollett's *History and Adventures of an Atom*, a metaphor of mind would seem to anticipate the busy settings explored in *Evelina*. The distracted, weak brain is likened to a Mile End assembly, thronged by city milliners. As words and ideas "press in promiscuously," partners are uncoupled and the "puny master of ceremonies" is unable to distinguish the quality of the assembled and order the dance—"anarchy ensues."[46] In the late eighteenth-century novel of manners perfected by Burney and Austen, the ballroom is a space intricate with intentionality. It is not surprising to find in earlier verses dancing ideas: for example, in Allan Ramsay's "Epistle to James Arbuckle" (1719), Christopher Pitt's epistle "To Sir James Thornhill" (1727), and in Francis Fawkes's ode "To the Archbishop of Canterbury" (1756).

Is the experience of being "long in populous city pent," peculiarly modern?[47] Looking for precedents, I find that Michel de Montaigne, in his own essay titled "Of Solitude," avers that solitude may be enjoyed in the midst of a city and that mere retirement may not be enough to escape from marauding worry, ambition, fear, and lust. The soul cannot escape itself. It must be sequestered from itself. Montaigne writes, "we must get away from the gregarious instincts that are inside of us."[48] We must "reserve a back shop all our own" where we can converse with only ourselves, where the soul's only company is itself (177). Introspection must be somehow conducted in that "back shop" so that not even the regular customers, apprentices, or a wife might intrude. Somehow the soul is to be withdrawn deeply into itself to escape self-pestering. Montaigne seems to believe this is possible, but many of the eighteenth-century writers I have encountered in collecting metaphors are not so sure.[49]

In Jane Barker's *A Patch-Work Screen*, the narrator, Galesia, situated in her "Garret-Closet," attempts to flee the "Noise and Bustle" of London.[50] In solitude she tumbles over volumes of Harvey and Willis. She writes, "My impertinent Muse here found me; and here we renew'd our old Acquaintance" (65). Galesia alone and yet not yet alone confuses her new interior with her interiority. (It is an eighteenth-century commonplace that one is never alone when books are near.) Her muse takes possession of her: "Poetry being one of those subtle Devils, that if driven out by never so many firm Purposes, good Resolutions, Aversion to that Poverty it intails upon its Adherents; yet it will always return and find a Passage to the Heart, Brain, and whole Interior" (66).

Robinson Crusoe in the Street

Several population metaphors of mind are highly articulated and of a piece with the text in which they appear. Others generate surprising implications when we consider them carefully. Many of the metaphors have a paradoxical flavor. Consider the mind of Robinson Crusoe. Isolated for more than twenty-four years on his desert island, Crusoe is unable to sleep one night. He explains his insomnia retrospectively: "It is as impossible as needless to set down the innumerable Crowd of Thoughts that whirl'd through that great thorowfare of the Brain, the Memory, in this Night's Time."[51] Crusoe's mind in isolation is figured as a busy place—a crowded thoroughfare. Lonely Crusoe (that literary, that mythical paradigm of the solitary individual) owns a populated mind.[52]

A surprising way of being alone is articulated in Defoe's prose: being alone in a crowd, alone with others and in the presence of strangers. In "Of Solitude," the first chapter of the third volume of his story, Crusoe himself offers an explanation of how "All Reflection is carry'd Home" to the self so that "Man may be properly said to be *alone* in the Midst of Crowds and Hurry of Men and Business." His reflections are his own: "all that is pleasant, he embraces for himself; all that is irksome and grievous, is tasted but by his own palate."[53] Pleasures and flavors—even our reflections—are private, confined to an isolated palate, cast away.

But urban solitude is even harder to understand when we find that the crowd crowds *within* an individual's mind, multiplying the number of strangers at home. This crowd is a paradoxical figure. One may be alone in the midst of it, but when alone one finds the mind crowded with thoughts. Crusoe admits that he enjoys "much more solitude in the middle of the greatest collection of mankind in the world" than he did in his "eight and twenty Years Confinement to a desolate Island" (*Reflections* 4).

Likewise, René Descartes explains in his *Discourse on the Method* how he moved away from all his acquaintances and retired to Holland in order to live among strangers and find more certain foundations for philosophy.[54] He writes, "Living here, amidst this great mass of busy people who are more concerned with their own affairs than curious about those of others, I have been able to lead a life as solitary and withdrawn as if I were in the most remote desert, while lacking none of the comforts found in the most populous cities" (1:126). Descartes, like Crusoe, is most alone while in the presence of others.[55] In eighteenth-century descriptive poetry focused not on introspection but on external nature, personification works contrarily, turning features of the landscape into persons. So Hugh Blair observes of poetry that by means of personification we "find ourselves always in the midst of our fellows."[56]

Literary loneliness involves strange and surprising reversals. As both Descartes and Crusoe note, it is easy to be solitary in the city because provisions are easier to obtain. Crusoe's urban life consists in solitude without rigors and mortifications—or funny getups (survivalist goatskin or hair shirt). It is meditation without monkishness. The idea is that the owner of an urban soul must "learn to retire into himself" (*Reflections* 13). The man who is thus alone can be company to himself. A man "can never want conversation who is company with himself, and he that cannot converse profitably with himself is not fit for any conversation at all" (5). Crusoe's is a "retired" soul, one that practices soliloquy in the midst of the populous city (9).

Reverie

The picture of the crowd of strangers within pervades eighteenth-century literature. Sixty years after the publication of Defoe's novel, James Beattie, in his *Dissertations Moral and Critical*, characterizes meditation and reverie by helping himself to the same imagery. Beattie defines reverie as that "state of mind . . . when, without attending to any one particular idea, we give full scope to our thoughts, and permit them to shift, as Imagination or accident shall determine . . . we are conscious of something like mental relaxation; while one idea brings in another, which gives way to a third, and that in its turn is succeeded by others; the mind seeming all along to be passive, and to exert as little authority over its thoughts, as the eye does over the persons who pass before it in the street."[57] Beattie may well be inspired by Defoe here, but he explicitly echoes his adversary Hume's language: "One thought chases another, and draws after it a third, by which it is expelled in its turn"—that from the theater of the mind passage in Hume's *Treatise* quoted previously (I.iv.6). Beattie and Hume, mortal combatants, avail themselves of the same language. In the eighteenth century consciousness is not so much a stream as a parade—and a man is not so much an island as a commonwealth.

The phenomenology of reverie is one shared among quite a number of writers. But a return to Crusoe's island hallucinations of Leaden-Hall market and his street scene insomnia provokes a specific serious reflection: cannibals frequent his island, all lurking just out of sight. Read allegorically, the island is an emblem of London; taken otherwise, a tropical solipsism that comes to be invaded by cannibals.[58] Crusoe's fortifications by which everything is "made double" suits the duplicitous threats of empiricism: Locke's simple ideas are invaders; the self is a territory with permeable boundaries.[59] To put it with more point: savage ideas terrify Crusoe, and Crusoe is *consumed* by his fears. In the sleepless night, as Crusoe's crowd of thoughts whirls over the history of his life, he plots an escape by canoe from the island and considers the station of his cannibal neighbors.[60] Later that same night Crusoe finally falls asleep and dreams he gains a servant (Friday is a stranger within). His next days are taken up with "secret Disputes with my self" as he tries to reconcile himself to shedding blood for the sake of gaining this servant and companion—a person he can talk to who is not his own self (236).

Familiar or Foreign

I have collected inhabitants and arranged them, as in a gallery, from familiar to more foreign. So, in the novel *Julia de Roubigné*, Henry Mackenzie has one of his characters retire to the "family of [his] own thoughts."[61] The passions are divided and more darkly domesticated in Pope's *An Essay on Man*: "Love, Hope, and Joy" belong to "fair Pleasure's smiling train," while "Hate, Fear, and Grief" are "the Family of Pain."[62] In *The Deserted Village* Goldsmith celebrates how "The soul adopts" simple pleasures "and owns their first-born sway;/Lightly they frolic o'er the vacant mind."[63] In Goldsmith's lines the people within are familiar, bucolic tenants, but as variously imagined interior populations may prove strange, with the savage ranking, in the eighteenth century, as a consummate stranger within. Even where innate ideas figure as indigenous, an interior landscapes may prove remote; as in the lines from Martial, inhabitants come into focus as near and far. Joseph Glanvill recycles the Delphic conceit in *Scepsis Scientifica* when he writes, "we are as much strangers to our selves, as to the inhabitants of America"; and William Collins conjures an image of uncolonized terrain when he writes of the "shad'wy Tribes of *Mind*" joining their murmurs in a "braided Dance."[64] The reader is referred to the reversible metaphors of **Empire**.

In the *Meditations* Descartes looks out the window and sees hats and coats, which he does not doubt could conceal automatons.[65] The stranger at home behind the casement, catching sight of herself in reflection, is likewise uncanny (*unheimlich*), and the eighteenth-century mind is increasingly haunted by its own reflections, its thoughts, dreams, visions, fears, and phantasms. In his writings on the occult, including his 1727 *Essay on the History and Reality of Apparitions*, Defoe identifies spectral apparitions with the imagination and calls the conscience "a frightful Apparition itself" (100). Crusoe, after discovering the mysterious footprint, appears to be "haunted with an evil Conscience" (166); and Samuel Wesley the Younger observes, "Care no Desert can exclude,/We haunt ourselves in Solitude."[66] The lover's mind is especially likely to be haunted by the image of his or her beloved. In Quixotic or Cartesian fashion, the mind may be imposed on by chimeras and other fantastical creatures: Pope invokes Oedipus in his adaptation of "The First Book of Statius his Thebais": a "thousand Furies haunt his guilty Soul."[67] These horror stories of imagination are historicized in Terry Castle's description of Enlightenment writers coming to "figure imaginative activity itself, paradoxically, as a kind of ghost-seeing."[68] The very ideas that are the centerpiece of "the theory of ideas" are variously termed "phantoms" and "phantasms." The novel is gothic, and its representations of experience are "self-haunting," involving—so the critic Frances Ferguson argues—the conflict between "experience and the formal construction of it."[69] There may well be ghostly figures in the machinery—although not quite the Cartesian sort that Gilbert Ryle's logical behaviorism identifies and exorcises.

Ralph Cudworth's *Treatise Concerning Eternal and Immutable Morality* is one of the rare works that personifies mental contents without resorting to structuring governmental metaphors. Here Cambridge Platonism mixes up foreign and domestic in extended analogy. In a great throng or crowd, the onlooker seizes on the familiar face of an acquaintance. Allowing this street scene to structure his line of argument, Cudworth asserts that the "Foreign and Adventitious" forms are necessarily interpreted by "something Domestick" (IV.i.2). Cudworth updates the theory of anamnesis (recollection) and revises the theory of ideas. His antimaterialist philosophy refers to the obstetric metaphors of Socrates in order to distinguish between *phantasms*, on the one hand, and *conceptions* of the mind, on the other—phantasms are impressed on the brain from without; conceptions or cogitations originate within. Cudworth figures the latter cogitations as conceived in and brought forth from out of the mind's "own womb" (IV.i.6). When this Neoplatonism is read against fellow Cantabrigian Laurence Sterne's *Tristram Shandy*, Cudworth's embodied descriptions of mental parturiency and his comparison of "Spermatick" to "Innate Cognoscitive" powers stand out in almost obscene anticipation of Sterne's novel.[70]

The Unconscious

In the period surveyed, crowd metaphors outnumber the more pastoral, primitive, and supernatural metaphors of mind. Crowds are thoughtless, headlong, madding. They are—to introduce a key modern term—"unconscious." The unconscious is not a typical feature in most accounts of eighteenth-century philosophy, but the figuration here surveyed shows that the eighteenth century had developed strategies for picturing it all the same. Foreign ideas pour across the sensorium, jostle and throng, and come to compose us (again, see **Empire**). The mind is a coalition of faculties and contents that are readily personified. And in that personification, certain contents are relegated to the status of laborer, savage, or specter. There is a political unconscious, but this is not to suggest that all of these metaphors are ideologically motivated. Some are; some only become so in literary analysis.

Metaphors are of long duration even if the situations in which they are put to use continually erode. Philosophers deploy personifications still and find them ready at hand when they would take up perennial problems in philosophy of mind. Unthinking agents—Ronald de Sousa calls them "rational homunculi"—seem to do the work of thought and prove handy in accounts of akrasia.[71] The struggles of ego and id are associated with Freud's partitioning of the mind, but rational homunculi are also to be found in the work of the cognitive scientist Marvin Minsky and the philosopher of mind Daniel Dennett.[72] The crowd is, I submit, in its way, an especially appropriate image of the self, one that captures the feel and phenomenology of mental processing and one that is fully exercised in the long eighteenth century. The theory of ideas locates the eighteenth-century population explosion inside. It proves impossible to be alone with one's thoughts. Ideas throng and crowd the mind. The strangers may stifle or overwhelm an Evelina, or they may prowl just at the edge of consciousness. The *hortus conclusus* is overrun with prostitutes and cutpurses—perhaps even cannibals.

8 Metal

Collocated Keywords: Alloy, Brass, Dross, Gold, Iron, Lead, Silver, and Steel

Count of Metaphors in Database[1] (1700–1799): 685

GRAVELLO: My aim is fixt at the Rich and Great, he that has Wealth enough, yet longs for more, Count *Pirro*, the Governour's Heir and Nephew, that rich Lord that knows no end of his large Fortunes, yet still gapes on, for Gold is a sure Bait to gain him, no other Loadstone can attrack his iron heart, 'tis proof against the force of Beauty, else I should not need this Stratagem, for Nature has not prov'd a Nigard to my Daughter.

—Susanna Centlivre, *The Stolen Heiress*, I.i (1703)

Every one has in him a natural Alloy, tho' one may be fuller of Dross than another: For this reason I cannot think it right to introduce a perfect or a faultless Man upon the Stage; not only because such a Character is improper to move Compassion, but because there is no such a thing in Nature.

—Joseph Addison, *Spectator* no. 548 (1712)

As Iron is to be hammer'd whilst it is hot and ductile, so Children are to be taught when they are young.

—Bernard Mandeville, *The Fable of the Bees. Part II* (1729)

After a weak mind has been duly prepared, and turned as it were, by opening a sluice or torrent of high-sounding words, the greater the contradiction proposed the stronger impression it makes, because it increases the puzzle, and lays fast hold on the admiration; depositing the small proportion of reason with which it was before impregnated, like the vitriol acid in the copper-mines of Wicklow, into which if you immerse iron, it immediately quits the copper which it had before dissolved, and unites with the other metal, to which it has a stronger attraction.

—Tobias Smollett, *Adventures of an Atom* (1769)

Virtue sleeps
While all the finest faculties of mind
Rust, like the iron long unus'd.

—Ann Yearsley, "To Frederick Yearsley" (1787)

See also **Coinage** and **Fetters**

THE MIND IS A METAL. The soul may be tempered or forged, thoughts and passions refined, and the heart steeled, melted, or coined. One's character and temperament, the very stuff one is made of, is "mettle "or "metal," two variants that the *OED* records as more or less semantically differentiated by the middle of the eighteenth century.[2] A hero may show his or her mettle (or metal) and one's metal (or mettle) may be tested; the spirited creature is mettlesome. A coin bounced off a hard surface may ring out in testament to its quality, and a precious metal may be rubbed against a touchstone to test its softness. But character, or *mettle*, demands a different sort of test or touchstone to be tried.

The differences between "metal" and "mettle" immediately introduce issues in the history and the philosophy of language. Samuel Johnson observes that "mettle" is a corruption of "metal" "but commonly written so when the metaphorical sense is used" ("METAL"). Orthography indicates figuration, but how is it that the new, differentiated word—a word that bears a "metaphorical sense"—is a metaphorical word? Are we to believe that "mettle" has no literal meaning? Johnson uneasily gives "Substance" as the secondary sense of "METTLE" and observes in an illustration chosen from Shakespeare's *Timon of Athens* that "mettle" should be spelled "metal" ("METTLE").[3] Johnson's desire to correct Shakespeare's spelling, if not his meaning, indicates the difficulty of making distinctions between literal and figurative when dealing with a linguistic unit smaller than the sentence. Arbitrary distinctions between the two senses of "metal"—or rather, between "metal" and "mettle"—encourage the arbitrary assignment of figurative and literal at the level of the word.[4]

Courage and spirit are traditionally associated with the arms and armor with which those practiced in war are outfitted. Metal metaphors are militant. Victors inherit the spoils and are victorious because they bring better weaponry to the fight: might and metal are self-perpetuating. Luster, firmness, sharpness signify virtue, while inactivity brings a rust on the faculties and a corrosion of the self. Hudibras prepares "Both kinds of mettle . . . Courage and steel" before going into battle.[5] In *Amelia*, Fielding describes the mind of Colonel James as "formed of those firm Materials, of which Nature formerly hammered out the Stoic, and upon which the Sorrows of no Man living could make an Impression."[6]

But too much firmness is a mark of steely, cold, hard hearts: Colonel James's friendship is not to be depended upon. The eighteenth century distrusts standing armies and professional soldiers. To produce the well-tempered heart, neither too hard nor too soft, neither brittle nor insensible is a concern of the so-called Age of Sensibility; and one might note with a sidelong glance at eighteenth-century innovations in the production of steel that it is also an *industrial* concern. Mettle must be formed with a proper degree of hardness: a people too soft, too effeminate, too polite, too luxurious, or too corrupt are prone to conquest and enslavement and are unable to defend their liberties from the encroachments of corruption and foreign power; but a people too cold and hard-hearted will be plagued by internal strife, unfit for *le doux commerce*, and unable to enjoy the pleasures of sociability.

Such is the figuration that concerns us under this heading. Specific metals possess specific characteristics and must be taken up individually. In what follows I consider more closely the metaphorics of alloys and "base metals," the processes of the furnace, the value placed in precious metals, the production of iron and steel, and the minting of coinage. Politeness, polished surfaces, and refinements are treated, as are apocalyptic figures of refinement, in which the soul is purified, its drossy body burned away. The eighteenth century is a period in which imperial expansion devoured New World gold and silver and in which manufacturing and technical innovation marked contemporary ventures in mining, smelting, and the production of iron and steel. Translators and imitators of Hesiod, Plato, and other ancients reinvigorate alchemical and metallurgical metaphors. Britain exported lead and tin and spent gold and silver in wars. Mercantilist projects hoped to hoard precious metal even as the Bank of England experimented with paper money and political economists began to differentiate money from metal.

Myths of Metals

Metals are identified by more than rigidity and are valued differently or are assigned different "intrinsic" values depending on their scarcity, weight, and luster. By and large, gold has been valued more than silver, and silver more than other metals, while baser metals such as tin, lead, and copper have different values in different cultures and historical periods.[7] In Hesiod's *Works and Days*, four metals compose the outlines of a classical historiography. In Hesiod—and in Ovid's later revision of Hesiod—we find an account of the origin and races of men. Hesiod and Ovid detail a process of degeneration from an Age of Gold to one of iron, from metals precious to those practical.

The differentiation of precious gold and silver from useful bronze and iron is the old "noble" or supposedly "Phoenician" lie on which Plato's city in speech is founded. Citizens of the republic are told that they are all brothers, all born of the earth and fashioned by a god as a mixture of soul and metal: in one late eighteenth-century summary, "the divinity infuses into some men, even at their birth, a portion of intellectual gold; into others, a portion of intellectual silver; but . . . the third class, the peasants and artificers, are composed of brass and iron."[8] The Platonic myth—what the eighteenth-century denominates a *fable* or *allegory*—coordinates a class structure with a hierarchy of precious metals: classes are rigidly designated but not entirely inflexible. Because all are made of the same earth, it "*sometimes happens that he who is mix'd with Gold, has Children who are only mix'd with Silver, and he who is mix'd with Silver, hath Children mix'd with Gold, and so of the rest.*"[9] Unforeseen mixtures require that a guardian watch over the souls of children and assign youth to the appropriate classes, thrusting the iron child born to a silver parent out among the craftsmen and husbandmen or honoring a low-born child with promotion to the ruling classes.

John Adams, reviewing these famous passages in letter 33 of his *Defence of the Constitutions of Government of the United States*, disdains Plato's "astrological and mystical whimsies," and would instead provide a typological history of republicanism that is organized by metaphors of mind—in the first case by "the several species of geniuses, the golden, the silver, the brazen, and the iron." For Adams, there are as many species of soul as there are republics, and he describes as characteristic of the second, mixed-metal type, natural divisions (silver and gold, iron and brass) that threaten both the republic and the soul with sedition, as "government within" falls inevitably into the class war and contentiousness characteristic of ambitious spirit.[10]

Ore from the Mine

The ore that includes both metal and dross is, according to Samuel Johnson, "Metal unrefined; metal yet in its mineral state" ("ORE"). An alloy is a mixture of metals, and in the poetic diction of the period, alloys especially are base, gross, and sordid; metals are usually preferred pure rather than mixed.[11] However, alloy's associations are not always unambiguously negative: alloys have their uses, and a Will to Refinement is not always evidenced in the figuration of this Age of Politeness.

For example, in Dryden's formulations unalloyed gold is too soft to hold a stamp (see *Gold* and *Silver* below), and we find these lines from Pope's *Essay on Man* illustrating the second sense of "MERCURY" in Johnson's *Dictionary*:

'Tis thus the Mercury of Man is fix'd,
Strong grows the Virtue with his Nature mix'd;
The Dross cements what else were too refin'd,
And in one interest Body acts with Mind.[12]

More than an emblem for the embodied mind, the refinement of ore and alloy is a prominent trope in devotional literature. The metaphor is a favorite of the Baptist minister Benjamin Keach and pervades his writings on baptism. In his poetic paraphrase of the book of Job, William Langhorne describes how "Racks of Pain" and "rapid Fever" are a "potent Fire" that refines the "drossy Souls . . . Till the bright Ore in polish'd Beauty shines."[13] In many devotional contexts, death is the ultimate refiner, separating the soul's precious metal from the coarse, drossy body.

Metaphors of refinement have their secular uses as well. Historians of Britain characterize the eighteenth century as both a period of increasing bourgeois refinement and a period of industrial revolution—in John Adams's retelling of the Platonic fable, iron and steel ambition can't help but seek wealth in the form gold and silver. And as dross is separated from raw ore in the furnace of experience, one gains in temper like the iron ore that is alloyed with carbon to become steel. Plays and novels in which a rude and earthy country girl learns to comport herself in the beau monde are, in an important sense, narratives of refinement, a refinement repeatedly figured by way of metallurgical process. It is the heat of the assembly, the flush of embarrassment, and the burning cheeks of the heroine that temper and refine her manners.

Wit and taste are signs of fineness—or may be refinements in themselves. Thoughts, happiness, and love may be refined from all "gross alloy" or "earthy dross." Wit and genius sparkle like gems or "gold refined." In her poem "Hypatia," Elizabeth Tollet, for one, figures reason as refining wit after it disengages the raw "Metal from the Mine." Lady Mary Chudleigh uses a similar metaphor when she notes that those "whose Fire does dimly shine . . . cannot their Dross refine,/Nor chase thick Vapours from their Brain."[14] The playwright and actor Frederick Pilon expresses a dubiously egalitarian sentiment in his comedy *He Would be a Soldier* (1786) when a character claims "uncouth men" may have "minds like rich metals, as yet unpurify'd from alloy; but let it once be known that the ore is gold, and the refiner's hand will soon bring forth the bullion."[15]

Many eighteenth-century authors lightly adjust the metaphor, treating the self as a marbled block that is veined and fissured.[16] An empiricist may prefer the new description (unhewn stone is shaped by experience), although Thomas Burnet, critic of Locke, compares innate impressions to "Gold in the Oar, that may be refin'd; or rough Diamonds, that by polishing, receive a further lustre." In his *New Essays Concerning Human Understanding*, Leibniz substitutes for the Lockean tabula rasa an image of veined marble.[17] Rather than by experience writing on a clean, blank sheet of paper, implicit knowledge is discovered by the sculptor who works to discover the contours presented in the veined marble.[18]

In a kind of synecdoche, we see that the self is also a quarry or mine. Tollet, quoted just above, plays on the words "mind" and "mine" in her recommendation that reason should "disengage the metal from the mine." This figuration of inwardness finds its way into both authoritarian and egalitarian metaphorics. As in the example from Frederick Pilon above, the mind may harbor veins of precious or useful metals that only become available when "disinterred."[19] Like the earth, the mind's treasures are interior and located deep within the self: "Full many a Gem of purest Ray serene/The dark unfathom'd Caves of Ocean bear," as Thomas Gray writes.[20] His "Village-*Hampden*," mute Milton, and innocent Cromwell are buried in the ground and imaginatively exhumed by the poet.

In the 1754 poem "A Description of Chedder-Cliffs; And Part of Mendip-Hills near *Wells*, In *Somersetshire*," Samuel Bowden explicitly figures the laboring-class mind as a mine. Bowden describes a bleak and savage scene in Somersetshire, before identifying the mind "disguis'd" by poverty with the ore concealed beneath the rugged mountains: "Thus oft' disguis'd, in poverty we find/Bright genius sparkle thro' an humble mind." He observes that though the mine may not harbor "gold," "diamonds," or "glittering strata," still "useful minerals" like calamine and lead (metals "of various birth") "Lodge in the fruitful bowels of the earth."[21]

Brass and Bronze

Bronze and brass are two "base" alloys put to figurative use in the eighteenth century. Johnson notes that "brass" does not strictly differentiate brass from bronze but is used "in popular language for any kind of metal in which copper has a part" ("BRASS" and "BRONZE"). Brass is a metal of impudence so that "BRAZEN" is defined by Johnson, in this case without comment on the term's figurative or literal status, as "impudent." Brass has a bright luster but not the heft of a precious metal; it is show without value, glister without the gold. So Sir Robert Walpole was nicknamed "Sir Robert Brass" by the opposition.[22] Brazen Pamela is called a bold-face, a pert, a saucebox, and an impudent hussy. But when Mr. B. decides to marry her, he warns that it will be easier for him than for her to pass in society because "Woman shines not forth to the Publick as a Man; and the World sees not your Excellencies and Perfections."[23] Where Mr. B. can "brazen out the Matter" of their marriage with his companions of "the Chace, the Green, and the Assemblee" (60), Pamela cannot. Feminine brazenness is impudence—not virtue, but Shamela's "vartue."[24]

Brass and bronze provoke other associations besides impudence. Hesiod's "bronze race" was terrible, strong, and warlike. Thomas Cooke's 1728 translation of Hesiod's *Works and Days* depicts these "brasen" people: "Savage their Nature, and their Hearts of Stone; / Their Houses Brass, of Brass the warlike Blade."[25] That the brass arms and armor match the brass homes of these brazen people implies that their warlike savagery is not tempered in any domestic space. As will become apparent in what follows, brass and bronze are unlike iron and steel insofar as there are few, if any, metaphors of softness, well-tempering, or melting associated with brassy, brazen metals.

Horace's book I, ode iii, which describes the oak-hearted, brazen-breasted mariner who first sailed the seas, is a favorite of those eighteenth-century British audiences that pride themselves on their nation's naval victories. The ode is imitated or alluded to by Dryden, Thomas Brown, William Oldisworth, Leonard Welsted, Allan Ramsay, Edward Young, Arthur Murphy, Christopher Smart, and William Combe. Brown describes mariners' hearts as "immur'd with triple Brass,"[26] but the metal is not always translated as brass, so that Dryden, for one, renders the lines as

> Sure he, who first the passage tried,
> In hardened oak his heart did hide,
> And ribs of iron armed his side. (ll. 13–5)

The figure of triple plating, which is found in Horace's original ode, attracts other metals to itself and is found in other contexts. In the sixth edition of *The Theory of Moral Sentiments* Adam Smith borrows from Milton's *Paradise Lost* when he describes how ancient philosophers were able to "arm the obdured breast with stubborn patience, as with triple steel."[27]

While the brass in Horace is put to jingoistic uses, it is also used to figure other, non-British peoples. It should be emphasized that Hesiod describes the *races* of men and not ages, and in the eighteenth century we find bronze, brass, brazen, and copper faces in travel literature. The peoples of India, Turkish and Arab Muslims, and Native Americans especially are figured as darker base metals. In *The Votary of Wealth*, the character Sharpset says he likes the look of Gangica, a "Gentoo" servant, and calls her a little marigold. When Gangica responds to his flirtations in halting English, "Oh, you moc.—You not like my copper face," Sharpset banters with her: "In my mind a lady looks better with a face of copper, than of brass—And that is all the fashion."[28] But when she returns a compliment, he blushes and speaks aside, "This girl's simplicity has done more than all the bronze of her sex could ever accomplish" (29). Gangica's copper is softer than the brass of fashionable London ladies, and although she cannot blush or guard her asides, she demonstrates she has "the fairest mind in a dark coloured case" (48). Her simplicity serves as foil to the plots unfolding around her. Sharpset, for one, finds something fascinating "in this dusky piece of disinterestedness" and marries her at the end of the play (30). So, too, must audiences have seen something in the affair of Sharpset and Gangica: an excerpt from their initial exchange, in which Gangica refuses to take a purse full of money from Sharpset, appears under the heading "DISINTERESTEDNESS" in a treasury of quotations from modern drama in 1800.[29]

Gold

Eighteenth-century poetic diction is stocked with golden virtues, golden means to be mindful of, golden dreams that tickle the imagination, and cupid's darts that are tipped with gold. Hearts are tied in matrimony with threads or bands of gold. Happiness without alloy is pure happiness; like pure gold or pure silver, it is refined and without impurity. Golden crowns perch upon golden tresses or weigh heavily on silvered heads. A person otherwise impecunious may own a heart as pure as gold refined. Shakespeare's Pistol tells us that Henry is "a Bawcock and a Heart of Gold" (*Henry V* IV.i).[30] Throughout the eighteenth century commanding officers (in dramas especially) encourage their men to soldier on, calling them "hearts of gold."

But **Coinage** may be clipped and light, tokens and baubles worthless; voices and appearances may be counterfeited, actions performed without the underwriting of golden virtue. It is proverbial that all that glisters and glitters is not gold. Thomas Gray, of course, updates the well-worn commonplace (available in Chaucer, Spenser, Shakespeare, and Milton) in his monitory ode on Horace Walpole's drowned cat and warns presumptuous maids of the impossibility of retrieving false steps. Likewise, Locke warns the philosopher not to take another thinker's principles on trust because "Such borrowed wealth, like fairy-money, though it were gold in the hand from which he receives it, will be but leaves and dust when it comes to use" (*Essay* I. iv.23). In the satirical poems and songs that follow his *Drapier's Letters*, Swift warns that the shining, glistering halfpence made by the iron- and copper-monger William Wood are worthless brass that will not pass in circulation.[31] Evelina, shown the glittering automata at Cox's museum, judiciously dismisses them as "mere shew, though a wonderful one."[32] In making such an accurate judgment of taste, she succeeds in displaying her own worth.

British moralists take up the issue of inner worth explicitly, trying to locate the source of ethical value, whether in action or in intention. Value is located either intrinsically or conventionally. Moral actions must be measured and weighed, and if their quality is not confirmed in the end by God's stamp, convention must discover the valuation. True, justified knowledge is valued in circulation. In a 1695 letter to William Molyneux, Locke compares "Meditating by one's self" to "digging in the Mine"—whether the "maiden Earth" brought up "contain any Metal" requires conversation and the "Touchstone" of another.[33] Likewise, Locke writes in a famous passage from the dedication to his *Essay*, discussed in **Coinage**, that "Truth, like Gold" is given its "price" or "publick stamp" by "Trial and Examination" (*Essay* p. 4).

True gold, like all metals, is known by its qualities. It is scarce and valuable. It is malleable, ductile, and incorruptible in fire. Gold is the "king of metals"[34] and only dissolves in aqua regia. Though regal, the metal is soft and easily worn by rubbing. Gold's salient features are reproduced in metaphor. The majority of gold metaphors specify purity and value. "Pure as gold refined" is a typical formulation. The Wesleys compose a hymn based on Job 23:10: the hymner sings "try me still / In the furnace of distress" so that "I shall at last come forth as gold."[35] This pure gold is soft and malleable. In his *Palamon and Arcite* Dryden observes that the "softest Metals are not slow to melt / And Pity soonest runs in gentle Minds."[36]

Adam Smith describes the imagination as ductile: "The frame of my body can be but little affected by the alterations which are brought about upon that of my companion: but my imagination is more ductile, and more readily assumes, if I may say so, the shape and configuration of the imaginations of those whom I am familiar."[37] A more extreme example of ductility may be found in Cowper's poetry. In "The Flatting Mill," Cowper details the industrial process by which an ingot of gold or silver is rolled, flatted, and beaten thin with mallets. The processes are recommended to the poet who would "urge reformation of national ill":

> If he wish to instruct, he must learn to delight,
> Smooth and ductile, and even his fancy must flow,
> Must tinkle and glitter like gold to the sight.[38]

Cowper demands the fancy must be beaten as fine as the "gold leaf" that is used to coat pills taken by invalids. But this sort of extreme ductility need not signal intellectual or rhetorical virtue. Cornelius Scriblerus, the father of Martin in *The Memoirs of Martinus Scriblerus*, is described as having a reason "so pliant and ductile that he was always of the opinion of the last [ancient authority] he read."[39] Other extreme cases of impressibility are remarked upon under the heading **Impression**.

As noted, it is easy enough to move from the consideration of metals to the consideration of morals. In Thomas Amory's novel *John Buncle*, "little *Ribble*, the *Chemist*" discourses long on semimetals, antimony of liver, bismuth, and aqua fortis before bringing his disquisition to a devotional conclusion.[40] It is gold that facilitates the transition. Ribble, too, notes the significance of gold's characteristic ductility: "And as to *gold's* being so yielding and *ductile* by human art, it is to be observed, that in return it exerts a greater power on the human mind." Ribble continues, "Passive it is in its ductility, but more active in its influence on man. It is a *greater tyrant* than a *slave*" (2:357). Ribble concludes his moralizing, "Too much gold most commonly inverts this order, and produces an apostasy that sets the inferior powers in the throne, and enslaves the mind to the body: It gives the *passions* the *commanding influence*, and makes *reason* receive *law* from *appetite*" (2:358). Here we see the well-worn dialectic discussed in **Empire**. As the discourse on metals and semimetals modulates into an ethical and devotional conclusion, the narrator admits, "It is an odd conclusion, I own, to a discourse on *metals* and *semi-metals*" (2:361). After tracing a line from the purity of gold to the purity of conscience, Ribble delivers his moral, "nothing can be given in exchange for the soul" (2:360), and would seem to have in mind the invaluable soul invoked in Mark 8:36: "For what shall it profit a man, if he shall gain the whole world, and lose his own soul?"

Silver

Silver follows gold in the schemes of Hesiod and Ovid, perhaps because it is less lustrous or mistakenly thought to be the softer metal.[41] Certainly silver is a less popular material for representing the immaterial self: in the database there are almost four times as many gold as silver metaphors (over ninety instances of gold, twenty-five of silver and sterling). If gold is identified by its ductility, silver is figured as fully liquid. In the poetry of the period, we find silver floods, streams, tides, rains, and descriptions of the silver Thames. Less obviously flowing are silver moonbeams, silver tongues, and silver fields of barley. All this quicksilver liquidity is readily associated with circulating coinage by writers concerned with money and political economy (again, see **Coinage**).

We may move between economic and religious discourses and note, despite Ribble's insistence that "nothing can be given in exchange for the soul," that slaves were sold, on average, for about £30 sterling in the British West Indies at the middle of the century. Or perhaps the soul is invaluable because alienable labor is so easily priced in gold or pounds sterling. In a poetic epistle Mary Mollineux urges her reader to "seek the Piece of Silver, hid within/The House, thy Heart."[42] Mollineux's poem alludes to the parable of the servant rejected by his master because he did not increase the one silver talent with which he was entrusted. Max Weber's model of Protestantism and the spirit of capitalism prepares us to identify these discourses in which the religious and economic overlap and to reconcile the inestimable, invaluable soul with metaphors that suggest its value may be specified in the same way as the value of precious metals is specified. It is the duty of the Christian to increase his talents. Wealth is a sign of grace: "unto every one that hath shall be given" (Matthew 25:29).

Those that have not—or whose talent is only a lump of base metal—must seek comfort in the technologies of refinement. Ephraim Chambers, author of the 1728 *Cyclopaedia*, cites Boerhaave in a discussion of the science of "METALLURGIA" and describes how the metallurgist may "work, gild, polish, and imitate the finer Metals in the coarser."[43] The entry is followed immediately by another more provocative: "METAMORPHOSIS, The Transformation of a Person." Blessed indeed are the poor in spirit and pure in heart, for in the British eighteenth century, silver is produced by smelting lead. Molten lead is oxidized into a compound called litharge. As hot air is pumped across the lead with bellows, the litharge is blown off, leaving behind a button of pure silver.[44] The process is ancient, and metal metaphors that detail refinement are found in the Bible. Psalm 12:6 reads, "The words of the Lord are pure words: as silver tried in a furnace of earth, purified seven times," and Psalm 66:10 reads, "For thou, O God, hast proved us: thou hast tried us, as silver is tried." The refinement metaphor may be found in at least four different hymns composed by the Wesleys and in several other eighteenth-century devotional poems. Methodism made special appeals to the laboring classes, and to miners in particular, so that both John Wesley and George Whitefield may have found metallurgical figures of speech a particularly effective way to communicate to their audiences. In 1739 Wesley and Whitefield preached to the miners of Kingswood near Bristol. That same year John Wesley purchased an old foundry in Moorfields, London, and organized the Methodist Society there. The building served as the headquarters of Wesley's society until 1779. In his *Journal* Wesley registers his awareness of the building's symbolic value in a quiet play on words dated August 8, 1779: "This was the last night which I spent at the Foundry. What hath God *wrought* there in one and forty years!" (emphasis added).[45] The Methodist congregation is so much metal, wrought by the preacher and stamped as silver by the Lord.

Iron and Steel

In a sermon on the prodigal son, Laurence Sterne wonders at the iron heart that first must be "heated" by fiction and fable before it can be "wrought upon."[46] The distance between what may be wrought in silver and gold and what may be wrought in iron is remarkable. We have seen that gold and silver suggest value, softness, and refinement. Metaphors of iron and steel yield very different associations. This is not to suggest that the working of iron is valueless or entirely distinct from social refinements: high-quality crucible steel was used to make fine cutlery, and Adam Smith famously details the "very trifling manufacture" of pins in his *Wealth of Nations*.[47] However, the majority of wrought iron was used to make nails, agricultural tools, and basic cutlery, and the majority of cast iron was used to make cooking pots and guns.[48] Before the Methodists moved in, cannons were manufactured in the building that housed Wesley's Foundry Church.

In the eighteenth century, iron is identified as the hardest metal and the lightest, except tin. It is malleable when pure but "in a less degree than gold, silver, lead, or copper" and requires "the strongest fire of all metals to melt" (see Johnson's *Dictionary* "IRON"). Iron is valued not for its softness or ductility but for its tensile strength, and the hardness of iron is used to figure hardness of heart.[49] Iron may be worked against a grindstone to set a sharp edge, and men of wit figure their wordplay as swordplay. Iron is put into a furnace to be refined, purified, tempered, and strengthened; flint and iron struck together throw sparks. Poets recruit all of these features in metaphorical uses.

About one hundred iron and steel hearts from eighteenth-century verse, prose, and drama are collected in the database. Death is iron-hearted. So too are slave masters and misers. Monsters gnash iron teeth. Iron hearts are found in both amatory and military contexts: lovers and soldiers both possess iron hearts.[50] An iron heart may be melted or rent. Insensible hearts become so by being *steeled* by courage, love, principles, and maxims, or rancor, habit, scorn, and revenge. Steel is itself understood not as a distinct metal in the eighteenth century but as a kind of iron and is often paired with brass in the figuration of insensibility.[51] The lines discussed above from translations of Horace's book I, ode iii (above, under *Brass and Bronze*) describe the feeling heart enclosed in plates of "triple brass" or "triple steel." The connotations are fully military, and Johnson notes that "steel" is "often used metonymically for weapons or armour" and "proverbially" for hardness (*Dictionary* "STEEL"). Pope's Baron in *The Rape of the Lock*, after cutting one of Belinda's curled locks of hair, glories in "The conqu'ring Force of unresisted Steel."[52]

In this context Frances Burney's character Evelina has a suggestive anagram for a last name: Anville. A bar of bright red steel quenched in cold water increases in hardness and may be reheated and worked on an anvil, improving its ductility and toughness in the process of "tempering."[53] A great number of the steel metaphors I have collected that involve the verb "to steel" should be associated with this process of tempering. Johnson writes of the verb, "It is used, if applied to the mind, very often in a bad sense" and cites examples from Shakespeare, Addison, Prior, and Tickell ("STEEL"). But I find Johnson somewhat exaggerates the prevalence of this "bad sense" of "to steel": there are a great number of honorable, steely soldiers in the poetry of the period and maidens are often advised to steel themselves against the advances of libertines. A ready example is available in the 1743 edition of the four-book *Dunciad*: the "heavy and lumpish" enthusiast is compared to lead, which "on the least application of *heat*" melts and runs, and "which of all metals falls quickest into fusion," whereas fire in a genius is "truly Promethean" and "fits it (as it does well tempered steel) for the necessary impressions of art."[54]

Tempering in the Forge

Indeed, "temper" is a key term in Adam Smith's revised *Theory of Moral Sentiments*.[55] As men are subject to inequalities of temper (some are colder, some harder than others), a major aim of Smith's *Theory* is to coordinate unequal temperaments in civil society so that one impartial spectator can enter into the feelings of another. Much concerned with delineating a virtuous temper of mind, Smith often uses the word "temper" in a manner clearly suggestive of metallurgy in the later editions of his *Theory*. For example, in the third section of his discussion of the character of virtue titled "Of Self-command,"

Smith treats the commonplace that "war and faction are certainly the best schools for forming every man to this hardiness and firmness of temper." And Smith describes self-command as "not only itself a great virtue" but also the virtue from which "all the others virtues seem to derive their principal *lustre*" (emphasis added).[56] Of course, "temper" ("temperament") also has musical associations, and another cluster of important terms ("tone" and "tenor" and "pitch") is employed in the earliest versions of the *Theory*.[57] In revising, Smith ingeniously employs a single word to cover both sensibility and stoicism, both steely self-command and melting, musical feeling. To combine the metaphorics of Stoicism and sensibility: nerves must be hardened, like the wires of a harpsichord, so as to vibrate well, each with each.[58]

Iron is worked in a forge or a smithy, and steel is tempered in a furnace. Johnson notes that "forge" may describe "any place where any thing is made or shaped" ("FORGE"). Internal furnaces and forges abound in seventeenth-century literature: Shakespeare writes of "the quick Forge and working-house of Thought" in *Henry V* and figures "imaginations . . . as foule / As Vulcan's Stithe" in *Hamlet*;[59] Descartes drew on a Galenic tradition in his explanation of the heart as a kind of furnace;[60] and in *Paradise Lost*, Milton describes Satan squatting like a toad "close at the ear of Eve" and using "the organs of her fancy [to] forge / illusions" (IV, ll. 802–3). The Presbyterian minister John Flavel writes, "Look, as iron put into the fire becomes all fiery, so the soul dwelling in the God of love, becomes all love, all delight, all joy."[61] The metaphors of the forge and smithy, here located in Shakespeare and Milton, continue to appear in eighteenth-century poetry.[62] William Cowper, for one, employs the metaphor: a "Strong Genius, from whose forge of thought / Forms rise, to quick perfection wrought."[63] It is the imagination that forges ideas, fancies, and illusions. To invoke Smith's project of tempering once again, the ductile imagination is the central and most important faculty of the mind in Smith's *Theory*.

Change over Time

In the final analysis, metaphors of iron and steel prove an unusual case in this study. In most entries, the distribution of metaphors I have collected varies "noisily" from decade to decade, with high-count clusters of metaphors typically correlating with individual authors or specific works. While in some cases I have suggested that further investigation might ratify variation as significant (**Empire, Fetters**), under this heading, I more confidently identify a trend. In short: iron and steel metaphors increase visibly across the century. The increase is not only in the raw counts of metaphors but also holds for

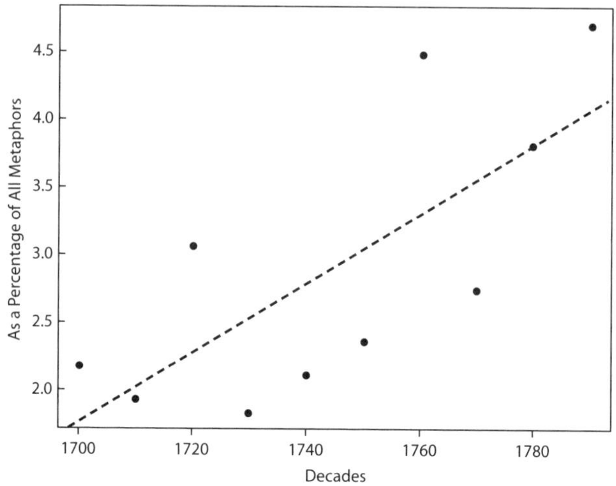

Iron and steel metaphors as a percentage of all metaphors collected, counted decade by decade, from 1700 to 1799.

frequencies of iron and steel metaphors as calculated as a percentage of the total number of metaphors collected decade by decade. I discover an increase in the number of iron and steel figures of speech—again, taken as a percentage of all metaphors collected and as used to figure minds, hearts, and souls. By contrast, analogous plots of gold, silver, or other metal metaphors fail to show a linear relation.

Where do these metaphors come from? Many may be assigned to the discourse of the Age of Sensibility: iron and steel hearts are complained of in the poetry and melted in the more melodramatic moments in novels and on the stage. To accuse someone of insensibility, inflexibility, and inhumanity is to accuse them of harboring an iron heart. But then, not all steely inwardness is reviled. As noted above, steel, especially, has positive connotations, and many late eighteenth-century individuals are congratulated on their "hearts of steel."[64]

The increase in steel and iron metaphors may be most visible in the 1790s. In this momentous decade, fetters, chains, bonds, and irons feature prominently in Jacobin and antislavery metaphorics (see **Fetters**), while jingoist, military metaphors appear in Anti-Jacobin metaphorics. Keyword search carries the reader to the relevant passages, aiding in the apprehension of disparate similitudes. Metaphors involving magnets and lodestones—common enough throughout the century—take on new significance as the public becomes interested in and then suspicious of Doctor Mesmer's theories of "animal magnetism." Many of the collected iron and steel metaphors appear in drama: John O'Keeffe's 1797 play *The Wicklow Mountains* includes references to late eighteenth-century Steelboy agrarian movements in Ireland.[65] In addition, metaphors are imported from abroad, and translations of Schiller and Kotzebue account for several variations on domestic iron and steel metaphors. In the more sentimental works of the Age of Sensibility, metallic hearts are melted down by impassioned rhetoric or suffering innocence. The historian G. J. Barker-Benfield describes a fusion of evangelism and sensibility in the 1790s ultimately producing reforming females who manifest "the degree of tough-mindedness with which so many late eighteenth-century female writers had insisted that sensibility be tempered."[66]

The determining context, obviously, is industrial revolution, but the metaphors seen in the aggregate take the same, traditional form, even as more of them appear in the literature. There *is* significantly more iron and steel produced in the later eighteenth century than in the earlier part of the century. The national output of iron in Britain in 1720, about 20,000 tons per year, increased to over 250,000 tons by 1806; between 1737 and 1802 the production of steel in Yorkshire alone increased twentyfold.[67] However, the increased number of metaphors does not explicitly reference the new industrial processes developed by Benjamin Huntsman, Matthew Boulton, or Henry Cort. It is, perhaps, not surprising that an increase in materials correlates with an increase in metaphors, although it is far from obvious how substance and discourse interact specifically. More metal means more metaphors? Perhaps, but this correlation is an exception to the norm explored elsewhere in these entries and refuses to generalize as some sort of (iron) law that governs discourse and the discursive environment.[68] In other entries I have documented how a constellation of metaphors remained the same even while the social and technological practices figured by these metaphors changed (see **Impressions**, **Writing**). Certainly some poetic diction must operate independently from material reality; otherwise we would be hard pressed to explain the prominence of, say, the phoenix in the poetry of the seventeenth century.

But in the case of iron and steel metaphors, how significantly literature, philosophy, politics, and socioeconomic developments all seem to fit together. But what does it mean that the metal metaphors pile up without much variation in terms of diction or syntax across the course of the eighteenth century—that they simply increase in number? A steel or iron heart of the 1690s presents much the same set of rhetorical characteristics as a steel or iron heart at the end of the eighteenth century—even as the technology involved in the production of iron and steel is much improved and the economic basis of that production changes. I am not sure how to connect base to superstructure here, and am more than a little nonplussed to find that metaphors of gold, tin, or brass do not increase in frequency alongside those of iron and steel. Why, I ask, are such shifts in frequency so rare in the metaphors of mind collected for the purposes of this study?

Although I will return to them in the conclusion of this book, these questions invite a new and separate investigation. I refer once again to the various pronouncements on metaphor from Shelley, Nietzsche, Derrida, Rorty, and Lakoff and Johnson cited in the introduction of this dictionary and referred to throughout. It is an unspoken—and not unreasonable—first principle of cultural studies that literature and its material environment interact, one with the other; that literary language is both constitutive and representational; or, to speak with Nietzsche, that commonplace truths are only "metaphors that are worn out and without sensuous power; coins which have lost their pictures and now matter only as metal."[69]

If, as historians so often insist, the long eighteenth century witnessed a radical change in the conceptualization of the self and the social structures inside of which the self is conceptualized, why doesn't this revolutionary change register more clearly in the majority of its metaphors for the mind treated in this dictionary? Most theories of metaphor would lead us to expect the strong correlations between literature and its context explored under the subheading *Iron and Steel* to be the rule and not the exception; that exception and rule are reversed for the majority of metaphors of mind in the eighteenth century—that ideological change in the eighteenth century seems to be happening behind or in spite of a stable poetic diction is a major discovery resulting from this research. Relentless empirical efforts, based in search technology and data mining, challenge and complicate theoretical commonplaces. It is not mirrors or lamps or Aeolian lyres that serve as our best markers of literary change (see the following entry, **Mirror**): the most unexpected metaphors serve to discover the veins and contours of literary history.

9 Mirror

Collocated Keywords: Glass, Mirror, Reflection, Speculum

Count of Metaphors in Database[1] (1700–1799): 237

Your Glass will not do you half so much service as a serious reflection on your own Minds; which will discover Irregularities more worthy your Correction, and keep you from being either too much elated or depress'd by the representations of the other.

—Mary Astell, *A Serious Proposal to the Ladies* (1694)

By these Allusions a Truth in the Understanding is as it were reflected by the Imagination; we are able to see something like Colour and Shape in a Notion, and to discover a Scheme of Thoughts traced out upon Matter.

—Joseph Addison, *Spectator* no. 421 (July 3, 1712)

Wherefore that we may the better understand how far the Passion of Sense reaches, and where the Activity of the Mind begins, we will compare these three Things together: First, a Mirror, Looking-glass or Crystal Globe; Secondly, a Living Eye, that is, a Seeing or Perceptive Mirror or Looking-glass; Thirdly, a Mind or Intellect Superadded to this Living Eye or Seeing Mirror.

—Ralph Cudworth, *Treatise Concerning Eternal and Immutable Morality* (1731)

I advised our Miss H—to the same remedy, but have a notion her mind is haunted by one particular image; if so, nothing will cure her; for if the heart be broken 'tis broken like a looking-glass, and the smallest piece will for ever preserve and reflect the same figure till 'tis again ground down into a new mass.

—Hester Thrale, letter to Samuel Johnson (August 30, 1783)

> ORSASMYN.
> Oh! that superior mind is gone for ever!
> —Yet still, thus ruin'd, like a broken mirror,
> It gives a perfect image in each fragment!
>
> —Sophia Lee, *Almeyda, Queen of Granada* (1796)

> To this knowledge which all men carry about with them, and to these sympathies in which without any other discipline than that of our daily life we are fitted to take delight, the Poet principally directs his attention. He considers man and nature as essentially adapted to each other, and the mind of man as naturally the mirror of the fairest and most interesting properties of nature.
>
> —William Wordsworth, preface to *Lyrical Ballads* (1800)

See also **Animals**, **Coinage**, **Court**, **Empire**, **Impressions**, **Inhabitants**, **Metal**, **Mirror**, **Rooms**, and **Writing**

In his classic study of metaphors of mind, *The Mirror and the Lamp*, M. H. Abrams describes the mirror as one of two antithetical metaphors—the other, also indicated in his title, being the lamp. Enlisted in his periodization of the eighteenth century, the paired title terms soon make visible Abrams's preferences as he contrasts passive mirrors, associated with eighteenth-century empiricism, with the active, radiant lamps associated with Romantic idealism. To reduce Abrams's ambitious study to barest narrative: lamps *replace* mirrors at the end of the century; and in the most compact statement of his argument, the claim made is that literary history progresses by metaphorical substitution. In connecting aesthetics to epistemology, Abrams's survey offers one of the most famous answers to the question posed in this dictionary's introduction—what difference does it make when we change the metaphor?

For Abrams, metaphors change alongside literary periods, with the metaphors of mind serving as an index to the spirit of the age. But the ratios are unbalanced from the outset, as Abrams describes the mirror giving way to multiple metaphors almost at once, as if the lamp image actively radiated new analogues, including the overflowing fountains and growing gardens that signal Romantic paradigms by means of proliferation.[2] By contrast, the *camera obscura* and tabula rasa (linked to Locke and discussed in the following entries, **Rooms** and **Writing**) are taken to define the reflexive imagery of neoclassical poets and critics if not to confine their practice to the play of light on a surface. In Abrams's exposition, the passive metaphorics of interiority and impression contrast schematically with the expressive, lyric practice of the Romantic poets, who favor fountains, radiating lights, and Aeolian harps in figurations of the mind. This putative shift in aesthetics (from imitation to expression, inwardness to projection) corresponds with—or *mirrors*, as it were—"a corresponding change in popular epistemology" (57).[3]

Like other readers of Abrams, I am not so sure that it is possible to distinguish an Enlightenment metaphorics of reflection from a Romantic one of projection without much special pleading for Wordsworth and Coleridge and adverting, in advance, to the schematic period differences that the metaphors are supposed to give rise to.[4] Worse, the emphasis on optics is blinkering, distracting from the prevalence of more prominent metaphors. In literary history the metaphoric field cannot be schematically reduced without distortion. Any metaphorics, taken in its details, is multiple and contradictory. The result of schematizing by "archetypal analogy" is unsurprisingly preposterous: in Abrams's account, the lamp, an Enlightenment emblem if ever there was one, is displaced and belatedly associated with Romanticism. Abrams's mirror metaphors are readily lost in the funhouse of mutually reflecting metaphors, the reflex images selected, after all, in order to illuminate literary history.

The Optics of Periodization

By means of reflection an object is displaced, its image readily reversed. Mirrors and lamps are not easily exhibited as antitheses because the figurative optics of the so-called En*light*enment is incredibly multifarious, alternately reflective and projective, penetrating and luminescent. Or, in at least one case, "obfuscated" with "fuliginous" matter, as when Laurence Sterne's Walter Shandy illustrates Locke's theory of ideas with a "lanthorn" simile. Toby Shandy, Walter's brother and interlocutor, objects that his own ideas whirl round more "like a smoak-jack" than those projected by a magic lantern. In the contrasting emphases on candlelight and funnel soot (between metaphors of reflection and those of convection), there is matter for discourse, but Toby and Walter fail to elaborate their competing images. Dismayed, Sterne's narrator, Tristram, cries out: "What a conjuncture was here lost!"[5] The opposition and Tristram's outburst serve my larger methodological point: metaphors must be taken together—in *conjuncture*, in the politico-historical sense of that term.

Toby's idea of a roasting jack turns all of Walter's ideas upside down, and I would have my discussion of mirror metaphors do the same. Following the installation of mirrors and chandeliers by seventeenth-century royalty and nobles in palaces and country homes, mirrors are increasingly hung in eighteenth-century interiors in order to *illuminate* the room, reflecting sunlight from without and multiplying the candles lit within.[6] Moreover, the mirror is as much an emblem of early modernity as it is of Enlightenment.[7] Even canonical Romantic texts can be marshaled against Abrams's argument: in the final epigraph to this entry, Wordsworth in the preface to *Lyrical Ballads* claims the mind of man is "naturally the mirror of the fairest and most interesting properties of nature" (any discussion of this metaphor is conspicuously *absent* from Abrams's study).[8] But more tellingly, the number of mirror metaphors tallied in my own investigation of eighteenth-century metaphorics is slightly *increasing* even as the eighteenth century comes to its close. One metaphor does not replace another, because literary history is ever making room for new metaphors and finding new uses for old ones.

Plotinus influentially figured the soul as a mirror, but the origins of optical metaphors of mind are not easy to fix, asking to be read, in England, from at least their increasingly widespread use in the seventeenth century forward.[9] Thus Abrams investigates Cambridge Platonism as one possible "Romantic" origin and makes mention of the persistent Protestant discussions of inner light. Much of the best traditional intellectual history associates ubiquitous reference to the "light of nature" with this moment, and philosophers such as Gilbert Ryle blame Descartes for the inauguration of the official dogma of mind-body dualism, which works on a "para-optical model" in which the mind "illuminates itself by beams of its own light reflected from a mirror in its insides."[10] From antiquity on, mirrors and lamps are not easily separable in metaphorology: a disentangling of allusions and steady attention to material history is required if we are to make explicit that the succeeding centuries do anything more than reimagine creation as framed and figured by the ancient authors, who nested all the visible world within crystalline spheres and imagined its motions and matter as reflections of a divine idea of order.

Take Alexander Pope as an exemplary eighteenth-century allegorist of the cave, a poet of both mirror and lamps. Pope, who moved to rural Twickenham in 1719, built himself a Palladian villa and dug a subterranean tunnel and "Grotto" to effect passage from the cellars of his house to his garden. In a letter, he describes this grotto functioning as a "*Camera obscura*" (an eighteenth-century figure of passive mimesis in Abrams's scheme) when the doors are shut; but, he continues, when one has "a mind to light it up, it affords a very different scene," as it is "finished with shells interspersed with pieces of looking-glass in angular forms, and in the ceiling is a star of the same material, at which when a lamp (of an orbicular figure of thin alabaster) is hung in the middle, a thousand pointed rays glitter and are reflected over the place."[11] The scene of writing is dazzling and heterocosmic: a fountain splashes, iron ores sparkle, an array of fragments center on a starry pendant of illumination. In the headquarters of neoclassical production, a lamp is already lighted.

While Abrams's study remains invaluable as a schematic and summary introduction to literary history, one that will long be read as a scholarly compendium of examples (and one that has obviously influenced and informed this dictionary), I take aim in this entry, as in the book, at Abrams's suggestion that new literary periods will be indicated by a parallel "mutation of metaphors" in discussions of mind and discussions of art.[12] In making the mirror a reflex image of a period, Abrams's critical practice stands, perhaps ironically, as an example of reflection or correspondence. He is then, as he says of Wordsworth, conflicted: perhaps better in his poetic assertions than in his critical method.[13] The supposed correspondences do not hold up to the scrutiny of keyword search; mirrors and lamps serve better as emblems of a canon defined post hoc than as leading indicators of change. And a fin de siècle turning point, as argued in the previous entry, may be better indicated by the rise of **Metal** than the decline of **Mirror** metaphors. At the least, a new attempt to revise Abrams's history of Romanticism in terms of the industrial revolution and its metaphors may break the reflex image that intellectual history has too long assigned to the eighteenth century.[14]

Of course, Abrams is not the only historian to advert to optics in periodization: William Ivins's and Erwin Panofsky's studies of perspective stand as influential models of modern rationalization.[15] Herbert Grabes's study of mirror-metaphors, titled *The Mutable Glass*, focuses on the century between 1550 and 1650, in which the mirror metaphor is described as occurring "with especially marked frequency."[16] More recently, Richard Rorty, rereading Grabes and others with Ryle's philosophical concerns foregrounded, strongly associates the mirror with a correspondence theory of truth: "The picture which holds traditional philosophy captive is that of the mind as a great mirror, containing various representations—some accurate, some not—and capable of being studied by pure, non-empirical methods."[17] Locating a decisive shift in the seventeenth century, Claudio Guillén observes that perspective becomes a philosophical metaphor at the same time that Newton incorporates optics among the laws of nature. Similarly, Dan Edelstein suggests that the new instruments of optics (microscopes and telescopes) sparked the ancient-modern quarrel in France, precipitating the new Enlightenment narrative.[18]

Certainly, mirror metaphors of mind have a very long history and appear even to transcend Western cultural uses, but I hope to have pointed up other metaphors as prevalent, if not more so (**Empire** and **Inhabitants**), in the eighteenth century.[19] Why the fascination with mirrors, lamps, lenses and periodization? Is it because periodization would work by means of reflection that it cannot help but regard itself in the figure of the mirror? If, for Abrams, Romanticism is "an attempt to overcome the cleavage between subject and object" (65), then almost any metaphor should do (mirror, lamp, camera obscura, fountain, harps, and breezes) because almost all metaphors of mind identify mind and matter.

Mirrors All Round

Mirrors are increasingly available in England in the late seventeenth century. Lord Foppington, in John Vanbrugh's *The Relapse*, typifies a new involvement with one's own reflection in both private and public. Foppington's library is furnished with books and mirrors, and when he leaves home, he goes to a coffeehouse where he can promenade with "Looking-glasses all raund." That his vain reflections are not reliably accurate is performed, in part, by his vowel shifts. His pretention repeatedly converts *o* to *a*, and his life is reported to be "an eternal raund O of Delights."[20] Foppington's superficies, his affectation of affectation, are typical of Restoration theatrics and significant in the self-reflexive comedy (a self-aware sequel) in which another of its characters, Loveless, goes to the theater only to find his "very Character" represented on the stage (24). That the theater is a mirror is an early modern commonplace, but as discussed below, the metaphor, as in Vanbrugh's text, may be turned right round and prove disorienting in application.

"How then can we represent, by a sensible image, the mind as a theatre to its own actings?" Boswell asks in a periodical essay, late in the next century, only to answer in a way that mixes cameral interiority and mirroring: "Let us conceive a spacious saloon, in which our thoughts and passions exert themselves, and let its walls be encrusted with mirrour, for the purpose of reflection, in the same manner that rooms in voluptuous oriental countries are said to be finished for the purposes of increasing sensual delight."[21] Voluptuous and masturbatory in its sensibility, Boswell's image is self-involved but may also reflect on a satirical number of the *Spectator* in which, in a dream vision, a beau's pineal gland is dissected and found decorated with a thousand little "Faces or Mirrours," in which the vain soul must "have been always taken up in contemplating her own Beauties."[22] Or it may allude to Versailles's famous *Galerie des Glaces*, which was opened in 1682 for court functions. In Boswell's vision of silvered interiority, subjectivity looks outward to itself; it is a confusing scene, glimpsed in a paragraph in which the metaphor appears, that mixes mirrors, windows, stage sets, and painted surfaces: views through and views reflected back. But for Boswell, especially, as a biographer of Johnson and an author of personal journals, the mirror imagery is apt. In *The Life of Johnson* he records himself making "pretty" allusions: "LORD TRIMBLESTOWN. 'True, Sir. As the ladies love to see themselves in a glass; so a man likes to see himself in his journal.' . . . BOSWELL. 'And as a lady adjusts her dress before a mirror, a man adjusts his character by looking at his journal.'"[23]

Boswell's imagery may be multiply reflected, catching its conceit from still other works in which stage and page correspond and serve as mirrors to the mind. Reading Boswell's journal against Addison and Steele's journalistic and dramatic writing, one recent critic would have us gloss "reflection" in this context as closer in meaning to "mediation" than mirroring; one genre is as a mirror held up to another.[24] The point is taken: in Steele's *Conscious Lovers*, Bevil Junior walks onstage reading *Spectator* no. 159 ("The Visions of Mirzah") and declares, "Such an Author consulted in a Morning, sets the Spirit for the Vicissitudes of the Day, better than the Glass does a Man's Person."[25] The irony that Steele's character is reading Steele's sometime coauthor Addison's essay would not have been lost on the audience. Such recognition crosses further generic distinctions. Reportedly finding his mirror-journal conceit in a 1698 funeral sermon delivered by Bishop Atterbury (the admission comes just after the exchange with Trimblestown), Boswell pleads coincidence, not plagiarism. Indeed, in Atterbury's oration, the gender lines are drawn differently: the journal is that of the deceased Lady Cutts, a manuscript that is both a "true naked History" and the "Glass" in which "she every Day dress'd her mind."[26]

Because books and plays are conventionally figured as mirrors, **Writing** metaphors and mirror metaphors may overlap. In Oliver Goldsmith's *Citizen of the World*, the "looking-glass of Lao," a fictional prop that "reflects the mind as well as the body," is employed in a moralized dream vision related by Goldsmith's narrator, Lien Chi.[27] A series of women peer into the "magic lanthorn, by which folks can see themselves on the inside" and are variously repulsed by the deformities discovered (1:197). When the final woman tried by the instrument returns an unblotted image, white as an "unwritten page," the punch line comes quickly to conclude the fiction: she is deaf and dumb, "a fool from her cradle," and we are to imagine her without experience (1:201).

From Addison and Steele's *Spectator* papers to Henry Mackenzie's *The Mirror* and after, such reflectors multiply in periodical writing.[28] In this last publication, Hamlet's instructions to the players, concerning the "mirror held up to nature," is explicitly quoted in the first number, while in the eighth number, Goldsmith's "mental reflector" may return as a pocket mirror "of a convenient size."[29] The author (Mr. Mirror) receives a letter from an unknown correspondent named Vitreus about a "Dervise" or "Mussulman" and a magical mirror—here too is more of Goldsmith's Orientalism, in which an Eastern character gives back an image of the West. Looking into the mirror, one sees one's own motives or the true character of others; give the mirror a tilt and the self-image by which people "reckon themselves" appears.

The Mirror and Philosophy of Mind

Eighteenth-century mirrors, like those of the previous century, are characteristically small, rarely affording full-length views. Accordingly, as with other metaphors of mind recorded in these pages, mirror metaphors center in various faculties: the conscience is a place of reflection, the lover's heart a looking glass. Julien Offray de La Mettrie depicts a person of weak judgment as having an imagination "abandoned to itself"—or too much employed in "looking at itself in the mirror of its sensations."[30] The metaphor is available as behaviorist optics: the eyes are figured as mirrors of the heart in several poems, the face the mirror of interiority, and D'Urfey describes habit as the mirror of the mind. Writing and speech likewise mirror thought and the imagination, with Shaftesbury playing powerfully on the figure in his essay on soliloquy, in which authors are encouraged to talk to themselves, developing the speculative habit, "so as virtually to carry about with 'em a sort of *Pocket-Mirrour*."[31] Adam Smith—with Shaftesbury surely in mind—describes "society," or rather "the countenance and behaviour of those [one] lives with," as a mirror in which the "propriety and impropriety" of one's own passions and the "beauty and deformity" of one's mind may be viewed.[32] (Smith's figure, with looking-glass logic, makes the face a kind of mirror.) Devotional writers carry reflex still farther, with wisdom or the soul made a mirror of God—made in his image.

The mirror, as emblem, equivocates. In engravings, both Vanity and Prudence consider their reflection in hand-held mirrors, the same posed figure proving allegorical of vice and virtue.[33] The critic Jean Hagstrum notes that Samuel Johnson's definitions divide "MIRROR" into two conflicting senses: particular reflection and ideal pattern. The mirror figure, of course, has a long and complicated prehistory inflected by any number of Neoplatonic and Pauline assertions (1 Corinthians 13:12 and 2 Corinthians 3:18) and invested, because of developments in glassmaking, with new meaning in the early modern moment. The metaphors of mind, premised in duplicity, promote paradoxes: competing images (mirror and mind's eye) confuse spectator and spectacle, idealism and realism.[34] As Richard Rorty explains, simplifying in order to focus on epistemological implications, the mind is "glassy—mirror-like—for two reasons": first, "it takes on new forms without being changed," and second, "mirrors are made of a substance which is purer, finer grained, more subtle, and more delicate than most."[35] Indeed, in such philosophical uses the mirror metaphor is often used to mark a difference between the object and reflected image.

Self-consciousness requires self-regard and results in multiplication by way of division (see **Inhabitants**). Walter Charleton, for one, in his *Natural History of the Passions*, pictures the rational soul "speculating the impressions, or images represented to her by the Sensitive, as by a mirrour."[36] Ralph Cudworth would sharpen the differences between sensation and intellection, arguing ad absurdum that if intellection were "mere Passion from without, or the bare Reception of Adventitious Forms, then no Reason could be given at all why a Mirrour or Looking-glass should not understand."[37] And in the triple comparison cited from Cudworth among the epigraphs to this entry, the mirror, the eye, and the mind are compared and contrasted, with the eye proving to be "nothing else but a Mirror or Looking-glass" but one that Cudworth cannot help but personify in the discussion that follows so that it might, in a strange passage, "dispute with the Mind or Intellect" about the workings of a watch—"a *Self-moving Machine*"—reflected in a mirror (151, 155). Forbes of Pitsligo makes the same point but with more humor: "a Glass, tho' it may be said to receive the Image of a Beau, and he really sees somewhat of himself in it; yet it can hardly be said to see any thing of him."[38]

As if to controvert Cudworth and Forbes of Pitsligo and illustrate the difficulty of such figures for reflection, an anonymous it-narrative, titled "Adventures of a Mirror" and published in the *Lady's Magazine* (January 1791), presents a fictional mirror that is both narrator and narrative object. Installed in a stately mansion, the mirror meets the human inhabitants and reports on them, and subsequent owners, in a series of letters. Believing at first the lady of the house, whose eye beams with delight, admires the narrator-mirror and not her own reflection, the mirror explains to the reader its initial and embarrassing confusion of image and object: "my silly fancy represented that she was admiring *me*." When in a few days the mirror must listen to "My lord" practicing a speech, unable to "consent" ("what I cannot, in such cases, refuse"), domestic satire turns more political. In the next letter, the mirror repurposes a pun from the first: placed in company, "seeing all that were present, and every minute circumstance that passed. How could I then avoid making *reflections*?"[39]

In Locke—to take up the most studied example—the mind is itself a kind of mirror and the understanding an eye. In the one passage much cited in discussions of the philosopher, simple ideas, when offered to the mind, "*the Understanding can* no more refuse to have, nor alter, when they are imprinted, nor blot them out, and make new ones in it self,"—no more, that is, "than a mirror can refuse, alter, or obliterate the Images or *Ideas*, which the Objects set before it, do therein produce" (*Essay* II.i.25). The reading of Locke's conception of the mind as passive, in Abrams as elsewhere, centers here. But not often remarked on is the syntax of Locke's analogy, which on closer inspection presents difficulty: tenor may be mistaken for vehicle in mutual comparison as we read that in *mirrors* are produced "*Ideas*" when objects are set before them.[40] And then the mirror may be construed, if only momentarily, as a mind, and Cudworth's and Forbes's counterintuitive examples appear vindicated of absurdity. Or perhaps, Locke's verbs "blot" and "obliterate," as Goldsmith seems also to have recognized, suggest the proximity of **Mirror** and **Writing** metaphors. Or—but this association is still farther fetched, perhaps over literalized—the early modern practice of scratching poetry and other messages onto glass surfaces is involved by remote association.

The mind is a mirror. Yet Locke pointedly refuses the mirror metaphor a few chapters later in his discussion of primary and secondary qualities. Secondary qualities (heat, color, and flavor), while "commonly thought to be the same in those Bodies, that those *Ideas* are in us, the one the perfect resemblance of the other, as they are in a Mirror" (II.viii.16), are the effects of bulk, figure, number and motion and therefore *not* in fact so resembling. Indeed, reflection is literalized and located without in Locke's analysis: light "rebounding" from the object provides us with an idea of its color (II.viii.19).

Still elsewhere Locke analogizes ideas to anamorphic pictures, made coherent by the introduction of a cylindrical mirror (II.xxix.8).[41] Citing this instance alongside other optical metaphors, Peter Walmsley has suggested that for Locke the mind is not a surface of reflection but a kind of "experimental machine," like Hooke's microscope or Boyle's air pump, "a place where the anomalous becomes expected."[42] Such complicated and conflicting structures of optical analogy have been carefully treated by William Walker, whose close readings of the *Essay* remain a sure guide to the shifting metaphorics of vision sketched above. The critic Joanna Picciotto, likewise, characterizes lens metaphors, which are frequently appropriated in the high and low literature of the period, as interposed between Abrams's binary literary models (the mirror and the lamp), emphasizing further that much of the experimental optics of the seventeenth and eighteenth centuries was influential *textually* "through the virtual witnessing enabled by print."[43] Locke is hardly the case in point that Abrams and others might make him.

False Mirrors

Because early modern mirrors are small, dull, and dim, and therefore provide unreliable reflections, a great preponderance of eighteenth-century mirror metaphors are delivered with concern. In Locke, demonstration, as opposed to direct intuition, involves dimmer reflections and the lessening of "clearness and distinctness" (IV.ii.6); and in Hume, likewise, when we reflect on past sentiments, "our Thought is a faithful Mirror," but "the Colours which it employs are faded and dead."[44] The figure of the false or dark mirror calls up Corinthians 13:12, "For now we see through a glass, darkly," but Francis Bacon is another locus classicus; for it is Bacon who, in 1605, likens the mind of man to "an inchanted Glasse, full of Superstitions; Apparitions, and Impostures."[45] The metaphor proves proverbial by 1678, when it is collected by John Ray (as a Scottish proverb: "A mirk mirrour is a man's mind").[46] In his popular *Essay on Human Life*, Lord Paget figures bias as a mirror in the mind: "Thro' this, as in a false or flatt'ring Glass/Things seem to change their Natures as they pass."[47]

When Pope writes, "Wit's false Mirror held up Nature's Light," he identifies reflection and illumination; the mirror of art returns and even supports ("holds up") the light of nature.[48] To mix and match language from this famous line from *Essay on Man* with a more famous one from the *Essay on Criticism*, by means of a "false Mirror," "True Wit . . . gives us back the Image of our Mind."[49] But taking Pope's claims as image and index, the mirror can be particularly hard to locate: do we identify it with lines of verse or with the mind that frames them? Is it within or without? The poem or the poet? Mirrors figure depth and erase boundaries, tricking us out of ourselves. Pope imitates classical models but also contributes influentially to poetic diction, the neat reversals effected in his couplets reflected and refracted by poet after poet.

Although the phrase is not found in Pope, "fancy's mirror," like the near bigram "false mirror," is a regularly recurring fragment of poetic diction, easily searched for and located in online text collections. In fact, I have collected over thirty examples, frequently finding the phrase filling out two iambic feet of unexceptional verse. Thomas Warton and Henry Jones, to select two of the better poets, almost echo each other: "But still in Fancy's mirror sees" (Warton's "Ode on Approach of Summer") and "Still to my Sight, in Fancy's

Mirror seen" (Jones's *Merit. A Poem*).[50] In these contexts, fancy's mirror is associated with dreams, memory, and forecasts. In William Somervile's popular, much-reprinted hunt poem *The Chace*, "Fancy's Mirrour" makes visible past glory. The teenage Falconar sisters vary the phrase by the insertion of a commonplace adjective: "fancy's vary'd mirror" shows future prospects in the Falconars' poem and in other verses. When the faculty is fully personified, fancy's mirror becomes an attribute. "Young Fancy" is arrayed in a "rainbow vest" and made to carry a mirror in a minor poem by Henry Headley.[51] In a set piece by the perhaps even more minor Edmund Rack, Queen Fancy, also rainbow-vested, looks into her "oval mirror," of a "wondrous texture . . . surpassing human thought." The mirror gives back Fancy's changeful mind as she looks on her own "airy visions." In still another poem, personification works more strangely when William Hayley figures Shakespeare's mind as Fancy's "bright mirror."[52]

As noted above, mirror metaphors may be slightly on the increase in the later part of the century. Sentimentality polishes the mind's mirror, improving a surface for images to float upon. So Sterne would clarify the understanding of the "motes, or specks of opacular matter, which if left swimming therein, might hinder conception and spoil all"; and Harley, the protagonist of *The Man of Feeling*, has a mind like "the mirrors of the ladies," which "have a wonderful effect in bettering their complexions."[53] Sensibility and sympathy lead to sublime reflection. Goethe's Young Werther, glowing with enthusiasm, imagines that paper he writes on might become a mirror of his soul as his soul is the mirror of God (*der Spiegel des unendlichen Gottes*). But the earliest English translation is troubled by the enthusiasm of the figure, reducing it to a wish that great conceptions might be described with the same warmth as they are *impressed* on the soul.[54]

Reflections in Nature

In Ann Radcliffe's novels, reversals of interior and exterior are dramatized in passages of description. Reflective surfaces of lakes are personized with bosoms that glow with reflection; cliffs have heads and faces; lakes, bosoms; and trees wave their arms. Almost any surface may focalize another, and a blurriness results that is written directly into the grammar and syntax. In *A Sicilian Romance* a lake is personified, or rather a character's perceptions are hypostatized: "A shadowy sequestered dell appeared buried deep among the rocks, and in the bottom was seen a lake, whose clear bosom reflected the impending cliffs, and the beautiful luxuriance of the overhanging shades."[55] Who or what is mirrored, lake or duke? If, as many critics suggest, Radcliffe's novels are an early locus of the development of free indirect discourse, it is this sort of ambiguity that encourages the subtle elisions of landscape and mindscape.

The "projective," "creative" mind of the eighteenth century is centered on a fancy or imagination, which is readily personified (**Inhabitants**) or figured in images drawn from both optics and visual art: in many cases to look into a mirror is to discover a face. Mirror-minds are found throughout Radcliffe's fiction, but I will seize one in particular in order to bring this entry to its conclusion: in *The Italian*, Vivaldi's mind resembles "the glass of a magician, on which the apparitions of long-buried events arise, and as they fleet away, point portentously to shapes half-hid in the duskiness of futurity."[56] The gothic mode, as Terry Castle has emphasized in "The Spectralization of the Other" and "Phantasmagoria and the Metaphorics of Modern Reverie," involves the supernaturalization of the world of thought: the brain is haunted by phantoms, fancy paints magical scenes, mixing colors juxtaposing will-o'-the-wisp lights with lengthening shadows; it is these visual metaphors, uncanny in being both reflective and projective, that invest the popular subgenre with special interest.[57]

Castle's essays move confidently from Radcliffe's metaphors to devices of another sort: the lamps, lenses, and mirrors rigged up by eighteenth-century impresarios and showmen in popular specter shows and other magic-lantern demonstrations. Castle makes us see the former (Radcliffe) as related to the latter (phantasmagoria), and her literary-historical case is made most convincingly. Of course, critics of all stripes almost cannot help but take literature as a mirror of history: an imaginary form of the real conditions of existence.[58] But the metaphorics of reflection as set forth in the foregoing pages should give us pause when we reconcile the representations of long-buried events and their eventual reception, and here is where Terry Castle's criticism excels. A gothic novelist like Radcliffe sets her anachronistic romances in a darkly imagined past while, at the same time, allowing her narrative events to stand in portentous relation to her own half-hidden present. Castle's analysis works similarly, and in doing so, it upends Abrams's intellectual history.[59] Turned about in perspective are the image and its object: the mirror is promoted as a thematic and, at the same time, located as an historical artifact.

How should intellectual history pinpoint a change in what M. H. Abrams calls "popular epistemology"? In the last decade of the eighteenth century, the French philosopher Destutt de Tracy founded the study of ideology, imagining a superscience in which the metaphors of painting and mirrors might mix (his ideological analyses are figured as "miroirs où les objets se peignent nettement et dans leurs justes proportions"[mirrors in which the objects are painted distinctly and in their correct proportions]).[60] From Tracy to Marx to Althusser and after, ideology and its critique is continually figured in terms of mirrors, lanterns, and cameras.

Periodizing in the French revolutionary moment, Edmund Burke invokes an age of chivalry and romance, figured as past, and a succeeding age of "sophisters, oeconomists, and calculators."[61] But *which* is the age of Enlightenment? If we must take the measure of the competing periods, let us tally the mirror metaphors and consider the frequencies as an opportunity for further reflection. But I count not more than two hundred mirror metaphors and observe that a surprising percentage of them fall on the near side of 1789.[62] With final apologies, then, to Richard Rorty and M. H. Abrams, these metaphors, when sorted through, are rarely straightforward examples of correspondence theory and should not simply be taken as emblems of an empiricist moment. What imaginary relations to real conditions are reflected in the collection of metaphors remain to be determined. This entry is submitted not as the final word on the matter, but as a prompt to better, more thorough accounting.

10 Rooms

COLLOCATED KEYWORDS: Cabinet, Cell, Chamber, Closet, Interior, Room, Window

COUNT OF METAPHORS IN DATABASE[1] (1700–1799): 550

And now am I to the *third Story* come;
The highest, and, alas, the weakest Room!
That once Experience would but cross the Jest,
And prove the highest *Chamber* furnisht best.
For *Knowledge (Nature's guide)* should quarter there,
And *Judgment*, her most trusty *Councellour.*
Invention, *Memory*, and *Wit*, should stay;
And all their Treasures in this *Turrit* lay.
But for such *Guests* I have no fitting Room;
Or if I had, I've no such *Guests* to come.

—Thomas Shipman, "The Rent Due," 1683

In this Design of Martin to investigate the Diseases of the mind, he thought nothing so necessary as an Enquiry after the *Seat* of the *Soul*; in which at first he laboured under great uncertainties. Sometimes he was of opinion that it lodged in the Brain, sometimes in the Stomach, and sometimes in the Heart. Afterwards he thought it absurd to confine that sovereign Lady to one apartment, which made him infer that she shifted it according to the several functions of life: The Brain was her Study, the Heart her State-room, and the Stomach her Kitchen. But as he saw several Offices of life went on at the same time, he was forced to give up this hypothesis also.

—Alexander Pope and John Arbuthnot, *Memoirs of Martinus Scriblerus* (1741)

Yet not even these can find an asylum from cares;—though the soul, like a hermit in his cell, sits quiet in the bosom, unruffled by any tempest of its own, it suffers from the rude blasts of others faults.

—Eliza Haywood, *The History of Jemmy and Jenny Jessamy* (1753)

SIR THOMAS
I suppose, Gentlemen, my memory, or mind, to be a chest of drawers, a kind of bureau; where, in separate cellules, my different knowledge on different subjects is stor'd.

—Samuel Foote, *The Patron* (1764), II.ii

My pineal gland could you but view,
You'd scarce believe your eyes see true:
There's such a jumble; good and bad,
All sorts of thoughts, may there be had;
Like broker's shop, where we may find
Goods that belong to half mankind.

—Mary Savage, "Letter to Miss E.B. at Bath" (1777)

See also **Inhabitants** and **Writing**

"People tend to identify their minds with the 'place' where they conduct their secret thoughts," or so claims the twentieth-century philosopher of mind Gilbert Ryle.[2] In the eighteenth century, the closet or study is the most readily identifiable place in which secret thoughts are conducted. It is a place of withdrawal and meditation—a place of retreat and retirement and a scene associated with prayer, letter writing, and reading. A secretarial space, a room within a room, an eighteenth-century closet is furnished with bureaus and cabinets; locked drawers contain secret contracts. But, as Ryle, Stuart Hampshire, and "extended-mind" philosophers have emphasized, secret thoughts may also be located in public places: covert agents pass notes, sharps win card games with winks and legerdemain, Freemasons know each other by grips and handshakes, stockjobbers trade "inside" information, conspirators plot plots just out of earshot, and soliloquists learn strategies of abbreviation and silence.

After the Great Fire of 1666 burned away much of London's core topography, the subsequent period seized the city as a carte blanche and redrew the map, imagining new spaces and building new churches, new pleasure gardens, new shopping districts, and new homes.[3] With architectural history of the long eighteenth century serving as an index of developments in *mentalité*, critics and historians link domestic interiors and deepening psychological interiority.[4] Bourgeois interiority depends on the construction of bourgeois interiors, and one literary historian claims, in a by-now standard formulation, that "imaginative interiority" is an effect of civil war and revolution, "produced in the interests of the bourgeois class which came to power in the second half of the seventeenth century."[5] Early modern literary critics would postpone the emergence of interiority to the eighteenth century; many eighteenth-century scholars defer its arrival further still.[6]

Taking my cue from a distinction between inwardness and interiority neatly drawn in an essay by the philosopher Stephen Toulmin, I examine the ways in which the mind, the soul, and the heart are variously imagined in or as different rooms, both private and public.[7] The analysis of these metaphors discovers inwardness as a rhetorical practice in the figuration of *interiors* and cannot be taken as representations of *interiority*—which is another metaphor for the mind. Simultaneously, I revisit the critical commonplace in which interiority is supposed something that emerges in the long eighteenth century (often in the eighteenth-century novel). What emerges, in fact, are the metaphors, which are to be enumerated. To be sure, *interiority* is most awkwardly said to emerge (from where? from within what?). Specified metaphorically, its location (temporal, spatial) is both obvious and abstruse, indoors or intracranial.

In literary histories, fiction is said to be concerned with representation of an interiority that cannot be located outside of fiction. Here a room is an interior that figures interiority; interiority, the aspect of an interior. Beginning with lonely cells, private closets, and other "inmost" rooms, and concluding with crowded theaters and tea rooms, I will explore putatively secret or purely private spaces as they become available—in figures and fictions—to the pryings of publicity. The inability of inwardness or interiority to secure a private place is read as fact of the matter as much as of metaphysics: any interior, almost by definition, is subject to invasion.

Because I am convinced that any inner process must needs be located by outward criteria, I will maintain that no room is truly private.[8] Interiority is ever little more than a metaphor. Syllepsis proves a helpful figure for breaking and entry, and metaphors of furnishing—of the "furniture of the mind"—will also be useful for marking metaphorical distinctions and situating acts of thinking. Where citations of revisionist histories of subjectivity and interiority appear in the text below, I would complicate and deny claims for the arrival of interiority (bourgeois or otherwise), whether in the late seventeenth or early eighteenth century or later (in any century, really). The revisions are revised lest they literalize interiority.

Interiority and Inwardness

"INTERIOUR" is defined by Samuel Johnson as "internal; inner; not outward; not superficial." The word appears in the titles of early modern travel literature (as in the *interior* of America or Africa) and in geometry textbooks (*interior* angles). It does not reliably connote architectural interiors (*interior* design) until the beginning of the nineteenth century. Many are the varieties of interiority, but the earliest attestation of "interiority" in the *OED* is from John Norris's 1701 *Essay Towards the Theory of the Ideal or Intelligible World*, which quotes from Norris's discussions of Augustinian "interiority" and "community" of truth.[9] In his metaphysical *Essay* Norris describes an "interior Truth, whose *School* and *Oracle* is within our Breast" (2:170). The most "direct and natural Way" to knowledge is "to retire into our selves, and there with humble and silent Attention, both to consult and receive the Answers of interior Truth, even that Divine Master which teaches in the School of the Breast" (2:571). One retires or retreats to the interior, which is figured as a schoolroom. The Platonizing churchman, philosopher, and poet Norris is openly indebted to Augustine here and quotes from the *De Vera Religione* (xxxix.72): "*Nolie* [*sic*] *foras ire, in te ipsum redi, in interiore homine habitat veritas*" (2:573). Interior man (*interiore homine*) is obviously not an eighteenth-century invention, or even an early modern invention. Inner and outer are used to structure distinctions between spirit and matter as early as the fourth century.[10]

But I would begin with the closet or cabinet—a private, domestic interior—and not Norris's more ambiguous "School of the Breast," in which the self masters and is mastered by divine teachings. In this entry the closet, study, back-shop office, or cabinet is the privileged space of retreat from public education, business, and social relations but also the private space in which the public is reflected upon. It is the reflective, inside-out structure that will feature in what Kant will characterize as a "Copernican Revolution" that transposes inner and outer, subject and object. The eighteenth century is recruited in the stories literary historians tell about the appearance of "deep subjectivity." Between empiricism and idealism, the novel is supposed the paradigmatic literary practice that "publicizes the private."[11] Monographs by Armstrong, Bender, Gallagher, Lynch, Varey, and Wall focus on the novel's representations of interiority, in one way or another expanding upon or complicating Georg Lukács insight that "the novel tells of the adventure of interiority."[12]

While I have discovered the bulk of my room metaphors in verse, I acknowledge the novel does reliably deliver representations of domestic spaces honeycombed with rooms. Closets, cabinets, and private rooms figure importantly as interior spaces into which characters withdraw.[13] In the seventh chapter of *Don Quixote* the barber and the curate wall off Quixote's study in an attempt to cure him of his madness. Robinson Crusoe's fortifications include the construction and furnishing of a house, a fort, and a cave—his main residence—walled in and walled in again. Pamela and Clarissa lock themselves up in their closets, these private spaces often read as "metaphors for private consciousness" or as "an image of the mind."[14] Arabella, the female Quixote, discovers her mother's romances when they are brought out of her mother's closet and placed in her father's library; but the books are soon relocated to Arabella's own closet, producing a quixotism that will not lift until they are banished from her private chambers and her constant study. Much of the self-reflexive drama of *Tristram Shandy* is located in the closet in which the narrator's life and opinions are penned. Caleb Williams becomes obsessed with a trunk that his employer keeps locked up in his closet. Lady Delacour admits Belinda into her closet and into her secret only after Belinda has proven herself trustworthy.

Architectural historian Mark Girouard argues that the latter half of the seventeenth century witnessed an increase in interior privacy; that is, a recessed "withdrawing" room—the closet—became an increasingly important space in English houses.[15] This closet is a place of confidence and a place in which a prince traditionally only meets with his most trusted advisors. It is a private place where secrets are shared and kept. Virtuosos store their instruments, coins and medals, specimens, notes, and books in their cabinet or closet. The young lady hides her letters in an *escritoire*.[16] One retires to a private place, an "inmost room," for any of a variety of reasons: to read, to study, to meditate, to conduct business, to write letters, or to pray. Scripture endorses the last activity explicitly: the King James translation of Matthew 6:6 instructs, "When thou prayest, enter into thy closet."[17] It is this private space that, in part, affords a private life—and *affording* is very much to the point, as not everyone can afford a room of his or her own.[18] The practices and exercises that mark "private" thought are especially suited to the interior world of the Protestant bourgeois home. (Although, as is evident in many of the metaphors collected under this heading, spaces inward and private may be as easily troped academic or monastic.)

So it is in our histories of early modern culture that the *withdrawing* bourgeoisie indicates an *emerging* interiority. The literary critic follows developments in architectural history in order to understand the practice of inwardness or the "technologies of subjectivity," but in doing so he or she should be careful to avoid the oxymoronic narrative of withdrawal and emergence and not fall prey to the metaphor of interiority in question. New cultural practices arise or emerge; *bourgeois interiority* as such cannot. It will not do to discover a new phenomenological depth of subjectivity in the seventeenth and eighteenth centuries and claim that novelistic characterization or free indirect discourse is developed thereafter to represent it. People have long identified their minds with secret, private spaces, but the mind does not emerge as its own place. Interiority is always and only metaphorical insofar as there is no special objectless, inner place in which thought happens. There are, obviously, interiors, and these are often favored sites for meditation, contemplation, and prayer. People identify their minds with the places where they conduct their secret thoughts, and while I am sure that there have been secret thoughts and secret places for as long as there have been secrets, not all secret or private spaces have been bourgeois. Indeed, many of the spaces discussed thus far belong in elite, aristocratic, even monastic settings. In documenting the history of these metaphors, one must be careful not to conflate bourgeois interiors and bourgeois interiority.

Interiority is at the center of many literary histories of the eighteenth century, and yet interiority itself is a concept that too often remains unanalyzed. Theorists of interiority may be prone to mistake a metaphor of mind for an explanatory device, confusing the practice of a silent, internalized version of a public activity with a figurative representation of that activity in some strange (often ostensibly literal) space.[19] Inwardness is taken for interiority. A version of the mistake is native to the period: Stephen Toulmin faults a "literal-minded" tradition of early modern natural philosophy, one that includes Descartes, Locke, Newton, and Harvey, with making interiority not just a matter of being in the mind "but, quite literally, [in] the interior of our *heads*" ("Inwardness" 4). Newton, who pictures the floor plan of the brain as designed around "little Sensoriums" into which images of the external world are carried, is identified as a key figure in this tradition.[20]

In Toulmin's analysis, the inwardness of mental life involves those practices—often literary practices—that strain our language; interiority signals a mistaken position in the philosophy of mind. Inwardness is "an acquired feature of our experience, a *product*, in part, of our cultural history but in part also of our individual development" (5); interiority belongs to a tradition both theoretical and literal-minded that locates the life of the mind in "not just the interior of our *minds* but, quite literally, the interior of our *heads*" (4). The trouble with interiority, claims Toulmin, is that it "telescopes *for purposes of theory* half-a-dozen distinctions that *in practice* cut along quite different lines: the private as against the public, the internal as against the external, the moral as against the physical, the mental as against the material, and so on." To recast Toulmin's distinction in the terms of this text: notions of interiority produce mind-body dualism and its attendant metaphors.

The Pineal Gland

One amusing literal-minded fable of interiority can be found in *Spectator* no. 275, in which Addison, taking a hint from Swift's *A Tale of a Tub*, describes the dissection of a brain.[21] After spending a day engaged with an assembly of virtuosos, microscopists, and dabblers in anatomy, Mr. Spectator dreams of attending the dissection of a beau's head. As the "imaginary Operator" opens up the beau's head for inspection, Mr. Spectator reports, "The *Pineal Gland*, which many of our Modern Philosophers suppose to be the Seat of the Soul,[22] smelt very strongly of Essence and Orange-Flower Water, and was encompas'd with a kind of Horny Substance, cut into a thousand little Faces or Mirrours, which were imperceptible to the naked Eye; insomuch that the Soul, if there had been any here, must have been always taken up in contemplating her own Beauties" (2:570–1).

The beau's pineal gland is figured as a fop's private dressing room. As the men of science explore the brain, they observe cavities packed with frippery, love-letters, and pricked dance cards. They observe two large cavities located on either side of the head, "that on the right Side filled with Fictions, Flatteries and Falsehoods, Vows, Promises and Protestations; that on the left with Oaths and Imprecations" (2:571). The architecture of the brain is pictured, as if the Spectator were giving us a tour of the beau's lodgings and not of his brain: here is where he keeps his handkerchiefs, here his billets-doux. The most private, interior of "places" is identified with a private interior. The picture is made explicit in the final paragraphs of the issue as the Spectator reports, "When we had thoroughly examin'd this Head with all its *Apartments*, and its several Kinds of *Furniture*, we put up the Brain, such as it was, into its proper Place, and laid it aside under a broad piece of Scarlet Cloth" (2:573, emphasis added).

Although the architectural metaphors are a departure from strict linguistic propriety, the brain, in the end, is returned to its "proper Place." But the logic of dream dissection further complicates the question of interiority: whose inside do we explore? The sleeping Spectator, whose dream vision furnishes the details of the beau's anatomy, is surely at home in bed (sleeping under scarlet bedclothes?). Were this a *Tatler* paper—a publication that explicitly conflated topicality, literary topoi, and topography by printing news under headings that named different locations in London ("From Will's Coffee-house,"

"From St James's Coffee-House," "From the Graecian")—its dateline would read "From my own Apartment."[23]

The conceit of the pineal gland as the seat or apartment of the soul is Cartesian. In November of 1619 René Descartes, theorist of the pineal gland, on his way back from the coronation of the Ferdinand II in Frankfurt and held up by the onset of winter, spent a whole day by himself in a *poêle*, or small stove-heated room. Descartes describes the setting in the second part of the *Discourse on Method*. The scene is well known in the history of philosophy, for it is the setting in which the rudiments of modern epistemology were famously worked out, where Descartes's mind turned inward and discovered itself as a thinking thing. Withdrawal is the key strategy of Cartesian epistemology.[24] In the dedicatory epistle to the *Meditations*, Descartes worries that his proofs will not be understood by many, because "they particularly demand a mind quite free from prejudices—a mind that can withdraw itself from commerce with the senses [*détacher du commerce des sens*]."[25] Cartesian meditation is a fantasy of withdrawal, and Descartes declares that he must "withdraw into solitude" before he can begin again from "first foundations" (57). A withdrawal from the senses is best achieved by this withdrawal into solitude. The mind is first identified with a space of retirement and is then identified with the pineal gland, the site or seat of thought.

Descartes wrote the *Meditations* in response to the queries provoked by the *Discourse*, and even though we visit no *poêle* in the *Meditations*, we are again conducted into the depths of inner space. Four years after the publication of the *Discourse*, Descartes rehearses the same rhetorical scene he used in that earlier work. In the first meditation, Descartes begins at fireside with a catalog of what can be doubted—"that I am here, sitting by the fire, wearing a winter dressing-gown, holding this piece of paper in my hands" (2:13). From this doubtfully described fireside where Descartes is writing out his thoughts, the reader is conducted to the most interior kernel of certainty: "I am, I exist" (61). Only when the world recedes, only when we work our way inward, is the *res cogitans* found.

The Inmost Room: Apartments and Private Cells

There are interiors within interiors, figures nested in literal spaces. The practice of retirement may be read both figuratively and literally, and the Quaker poet Mary Mollineux expresses these two parallel varieties of inwardness in the line "*In Heart, and in thy private Closet bow.*" Stephen Duck writes of Musidora, who "In her own Breast . . . seeks a calm Repose, / And shuns the crowded Rooms of *Belles* and *Beaux*."[26] As seen in **Inhabitants**, Montaigne figures the self as a crowded space and urges us to "reserve a back shop all our own," where we can converse with only ourselves, where the soul's only company is itself.[27] Montaigne's figuration gives a commercial twist to the *beatus ille* tradition.[28] (Recall Descartes's "commerce of the senses" quoted above.) More typically the retirement counterposes country life and court life; the happy man in retirement is pictured as having withdrawn to his country estate, the freehold that qualifies him as a full rights-bearing person under eighteenth-century law.[29] Wollstonecraft writes of man erecting "a pavilion in his own mind" to retire to, to evade rumor.[30] It is in the country that one flees the bustling city throngs and devotes time to reading the classics or to cultivating his garden—but perhaps a back shop will suffice for the middle-class merchant who has not yet made his fortune.

The mind or soul is identified as an inmost room or is there located, and therefore, like the French *appartement* or the beau's head, partitioned. To move inward is to move closer to a central closet or cabinet.[31] The "inmost rooms" in Blackmore's *Nature of Man* are the seat of government and consciousness. The inmost room may also be at the pineal center of things, where a sovereign presides from her "imperial seat" in the brain's "Presence-chamber"[32] over a court of sensory information (see **Empire**). Here again interiority is figured not in bourgeois terms but royal or aristocratic ones. If we are, as historians of consciousness, to associate interiority with a rising middle class, we must be prepared to explain how aristocratic floor plans newly structure middle-class heads.[33]

Fielding, in a well-known demurral, warns that it would be "an ill office in us to pay a Visit to the inmost Recesses of [Blifil's] Mind, as some scandalous People search into the most secret Affairs of their Friends, and often pry into their Closets and Cupboards only to discover their Poverty and Meanness to the World."[34] Fielding's use of a metaphor of mind stands almost as an ironic emblem of his narrative technique: to represent a character's thoughts and feelings is equal to prying in their "Closets and Cupboards." By contrast, in the same year *Tom Jones* was published, Thomas Edward sent a sonnet to Richardson, celebrating the novelist "whose magic skill / The close recesses of the Soul can find" (ll. 1–2).[35] Of course, Fielding's narrator is not wholly above invasion, and we see into Tom's mind and motives—into Sophia's too, on occasion. But then these two characters, unlike Blifil, seem to have interiors as well furnished as their facades are attractive. Prying will discover no meanness. Elsewhere in *Tom Jones* Fielding literalizes his metaphorics. Molly Seagrim, whose garret room "wanted the Conveniency of Closet," tries to hide the philosopher Square in a "little Hole" or "inclosed Place," but he is revealed by an accident of plot when a "wicked Rug [gets] loose from its Fastning" and discovers her lover to Tom Jones (2:144–5). A private place may quite suddenly become public, as when a blush or awkward lie betrays the unfaithful lover.[36]

To each mind, a room of its own. Hack writers, not unlike Molly, occupy garrets. As emphasized by sneering Augustan satirists, Grub Street writers with mean and narrow minds live in mean and narrow rooms; in rich contrast to the bare cell, gentlemen and virtuosos retire to well-furnished cabinets and closets.[37] In *Guardian* no. 39, attributed to George Berkeley, the narrator, named Ulysses Cosmopolita, takes some magical Cartesian snuff and leaves his "Body locked up safe in [his] Study" and repairs to the freethinking Grecian coffeehouse, "where, entring into the *Pineal Gland* of a certain eminent *Free-thinker*, [he makes his way] directly to the highest part of it, which is the Seat of the Understanding."[38] Expecting to find there "comprehensive Knowledge of all things Humane and Divine, . . . to [his] no small Astonishment," he finds "the place narrower than ordinary," with no "room for a Miracle, Prophesie, or Separate Spirit." The narrow philosophical soul has no room for God's oversized furniture or home visits from Jesus and the Holy Spirit. Descending "a Story lower, into the Imagination," Ulysses finds the room to be "larger indeed, but Cold and Comfortless" (1:155).

William Shenstone complains that "selfish sages" are cloistered, "Proud that their heart is narrow as their cell!"[39] The garret or cell is a poorly lit and poorly furnished space, and the hermit's or monk's cell is then a standard emblem of dangerous—often popish—isolation. In one ironic exception, John Tutchin, an outspoken anti-Catholic Whig writer, describes Virtue finding "Refuge in an honest Mind," the pentameter lines narrowing to trimeter: "There it securely dwells / Like *Anchorets* in Cells."[40] In Locke's *Essay* ideas are "rouzed and tumbled out of their dark Cells, into open Day-light, by some turbulent and tempestuous Passion" (II.x.7).[41] Cells are also found, often literally, in the mind or brain.[42] "Cell" and "dwell" supply internal or end rhymes in any number of philosophical poems, so that the mind or soul is personified as an inhabitant or guest who *dwells* in a *cell*—in more medical works, the brain's cellules.

In his poem "The Causes of Dreams," Henry Needler describes how the soul "by drowsy sleep oppress'd" retires "Into her private Cell . . . to Rest," while ideas revisit the "Traces of the humid Brain" and "Thro' beaten Paths their wand'ring Courses take, / And Images confus'd of things awake." Nocturnal bustling (the motions of a "liquid spirit'ous Train") outside the soul's bedroom is the stuff of dreaming, and dreams themselves are often figured as spirits or ghosts that haunt the house of the mind.[43] In Needler's poem, the self that withdraws to a private room to rest is duplicated within (at one recursive regress or figurative remove) by the parallel self, or soul, that withdraws into a metaphorical space. Needler does not so much explain the causes of dreams as picture for us a dreamer, locked in, besieged by noisy servants or spirits who haunt the hallways. Repeatedly, this association, if not conflation, of interiors and interiority presents itself—often in a syllepsis or zeugma, as in Mary Mollineux's parallel "heart" and "closet" noted above.

Charlotte Lennox, for example, writes, "But, in order to place this momentous Affair in a true Light, 'tis necessary to go back a little, and acquaint the Reader with what had passed in the Apartment; and also, following the Custom of the Romance and Novel-Writers, in the Heart, of our Heroine."[44] It is the custom of fiction to acquaint readers with what passes in both the apartment and the heart. The structure of Lennox's sentence fascinates—"what passed in the Apartment" and also "in the Heart" of our heroine—the metaphor of mind is split across the conjunction "and." The critic Ian Watt spells out a similar syllepsis and claims of privacy that "the domestic life and the private experience of the characters who belong to it: the two go together—we get inside their minds as well as inside their houses."[45] The eighteenth-century novelist, like Ulysses Cosmopolita in the *Guardian* or Mr. Spectator, can enter without detection into both the apartment *and* the heart of her characters. The telling of what passes in each of these spaces is captured in Lennox's verb "acquaint," a verb that has a quite specific technical sense in early modern epistemology.[46] Lennox runs "Heart" and "Apartment" together playfully; in the works of philosophers metaphors of interiority may be taken too seriously.

The situation of a self in an interior and the identifying—or rather *mistaking*—of that scene as a scene of interiority is a central element of dualism. The interior is just another space to think inside of; the metaphor in no way helps us to make sense of "interiority." The picture of the mind as an occupied space begs the question, because the metaphor of interiority includes an inhabitant with an unpictured, now second-order mind (see **Inhabitants**).[47] This is a classic case of the proposed explanation of a consciousness displacing the real issue into a homuncular, Cartesian tenant.[48] How are we to understand what goes on in the head of the personified soul, locked in its "private Cell," asleep and dreaming or awake and cogitating—perhaps even wandering through the rooms of the self? Does the soul dream too, or are we to understand our dreams as occurring outside of us—outside of the brain's inmost room? Our metaphors of mind generate vicious circles.

Camera Obscura

Two of what are now the best-known eighteenth-century metaphors of interiority are found in Locke's *Essay*, a work filled with architectural metaphors.[49] In the preliminary argument against the existence of innate ideas, Locke explains that we have ideas because we have sensations: "The Senses at first let in particular *Ideas*, and furnish the yet empty Cabinet" (*Essay* I.ii.15). Locke gives up his blank paper metaphor for an empty room, but this cabinet is also the scene in which all of the mental scribbling described in **Writing** may be pictured taking place. In book II of the *Essay* the cabinet reappears as a "Closet wholly shut from light" (II.xi.17). Here, Locke again makes the assertion that "external and internal Sensation, are the only passages that I can find, of Knowledge, to the Understanding. These alone, as far as I can discover, are the Windows by which light is let into this *dark Room*" (II.xi.17).[50] The paragraph continues, "would the Pictures coming into such a dark Room but stay there, and lie so orderly as to be found upon occasion, it would very much resemble the Understanding of a Man, in reference to all Objects of sight, and the *Ideas* of them." It is clear that Locke is describing a camera obscura. The window that lets in light is like the pinhole in a pinhole camera. *Camera* is Latin for chamber—which makes the mind a dark chamber.

Locke's dark room may be identified with the "dark closet" in which Newton conducted his optical experiments.[51] The Baptist preacher Benjamin Keach describes the "dark room" of the heart in his "Dialogue between a Young Professor and a Quaker," into which the door or window of faith lets in light.[52] And, as we have already seen under the heading **Animals**, a "dark Room" also appears in Dryden's *All for Love*: "*And yet the Soul, shut up in her dark Room, / Viewing so clear abroad, at home sees nothing.*"[53] In the letter that treats Lockean pedagogy and "home education," Pamela transcribes these same lines from Dryden "for the Beauty of the Thought."[54] The "dark Room" in Dryden's formulation is featureless—a dark, blind metaphor of an interiority that refuses to be pictured. The "Beauty of the Thought" derives, in part, from this particular opposition of "at home" and "abroad."[55] Home is a figment of being abroad; a dark, uncanny place, it is no place at all. "Without the help and the assistance of the senses," writes Locke elsewhere, the mind "can achieve nothing more than a labourer working in darkness behind shuttered windows."[56] What sort of work is this?

In the eighteenth century a "dark closet" is also a room in which a chamber pot or close stool is stored. The resulting scatological metaphor of mind is found in Swift (of course), who writes of the "human Understanding, seated in the Brain" that is troubled by those "vapours ascending from the lower faculties," which are comparable to the "fumes" that issue, as it were, "from a Jakes." And the metaphor returns in Fielding, who figures philosophical self-study similarly: "having raked out that *Jakes*, his own mind," the nasty, introspecting truth-finder, may not discover any "Ray of Divinity."[57] The Scriblerians favor the metaphor for their satires of hack writers who clench and strain at literary production as if at a stool. Here is activity, a working in the darkness. The seat-of-the-soul metaphor should never have recovered from Swift's picture of squatting cogitation or Fielding's picture of the philosopher who keeps pornography in his closet and inspects his own feces. Romantic interiority must forget its Augustan ancestry.

Soame Jenyns's poem "A Translation of Some Latin Verses on the Camera Obscura" captures the interaction of Locke's paper and optical metaphors, locating Locke's "white Paper" in Newton's "dark closet":

> Divine Apollo! let thy sacred fire
> Thy youthful bard's unskilful breast inspire,
> Like the fair empty sheet he hangs to view,
> Void, and unfurnish'd, till inspir'd by you;
> O let one beam, one kind enlightning ray
> At once upon his mind and paper play![58]

Although the poem is advertised as a translation of Latin verses, the scene is Newton's exactly: a dark chamber, a hole that lets in a focused beam of light, and a sheet of paper on which to observe the results when a lens, prism, or piece of hair is interposed between the hole and the sheet of paper. In the next stanza of the poem, Jenyns seems to versify Isaac Newton's instructions for arranging the "silver sheet" and "convex, round, transparent glass" (177).[59] Lockeans, at least, can have *both* their blank slates and this "*dark room*" because in Jenyns's lines the two metaphors are rendered compatible.[60] Locke and others explicitly figure the mind as an interior space, a cabinet or a closet; the understanding is structured as an interior, and in that interior **Writing** occurs.[61] Ideas are imprinted on the mind, or light paints itself on white paper as in William Gilpin's essays on the picturesque, in which the imagination "becomes a camera obscura" by means of which scenes of fancy are painted within as well as literally sketched out.[62]

The senses are figured as inlets: analogous to those holes that Newton pokes in a sheet of lead or cuts in a black felt cloth to let a beam of light shine into a dark interior, analogous to the windows that let light into Locke's dark room. Allegoresis plumbs a much deeper tradition that follows Origen's and Bernard of Clairvaux's readings of the wall and latticed window in the Song of Solomon 2:9 in terms of the body and the senses.[63] Traditionally, in poetry and fiction, eyes are the windows of the soul—or the mirror of the heart.[64] This figuring of thresholds (windows and doors), demarcates interior and exterior, foregrounding the embodiment of mind or soul.

In eighteenth-century figuration a "glass" (both window and mirror) is repeatedly imagined in the breast; and allusions to Momus, who criticized the gods for not placing a window in man's breast, are commonplace. Pope writes to Lady Mary Wortley Montagu of carrying the Momus project further and installing modern "Casements" so that "while a Man show'd his Heart to all the World, he might do something more for his Friends, even give it them, and trust it to their Handling."[65] The window is made conspicuous several times in its absence: "Men have no Windows in their Breast," writes the dramatist John Wilson. But John Wesley, visiting Methodists in Oxfordshire, reports that they "did 'open the window in their breast'" so that "it was easy to discern that God was there, filling them with joy and peace in believing."[66]

Included in the first volume of *Tristram Shandy* is a well-known set piece on the Momus glass (1:23).[67] Sterne elaborates the conceit vividly, worrying about paying taxes or "window-money" and imagining how one might take a man's character by looking into this "dioptrical bee-hive." In Sterne's figure, the brain's cells (rooms within rooms) are implicitly honeycombed, and the thoughts are, both literally and figuratively, "maggots" that may be traced "from their first engendering to their crawling forth" (53). (See **Animals**.)

Johnson defines "INLET" as "Passage; place of ingress; entrance" and cites Milton: "She through the porch and *inlet* of each sense / Dropt in ambrosial oils till she reviv'd." Locke describes internal as well as external sensation as "the only passages I can find of knowledge to the Understanding" (*Essay* II.xi.17). The brain or heart—as was the case in the Spectator's dissections—is often figured as a maze of passages. Mandeville writes, "So that all we can know of this Consciousness is, that it consists in, or is the Result of, the running and rummaging of the Spirits through all the Mazes of the Brain, and their looking there for Facts concerning ourselves." Burney, in a canceled preface of *Cecilia*, paraphrases Addison: "the Mind of Man is 'Dark & Intricate, / Filled with wild Mazes, & perplexed with *Error*.'"[68]

Furniture of the Mind

The "silver paper" of the mind in Soame Jenyns's poem is "empty," "void," and "unfurnished." The room is, like Dryden's dark room, featureless. But the metaphor of furnishing may be misleading because not all furniture should be pictured as upholstered. As C. S. Lewis points out, "furniture" need not always "admit 'domestic movables' as one of its senses. . . . [I]t must have become one of the word's meanings by being a very common speaker's meaning."[69] In my collection of metaphors, the "furniture of the mind" most often takes on the sense of "domestic movable" by appearing in proximity to a metaphor of interiority. Jenyns's poem is here an exception. More often we find examples like the following simile from Mandeville: those who would "extricate themselves from all worldly Engagements" and "purify the Mind . . . must divest themselves of their Passions, as Men take out the Furniture when they would clean a Room thoroughly."[70]

Few interiors are unfurnished. Indeed, the metaphor of interiority invites interior decoration. The eighteenth century came to favor light moveable chairs and tables, readily arranged as social occasion necessitated. The retail furnishings produced by the furniture maker Thomas Chippendale and the designers William Kent and Robert Adam began to appear in the interior descriptions afforded first in travel writing and then in the novel.[71] And although most eighteenth-century rooms are not yet cluttered with furniture as nineteenth-century rooms will be, eighteenth-century minds are crammed with the bric-a-brac of ideation. Most notably, Alexander Pope writes of the "moving Toyshop of [the] Heart."[72] But Mary Savage—cited among the epigraphs—likewise pictures the pineal gland as a jumbled "broker's shop,"[73] and in a Thomas Holcroft play, a character complains his brain is like "a broker's shop; the little good furniture it contained all hid by lumber!" (II.iii).[74] Cynthia Wall notes that Defoe, the novelist, in his *Tour thro' the Whole Island of Great Britain*, is interested more in exteriors than interiors (*Things*, 191). But a facade may not immediately advertise the furniture within: in *Clarissa*, Belford asks Lovelace, "what sort of sign must thou hang out, wert thou obliged to give us a clear idea, by it, of the furniture of *thy* mind?"[75] This dialectic of inner and outer occupies eighteenth-century writers. John Hookham Frere writes of the sumptuous villa that like "many a beau," has an "Outside and front all fine and burnish'd,/But the inner rooms are thinly furnish'd."[76]

In his study of keywords, C. S. Lewis cites George Berkeley's phrase "all the choir of heaven and furniture of earth" to make the point (against Empson) that "furniture" need not be metaphorical. The larger meaning of the word "furniture" includes "whatever 'furnishes' in the sense of stocking, equipping, or replenishing" (*Studies in Words* 15). Lewis identifies an uneasiness here. The sense of the word is conditioned by the history of its usage. Different speakers may deploy a term metaphorically, or they may use a term in a different sense. We may number almost as many senses as there are speakers and intentions, although it is usually the case that many uses may be easily bundled together, numbered, and fit under an appropriate rubric in our dictionaries. To discover a metaphor—to decide that Berkeley's use of "furniture" is metaphorical—we must stipulate which senses are available to an author and be prepared to make the case that the author is inventing a new sense, playing with a newly developing sense, or abusing an established sense of the word. The metaphor appears only in analysis. It may also disappear in analysis—as it does in Lewis's discussion of the line from Berkeley. In this book I include several instances in which a figurative sense disappears in a properly understood historical context or in which a piece of context enlivens a seemingly dead figure of speech.[77]

But the example of "furniture" is more complicated than Lewis would allow. It will not do to decide that the sense of a word is figurative or literal, as these are distinctions best drawn at the level of the sentence. And there is a Rylean argument to be made here as well: the furniture of the mind may be no metaphor at all but rather the domestic movables that furnish the scene of meditation. When we give up the pictures of interiority, we are left with a pictured interior. Furniture is an appropriate term because the setting of writing, thinking, and philosophizing is a furnished one. Melancholic and sedentary, philosophers sit, think, and write to the moment. When the philosopher, lost in thought, pulls himself up short and checks his surroundings, what does he find? The walls of his closet, his desk, the paper he is writing on. People identify their minds with the place they conduct their thoughts, and what we know stands as plain as a wardrobe. The furniture of the mind may even prove literal, like the "cane-chair" in *Tristram Shandy* with its two knobs that come to figure wit and judgment (3:146).

The philosopher who writes to the moment, like a Tristram Shandy perched over his papers in his study, finds himself surrounded by furniture. David Hume conjures a room in his *Treatise*: "I survey the furniture of my chamber; I shut my eyes, and afterwards open them; and find the new perceptions to resemble perfectly those which formerly struck my senses" (I.iv.2). It seems Hume first surveys his furniture and then his perceptions, the original thing and then its copy. After shutting and opening his eyes, Hume has withdrawn behind his own sensations: the interior scene figures interiority.[78]

Compare Berkeley: "The Objects of Sense Exist only when they are Perceived: The Trees therefore are in the Garden, or the Chairs in the Parlour, no longer than while there is some Body by to perceive them. Upon shutting my Eyes all the Furniture in the Room is reduced to nothing, and barely upon opening 'em it is again created."[79] The chairs in the parlor exist because they are perceived, by God, by Berkeley, or by both God and Berkeley. Furniture for Hume is sometimes just furniture, but Berkeley is more likely to use furniture to describe the outfittings of Creation (the chair and the tree inhabit parallel constructions). The metaphysics matters here—as Lewis might well admit. For Berkeley everything that can be said to exist is furniture of the mind (our mind or God's mind). But then idealists have an unusual relationship with metaphor. They do not separate sense impressions and furniture *in se*. Perception is the perception of some *thing*—some piece of furniture, say. *Esse est percipi*; to be is to be upholstered.

Locked In

In toy shops and broker shops, the collector may shop for curiosities to stock or furnish his cabinet. The poet James Woodhouse figures Fancy wandering the world in order to "crowd Imagination's rooms, immense."[80] "Furniture," so construed, recalls the objects of virtuoso collection. The modern critic Michael McKeon connects the Royal Society's "repository" with Locke's image of the mind's cabinet. The interior is a cabinet of curiosity, in McKeon's words, "stuffed with natural and cultural rarities" (*Domesticity* 218).[81] "Cabinet" also has connotations of secrecy, and information is often reposed in the cabinet of another's breast. In *Gulliver's Travels*, Swift—using a single verb to govern two incommensurable spaces—complains that some writers pretend to "unlock the Thoughts and Cabinets of Embassadors and Secretaries of State."[82] "Cabinet" is a term that is also used to figure the body, especially in devotional writing, as in Katherine Philips's poem on the beauties of the interior, "when you with her Mind acquaintance get,/You'l hardly think upon the Cabinet." Penelope Aubin introduces a character named Ardelissa whose mind "well suited the fair Cabinet that contain'd it."[83]

The mind, and often more specifically, the memory, is a repository or storehouse. So, in the *Essay*, Locke defines memory as "the Store-house of our *Ideas*" (II.x.2).[84] The image is so conventional as to find its way into children's literature and John Newbery's popular Tom Telescope books at midcentury.[85] Learning stores the mind with acquired knowledge. The image of the storehouse is often connected to theories of possessive individualism in eighteenth-century studies, but the underlying figure is, like many of the figures here surveyed, of more ancient vintage. Epictetus avails himself of the metaphor in his *Discourses*. It should be stressed that the metaphor is not unequivocally empiricist. In Epictetus the storehouse is stocked before the soul comes into the world. Likewise, in his *Meditations*, Descartes uses the metaphor of the "treasure house," from which the idea of God is retrieved, without concern that it will undermine his argument (*Philosophical Writings*, 1:46).

All these valuables must be made secure, and the mind locked shut. Pope writes in *The Dunciad* of a youth at the "door of Learning" forced to memorize rhyming mnemonics. His thought is confined, and "We hang one jingling padlock on the mind."[86] Deeper subjectivity is figured by the interior unavailable to prying. Matthew Prior deploys the padlock metaphor for the other sex in his poem "An English Padlock." The jealous husband who keeps his wife locked up—"The Key, look here, is in this Pocket"—is corrected by his interlocutor. Her pen and paper confiscated, the wife will still "prick her Mind" to correspond with a lover, thrusting her letter through the keyhole. The only way to prevent cuckoldry is to let her see the world for what it is, to "Let all her Ways be unconfin'd: / And clap your *Padlock*—on her Mind."[87] Among the secret thoughts conducted in secret places, sexual fantasy and sexual fears loom large, and the oscillation between what might be thought of as literal and figurative in these lines is dizzying. A figurative prick, a literal padlock, or a mind padlocked (figuratively, one presumes), a key kept in a pocket (literally)—that same key, or "key," kept out of the wife's keyhole ("keyhole"). The jealous husband must be more a master of metaphor and double entendre than a master of his mistress.

As Prior's poem illustrates, there are no secure private places—any room is open to invasion. Hundreds of books purporting to contain secret knowledge are published in the eighteenth century that invoke cabinets unlocked or closets broken open.[88] A keyhole is inlet enough—any gap, fissure, crack. Walter Shandy believes that there are "a thousand unnoticed openings, . . . which let a penetrating eye at once into a man's soul"; the self is porous and "a man of sense does not lay down his hat in coming into a room,—or take it up in going out of it, but something escapes, which discovers him" (Sterne, *Tristram Shandy* 6:13–4).[89] Entering and exiting a room suggests the vulnerability of interiority. One worries that he or she will be seen into. The self is porous, if not open to invasion (see **Empire**). An interior, whether locked or barricaded, is never truly private.

Worse yet, there may be inlets but no real exits. The something that "escapes" in Walter Shandy's metaphor is not the self but some characteristic or meaningful gesture. The self cannot escape. Confinement again emphasizes the foundation of the body. In another poem by Prior, *Alma: Or, The Progress of the Mind*, the mind finds itself "confin'd" to "upper Rooms" in old age.[90]

Liquor may also serve as warden, as in Charles Darby's *Bacchanalia*. Bacchus may take over for Morpheus, having

> Legal Right, to lock up each mans Brain:
> Since every Room
> His own Goods did contain,
> And was his proper Wine-Cellar become.[91]

The brain's cells, or cellars, may be well stocked with wine, the furniture of the mind sodden, the whole locked up and claimed by the god of wine. But more troubling than being locked up is being locked in. Metaphors of confinement are doubled in the dualisms of the eighteenth century. The theory of ideas locks the soul away in her sensorium and leaves the mind no immediate object but its own ideas, while an older tradition further imprisons the self in the body.[92] The latter tradition may be very old indeed, as William Godwin claims the notion "that the body is the prison of the mind . . . has been entertained ever since the birth of reflection and logical discourse in the world."[93] In the Neoplatonic, Christian tradition the body is the soul's prison, and the sentiment is much exercised in devotional writing. Edmund Arwaker writes in his translation of *Pia Desideria* that "When first my Soul put on its fleshly load, / It was imprison'd in the dark abode." The mind may be confined within "the silent gates of sleep."[94] Incarcerated and encarcassed, the dark room is traded, finally, for a grave and eternal rest; death releases the faithful from the imprisoning clay of the body. Until then, the body is a tenement, a tent, or a tabernacle that we cannot readily leave.

The disabled politician William Hay works a variation on the theme, writing of the body in *Deformity, an Essay*: "let every deformed Person comfort himself with reflecting; that tho' his Soul hath not the most convenient and beautiful Apartment, yet that it is habitable: that the Accommodation will serve in an Inn upon the Road: that he is but Tenant for Life, or (more properly) at Will: and that, while he remains in it, it, he is in a State to be envied by the Deaf, the Dumb, the Lame, and the Blind."[95] Hay lightly admits, "there is no deformed Person, who does not wish that his Soul had a better Habitation" or does not repine that his "Tenement" was not constructed along Palladian lines, in a "more regular style of Architecture" (71–2).

The feeling of being imprisoned may be nothing more than "an ontological illusion" or "a consequence of confusing the interiority of neurological processes with the inwardness of mental experience."[96] Gin, sin, debt, and madness lead to real confinements in the eighteenth century. But the *mind* is readily figured as a prison. In Henry Mackenzie's *Man of Feeling* the passions are figured as "temporary madhouses."[97] Wollstonecraft equates female beauty with a "gilt cage" to which the mind comes to shape itself.[98] In a claustrophobic figure, Henry Fielding analogizes reason and a window: "Of what Use is Reason then? Why, of the Use that a Window is to a Man in a Prison, to let him see the Horrors he is confined in; but lends him no Assistance to his Escape."[99]

In Elizabeth Inchbald's comedy *Every One Has His Fault*, a character resolves to flee his room as his "thoughts are too confined."[100] His interlocutor asks, "are London streets calculated for reflection?" and he responds, "No;—for action. To hurry the faint thought to resolution." The project of much eighteenth-century popular writing is to drag the philosopher out into the public sphere, into the hurry of the streets. In Lord Shaftesbury's *The Moralists*, Philocles (Shaftesbury's proxy) complains that philosophy is no longer active in the world because she has been "immur'd . . . in Colleges and Cells" and calls for her to be brought "on the public stage." A similar sentiment is expressed in a well-known formulation of Addison's Spectator: "It was said of *Socrates*, that he brought Philosophy down from Heaven, to inhabit among Men; and I shall be ambitious to have it said of me, that I have brought Philosophy out of Closets and Libraries, Schools and Colleges, to dwell in Clubs and Assemblies, at Tea-Tables and in Coffee-Houses."[101] Godwin ambiguously mixes figurative and literal when he asserts, "the only means by which truth, however immutable in its own nature, can be communicated to the human mind is through the inlet of the senses. It is perhaps impossible that a man shut up in a cabinet can ever be wise."[102]

Theater, Censorium

The mind is also a theater filled with actors, an audience, and impresarios; in an image from *The Life of Johnson,* it is a Roman *amphitheater.*[103] There are performances within. Consciousness is a stage-show; the self is seated in an inner Cartesian Theater[104]—or, in Hume's articulation of the metaphor, "The mind is a kind of theatre, where several perceptions successively make their appearance; pass, repass, glide away, and mingle in an infinite variety of postures and situations" (*Treatise* I.iv.6). Complicating clear distinctions between inner and outer, the critics Joseph Roach and John O'Brien have explained the staging of thought and the machinery of mentation in the eighteenth-century theater in Cartesian contexts.[105] Public interiority and private performances are not clearly separable. Various devices are found for displaying those emotions or intentions that a character would prefer remain merely private flutterings or inward fears.

Richard Steele seems to pun on "sensorium," when he names his private theater in the great room of York Buildings the "Censorium" and promotes private theatricals there.[106] Steele's spelling, which conflates censorial judgment and common sense, is preferred by Charles Johnstone in his *Chrysal*, in which the narrator mounts to the "censorium" of a brain to talk with the personified "spirit of consciousness" about the nature of personal identity.[107] Later the theater metaphor will return by way of tart reference in James Ramsay's seminal abolitionist work, *An Essay on the Treatment and Conversion of African Slaves* (a student of Reid, Ramsay snipes at Hume throughout): "It is said of negroes, that their brain is blackish, and the glandula pinealis wholly black; a remark of which the Cartesian, with his audience-hall of perception, might make much."[108]

Public Interiors

We might designate an eighteenth-century metaphorics of public interiority and list the public places that figure mental spaces. Mahmut, the narrator of Giovanni Marana's international blockbuster, *The Turkish Spy*, writes that he makes "a *Mosque* of my Heart, where Friends are ever present," even as he lives undercover in Paris.[109] In *The Temple Beau*, Fielding's Lady Gravely accuses Lady Lucy Pedant of having a heart "like a Coffee-House, where the Beaus frisk in and out, one after another."[110] There are both public houses and public spaces in the house. Guests drop in on us and disturb our meditations. In Mary Davys's *The Reform'd Coquet* Amoranda's heart is "like a great Inn, which finds room for all that come."[111] In *Alma* Prior compares olfactory bits that flow up the nasal passages to footmen who run before "Coaches, / To tell the Inn, what Lord approaches."[112] Many rooms accept visitors, and the heart and the breast especially are figured as guest rooms. One may come to inhabit the breast of another or may reserve a room for a beloved. One may also make room for God, who is often figured as a guest or tenant (see **Inhabitants**).[113] Indeed for almost every metaphor numbered in **Rooms**, I find several corresponding **Inhabitants**. Private spaces are traversed by public figures.

Inwardness is practiced in public. We retire and comment inwardly on the passing show, and one removes himself from public proceedings by withdrawing attention from the scene. In the hurry of the world, retirement is more clearly figurative. Considering the case of a "city mind" that is typically to "commercial incidents confined," Thomas Chatterton sketches a merchant, puzzled by unfathomable equity and law proceedings: "Into their inner room his senses draw" and "snore in consultation deep."[114] The somnolent senses pantomime the courtroom consultations without.[115] In a more complicated metaphor near the conclusion of *The Vicar of Wakefield*, Dr. Primrose prepares himself and his family for imprisonment for unpaid rent. He blithely instructs, "wherever we are thrown, we can still retire to a charming apartment, and look round our own hearts."[116] (In this sentimental fiction, it is the heart, not the mind, that is the preferred interior. In later editions, Primrose's metaphor is activated by a subjunctive *when*: "when we can look round.") Multiply dislocated by the plot, the evicted Primrose still retains, in prison, a separate abode in good conscience. Coincidentally, in the novel's county gaol—a setting more penitentiary than prison, as John Bender has observed—each prisoner is assigned a separate cell.[117] As emphasized repeatedly in this entry, public and private cut in unpredictable directions.

As a scene of thought, the eighteenth-century mind is often a public place. Across the period, our distinctions between indoors and out, public and private, do not consistently match up, as theorists of bourgeois interiority had best come to recognize. In the literary and cultural history that connects Richardson to Austen, the action of the novel moves out of the closet and into the parlor; private people come together as a public, and there are both public interiors and private landscapes.[118] I opened this excursus with a quotation from Gilbert Ryle, and so I will close with another: "the mind is not even a metaphorical 'place,'" asserts Ryle. "On the contrary, the chessboard, the platform, the scholar's desk, the judge's bench, the lorry-driver's seat, the studio and the football field are among its places" (*Concept of Mind* 51).[119] We may have our inward practices, but we have no interiority within which to rehearse them. Minds are extruded and extended so that metaphysically flavored privacy—private language, private thought, deep interiority—implied by our metaphors is nowhere available. Privacy, in this case, is only privation. Our pictures of interiority fail us. We are, in truth, almost entirely *out* of our minds.

11 Writing

COLLOCATED KEYWORDS: Blot, Engraving, Ink, Paper, Pen, Table, Tabula Rasa

COUNT OF METAPHORS IN DATABASE[1] (1700–1799): 525

Let us then suppose the Mind to be, as we say, white Paper, void of all Characters, without any *Ideas*; How comes it to be furnished? Whence comes that vast store, which the busy and boundless Fancy of Man has painted on it, with an almost endless variety? Whence has it all the materials of Reason and Knowledge? To this I answer, in one word, From *Experience*: In that, all our Knowledge is founded: and from that it ultimately derives it self.

—John Locke, *An Essay Concerning Human Understanding* (1690)

But should some swain more skillful than the rest,
Engrave his name on this cold marble breast,
Not rolling ages could deface that name—
Through all the storms of life 'tis still the same:
Though length of years with moss may shade the ground
Deep, though unseen, remains the secret wound.

—Lady Mary Wortley Montagu, "Epistle [To Lord Bathurst]" (written ca. 1725)

Live then upon the paper, and upon my memory, every stroke of his pen! For there is no gall in his ink, but only precious balm, and honied drops of salutary counsel.

—Hester Mulso, letter to Samuel Richardson (January 3, 1750–1, publ. 1807)

Sir Charles Grandison's heart is the book of heaven—May I *not* study it?

—Samuel Richardson, *Sir Charles Grandison* (1754)

STEPANOFF.
An excellent fellow this Wasili! There are occupations in the world, which mould a man into a certain form for life, like a piece of paper which has once been folded, its marks are never obliterated. Does not one discover at the first sight, that this man has been a page of the bed-chamber? He announces those that arrive, he conducts them when they depart, he busies himself in carrying news, he knows how to set out a table, he is as idle as a fat lap-dog, and the inside of his head is like a woman's work-basket.

—August von Kotzebue, *Count Benyowsky*

See also **Impressions** and **Rooms**

In this final entry I concentrate on a picture of the soul or mind as something written upon—in the main instance, as a sheet of paper.[2] While Locke and Richardson are paradigmatically invoked in this context, I mean to multiply metaphors and consider other writers. For example, Wasili, the *page* boy described in the fifth epigraph above is the occasion for the observation that certain professions mold a man "like a piece of paper," which once "folded, its marks are never obliterated." That page boys are themselves stock conveyers of letters in epistolary fiction and that a "mould" is a rectangular sieve of wood and wire employed by a papermaker only adds further creases for the literary critic to consider. The metaphors in this concluding entry split differences of matter and meaning and bring forward metaphor in its materiality. As the previous generation of literary theorists emphasized, the substance of writing is legible in terms both literal and figural, "mimetic and antimimetic at the same time."[3] Writing, brought into focus in the form of letters, must appear as marks on a page or operate less visibly, transcending the conventions of typography.

In the first section that follows, I treat eighteenth-century variations on the tabula rasa. In the concluding pages of this entry, I look closely at the writing metaphors in Samuel Richardson's novels and say more about epistolary fiction at large. Richardson contributes influentially to an increase of writing metaphors in the 1750s and 1760s that conflate thought and letter writing. I work to loosen associations, by literary and intellectual historians of the eighteenth century, of Locke's philosophy with the metaphor of the tabula rasa, or blank slate. I argue that the blank slate does more than function narrowly as an empiricist metaphor of mind. It is available to both innatists and empiricists, to skeptics and theologians, to natural lawyers and pyrrhonists, radicals and Royalists, pedagogues and misogynists, poets and novelists, and many others besides. The blank slate is, as it were, a blank slate.

Experience inscribes a blank slate, memory is like a written record, the heart or soul is engraved with tenets of belief—we read both novels and the book of the self (related metaphors have been collected in **Impressions**, as the keyword "engraving" finds both writing and printing metaphors).[4] I suggest that metaphor provides content to claims about the novel's instrumental and ideological impact in the history of so-called modern subjectivity.[5] In eighteenth-century Britain there is a special relationship between letters and what goes on inside a letter writer.[6] Minds and letters share certain salient features. The relationship is in large part figurative, but epistolary fiction, in particular, works to literalize its own metaphors. The materials used to picture the immaterial self are tablets, paper, pen, and ink. I take up these materials in that order, more or less.

White Paper or Tabula Rasa

In his *Essay Concerning Human Understanding*, Locke writes, "Let us then suppose the Mind to be, as we say, white Paper, void of all Characters" (II.i.2). In the three centuries that followed the publication of Locke's *Essay* in 1690, the terms "blank," "tabula rasa," and "white paper" have come to be so powerfully associated with Lockean philosophy that the name Locke and the phrase "blank slate" now travel together, almost inseparably. Critics and historians treat the blank slate as the structuring image of Locke's project, and it is, no doubt, a handy emblem: a picture occupies the foreground, but the picture's sense and application are not as easy to survey.[7] This most famous of metaphors for the mind, of course, was not a new one in 1690, and Locke himself would seem to admit as much by qualifying his supposition with the parenthetical "as we say." Students of ancient philosophy will know that Aristotle pictures the mind as a blank slate and that the idea of a mind that is written upon by experience was pervasive even before Aristotle.[8] E. R. Curtius reports, "Pindar and the tragedians are the first to conceive of memory as a written record."[9] The mind is figured as a wax tablet in Plato's *Theaetetus*—and Plato is careful to cite a Homeric precedent (see **Impressions**). Elsewhere, in the *Phaedrus*, dialectic is likened to the engraving of words in the soul of a learner, a writing prior to or truer than book matter.[10] Laws written in the heart are found in Old and New Testaments alike. Proclus and Aquinas echo Aristotle, and the metaphor is commonplace in medieval literature.

As a print-culture remediation of the tabula rasa, the metaphor of "white paper" appears in two Renaissance conduct manuals reprinted and retranslated in the seventeenth and eighteenth centuries. In a 1589 translation of Pierre de la Primaudaye's *Académie Française*, we read, "The minde is as a white paper, wherein as a man groweth in age and judgement, he writeth his cogitations and thoughts, which the studie of letters and learning do affoord him" (83).[11] Remediation is dramatized in two translations of Stephano Guazzo's *Civil Conversation*: in a 1581 translation, the mind of an infant is "like a payre of tables, wherein nothing is written," while a 1738 translation of the same work gives "like a white Sheet of Paper" in the place of "payre of tables."[12] Tablet or paper, the early modern mind is a commonplace book. In his influential, best-known work on ecclesiastical polity, Richard Hooker writes, "The soule of man being therefore at the first as a booke, wherein nothing is, and yet all thinges may be imprinted."[13]

A very different use of the picture is available in the skeptical writings of Michel de Montaigne and Pierre Charron. In an *Apology for Raymond Sebond*, Montaigne claims that the Pyrrhonist's mind "is a white sheet prepared to take from the finger of God what form soever it shall please him to imprint therein."[14] In Guazzo, La Primaudaye, and Hooker, the white paper images the infant soul. Hooker in particular emphasizes perfectibility: man grows from "vtter vacuitie" to "perfection of knowledge,"[15] whereas in the skeptical tradition the skeptic erases error and opinion to become a blank slate before God—the skeptic becomes, so to speak, "as a little child" (Mark 10:15). At the turn of the eighteenth century, John Pomfret echoes earlier skeptics on the efficacies of the "fair Unwritten Blank"—those "who Truth from Falshood wou'd discern; / Must first disrobe the Mind, and all Unlearn."[16]

In the seventeenth century, Locke's "white Paper" is anticipated in John Earle's *Microcosmographie* and in the poetry of Samuel Speed. Both writers figure the infant soul as white paper and would seem to borrow from Guazzo, La Primaudaye, or a similar source.[17] Locke's precursor, Pierre Gassendi, invokes the tabula rasa in a response to Descartes (although Locke used the tabula rasa metaphor before he read the works of Gassendi: the metaphor appears twice in his *Essays on the Law of Nature*, which were written in the years 1660–4). The metaphor appears multiple times in the philosophy of Thomas Hobbes.[18] In his *Elements of Law*, Hobbes uses it twice: he first grumbles that if the minds of men were "all of white paper" they would be more disposed to recognize "right ratiocination," but then, later in the same manuscript work, he more optimistically imagines the minds of incoming university students as "white paper, capable of any instruction." He writes in *Leviathan* also of "Common-peoples minds," which, "like clean paper," are "fit to receive whatsoever by Publique Authority shall be imprinted in them" unless "they be tainted with dependance on the Potent, or scribbled over with the opinions of their Doctors."[19]

Even from this incomplete, preliminary inventory, we can see that the metaphor has multiple applications in the seventeenth century: the blank slate is used to emphasize the plasticity of the infant mind, to underscore the perfectibility of man, to make a case against the existence of innate ideas, to picture the ease with which right reason or ideology is scribbled in the minds of educated young men and unprejudiced "common" people, and to picture the state of the skeptically devout soul that is ready to be imprinted with the image of God. A metaphor proves multifarious in its application; the totality of usages is not easy to survey.

Papery souls and selves abound in the seventeenth and eighteenth centuries. And yet the so-called blank slate has become associated with Locke's philosophy to such a degree that Locke's invocations of the tabula rasa eclipse uses by Aristotle, Aquinas, Montaigne, Bacon, and Hobbes—all figures of equal or greater stature in the long history of philosophy.[20] As in other entries in which I follow a metaphor through works by canonical and noncanonical writers, I work here to correct the mistake of treating the picture as the exclusive property of John Locke. Some of this work has already been done: Philip Vogt notes that Locke makes reference to "white paper" only four times in the *Essay*, and only twice is the white paper used to picture the mind. Many commentators have noticed that Locke's other metaphors are much neglected by intellectual historians, one critic emphasizing that the phrase "tabula rasa" does not even appear in Locke's *Essay* and arguing that the tabula rasa metaphor, where it does appear, "is consistently displaced by other things to figure the mind."[21] The blank slate has a long history in poetry, drama, novels, philosophy, and politics. A commonplace metaphor persists even as the technologies it references change. In many ambivalent instances, the change from one medium to another is explicitly signaled by a disjunctive phrase: "tabula rasa or clean sheet of paper."[22] The wax tablet survives the print revolution; its metaphorics remediated as—and inscribed on—blank sheets of paper.

The Character of Innate Ideas

As has been demonstrated by John Yolton, Locke's specific image—"white Paper, void of all Characters"—is a calculated modification of a popular seventeenth-century image. The image of the white paper concedes the broad outlines of that picture while altering its details. Locke, of course, picks a fight with a host of Cartesian rationalists, Cambridge Platonists, and theologians. Typical of his antagonists' position is Richard Carpenter's comparison of the conscience to a book that is "even in thine owne bosome, written by the finger of God, in such plaine Characters, and so legible, that though thou knowest not a letter in any other booke, yet thou maist reade this."[23] Likewise, Henry More denies that the mind of man is "a Table book in which nothing is writ"; rather, the mind includes an indelible idea of an absolutely perfect being.[24] As in More, the blank page appears in most theological contexts only to be denied; therefore, insofar as the metaphor appears in these texts only to be negated, Locke reverses his adversaries' negations.

Locke denies that "the *Ideas* Men have of God, are the Characters, and Marks of Himself, engraven in their minds by his own finger" (*Essay* I.iv.14). And in the preceding chapter of book I, Locke proceeds by entertaining the possibility that the innate principles inscribed or engraved in the soul might not be "blotted out" in infants, imbeciles, and savages (I.iii.20). Often the writing metaphors are associated with (if not openly attributed to) innatist and Cartesian opponents. Locke proceeds in book I of the *Essay* by considering whether the innate principles that are inscribed or engraved in the soul might not be "blotted out" in infants, imbeciles, and savages. Indeed, the literary critic William Walker would have it that in the majority of cases, Locke claims a "containment metaphor" (i.e., the mind is a container) "for himself while relegating the imprinting metaphor to the innatists."[25] Arguing that the soul thinks not always, Locke asserts that the thoughts of a soul that perish in thinking are no more useful than "Characters drawn on Dust, that the first breath of wind effaces" (II.i.15). But Locke also uses related metaphors even as he fusses with the pictured media and materials. In the sentence that follows the supposition that the Mind is "white Paper," Locke personifies the fancy as a painter; and in his discussion of memory, Locke describes the ability of the mind to "revive" ideas and "as it were paint them anew on itself" (II.x.2). Later in the same chapter, he pictures the mind as a tomb "where though the Brass and Marble remain, yet the Inscriptions are effaced by time, and the Imagery moulders away" (II.x.5).

The metaphor of paper need not signal an anti-innatist argument. Often a paper metaphor is used to picture innocence. Fair, clean paper may be marked, blotted, or even crumpled. Sir Robert Howard in *The Vestal Virgin* has a character claim,

> Minds like smooth paper never writ upon,
> When folded up, by some impression
> Marks will remain it never had before,
> And ne're return to former smoothness more. (III.i)[26]

Here the paper remains blank and yet is marked. There are any number of ways of adjusting the metaphor of smooth or white paper to stress one or another salient feature of paper, and a count of blank slate and innatist metaphors does not show one set of metaphors predominating over the other. Furthermore, blank slate metaphors are not always deployed in anti-innatist contexts, and descriptions of what God has written in the heart, mind, and soul do not always specify that writing's status as innate. Quite often the blank slate appears only to be denied, negated, or questioned. It is therefore inaccurate to characterize the British eighteenth century as a period in the grips of Locke's metaphor; rather, Locke and the other writers who use the metaphor of white paper put one of the period's available metaphors to one of a variety of uses.

Monograms and Watermarks

The metaphor remains a site of controversy for Locke's critics. For example, Thomas Burnet, a proto-moral-sense theorist who wrote three sets of remarks on the *Essay*, complains that Locke recasts the natural principles of morality as "Idea's" and inappropriately figures them as "*Characters, fair Characters, indeleble Characters, stampt, imprinted, engraven* in the Mind."[27] Burnet switches metaphors on Locke at first, likening natural conscience to "gold in the Oar" or a rough diamond (see **Metal**). He then engages Locke more directly, picturing what he calls "Natural" or "Original" impressions—that is, innate ideas—as "Monograms or Sketches, that want their full Lines and Colours to compleat them; and yet one may discern what or whom they are made to represent, though imperfectly drawn" (8).[28] Burnet's figuration partly suggests visual arts metaphors, but his "Monogram" is also a mark of ownership or a maker's mark. As glossed in Edward Phillips's *New World of Words*, a dictionary contemporary to Burnet's and Locke's exchange, a "Monogram" is "a Cypher, or Character, consisting of one or more letters interwoven together, which was formerly the Abbreviation of a Name, and served for a Seal." Some owners of books inscribed initials and other letters in difficult-to-decipher alphabetic tangles.[29] One imagines, with Burnet, whole innate monogrammatic inscriptions, divine ciphers awaiting later decoding.

In truth, Locke and many of his innatist opponents appeal to a similar picture, and the outlines of that picture are altered little, if at all, whether the writing is attributed to God or experience.[30] Throughout the eighteenth century, writers continue to claim that savages and infants show the stamp of moral sense (if not innate principles) and that the law of nature is written in the soul or in the heart. In quarreling with Locke, Burnet paraphrases Romans 2:14–5: "Those that were without a Law were a Law unto themselves, doing by nature the things contained in the Law, *which shows the Law written in their hearts*."[31] By implication, those who would deny innate ideas contradict scripture. But many writers avail themselves of both (seemingly contradictory) versions of the picture: William Coward in his *Abramideis* (1705) and Gilbert Burnet in his *Exposition of the Thirty-Nine Articles of the Church of England* (1699) help themselves to both blank slates and innate ideas.[32] Locke himself claims in his *Second Treatise* that the "Law of Nature" is plain "writ in the hearts of all mankind" (II.ii.11),[33] and in his discussion of innate principles, he allows in the *Essay*, "That *if* there were *any Ideas* to be found *imprinted* on the Minds of Men, we have reason to expect *it should be the notion of his Maker*, as a mark GOD set on his Workmanship" (I.iv.13).

The question of just what sort of watermark or monogram we might find on the clean, white paper of the mind remains very much disputed in eighteenth-century philosophy, while the paper Lockean arguments are printed on provides contradictory evidence. Handmade paper is marked by the wire mold handled by the vatman, who is also called "the maker," and a close inspection of most eighteenth-century paper reveals a sheet crisscrossed by chain lines and wire lines and decorated with watermarks and countermarks. Innatists metaphors of marking and stamping persist in the language of the moral sense theorists, in spite of seemingly Lockean invocations of the mind as a piece of "white Paper, void of all Characters." In **Impressions**, I claim Locke's metaphor is complicated by the passage of Stamp Acts in the eighteenth century. The extension of "tabula rasa" metaphors—that which is picked out in the material environment—changes from Aristotle to Aquinas to Locke as the textual technologies change. Those moral and religious writers who worry that the tabula rasa conflicts with scripture may well avail themselves of those stamped marks that predate later impressions, and watermarks (which often include Christian or royal imagery) may be appealed to in the same fashion. The vocabulary of innatists, moral sense philosophers, and literal interpreters of scripture is crowded with "stamps" or "marks" or what Burnet has called "Monograms."

Locke's Metaphor

I have discovered almost thirty Lockean citations in my keyword investigations of blank slate and paper metaphors, but more than half of these citations are negations, denials, or qualifications of the figure. It is not at all obvious that it is Locke, to quote M. H. Abrams, "who more than any other philosopher established the stereotype for the popular view of the mind in the eighteenth century."[34] The great majority of the almost two hundred instances of "white paper" or "tabula rasa" I have collected do not reference

Locke's use of the metaphor at all. Often attribution is oblique: the mind has been compared to a blank slate by "some," "some authors," or "some philosophers."[35] John Grose, for example, writes in his *Ethics*, "The wise philosopher tells us, that the soul of man is *rasa tabula*, like a white sheet of paper, out of which it must be more than common art to erase the first impressions."[36] In fifteen instances the metaphor is attributed to some philosopher *other* than Locke: Aristotle is named by Robert South, John Hartcliffe, Leibniz, Berkeley, J. Richardson of Newent, William Warburton, and James Harris. Epicurus is credited in Creech's translation of Lucretius, in a translation of Fenelon, and in a poem by Soame Jenyns.

Throughout the eighteenth century the metaphor of the blank slate may be readily associated with Epicureans, Socinians, materialists, atheists, freethinkers, and Hobbists. In Ralph Cudworth's posthumously published *Treatise Concerning Eternal and Immutable Morality*, the metaphor of the "meer *Rasa Tabula*" is negated.[37] The appearance of the adjective "meer" is a particularly reliable indication that the metaphor has been deployed only to be denied, by signaling that the mind is *merely* passive and that anyone who would help himself to the metaphor of the blank slate courts materialism, atheism, and worse. Cudworth may seem to address Locke in this passage, but the work was written before Locke published his *Essay*.[38] It becomes clear in the sentences that follow, that the intertext is not Lockean at all; rather it is Thomas Hobbes's *Leviathan*.

Perhaps most surprisingly, in the preface of a translation of Giovanni Marana's international best seller *The Turkish Spy*, the blank slate is associated with the philosophy of René Descartes! Where Gassendi and Locke employ the blank slate metaphor in order to qualify or overturn a Cartesian model of the mind, the preface details how the Cartesian practice of hyperbolical doubt cleans and polishes the soul so that it becomes a "Tabula Rasa."[39] Moreover, the translation of Marana's epistolary novel is not alone in its association of Cartesian philosophy with the tabula rasa. In the entry on John Maldonat in an eighteenth-century English translation of Pierre Bayle's *Dictionary*, we find the following assertion: "We must examine every thing, as if we were a *tabula rasa*. . . . This is doubtless what Des Cartes intended, when he would have his Philosopher doubt of every thing, before he examines the reasons of the certainty of it."[40]

Throughout the century the metaphor recurs in skeptical and devotional contexts in which the skeptic or sinner prepares him- or herself to receive the impress of divine truth by erasing or blotting all the false, worldly opinions that have been scribbled in his or her soul. In a 1712 sermon, Matthew

Henry exhorts his auditors to address themselves to God with entire resignation: "The Heart must be *Tabula rasa*, white Paper to *his Pen*, soft Wax to *his Seal*: Let him *write* upon me what he *pleaseth*, and make what *Impressions* he *pleaseth* upon me."[41] Similarly, in a 1692 collection of sermons by Robert South, a collection that went through several eighteenth-century editions, we learn that "Impartiality strips the mind of prejudice and passion, keeps it tight and even from the Byass of Interest and Desire, and so presents it like a *Rasa Tabula*, equally disposed to the Reception of all Truth."[42]

As should now be obvious, a metaphor functions in various, often opposed discourses. The blank slate appears in materialist, natural philosophical contexts and in theological or devotional contexts. The picture may be associated with the repudiation of innate ideas, but it is also used to picture the mind of the Cartesian doubter or the soul of the true believer. The metaphor is used to figure the infant mind but is also, as it appears in William Sherlock's *Discourse Concerning Happiness*, used to figure the mind of an old or sick man who has "no Ideas left in his Mind" and is "become a *Rasa Tabula* again."[43] To emphasize the diverse contexts in which a blank slate might be deployed, I will cite two competing examples, the first materialist and the second Neoplatonic. The metaphor is taken up by Bernard Mandeville in *The Fable of the Bees* where the *brain* of an infant is figured as a "Charte Blanche." In an entirely different register, when Abel Evans employs the metaphor in his poem *Prae-existence*, the blank slate metaphor is used in a description of the soul's transmigration.[44]

It is not easy to date a moment in the eighteenth century when, if ever, the blank slate metaphor became definitively Lockean. Perhaps an increasing association of Locke with white paper may owe something to changes in the history of papermaking. Around 1755 James Whatman produced "wove paper" for the printer and typefounder John Baskerville (sheets of which were used in Baskerville's 1757 edition of Virgil, his 1759 edition of Milton, and his 1761 edition of Dodsley's *Fables*). The tightly woven brass mesh used in Whatman's paper mold resulted in a smooth blank sheet unmarked by laid wire lines, watermarks, or countermarks. But because the paper was difficult to make, it was not commonly used by printers before the last decade of the century.[45] At the turn of the nineteenth century, many fine editions of eighteenth-century authors surveyed under this heading, from Addison and Watts, are printed on finely woven paper, but I have yet to discover an edition of Locke's *Essay* on otherwise unmarked paper.[46] However, increasingly advertised after 1770 are printed and bound commonplace books designed on principles recommended by Locke in a letter to a Mr. Toignard. (The letter was translated and published posthumously in 1706.)[47] To be sure, one of these Lockean blank books, sold by John Walker, is advertised as containing "superfine Wove Paper."[48]

Engraving Letters

The picture of the soul and what is written and painted on it is continually revisited, contested, and altered in the eighteenth century, and it has currency outside of philosophical dispute. As demonstrated, writing metaphors both predate Locke's *Essay* and outrun Locke's application of them. In the amatory novels of the early eighteenth century, the contents of a mind are scribbled out in a letter, and the contents of an important letter are reciprocally engraved on the mind. Typical is the avowal of a character in Eliza Haywood's novel *The British Recluse* who claims her correspondent's letter is "too deeply engraven in my Mind, ever to be forgotten."[49] After Richardson's *Pamela*, the commonplace contrast of writing and reading reinforces both the mimetic and antimimetic features for the reader of a fictional text made of *printed* letters.

From early amatory novels to later sentimental fictions, the identification of letters with the mind of the absent writer characterizes much eighteenth-century figuration.[50] Neither subject nor object, the letter itself mediates between sender and receiver as an intersubjective intermediate. The poet Robert Lloyd connects and confuses the mind and paper in a poetic epistle from a cobbler who decides "To set [himself] down and *think* a letter, / And without any more ado, / Seal up [his] mind, and send it."[51] A much-cited instance figures in Johnson's correspondence with Hester Thrale: "A man's letters [. . .] are only the mirror of his breast, whatever passes within him is shown undisguised in its natural process."[52]

Many writing metaphors rework or are reworked as engraving metaphors, doubling image and impression. The figuration frustrates the easy organization of metaphors under headings.[53] As noted, recurrent reference is made to the tables of the heart and the law engraved there, especially in devotional contexts. The devotional competes with the pedagogical in Sarah Scott's *Millenium Hall*, where a character asserts, "the foundation of most of our virtues, or our vices, are laid in that season of life when we are most susceptible of impression, and when on our minds, as on a sheet of white paper, any characters may be engraven."[54] Mr. Villars seems likewise to find an intermediate between paper and tablets when he writes to his ward Evelina in Frances

Burney's epistolary novel of the same name: "Yes, my child, thy happiness is engraved, in golden characters, upon the tablets of my heart! and their impression is indelible."[55] Villars's letter is intersubjective, both written out and capable of making further impressions; the multiple keywords employed point back to the metaphorics of **Impression** and **Metal**.

Marking Spotless Paper Souls

In pedagogical contexts the image of white paper is used to emphasize that the mind is plastic, shaped by custom, education, and experience. In the preface of the anonymously authored *Remarkable Trials and Interesting Memoirs, of the Most Noted Criminals* (1765), the reader is warned, "'tis a known Observation, that a young Mind is like a white Sheet of Paper, on which may be inscribed the most beautiful Images, as well as the ugliest Deformities."[56] "Sheet of paper" figures the mind as made of such stuff that any impression, wicked or virtuous, may be set in it—that it is extremely plastic, and that first impressions are therefore among the most important impressions that will be made. This use of the metaphor, I suspect, is the most traditional one. It follows from Guazzo, La Primaudaye, and any number of other writers who compare the infant soul to a blank piece of paper in the context of a theory of education. John Ray digests the sentiment as syllepsis in his 1678 collection of proverbs ("*Youth* and white paper take any impression").[57] Locke himself deploys the metaphor in this sense at the end of his *Some Thoughts Concerning Education*, a work written for the benefit of those gentlemen's sons who are "as white Paper or Wax to be moulded and fashioned as one pleases."[58]

In the 1741 poem *Hints to a Schoolmaster*, Stephen Duck, the autodidact farm laborer who learned to read Milton's *Paradise Lost* two or three times through with a dictionary "before he could understand the language of it," recommends,

> Ere Vice the spotless Paper foul,
> Imprint the Volume of the Soul
> With Vertue's noble Mark![59]

Eighteenth-century typography almost obliges the modern reader (if not the hasty eighteenth-century reader) to scan "spotless Paper foul" improperly as "spotless Paper soul." And possibly, the momentary misprision of a long *ſ*—a signifying *mark*—dramatizes anxieties of laboring-class literacy.[60] The visual, typographical rhyme is especially apt because the soul is itself a "Volume" to be imprinted prior to exercises that will subsequently blot and foul papers.

But in the next lines the metaphor is elaborated so as to suggest a different picture of the soul, as if the student practices his new skill with inscription out of doors:

> The Mark, extending by degrees,
> Shall grow like Letters carv'd on Trees,
> That widen with the Bark. (3)

Here the growth of the young plant increases the legibility of the mark.[61] Blank slate metaphors are often mixed with metaphors of cultivation, and not just by "thresher" poets. But again, the partisans of nature and those of nurture tease out those salient features of the images that best suit their system of belief, with innatists preferring to discourse on seeds, relativists on soil, air, water, and weeding. While Duck's picture of the soul might be tentatively characterized as Lockean, refinements of the tabula rasa metaphor do little to displace innatist figures of speech in eighteenth-century discourse—if only because they replace one writing metaphor with another. Here again is a "Mark" reminiscent of Burnet's "Monograms" or David Fordyce's "Stamp" (discussed in **Impressions**). Note that the medium is adjusted in various contexts as necessary: the slate or tablet is composed of tree bark, wax, paper, or stone. In Walter Harte's *Essay on Reason*, the white paper is transfigured as a "stretched canvas."[62]

The Politics of Paper

With Locke in mind, commentators often associate the blank slate with late eighteenth-century liberal political projects.[63] Thomas Jefferson thus observes (the context is architecture but the implications are political): "Every half century then our country becomes a tabula rasa, whereon we have to set out anew, as in the first moment of seating it"; and the third chapter of William Godwin's *Political Justice* opens with a denial of innate principles.[64] But the metaphorics of the blank slate is by no means unambiguously egalitarian, liberal, or radical, and we have already seen Hobbes employ the picture in authoritarian fashion. In the 1796 Jacobin novel *Memoirs of Emma Courtney*, Mary Hays puts a blank slate metaphor (smooth-woven paper may here be determinative) in the mouth of a chauvinist character who claims, "The mind of a young lady should be clear and unsullied, like a sheet of white paper, or her own fairer face: lines of thinking destroy the dimples of beauty; aping the reason of man, they lose the exquisite, *fascinating* charm, in which consists their true empire."[65] Because it is infants and children whose minds are often figured as white paper, the picture proves ready-made for those who would infantilize women.

Almost certainly Hays has Mary Wollstonecraft in mind, for in *A Vindication of the Rights of Woman* Wollstonecraft admits the reading of trifling novels is "better than leaving a blank still blank, because the mind must receive a degree of enlargement and obtain a little strength by a slight exertion of its thinking powers."[66] In Samuel Whyte's "Occasional Prologue to *Jane Shore*" (privately performed in 1790), the blank metaphor is more ambiguous: "If female minds are uninform'd and blank, / Whom, lordly sirs! are female tongues to thank?"[67] The project of maintaining a blank as a blank is obvious in any satirist, moralist, or author of conduct literature who recommends keeping pen, ink, paper, and books out of the hands of young ladies. The tabula rasa metaphor, so often cited by political historians tracing Lockean notions of radical equality in eighteenth-century political discourse, proves ambivalent: the blank page is an emblem of equality and therefore associated with reform and revolution, but it is also an emblem of oppression, of a blank kept blank and spotless until it is ready for the inscriptions of hegemony.

I return to strong claims made for metaphor (and quoted in the introduction of this dictionary and revisited throughout these entries) that pictures and metaphors determine most of our philosophical convictions. I ask in what sense can we say that the picture determines the uses to which it is put if Jefferson, Godwin, Wollstonecraft, and Hays—four late eighteenth-century writers whose political convictions might be said to largely overlap—all find different applications for the same picture? Jefferson associates the tabula rasa with perpetual revolution, Godwin—drawing on Hooker and Locke—bases his program of perfectibility on a denial of innate principles, while Wollstonecraft and Hays recognize that spotlessness is next to emptiness. Certainly the assembled writers' convictions are not simply determined by the picture they have employed, and certainly their convictions (political and otherwise) partially determine the uses to which they put the picture and the sense the picture is given in application.

Blank, Blotted Sheets

The blank slate metaphor proves a palimpsest of commonplaces. A mind may begin blank but ends up inked over, revised and rewritten. The reversible metaphor reorders the writing self as the mind spills out and inks up a blank page. Sentiments flow from the heart and to the pen, even as the motions of the pen circumscribe the mind's wanderings.[68] The words come smoothly or not. A line from *Ascham's Schoolmaster* illustrates the third sense of "BLOT" in Johnson's *Dictionary*: "Heads overfull of matter, be like pens overfull of ink, which will sooner *blot*, than make any fair letters at all." And for the second sense of the same headword, Johnson selects Locke's assertion that simple ideas appear in the mind in such a fashion that the understanding cannot "refuse, nor alter, nor *blot* out . . . or obliterate" them. Agnes, a minor character in Delarivier Manley's *Memoirs of Europe*, is typed as an "Idiot": "her *Mind*, 'twas all a *Blot*, nor had it ever been otherways; she had no *Notion* of Things, no *Discourse*, no *Memory*"; alternately, Charles Churchill warns, "Constant attention wears the active mind, / Blots out our powers, and leaves a blank behind."[69]

In the *First Satire of the Second Book of Horace* (1733), Pope depicts the satirist who can't stop writing: "My head and heart thus flowing thro' my Quill." The satirist can't sleep; he wakes at night. Advised not to write, he complains, "Not write? but then I *think*, / And for my Soul I cannot sleep a wink."[70] In this couplet is something like a Scriblerian response to Locke's protracted discussion and denial of the always-thinking Cartesian soul (Locke would have it that the soul "thinks not always"). If thinking is just another kind of writing, then the satirist is doomed to insomnia. Pope's verses anticipate characters like Pamela or Clarissa, characters who cannot stop writing.

The blank slate metaphor in narrative—especially in epistolary writing—initiates dialectics of blanching and blotting. In a scene from the fourth volume of *Pamela*, Mr. B., back from riding, breaks in upon Pamela in her closet and declares, "Here are Pen and Ink: Here too is Paper but it is as spotless as your Mind."[71] I detect a note of suspicion here: Mr. B.'s interest in papers still blank leads us away from the picture of white paper and what is written on it to a closer consideration of metaphors of ink. Spotless paper and spotless minds await the blot or inky stain of experience, and wives, like Pamela, who spend too much time scribbling secret notes may imperil their very spotlessness. Much of the early drama in *Pamela* involves Mr. B. trying to make out what Pamela is putting down on paper, but in the later volumes of the novel, Mr. B. continues to police Pamela's letter writing, both anxious and eager to find himself written out, checking Pamela's sheets of paper as if they belonged to the marriage bed, a context in which a stain is a guarantee of innocence and virginity.[72] We again see a tension between conservative and progressive implications of a metaphor for a mind. A metaphor fits into different contexts in different ways. Even within a single text, a metaphor can function in ambiguous, contradictory fashion. So various critics interpret Pamela's story variously as egalitarian, reactionary, or otherwise.

Blankness, of course, is not just a characteristic of women in the eighteenth century; a male variety is described by Joseph Addison in *Spectator* no. 10: "There is another Set of Men . . . whom I have lately called the Blanks of Society, as being altogether unfurnish'd with Ideas, till the Business and Conversation of the Day has supplied them."[73] Addison's "Blanks" recall Hobbes's university students who come to their studies as "white paper." Addison urges these Blanks not to leave their chambers until they have read his paper and been impressed with his print, implying that a gentleman may have a subscription to the *Spectator* in lieu of a mind. The type is legion at midcentury, jostling in the box lobby of a playhouse and at Vauxhall—or so it registers in Elizabeth Griffith's comedy *The Platonic Wife*, where these bodies without souls are compared to the white paper used merely to "make up bulk, and stuff of life's volume."[74]

The metaphors become more complicated in any number of works of literature as they come to interact with the commonplaces that structure eighteenth-century racial and gender hierarchies. In Edmund Arwaker's versification of Aesop's fables we find the following racialized use of an innatist metaphor:

> The Characters that Nature has impress'd,
> Keep their primaeval Stamp on ev'ry Breast;
> And he that wou'd, what's printed there, erase,
> As well might hope to blanch a *Negro*'s Face.[75]

Blank and black, or rather black and white, introduce a more complex constellation of associations. In innatist arguments the racist blanches and the leveling appeals to an egalitarian blank slate are blocked by the apparition of a black face. "Blank" tangles with "naked" in several instances, so it is not surprising that Arwaker connects his writing metaphors with skin color. In the race science of the eighteenth century—and in the popular imagination of that period—it is thought that "savage" infants are born white and only darken when exposed to air and light or rubbed with ashes and dirt. Buffon compares the color of albino "white negroes" to paper; and in a treatise on printing and dyeing, Edward Bancroft cites one M. Sennebier's studies on the tinting and darkening of African skin.[76]

Arwaker pictures racialization as irreversible: the slaveholding squire who would scour the "Sooty Face" of his purchased Negro finds he spends "his Labour, Soap, and Time, in vain" (114).[77] Although an uncolonized territory may be imaged as a tabula rasa, I have yet encountered only one eighteenth-century instance in which the apposite metaphor for the mind is evinced, in an epic simile from a late eighteenth-century travelogue: "as the great continents of Africa, amidst its seas of sand, occasionally show an Oasis or fertile isle, rising in each desert; so in analogy to the face of the country, does the blank and torpid mind of its people, display occasional notes of intelligence and philanthropy, rich spots of genius, and partial scenes of improved social establishment."[78] In denying the metaphor to the colonized, the colonizer would deny those native to a territory their minds. And yet Locke's argument against innate principles is partly supported by the evidence of travel literature and the example of "Hottentots" and other savages. The map is a blank on which imperial culture first writes; the African body, a spot or blot.[79]

I take the final example in this survey of blankings and blottings from the second act of Richard Sheridan's *The Rivals*. Mrs. Malaprop demands that her niece Lydia Languish promise "to forget this fellow"—the poor ensign Beverly—and asks Lydia "to illiterate him, I say, quite from your memory."[80] The malapropism is "illiterate" for "obliterate." Malaprop's request comes in a scene that opens with Lydia on a sofa, novel in hand, discussing the picked-over holdings of the Bath circulating libraries and that ends with Mrs. Malaprop and Sir Anthony Absolute debating the dangers of teaching a young girl to read. If experience is a kind of writing, forgetting is a kind of erasing or blotting; and so it is that a guardian like Malaprop may hold fast to the hope that a giddy girl who has read too many giddy novels may be *illiterated* and returned to a spotless and blank state of innocence, be made again "illiterate," in the eighteenth-century sense of "unlettered" or "unread."

Writing to the Moment

A metaphor has its applications in and is constitutive of cultural practice. A picture of thought is available in the moment of writing,[81] and there are several genres with which the foregoing writing metaphors are intimately involved. For example, philosophers of mind share their most private and profound thoughts with a readership. They *publish* their introspections, and we read them. Ralph Cudworth, for one, emphasizes the reading in the etymology of intellection (*inter + legere*): "according to the Etymon of the Word, *the Intellect* doth *read inward Characters written within itself*" (III.iii.4).[82] When reading eighteenth-century philosophers, we are referred repeatedly to the paper on which the writing is inscribed. We find ourselves sharing the space in which the philosopher sits as the philosopher muses about the ordinary objects he finds in front of himself.

In his *Essay* we find Locke experimenting with the white paper on which he writes while he writes upon it, investigating the line between sensation and reflection as it is figured in the mind and appears on the page; he finds his "Idea" to be *in*scribed *out* there (his term is "exhibit"):

> Thus I see, whilst I write this, I can change the Appearance of the Paper; and by designing the Letters, tell before-hand what new *Idea* it shall exhibit the very next moment, barely by drawing my Pen over it: which will neither appear (let me fancy as much as I will) if my Hand stands still; or though I move my Pen, if my Eyes be shut: Nor when those Characters are once made on the Paper, can I chuse afterwards but see them as they are; that is, have the *Ideas* of such Letters as I have made. (IV.xi.7)[83]

Berkeley experiments in a similar way with fleeting exhibitions, allowing us a glimpse of the room in which he is composing his *Treatise*: "Upon shutting my Eyes all the Furniture in the Room is reduc'd to nothing, and barely upon opening 'em it is again created."[84] Hume, given as he is to philosophical experiments, is a particularly interesting case.[85] We are invited to occupy Hume's perspective in several different passages in the *Treatise*; and in one particularly striking description, he shares his immediate impressions with us in a passage that realizes the material presence of the paper only to carry the reader away from the surface of inscription and outdoors: "The paper on which I write at present, is beyond my hand. The table is beyond the paper. The walls of the chamber beyond the table. And in casting my eye towards the window, I perceive a great extent of fields and buildings beyond my chamber" (1:333). These are perhaps odd passages to encounter in a philosophical treatise, and Sterne has much fun in *Tristram Shandy* and *A Sentimental Journey* parodically restaging these philosophical scenes (be they in his study or in a *desobligeant*). In one particularly well-known passage he literalizes the furniture of the mind, or at least Wit and Judgment, as the "two knobs" that are to be found "upon the back of this self same chair on which I am sitting."[86] As discussed under the headword **Rooms**, people identify their minds with the place they conduct their thoughts. And so the reader is asked to envision the setting in which the book he or she is reading was produced. The rhetoric has the full flavor of self-reflexive fiction but also serves to concretize the scene of writing for the reader, combining and literalizing in narrative the metaphorics explored in **Impressions**, **Inhabitants**, **Mirror**, **Rooms**, and **Writing**.[87] Hume's instructions point us *beyond* the legible, printed page to a hand (see Locke's "before-hand" above), a manuscript, an interior, a window. Where we have been following the writer's thoughts, his interior musings, we are suddenly repositioned alongside, or even within, the head of the writer. In the effected gestalt switch, we share a relation to a piece of paper (if not "*this*" piece of paper), and the deictic shift serves as invitation to the closet of the philosopher.

Locke, Berkeley, and Hume, good empiricists all, work from their own sense impressions—they believe they have no other impressions to work with. We can follow their reasoning easily enough, but when they would show us what they perceive—show us the very apparatus of perception—they must give up reasoning and depict sensation. "Thus I see," Locke writes, and we are meant to see with him. We open and close our eyes along with Berkeley or look over furnishings and out the window with Hume. We are brought right up to the moment at which the philosopher commits his musings to paper. More than that, the philosophers efface the presence of their own writing, printed as it is on the reader's page, and refigure it. The reader imagines a piece of a paper, a clean, blank sheet—Stephen Duck's "spotless Paper soul"—the very picture of a mind on which experience writes.

IN THE REMAINING PAGES OF this final entry, I would locate a single novelist's fictions—Samuel Richardson's epistolary novels—in the larger metaphorical field. These fictions both stand for and stand out against a wider whole as I consider how a metaphor may interact with and constitute a specific literary genre. This valedictory critical exercise further demonstrates how distant reading supports close interpretation by indicating the range of metaphors by which figure and ground may be defined. In short, the metaphors described above inform eighteenth-century epistolary fiction, the genre that most relentlessly literalizes metaphors of writing. As the rhetorical strategies employed by Locke, Berkeley, and Hume have already been associated with Richardson's technique of "writing to the moment," to Richardson's novels I now turn. The increase in the frequency of writing metaphors at midcentury should be attributed to the influence of Richardson's example.[88]

Both Lovelace and Clarissa are adept at writing to the moment. Richardson had used the technique in *Pamela*, but not to the extent that it is exploited in *Clarissa*. In his second novel, Richardson introduces two new letter writers who surpass Pamela's ability to put down on paper what has happened. Early in the first volume, Anna (Clarissa's main correspondent) reports of Lovelace that "his thoughts flow rapidly to his pen" (1:67; p. 74 in Angus Ross's single-volume edition).[89] Likewise, Belford (Lovelace's correspondent) reports of Clarissa "that there never was a lady so young, who wrote so much and with such celerity. Her thoughts keeping pace, as I have seen, with her pen, she hardly ever stopped or hesitated; and very seldom blotted out, or altered" (1368).

Recording their impressions almost as quickly they have them, the main characters almost spill or pour out their minds onto the paper of their letters. When a reader of these letters encounters this kind of writing—as in the empiricist philosophy discussed above—he or she is resituated by it. So when Richardson's heroine write to the moment, the reader is carried into her closet. As Lovelace prepares to seduce Clarissa, his "charming frostpiece," he writes to the moment—posed as if in supplication, he writes, "On one knee, kneeling with the other"—in a frozen cavern, picturing the "hoar frost" dripping and dissolving on his wig and linen (270, 145). This description would carry Clarissa out of herself, from the coolness of the "Ivy summer-House" from which she writes to him at his "Ivy-Cavern" on the other side of the garden wall, through which the two exchange letters (366, 271).

After Clarissa's rape, Lovelace lets Belford in on the secret of his writing: "Thou'lt observe Belford, that though this was written afterwards, yet (as in other places) I write it as it was spoken, and happened; as if I had retired to put down every sentence as spoken. I know thou likest this lively *present-tense* manner, as it is one of my peculiars" (882). In the pages that follow, Lovelace rewrites the moments just preceding his attempt on Clarissa, and as readers we are horrified to find ourselves right there with him. By way of contrast, Belford is incapable of matching Lovelace's speed and complains, "But do you think I can leave off in the middle of a conversation, to run and set down what offers, and send it to you piecemeal as I write?—If I could, must I not lose one half, while I put down the other?" (1357). Richardson shows us that Anna, too, cannot keep pace: "I have a vast deal to write. I know not what to write first. Yet my mind is full, and seems to run over" (406).[90]

Belford and Anna either are not in control of the metaphor of mind or are unwilling to close the gap between an event and the representation of that event.[91] As observed in the opening paragraphs of this entry, writing to the moment is both mimetic and antimimetic. As a realist convention, writing to the moment is an epistolary artifice—an aspect of epistolarity self-reflexively described by its fictional characters, who would have us see thought as it is set down; as it figures on the page, it is literalized in print.[92]

Early in the novel, Clarissa writes to Anna to affirm, "One of the first conditions of our mutual friendship was that each should say or write to the other whatever was upon her mind" (135). Richardson repeatedly encourages his readers to believe that his characters write out their whole being (and insofar as the characters are fictions, their whole being *is* written). So Sally Godfrey tells Pamela, "I can write my whole Mind *to* you"; and Lady Grandison writes to Mrs. Shirley, "in absence, we will not be divided; for we will mingle souls and sentiments on paper."[93] On the printed page we find Richardson mixing a picture of the mind with a practice of writing, and because the picture of the soul is a picture of paper, the picture and practice reinforce each other. Richardson's fictions involve many of his readers in further correspondence, perhaps most famously in the case of Lady Bradshaigh, whose early letters to Richardson she signed with the fictitious name "Belfour," performatively closing distance between herself and the characters of the novel.[94] In a letter to another of his real-life correspondents, Richardson writes of the pen "that makes distance presence; and brings back to sweet remembrance all the delights of presence; which makes even presence but body, while absence becomes the soul."[95]

Pens figure throughout *Clarissa* as instruments present to the body for figuring a soul in absence and abstraction. When her thoughts drift, Clarissa scolds herself: "But whither roves my pen" (82). Her pen grows tired and trembles as she grows ill (1005, 1318). During his illness, Lovelace loses control of mind and pen. He writes Belford that he "dare not to indulge in these melancholy reflections," and when he finds his "head strangely working again," he commands, "Pen, begone!" (1428). A page later he writes, "since my pen will slide into this gloomy subject, whether I will or not; I will once more quit it; nor will I again resume it till I can be more *its master*, and my own" (1429). When Lovelace is in a fit of love, he writes, "My heart, I see (on reperusing what I have written), has communicated its tremors to my fingers; and in some places the characters are so indistinct and unformed that thou'lt hardly be able to make them out" (936).

When Lovelace compares Clarissa's and Anna's handwriting and finds that Clarissa's "delicate and even mind is seen in the very cut of her letters," her writing, albeit absent, may come closer still to the reader in the "equal and regular" type-cast letters of the printed page, the letter forms of which were cut into punches before being cast as blocks of moveable type (811). After Clarissa's rape, her disordered mind is pictured as a disordered page, a literalized metaphor only a printer-novelist like Richardson could compose (893). Devious Lovelace writes in a coded "character"[96] that is likewise transformed by conventions of print; not represented literally, his hand is a figure until, in his indexing of Anna Howe's letter, his markings, multiplied in the margins of the "cursed letter," are represented as a manicule, or pointing printer's hand (743). It is relevant that when Clarissa escapes Sinclair's house, she moves above a glove shop (974).

Throughout *Clarissa* Richardson uses ink as both metonym and metaphor for thought. Specifically, ink often stands in for the emotions, those spirits and passions that circulate in the brain and give color and shape to ideas. Richardson's mixing of picture and practice is so complete that when a Clarissa or Pamela cries, her tears mingle with her ink and blot her page—a page, like the philosopher's, that we must imagine.[97] The equation of ink and emotion may be made casually: Clarissa, bothered by Anna's reflections on her family, chastises her friend: "you dip your pen in gall whenever you are offended" (236). Clarissa knows better and leaves off writing when she finds herself growing angry: "But it is time to lay down my pen, since my ink runs nothing but gall" (225).

I will end here, perhaps abruptly closing the distance between literal and figurative, by noting that much eighteenth-century ink is (quite literally) made from galls—that is, from the tumors that appear on oak trees when an insect wounds the branch of a tree and deposits its egg underneath the bark. The galls are harvested and ground up, soaked, and mixed with ferrous sulfate to make indelible ink. Clarissa dips her pen in ink, in gall, and writes. This writing is the theme and content both in a novel about a rape that is narrated by means of fictional letters composed by a man who makes a living putting ink on paper. Clarissa's linguistic codes seem ever alert to *Clarissa*'s bibliographic ones. Written in one moment, read in another, the indelible picture challenges our ability to discriminate figurative and literal. But whether all metaphors of mind must be spelled out in just this way is matter for the conclusion.

Conclusion
The Mind Is a Metaphor

Hyl. Explain to me now, O *Philonous*! how it is possible, there shou'd be room for all those Trees and Houses to exist in your Mind. Can extended Things be contained in that which is unextended? Or, are we to imagine Impressions made on a Thing void of all Solidity? You cannot say, Objects are in your Mind, as Books in your Study: Or, that Things are imprinted on it, as the Figure of a Seal upon Wax. In what Sense, therefore, are we to understand those Expressions? Explain me this if you can: And I shall then be able to answer all those Queries you formerly put to me, about my *Substratum.*

Phil. Look you, *Hylas*, when I speak of Objects, as existing in the Mind, or imprinted on the Senses; I wou'd not be understood in the gross, literal Sense, as when Bodies are said to exist in a place, or a Seal to make an Impression upon Wax. My Meaning is only, that the Mind comprehends, or perceives them; and that it is affected from without, or by some Being distinct from itself. This is my Explication of your Difficulty; and, how it can serve to make your Tenent of an unperceiving, material Substratum intelligible, I wou'd fain know.

—George Berkeley, *Three Dialogues* (1713), 141–2

In the eleven preceding entries, a literary history of metaphors is set out in detail. This book is a work of reference; its historical mode is descriptive. If read for story, the reader's impatience will be much fretted, as very little will be found in the way of turning points under any one heading. But as stated at the outset, that is the news I am breaking: the narrative of the eighteenth century is not one in which **Mirrors** yield to lamps or in which John Locke's adoption of the blank slate metaphor inspires declarations of independence and revolution. Instead, the collected metaphors (with important exceptions) accumulate in haphazard distributions, decade by decade, as they are put to various uses in various contexts. To be clear: I am not claiming, as J. C. D. Clark does, polemically, that the long eighteenth century is a period that displays persistent uniformity and internal coherence,[1] only that the diachronic slices of discourse I have sampled are relatively even, consistent, and regular, and if involved at all in what are surely the sweeping changes associated with the Enlightenment and its scientific and political revolutions, it must be as cover for what goes on in other quarters.[2]

The discovery and description of changing metaphorics is believed the main work of literary and cultural history.[3] Barbara Stafford usefully summarizes and complicates the sentiment: "Metaphors embody and configure both the abiding and the changing preoccupations of an age."[4] The methodological problem is, then, as I see it, to distinguish that which changes from that which is abiding and connect the figures of speech with the concrete materials and current events figured by them. As determinations, change and stasis are relative to one another; metaphors of mind persist even as they are enlisted in new arguments and put to new uses. And in the final tally of eighteenth-century metaphors, more abides than is expected.

After collecting and sorting thousands of metaphors of mind, I have come to place emphasis on imperial fortunes, the abolitionist moment, and contemporary industrial developments (**Empire**, **Fetters**, **Metal**). In other entries, less sanguine about drawing conclusions, I differentiate usages in a lexicographical mode and identify clusters of metaphors. Metaphors may collect in an author or genre, but it is difficult to discern more sweeping changes, at least by using keyword search and attendant discourse analysis. Future attempts (computational efforts, mining greater quantities of literature) may upset my findings, but in the meantime the findings demand explanation.

In coming to terms with the metaphors all in the lump, this final essay takes Berkeley's idealism as a point of departure and ends with an image of dialectical materialism. My effort is to get from stasis to change. I take the philosophical exchange from Berkeley's *Three Dialogues* cited in the epigraph to this section as motivating because metaphors of mind are themselves put in question by it. The exchange has been mentioned twice already in this work (in the introduction and under **Impressions**), and Philonous's insistence that metaphors belong to "the general Analogy of Language" has been enlisted as an informing warrant, a way of thinking about the structure of metaphor in the period at large. But the discussion of the origin of such metaphors from the analogy of thought to its objects has not yet been given sustained consideration. Nor has Berkeley's dialogue been put *in dialogue* with other eighteenth-century discussions of figurative language so that empiricism of the eighteenth century might be more generally characterized as a rhetorical formation. The pages that follow attempt both before turning to a different exchange, one between I. A. Richards and William Empson, in which Empson explains how metaphor may be made to yield to the literal through mutual comparisons of tenor and vehicle.

Why is it "common Custom" that we talk about thoughts as if they were things? Consider the prepositional phrase "in the mind," Berkeley's favorite metaphor.[5] When in the *Three Dialogues* Philonous (Berkeley's spokesman) is accused of abusing language by Hylas (a proxy for the bewildered reader), he retreats from his descriptions, refusing to be construed in "the gross, literal Sense" (141). Ideas, Philonous must admit, are not shelved *in* the mind as books in a study (**Rooms**); impressions are not made as *in* wax, with a seal (**Impressions**); but he retorts that "the Mind comprehends, or perceives them; and that it is affected from without" and continues, speaking so as to close down the objection conclusively: "Nor is there any thing in this, but what is conformable to the general Analogy of Language," by which thinking is signified by words borrowed from "sensible Things" (142).[6] Still, in speaking of *comprehension* and *perception*, Berkeley's spokesman may not have gotten entirely clear of the accusation of metaphor, because both words are rooted, etymologically, in the physical act of *seizing* something—or so Locke and Bolingbroke insist, and so Berkeley must realize.[7]

In the *Dialogues* as elsewhere, Berkeley acknowledges that philosophers speak of the objects of perception *as if* they were things, so the general analogy that obtains must coordinate, at minimum, two semantic realms. When Berkeley intimates that words have both literal (gross, original) senses and new senses that result when a word is borrowed and put to a new use, he appeals to an eighteenth-century understanding of metaphor that looks back to Cicero and Quintilian and the classical catalogs of tropes. But in the context of Berkeley's idealism, when the "literal" language of the commonly sensible is enlisted to describe the private, subjective character of experience, a peculiar, modern metaphorics of mind results, in which ideas *are* things.[8] Figuration is sited in the theory of ideas, as Berkeley resolves to "*Think with the Learned, and Speak with the Vulgar*," but his philosophical vocabulary is bifurcated, its terms, meant literally, refer only metaphorically.[9] "In common Talk, the Objects of our Senses are not termed *Ideas*, but *Things*," but properly speaking, "these Things are Ideas" (*Treatise* 143).

Identifying thoughts and things, Philonous will not quarrel "for a Word," and it can be hard to specify on which side (thought, thing) the metaphor falls. In Berkeley's idealism, the mind is a metaphor or a notion, and its ideas are real things. The dualities of mind and matter are shifted almost entirely into language, a matter of commonplaces and general analogy, which makes

Berkeley's an extreme, therefore clarifying, case in which the distinction between proper and improper language use (that is, more narrowly, literal and figurative use) is asked to do very heavy work in correlating "sensible Things" and "the immediate Objects of the Understanding."[10] The work of distinction demanded by Berkeley's idealism may indeed be so demanding that "language" fractures into two varieties, human and divine, with Berkeley proving too guarded to say definitively which is properly literal.[11] We are left, then, with the insuperable contradiction of word and object: the fact of general, linguistic analogy that is repudiated by Berkeley's main philosophical insight that "an idea can be like nothing but an idea."[12] In what sense, demands Hylas, are we to understand "those Expressions" that make the mind conformable to that which it is not like, to which it cannot be compared.

Later writers, such as Thomas Reid, deny resemblance more forthrightly in their appeals to common sense: the analogy of body and mind is the limit of comparison "because there are not two things in nature more unlike."[13] Analogy works, nevertheless, pervasively, in the period's empiricism. That ideas about the world derive from that world wins the assent of materialists (like Hobbes), low-key empiricists (like Locke), and idealists (like Berkeley). And yet, to imagine a complete intellectual world modeled on the physical world, populated by impressions and ideas, and governed by laws of thought entails something more: a philosophical disposition that Hume scholar Annette Baier names, in an inspired phrase, a full-blown "figurative empiricism"—a phrase I have taken on in these pages to designate my area of study.[14] The furniture of the mind, a census of its **Inhabitants**, and a survey of the laws that govern them will be stated by way of general analogy as empiricism assigns its metaphors of sense to the idealities described. Any history of such assignments contributes to the biography of mind or, more grandly (too grandly), to the study of what Hegel named *Geist*.[15] Its main method, as stated in my introduction, is a variety of linguistic phenomenology.[16]

I maintain that figurative empiricism is the unofficial corollary to the theory of ideas in the eighteenth century and is promoted implicitly or explicitly in any writing in which the facts of mental life are pervasively represented *as if* they were physical facts.[17] Sensuous particulars, stubborn and resistant, "nonidentical," are recruited by resemblance and organized in a general analogy that structures a world for the mind. Metaphors further advance false identity (A is B) and weld the two halves, mental and physical, of an ideological whole together.[18] Where physical facts crisscross and are crisscrossed by philosophical thought and literary language, the intersections invite rhetorical investigation and the recuperation of the literal by historical analysis.[19]

That the general analogy described in the preceding pages is, by and large, evenly distributed across the period surveyed indicates that eighteenth-century figurative empiricism is a coherent formation, resistant, on most of its fronts, to change. Eighteenth-century metaphors of mind are both constrained by canons of propriety and contested in their contexts.[20] Because of neoclassical decorum and its constraints, the metaphors recur; but because they are contested, the metaphors are repurposed. Working with the particulars, I number the appearance of a metaphor in print and speak as well to its varying senses and uses.

As pursued in the foregoing entries, figurative empiricism stands as but one episode in a longer history of category mistakes. Asserting that the mind is a metaphor is, I am afraid, putting the matter too baldly for many contemporary philosophers of mind[21] as well as those cognitivists who insist, straightforwardly, that mind is what the brain does. But I insist on intellectual and literary history in order to complicate contemporary philosophy and cognitive linguistics. For if the mind gives itself the appearance of an objective existence by drawing forms from material culture and applying them to itself, to what does "mind" refer but to congeries of metaphors, which themselves only obliquely signify that cultural origin?

Ambivalently metaphorical or theoretical in their moment of origin, many of the metaphors treated in these pages are no longer commonplace, while others seem to serve still reliably in references to states of mind. A history of metaphors of mind will tell us as much about meaning-making as it will about the ways of the world. Tenaciously strange metaphors survive in lyric poetry, while others "congeal into a technical term" in philosophical or scientific explanation.[22] The metaphors of mind collected in these pages therefore serve in the analysis of several varieties of figurative empiricism prevailing in the eighteenth century.

As I acknowledge in the opening sections and emphasize throughout, my scope has been abridged, the general analogy only glimpsed in the activity of collecting and sorting examples. In this dictionary, many likely entries are unwritten, and thousands of metaphors have been left behind in the database. An untold number of metaphors have not even been collected.[23] But that it is possible to track shifts in usage—in **Metal** metaphors especially—means that I am able to offer conjectural evidence of the interactions of material conditions and intellectual history, context and text. And even where frequencies show more stability, new studies might unearth fundamental, roiling change by attending separately to base and superstructure, vehicle and tenor, and describing the analogies.

To put it another way: stable metaphors give up their semantic impertinence and impropriety and enter the dictionary by way of convention, a process that has a history.[24] Taking a place among other concepts, a metaphor is converted to an established use and is lexicalized.[25] My reading against the grain of this semantic history for the metaphorical moments has proven to be remorselessly concretizing and materialist in its steady-on, example-by-example tracing of the mind and its objects (Berkeley's "immediate objects of understanding") to the matter (Berkeley's "sensible things") from which the terms for mental operations are borrowed and the place in which (the very page on which) a conversion was effected and a metaphor coined.[26]

In this, as in other things, I have tried to follow Samuel Johnson, who believed (at least when he wrote the *Plan* for his *Dictionary*) that each of his entries might tell the story of metaphor by locating the physical referent of a term *prior* to its psychological application.[27] To cite an example glossed by William Wimsatt and other readers of Johnson's *Dictionary*, "ARDENT" is a term the first meaning of which is "Hot; burning; fiery," while the second meaning is "Fierce; vehement; having the appearance or quality of desire."[28] But where does the word for "fire" come from in the first place? What Promethean speech act first sparks into language? And what poet first identified fire and desire, using the name of one to refer to the other? The act is equally incredible and promethean.

In its philosophical fables, the Enlightenment imagined original language users—savages in the state of nature—making an incredible, metaphorical connection that identified word and idea.[29] In the eighteenth century, perhaps especially, such meaning is incoherently explained as a matter of convention: language users come together to agree on the meanings of words, yet no agreement can be proposed or ratified until these users have established a common language.[30] At the beginning of a language, the first word is a metaphor, a founding or placing of sense in the flux of sensuousness: so the claim is made for the origins of conceptuality *as* metaphor. And the argument is put forward by Vico, Condillac, Rousseau, Herder, and later still by Nietzsche among others (and these writers feature in still later poststructuralist accounts of metaphor and meaning in the eighteenth century).[31]

But it cannot be so: a lexicalized metaphor is a new term in a vocabulary.[32] I say, no new metaphor without general analogy. I say, moreover, that there is no ready way of establishing priority in terms physical and psychological but by etymological fiat and just-so storytelling.

An early and influential assertion that our language for mental operations is, in its origins, metaphorical is found in Locke, who imagines "the first

Beginners of Languages" borrowing from the sensible to figure the invisible—the process as described is recognizably metaphorical as terms for "*obvious sensible* Ideas *are transferred to more abstruse significations*" (*Essay* III.i.5). For each idea in their minds, primitive speakers found the word that signified and therefore expressed that idea—making the mental manifest in speech.[33] Locke writes, "*Imagine*, *Apprehend*, *Comprehend*, *Adhere*, *Conceive*, *Instill*, *Disgust*, *Disturbance*, *Tranquillity*, etc. are all Words taken from the Operations of sensible Things; and applied to certain Modes of Thinking" (III.i.5). Through long use the terms of an original and poetic language came to be established as firm, customary, and obligatory as a philosophical lexicon was formed, expanded, and conventionalized. The fall from figuration and linguistic progress may even be encoded in Locke's list, departing as it does from the verb *imagine* to terminate in *tranquillity*. Or the list may be read as theory—indeed an anticipation of Wordsworth's theory of poetic imagination, in which emotion is recollected in tranquility.

The passage from Locke is much discussed, but from Hans Aarsleff to the present, commentators often overlook a strangeness, which I want to draw out. In short, Locke's theory of metaphors for mind juggles thought and thing and traces a double movement: from the obvious to the abstruse, and from the abstruse to the literal. Locke's pairing of invisible thought and sensible thing—to speak with Quentin Meillasoux—anticipates the "correlationist two-step" of post-Kantian philosophy, in which the relation of thinking to being is given priority over either of the correlated terms.[34] The relation of the invisible and the sensible is made impossibly if ineluctably in metaphor, a trope that makes a statement of identity (*A* is *B*) commensurate with an implication of resemblance (*A* is like *B*). The assertion of resemblance—as well as its denial—suggests that it is possible to stand outside of idea and object in order to judge of similarity and difference. But there is no such view from nowhere, no supreme **Court**, no standpoint from which one can construct such analogy and compare the world as it is in itself with the world as it is for us.[35]

When empiricism distinguishes between the mind and its ideas or between sensibility and understanding, it should discover a limit to what Kant called, at the end of the century, "the pretension of sensibility," because positive talk of things in themselves is "empty trafficking with words."[36] Conceptions of mind may be farthest-fetched metalepsis, if not (as Berkeley's Hylas suggests) catachresis.[37] Locke and other figurative empiricists would have us believe that there was once spoken a language without metaphors of mind. And here Locke's account of our psychological terms deriving from physical ones necessarily gives way to a rhetorical analysis that queries analogy as that which would bridge mind and matter.

Long use literalizes references to the immaterial as it converts words from original, obvious uses to more abstruse ones and then back again. And that is as far as it goes, the bridge to nowhere that metaphysics would build. This book, a work of literary history, has no remit to offer firm, new philosophical foundations—even should it want to. Rather, by restoration in the final entry (**Writing**) of mental significances to textual and cultural materiality, I would recover the privileged ground on which analogy is stated: literature. From my online index of eighteenth-century pages, I work back, critically and historically, through the figures of empiricism, investigating the general analogy of language metaphor by metaphor. Such work has required continually switching between meaning and reference in a manner that I associate with metaphor as such. The shift is concisely characterized by Donald Davidson in the essay "What Metaphors Mean," when he insists that identifying metaphor requires the ability to contrast new uses of old words with the use of words already understood: in the first case, "our attention is directed to language, in the other, to what language is about" (35).

I find this same shifting to be neatly illustrated in *The Philosophy of Rhetoric*, where I. A. Richards introduces his well-known distinction between tenor and vehicle.[38] Working with eighteenth-century materials (including Lord Kames's treatment of metaphor), the new terminology is fully exercised in a reading of the most famous quatrain from John Denham's poem *Coopers Hill*:

> O could I flow like thee, and make thy streame
> My great example, as it is my theme!
> Though deep, yet cleare, though gentle, yet not dull,
> Strong without rage, without 'oreflowing full.[39]

Denham's lines, on a first reading, may reduce to the literal, hydrological description of a river. The comparison may "flow," in one direction only—downstream, as it were. But the close reader who observes the elision and metrical containment of the word "overflowing" confirms a fullness of meaning. On closer consideration then, the lines may be understood in mutual terms (a liquid stream and a stream of ideas); or—and this is the strong reading promoted by Richards against eighteenth-century understandings of metaphor as merely decorative comparison—the river "may come to seem an excuse for saying about the mind something which could not be said about the river" (Richards, *Philosophy* 122).

On Richards's interpretation the poet's mind (the tenor) and the river (the vehicle) shift positions alternately in the final couplet. The words *deep* and *clear*, Richards claims, are "literally descriptive of the vehicle, the river; derivatively descriptive of the mind"; by contrast, the words *gentle* and *rage* belong to the tenor but are derivatively descriptive of the vehicle (121). For Richards, the comparison flows in two directions. The river's stream may be both "example" and "theme" (to recur to Denham's words); fluid motions exemplify both tenor and vehicle. The Thames and the activity of the poetic mind are mutually figured in the verses so that, according to William Empson, "it is not even obvious which is tenor and which is vehicle."[40]

Here I would add to Richards's and Empson's readings in my usual way, by reconstructing contexts in which the metaphor both means and matters. The tidal ebb and flow of the Thames, I suggest, underlies Denham's comparison and secures the best interpretation of these lines: the tide of the river turns every six hours or so, flooding inward and then ebbing seaward. Such reading foregrounds dialectic. It takes text and context, figure and ground as reversible.[41] As is so often the case in literary study, the metaphor comes to seem an excuse for saying something more about the world.[42]

That a description of a river could express two propositions brings out the duck-rabbit duality of metaphor as well as duality of mind and its objects. Neither the priority of thought nor that of the river is established in these readings of Denham's verses, and the root meanings of *dull* (sluggish, stagnant) and *rage* (a flood, a swell) complicate the isolation of a tenor. When Empson reads Richards reading the lines from Denham, he proposes a new term, "mutual metaphor," for cases in which "tenor and vehicle are treated as examples of some wider concept which transcends them, and upsets the ordinary scheme of interpretation." The term is probably inapt, Empson admits, as it is meant to mark "a virtual abandonment of metaphor." What is effected is a putting of tenor and vehicle on equal footing: "We are no longer interested in which is the vehicle and which is the tenor,"[43] and the two cases collapse into one.

I have grounded my inquiry in the general analogy of language. But when that which Richards called the "ground" of comparison is taken literally, general analogy intimates geography. Closer still to the closing methodological point I make here, Fernand Braudel evokes the river of time in his historiography (it is his foundational metaphor), distinguishing its deep, slow laminar flow from the eddies and back currents on the surface of *histoire événementielle*.[44] While it is a matter of method that Braudel's monumental history of the Mediterranean brings "geographic time" to attention by focusing on coasts and river basins, it is portentous that, in the current moment of climate change, new tidal rhythms threaten to become part of the history of events.

In time the Thames turns, and tenor and vehicle change places again as reading itself gives rise to new descriptions. More details may be brought in: Denham's poem opens with an invocation of the streams that flow from Mount Helicon, while on the page preceding the famous four lines expounded above, the river Thames, which would "pay his tribute to the Sea," is likened to "mortall life" hasting "to meet Eternity" (9). In this last, the desultory reader, idling away, is reminded that his reading has likewise its termination.

Richards cites Samuel Johnson's approval of the lines in *The Life of Denham* but not his critical suggestion that the quatrain may not be true wit: Denham's words, says Johnson, "thus artfully opposed, are to be understood simply on one side of the comparison, and metaphorically on the other; and if there be any language which does not express intellectual operations by material images, into that language they cannot be translated."[45] I am not sure I can myself get clear about which "side" of a comparison is which, but I admire Jean Hagstrum's explication of Johnson's comment and will allow that the "words have no literal and exact meaning which is independent of the river" and that, for Johnson, the poet's intellect can only be understood "by analogy."[46] The trouble is that Johnson, unwilling to compare mind and matter, censures such analogy. For purposes of appraisal Johnson imagines—the moment is arresting—a language without metaphors of mind.

Epilogue

BECAUSE THIS DICTIONARY arrays four-square superimpositions of mind and matter, metaphor and meaning, eighteenth-century thought and its social context, each becomes an excuse to say something about the other. Fixed for the moment in these pages, the dualities abide, find equal footing, and wait only for new readings to stir them.

In valediction then, I remind the reader that this book, too, is part of a double unit and points beyond itself to a database, the interface for which is located at http://metaphorized.net/. There collected are the many metaphors enumerated in these pages but not quoted.

Tenor and vehicle change places here, as this publication is made to stand as a *paper surrogate* for a *digital artifact.* Seen as such, every entry is also a portal, and the incompletely assembled quotations are provocation to query the database and return more metaphors.[1]

My book's surrogacy exemplifies what, in the sciences, has recently been called "an empty paper"—that is, a scholarly article whose main purpose is to publish a link to a database.[2] *Empty paper!* The two words are a happy combination, both ready-made periphrase and new-made idiom. I take them as both and more: an instance of eighteenth-century poetic diction, cast away in a new technoscientific context. For me, the phrase evokes the blank slate or tabula rasa, the metaphor with which this project began, the metaphor with which this epilogue concludes.

This page
was intentionally
left blank

Notes

About This Book

1. Please point your browser to http://metaphorized.net/ and continue reading.

2. Samuel Johnson, *A Dictionary of the English Language* (W. Strahan, 1755) vol. 1, preface. I have worked most closely with the AMS Press facsimile edition of 1967.

3. See Baier's *Death and Character: Further Reflections on Hume* (Cambridge, MA: Harvard UP, 2008), 138.

4. Pierre Bourdieu, *Outline of a Theory of a Practice* (Cambridge: Cambridge UP, 1977), 91.

5. Quoting Berkeley's *Three Dialogues* (G. James, 1713), 141–2.

Introduction

1. James Boswell, *The Journal of a Tour to the Hebrides* (Henry Baldwin, 1785), 27, 28.

2. Tobias Smollett, *The History and Adventures of an Atom* (Robinson and Roberts, 1769), 2:207–8.

3. A computer scientist reminds me that *all computation* can be done by hand, given time: "If a Turing machine can do it, I can do it" (Worthy Martin, personal communication). On the possibility of automating the identification and collection of metaphors, see Brad Pasanek and D. Sculley, "Mining Millions of Metaphors," *Literary and Linguistic Computing* 23:3 (2008): 345–60.

4. The favored terms of I. A. Richards, Max Black, and George Lakoff, respectively. See I. A. Richards, *The Philosophy of Rhetoric* (London: Oxford UP, 1936); Max Black, *Models and Metaphors* (Ithaca, NY: Cornell UP, 1962); and George Lakoff, "The Contemporary Theory of Metaphor," in *Metaphor and Thought*, 2nd ed., ed. Andrew Ortony (Cambridge: Cambridge UP, 1993), 202–51. Johnson's often-cited remark was recorded by Boswell, *The Life of Samuel Johnson* (Henry Baldwin, 1791), 2:157.

5. Roger M. White, *The Structure of Metaphor: The Way the Language of Metaphor Works* (Oxford: Blackwell, 1996), 79–80.

6. Anne Killigrew, *Poems by Mrs. Anne Killigrew* (Samuel Lowndes, 1686), 35; Matthew Prior, *Poems on Several Occasions* (J. Tonson and J. Barber, 1718), 320.

7. More than 3,800 metaphors were found by reading, but the plurality (a little over 5,500, or almost half the entries in the database) come from searches conducted with Hugo, a bespoke search interface designed by Stanford Libraries programmer Rick Wong and installed over the SGML-encoded Chadwyck-Healey text collections of English poetry, English prose drama, and eighteenth-century prose fiction. The

composition of the database and the distribution of my metaphors are detailed in the text that follows.

8. Alexander Pope, *An Essay on Criticism* (W. Lewis, 1711), 15.

9. The term "bifurcation" is associated with Alfred North Whitehead's *The Concept of Nature* (Cambridge: Cambridge UP, 1920), 26–48; "bipolar world" is Earl Wasserman's phrase. See "Johnson's *Rasselas*: Implicit Contexts," *Journal of English and Germanic Philology* 74 (1975): 9–10. On the Cartesian dichotomy as the foundation of other structural divisions, see Stephen Toulmin, *Cosmopolis: The Hidden Agenda of Modernity* (Chicago: U of Chicago P, 1990), 108–17. On organizing literary study in terms of dialectical divisions and conflations, see Michael McKeon, *The Secret History of Domesticity: Public, Private, and the Division of Knowledge* (Baltimore: Johns Hopkins UP, 2005), xxiv. Close reading discovers division at the level of the text. John Sitter describes Hume's dichotomies in book II of *A Treatise of Human Nature* as "a virtual banquet of two-pronged forks." *Literary Loneliness in Mid-Eighteenth-Century England* (Ithaca, NY: Cornell UP, 1982), 33. John Richetti describes Locke literalizing the world of experience while promoting a quasi-figurative theory of language in *Philosophical Writing: Locke, Berkeley, Hume* (Cambridge, MA: Harvard UP, 1983), 48–116.

10. Unless otherwise noted, citations from Locke's *Essay* are drawn from Peter Nidditch's Oxford edition, which is based on the fourth edition of 1700. *An Essay Concerning Human Understanding* (Oxford: Oxford UP, 1975). I have consulted earlier and later printings of the title and am careful to date the metaphors correctly.

11. Kenneth MacLean, *John Locke and English Literature of the Eighteenth Century* (New York: Russell and Russell, 1962), 20–1.

12. Abrams converts Locke into Wordsworth, his "epistemological opposite," in two moves, via Edward Young. *The Mirror and the Lamp: Romantic Theory and the Critical Tradition* (Oxford: Oxford UP, 1953), 63. In contrast, I would locate contradiction in Locke at the outset and multiply complications in the literature of the eighteenth century that follows after.

13. Abrams, *Mirror and Lamp*, 57. The main event—the comparison of eighteenth- and nineteenth-century metaphors—is beyond the scope of this book.

14. Alan Liu, "The Meaning of the Digital Humanities," *PMLA* 128:2 (2013): 409–22, 414. Liu takes an experiment done with "word cohorts" by Ryan Heuser and Long Le-Khac that resulted in the fourth pamphlet published by the Stanford Lit Lab as his object lesson.

15. "But as there is no such thing as an innocent reading, we must say what reading we are guilty of." Louis Althusser and Étienne Balibar, *Reading Capital* (1971; repr., London: Verso, 2009), 14.

16. Terry Eagleton says of Williams in a memorial lecture: "Words for him were condensed social practices, sites of historical struggle, repositories of political wisdom or domination; he had a Celtic feel for them, for their rich texture and density."

"Resources for a Journey of Hope: The Significance of Raymond Williams," *New Left Review* 168 (March–April 1988): 10.

17. On Browning and other dictionary readers, see Austin Dobson, "Dictionary Readers," in *Later Essays, 1917–1920* (London: Oxford UP, 1921), 160. Ammon Shea's *Reading the OED: One Man, One Year, 21,730 Pages* (New York: Penguin, 2008) is an alphabetically organized diary of reading the twenty volumes of the *OED*. Shea's and other "extreme reading" efforts are discussed in a recent issue of the *New Yorker* (June 9, 2014).

18. Austin's ordinary language methods are outlined in "A Plea for Excuses," in *Philosophical Papers*, ed. J. O. Urmson and G. J. Warnock (Oxford: Oxford UP, 1961), 175–204. See also Stanley Cavell, "Austin at Criticism," in *Must We Mean What We Say? A Book of Essays*, updated ed. (Cambridge: Cambridge UP, 2002), 97–114.

19. On the importance of metaphors of mind in Johnson's *Dictionary*, see William K. Wimsatt, *Philosophic Words: A Study of Style and Meaning in the Rambler and Dictionary of Samuel Johnson* (Hamden, CT: Archon Books, 1968), 42–9. For the exhibition of genealogy and intellectual history, see Johnson's preface to the *Dictionary*.

20. See Alan Liu, "From Reading to Social Computing," in *Literary Studies in the Digital Age: An Evolving Anthology* (MLA 2013), doi:10.1632/lsda.2013.2.

21. Dobson, "Dictionary Readers," 160. For an evocative one-paragraph description of dictionary reading, see Matthew Garrett, *Episodic Poetics: Politics and Literary Form after the Constitution* (Oxford: Oxford UP, 2014), 32–3.

22. Boswell, *Life of Johnson*, 1:400.

23. On alternating between these modes of reading, see Robin Valenza, "How Literature Becomes Knowledge: A Case Study," *English Literary History* 76:1 (2009): 238. Valenza's compelling essay influences my framing of this book in these opening pages. More recently Naomi S. Baron, Jim Collins, N. Katherine Hayles, and others have contributed to a discussion of our changing reading practices. See "The Changing Profession: Reading in the Digital Age," *PMLA* 128:1 (January 2013): 194–243.

24. Keith Thomas, "Diary," *London Review of Books* 32:11 (2010): 36–7.

25. These figures derived from the Literature Online interface. I located the initial bulk of metaphors by searching in the Chadwyck-Healey full-text collections through a now defunct search interface designed and maintained by Stanford University Libraries. The interface, called HUGO, was a system for browsing and searching texts encoded in Standard Generalized Markup Language (SGML). Stanford librarian Glen Worthey informs me that the principal programmer, Rick Wong, named the program after Hugo de Saint Caro, or Cardinal Hugo, compiler of the first concordance. A brief history of Stanford's Humanities Digital Information Service is available at www-sul.stanford.edu/depts/hasrg/hdis/about.html.

26. The databases are occasionally faulted for editorial choices and a reliance on the indispensable if out-of-date *New Cambridge Bibliography of English Literature* (Cambridge: Cambridge UP, 1969–72), which omits or slights many women authors,

African writers, and laboring-class poets now central in contemporary eighteenth-century studies (the newer, third edition still in preparation will be more comprehensive). On the first Chadwyck-Healey text collections, see, for example, John Sutherland's review, "When in Rom," *London Review of Books* 9 (June 1994): 7–8. Compare John Richetti's more positive but still skeptical review of the eighteenth-century fiction collection in *Eighteenth-Century Fiction* 10:1 (October 1997): 107–10. Because the text collections do not uniformly include first printings, I have done lots of backtracking, comparing later printings with earlier ones.

27. Raymond Williams, *Keywords: A Vocabulary of Culture and Society*, rev. ed. (New York: Oxford UP, 1983), 19. As stated in note 7, above, over 3,800 metaphors were found by reading, while a little over 5,500 were discovered searching in Chadwyck-Healey's databases of eighteenth-century fiction, poetry, and prose drama. Over 1,100 more metaphors were located in ProQuest's Literature Online collections, which supplement the original Chadwyck Healey collections. More than 450 metaphors come from searches in Google Books. I have also employed a variety of other electronic text collections: over 330 metaphors were discovered or reconfirmed in searches of Eighteenth Century Collections Online and over 350 more from ECCO-TCP. Over 220 entries were found searching the Intelex Past Masters text collection, 190 were found searching texts in the Liberty Fund's Online Library of Liberty, over 180 are from the University of Virginia Electronic Text Center, and over 110 from EEBO or its TCP full-text duplicate.

28. *The Architecture of Concepts: The Historical Formulation of Human Rights* (New York: Fordham UP, 2013).

29. Robin Valenza, principal investigator, with Michael Gleicher, Jonathan Hope, and Michael Witmore.

30. To be clear, eighteenth-century editions of Shakespeare and Milton and other early modern authors, although consulted and occasionally quoted, are not included in the counts arrayed at the head of each entry. Each metaphor is counted only once and dated to the moment it is first published or otherwise put into circulation. Serial publications are dealt with and dated by part. Metaphors from collections titled *Poems on Several Occasions* were hunted in ECCO and Google Books to establish or confirm, where possible, earlier dates of publication. Works that were revised over years are checked in their various states. A case in point: I have searched through both the first and third editions of Richardson's *Clarissa* but have counted metaphors that appear in both editions only once, dating them to the first edition. Works with complicated textual histories, such as Locke's *Essay*, Thomson's *The Seasons*, and Akenside's *Pleasures of the Imagination*, have cost me much time and trouble.

31. Online I have taxonomized over 14,000 metaphors, 10,015 of which belong to the period (1700–1800) here surveyed. Some 700 metaphors are quoted in main text of this dictionary; some 50 more appear in these notes.

32. Valenza warns in "Literature Becomes Knowledge": "Database learning amplifies the difficulties present in old-fashioned index-learning. First, generalizing on

the basis of this data requires a careful look at how the database is compiled. Although extensive, most databases are not exhaustive. Further, their search and indexing techniques reflect the limitations of any indexing process, even one based on a full text corpus. They often miss words that are in a different font (including chapter titles or italicized words); they produce false positives; variations in spelling and punctuation may or may not turn up; radically different outcomes may result from very slight differences in search terms. . . . These differences require some work and imagination to overcome if a project is to aim to be accurate and representative" (224).

33. See Sayre N. Greenfield's "ECCO-Locating the Eighteenth Century," *Eighteenth-Century Intelligencer* 21:1 (Jan 2007): 1–9.

34. See www.textcreationpartnership.org and www.18thconnect.org. Jerome McGann has forecasted that "the entirety of our inherited archive of cultural works will have to be re-edited within a network of digital storage, access, and dissemination." See Jerome J. McGann, "Literary Scholarship in the Digital Future," *Chronicle Review*, December 13, 2002.

35. See Jerome McGann, *Social Values and Poetic Acts: The Historical Judgment of Literary Work* (Cambridge, MA: Harvard UP, 1988), 122–4; and McGann, *Historical Studies and Literary Criticism* (Madison: U of Wisconsin P, 1985), 8–11.

36. Alexander Pope, *The Dunciad* (A. Dodd, 1728), 13. Roger D. Lund claims, "The index and its related forms—dictionaries, concordances, digests, translations and compendia—serve as convenient symbols for the transformation of 'ancient knowledge' into modern forms of information." "The Eel of Science: Index Learning, Scriblerian Satire, and the Rise of Information Culture," *Eighteenth-Century Life* 22:2 (May 1998): 21. See also Valenza, "Literature Becomes Knowledge," 218–9.

37. With reference to Fredric Jameson's heady speculations on the impossibility of new literary history: Jameson, "New Literary History after the End of the New," *New Literary History* 39:3 (Summer 2008): 375–87. An invocation of Pope's Smithfield muses requires alphabetical, indexical incantation and a carnival of carving, cutting, and pasting: see Franco Moretti's list of unread novels in the opening of his aptly titled essay "The Slaughterhouse of Literature," *Modern Language Quarterly* 61:1 (2000): 207–27. Eighteenth-century Smithfield was a scene of butcher stalls as well as the setting for Bartholomew Fair and its entertainments.

38. *Guardian* no. 60, Wednesday, May 20, 1713. The periodical essay almost seems to anticipate the opening of *The Life of Johnson*, in which young Johnson consumes "all literature," albeit irregularly, in his father's bookshop. Boswell explains, "he read a great deal in a desultory manner, without any scheme of study, as chance threw books in his way, and inclination directed him through them" (1:23). Markers of keywords will also have underlined the term "desultory" in the second paragraph of Boswell's *Life*.

39. See John Henderson, "Knowing Someone through Their Books: Pliny on Uncle Pliny (*Epistles* 3.5)," *Classical Philology* 97:3 (July 2002), 262–3, 272–4.

40. See Franco Moretti, "Style, Inc. Reflections on Seven Thousand Titles," *Critical Inquiry* 36:1 (Autumn 2009), 45, 152. The slogan "formalism without close reading" is from Jonathan Arac, "Anglo-Globalism," *New Left Review* 16 (2002): 41. Moretti approves it in "More Conjectures," *New Left Review* 20 (2003). But it may recall, with attendant irony, what Swift called "the *Art of being Deep-learned and Shallow-read.*" *A Tale of a Tub* (John Nutt, 1704), 119.

41. The phrase "distant reading" was coined by Franco Moretti in "Conjectures on World Literature," *New Left Review* 1 (2000): 56. In giving up close reading, Moretti imagines a "little pact with the devil." See also Moretti's *Graphs, Maps, and Trees: Abstract Models for a Literary History* (London: Verso, 2005), 1; and his *Distant Reading* (London: Verso, 2013).

42. Margaret Cohen, *The Sentimental Education of the Novel* (Princeton, NJ: Princeton UP, 1999), 23. See also Pierre Bayard's liberating, ironic polemics in *How to Talk about Books You Haven't Read* (London: Granta, 2007).

43. In this note, a reading list: Leah Price's scholarship is a good introduction to the history of reading in the eighteenth century and after. See her "Reading and Literary Criticism" in *Cambridge History of Victorian Literature*, ed. Kate Flint (Cambridge: Cambridge UP, 2012); Price, "From *The History of a Book* to a 'History of the Book,'" *Representations* 108:1 (Fall 2009): 120–38; and Price, "Reading: The State of the Discipline," *Book History* 6 (2004): 303–20. On slow reading, see Reuben Brower's classic "Reading in Slow Motion" in *Defense of Reading: A Reader's Approach to Literary Criticism* (New York: Dutton, 1962); and David Mikics's *Slow Reading in a Hurried Age* (Cambridge, MA: Harvard UP, 2014). Robin Valenza's "slow reading" of Richardson's *Clarissa* and Johnson's *Dictionary*, in "Literature Becomes Knowledge," contrasts interpretive work and indexical methods, in part by putting search indexes to interpretive ends. Srinivas Aravamudan also chooses the adjective "slow" to describe his acts of reading in *Enlightenment Orientalism: Resisting the Rise of the Novel* (Chicago: U of Chicago P, 2012), 7. On suspicious reading, see Rita Felski, "Suspicious Minds," *Poetics Today* 32:2 (2011): 215–34. For reparative reading, see Eve Kosofsky Sedgwick, "Paranoid Reading and Reparative Reading; or, You're So Paranoid, You Probably Think This Introduction Is about You," in *Novel-Gazing: Queer Readings in Fiction* (Durham, NC: Duke UP, 1997), 1–37. Michael Warner gives special consideration to Sedgwick's comments on paranoid readers in his overview of "uncritical reading"; more recently Malcolm Bull has recommended "reading like a loser" in his *Anti-Nietzsche* (London: Verso, 2011), and D. A. Miller has named and demonstrated a method called "Too Close Reading" in "Hitchcock's Hidden Pictures," *Critical Inquiry* 37 (Autumn 2012). The practice of distant reading was first articulated in Moretti's "Conjectures on World Literature."; but see also his *Graphs, Maps, and Trees.* A program for surface reading is outlined in Stephen Best and Sharon Marcus, "Surface Reading: An Introduction," *Representations* 108:1 (Fall 2009): 1–21. See also Heather Love's appeals to Bruno Latour and Erving Goffman in her call for a descriptive reading practice: "Close but Not Deep: Literary Ethics

and the Descriptive Turn," *New Literary History* 41:2 (Spring 2010): 371–91. See David Kazanjian's *Brink of Freedom: Improvising Life in the Nineteenth-Century Atlantic World* (Durham, NC: Duke UP, forthcoming 2015) on *over*reading archival texts, treating them as if they were making theoretical claims.

44. "How Scholars Read," *ADE Bulletin* 146 (Fall 2008), 14.

45. William H. Sherman, *Used Books: Marking Readers in Renaissance England* (Philadelphia: University of Pennsylvania Press, 2008), xv-xvi. See also Leah Price, *The Anthology and the Rise of the Novel*, 4. I muse on Frances Ferguson's remark as well (and the argument that follows): "We know that literature is a selection of language"; in "Planetary Literary History: The Place of the Text," *New Literary History* 39 (2008): 658.

46. Peter Stallybrass, "Books and Scrolls: Navigating the Bible," in *Books and Readers in Early Modern England*, ed. Jennifer Andersen and Elizabeth Sauer (Philadelphia: U of Pennsylvania P, 2002), 42.

47. On the commonplace book as a kind of database, see Peter Stallybrass, "Against Thinking: Responses to Ed Folsom's 'Database as Genre: The Epic Transformation of the Archives,'" *PMLA* 122:5 (October 2007): 1580–7. On reading and commonplacing, see Ann Moss, *Printed Commonplace-Books and the Structuring of Renaissance Thought* (Oxford: Clarendon, 1996); and Barbara Benedict, *Making the Modern Reader: Cultural Mediation in Early Modern Literary Anthologies* (Princeton, NJ: Princeton UP, 1996), 39–51. See also Ann Blair's *Too Much to Know: Managing Scholarly Information before the Modern Age* (New Haven, CT: Yale UP, 2010).

48. Michael Warner, "Uncritical Reading," in *Polemic: Critical or Uncritical*, ed. Jane Gallop (New York: Routledge, 2004), 20. Cohen responds to Franco Moretti's prescriptions for distant reading and Sharon Marcus's ideas about "just reading." See her "Narratology in the Archive of Literature," *Representations* 108:1 (Fall 2009): 51–75.

49. See Ramsay's *Reading Machines: Toward an Algorithmic Criticism* (Urbana: U of Illinois P, 2011); and his "In Praise of Pattern," *TEXT Technology* 14:2 (2205): 177–90. Compare Best and Marcus's claim that "computers are . . . potent describers, anatomizers, taxonomists," in "Surface Reading," 17. Best and Marcus's personification of the computer may betray some confusion about the workings of algorithms.

50. Ted Underwood, *Why Literary Periods Mattered: Historical Contrast and the Prestige of English Studies* (Stanford, CA: Stanford UP, 2013), 16. See also David Armitage on the return of the *longue durée* in intellectual history and the promise of digital collections and databases: "What's the Big Idea? Intellectual History and the *Longue Durée*," *History of European Ideas* 38:4 (December 2012): 493–507.

51. See Hugh Blair's *Lectures on Rhetoric and Belles Lettres* (Strahan, 1783) and Lord Kames's *Elements of Criticism*, 3 vols. (Edinburgh: A. Millar, 1762).

52. J. L. Austin, *Philosophical Papers*, 182. Compare Ernst Robert Curtius, who in all seriousness frames his particular research question as a "prolegomena to what I should like to call a phenomenology of literature." *European Literature and the Latin Middle Ages* (Princeton, NJ: Princeton UP, 1990), ix. Hegel describes his own

phenomenology as "a slow-moving succession of Spirits, a gallery of images." *Phenomenology of Spirit* (Oxford: Oxford UP, 1977), 492. See also John Michael Krois's discussion of Hegel's *Galerie von Bildern* as a collection of "linguistic images or metaphors." "*Ars Memoriae*, Philosophy and Culture: Frances Yates and After," in *Philosophy and Culture: Essays in Honor of Donald Philip Verene*, ed. Glenn Alexander Magee (Charlottesville, VA: Philosophy Documentation Center, 2002), 154.

53. The method of "literary montage" is associated with Walter Benjamin's literary history, in particular with the Arcades Project, in which Benjamin proposed a fine-grained Marxist historiography that would "assemble large-scale constructions out of the smallest and most precisely cut components." See *The Arcades Project*, ed. Rolf Tiedemann, trans. Howard Eiland and Kevin McLaughlin (Cambridge, MA: Harvard UP, 1999), 460–1. See also James Chandler's discussion of "scissors-and-paste history," Fredric Jameson, montage, and nominalism, in *England in 1819: The Politics of Literary Culture and the Case of Romantic Historicism* (Chicago: U of Chicago P, 1998), 53–60.

54. The plural of anecdote, it's been said, is data, but see Liu, *Local Transcendence: Essays in Postmodern Historicism and the Database* (Chicago: U of Chicago P, 2008), 112–37. Liu writes to criticize detailism (even as he ironically practices it) and playfully describes the "cement aggregate" of concrete detail that results in "the wet-cement quality of the reading experience" in the prose of contemporary cultural critics (120). Liu's major complaint is that cultural-critical methods are insufficiently tuned to both rhetorical considerations and history as such. Because I am writing explicitly about *metaphors* in the history of literature, I hope to escape Liu's critique by practicing a better kind of detailism. Reversing Liu's reading of "wet cement," I attend throughout these pages to figurative moments that turn unexpectedly literal and offer a view on material culture.

55. Introduction to Walter Benjamin, *Illuminations*, ed. Hannah Arendt (New York: Harcourt Brace Jovanovich, 1968), 47. Keith Thomas, who describes his own text as a kind of "collage of quotations," cites Arendt's discussion and confesses sympathy. *The Ends of Life: Roads to Fulfilment in Early Modern England* (Oxford: Oxford UP, 2009), 5.

56. See Marjorie Perloff on Benjamin and "unoriginal genius," in *Unoriginal Genius: Poetry by Other Means* (Chicago: U of Chicago P, 2010). See also Kenneth Goldsmith, *Uncreative Writing: Managing Language in the Digital Age* (New York: Columbia UP, 2011).

57. I am struck by the number of eighteenth-centuryists who find echoes of the postmodern present in the eighteenth-century past. See, for example, Wolfram Schmidgen's *Eighteenth-Century Fiction and the Law of Property* (Cambridge: CUP, 2002), 4; and Dror Wahrman, *Making of the Modern Self: Identity and Culture in Eighteenth-Century England* (New Haven, CT: Yale UP, 2004), xvii; and Ian Baucom, *Specters of the Atlantic: Finance Capital, Slavery, and the Philosophy of History* (Durham, NC: Duke UP, 2005), 21–3.

58. Quoted in Dan Edelstein's *The Enlightenment: A Genealogy* (Chicago: U of Chicago P, 2010), 50.

59. "Dictionary" is perhaps not *le mot juste* but has come to cover all the terms one might find for encyclopedic efforts in the eighteenth century and earlier: the "abecedarium," the "alveary," the "commonplace book," the *florilegium* or "garden of words," the "glossary," "maniple" or *medulla*, the "treasure-book" or "treasury."

60. See Bruno Latour's *Reassembling the Social: An Introduction to Actor-Network-Theory* (Oxford: Oxford UP, 2007).

61. Attempts to draw a distinction between dictionaries and encyclopedias goes back at least as far as d'Alembert. See Verena Haser, *Metaphor, Metonymy, and Experientialist Philosophy: Challenging Cognitive Semantics* (Berlin: Mouton de Gruyter, 2005). 44–5. As Haser notes, the difficulty in establishing a typology that separates dictionaries and encyclopedias parallels philosophical discussions of analytic and synthetic judgment, the best known of which is W. V. O. Quine's "Two Dogmas of Empiricism," *From a Logical Point of View* (Cambridge: Harvard UP, 1953), 20–46.

62. W. V. O. Quine situates his "intermittently philosophical" dictionary in "a loosely linked series of loose-knit books inspired by Voltaire's *Philosophical Dictionary*," which was, as "Voltaire remarked of the Holy Roman Empire, *mutatis mutandis*, . . . neither philosophical nor a dictionary." See Quine's preface to *Quiddities: An Intermittently Philosophical Dictionary* (Cambridge, MA: Harvard UP, 1987).

63. On metaphor and paraphrase, see Stanley Cavell, "Aesthetic Problems of Modern Philosophy," in *Must We Mean What We Say?*, 78–9. See also Donald Davidson: "There is no limit to what metaphor calls to attention." "What Metaphors Mean," in *On Metaphor*, ed. Sheldon Sacks (Chicago: U of Chicago P, 1979), 44.

64. The expression is associated with Gilbert Ryle's philosophy of mind but is usefully carried over to the theory of metaphor, connecting mind and metaphor. See Colin Turbayne revise Aristotle's famous definition of metaphor by quoting Ryle: "Metaphor consists in 'the presentation of the facts of one category in the idioms appropriate to another." *The Myth of Metaphor*, rev. ed. (Columbia: U of South Carolina P, 1970), 12. See also Nelson Goodman, who writes, "A metaphor might be regarded as a calculated category mistake" in *Languages of Art: An Approach to a Theory of Symbols*, 2nd ed. (Indianapolis: Hackett, 1976), 73.

65. Ricoeur, *Rule of Metaphor: Multi-disciplinary Studies of the Creation of Meaning in Language*, trans. Robert Czerny (Toronto: U of Toronto P, 1977), 97; Black, "More about Metaphor" in Ortony, *Metaphor and Thought*, 24.

66. See Blumenberg's *Paradigms for a Metaphorology*, trans. Robert Savage (Ithaca, NY: Cornell UP, 2010). Blumenberg defines "metaphorology" as ancillary to conceptual history: "Metaphorology seeks to burrow down to the substructure of thought, to the underground nutrient solution of systematic crystallizations; but it also aims to show with what 'courage' the mind preempts itself in images, and how its history is projected in the courage of its conjectures" (5). Blumenberg suggests that more

stubborn "absolute metaphors" will not be translated, even over the course of centuries, into clear and distinct conceptualizations.

67. *Elements of Criticism*, 3:111. Compare Janet Soskice's definition of metaphor as "that figure of speech whereby we speak about one thing in terms which are suggestive of another," in *Metaphor and Religious Language* (1985; repr., Oxford: Clarendon, 1992), 62.

68. See Boswell, *Life of Johnson*, 2:157.

69. See Richards's citation of Johnson in *Philosophy of Rhetoric*, 93, 96. His use of the phrase "double unit" appears on p. 98. On a metaphor's "implication-system" or "system of associated commonplaces," see Max Black, *Models and Metaphors*, 41–4, 46. The expression "implicative complex" appears in Black's "More about Metaphor," 28.

70. Lakoff, "The Contemporary Theory of Metaphor," 202–51. The conceptual metaphor theory was first widely published in Lakoff and Mark Johnson's *Metaphors We Live By* (Chicago: U of Chicago P, 1980). Again, as cognitive linguists, Lakoff and Johnson are most concerned with conceptual mappings, taking verbal or linguistic metaphor as a sign of deeper cognitive structures. See also the blending theory of Gilles Fauconnier and Mark Turner, which also emphasizes the conceptual. *The Way We Think: Conceptual Blending and the Mind's Hidden Complexities* (New York: Basic Books, 2002). While taking the measure of cognitivist approaches, I also read Robert Gibbs's *The Poetics of Mind: Figurative Thought, Language and Understanding* (Cambridge: Cambridge UP, 1994) with interest. The cognitivist line of research—especially its insistence on collecting and organizing examples—is compatible with my own, but I am, like Robert Fogelin, concerned that conceptual and cognitivist theories sacrifice linguistic and historical subtleties to the business of systematic mapping, thus shortchanging the complexity of metaphorical expressions or treating them only as symptoms of timeless conceptual structures and domains. For Fogelin's concern, see *Figuratively Speaking* (New Haven, CT: Yale UP, 1986), 85–6. A stronger critique of Lakoff and Johnson's "experientialist paradigm" is available in Haser, *Metaphor, Metonymy, and Experientialist Philosophy*.

71. Wayne Booth, "The Metaphor as Rhetoric: The Problem of Evaluation," in *On Metaphor*, ed. Sheldon Sacks (Chicago: U of Chicago P, 1978), 47.

72. See Donald Davidson's influential essay "What Metaphors Mean," collected with the other *Critical Inquiry* essays in *On Metaphor*, ed. Sheldon Sacks (Chicago: U of Chicago P, 1978), and reprinted in Davidson's *Inquiries into Truth and Interpretation* (Oxford: Oxford UP, 2001).

73. See Roger M. White's excellent and perhaps underappreciated study *The Structure of Metaphor: How the Language of Metaphor Works* (Oxford: Blackwell, 1996); and his article "Literal Meaning and 'Figurative Meaning,'" *Theoria* 67:1 (2001): 24–59. Davidson and White agree that a metaphorical sentence doesn't carry a metaphorical meaning *in addition* to its literal meaning, and all tropes preserve literal meaning to be understood. Wittgenstein writes in *Philosophical Investigations*, 3rd ed., trans.

Elizabeth Anscombe (Oxford: Blackwell, 2002): "Here one might speak of a primary and a secondary sense of a word. It is only if the word has a primary sense for you that you use it in the secondary one. . . . Only if you have learnt to calculate—on the paper or out loud—can you be made to grasp, by means of this concept, what calculating in the head is. . . . The secondary sense is not a 'metaphorical' sense" (184). The figurative is logically dependent (or "parasitic") on the literal. See also John Searle, who argues, "In a genuine metaphorical utterance, it is only because the expressions have not changed their meaning that there is a metaphorical utterance at all." "Metaphor," in Ortony, *Metaphor and Thought*, 91.

74. Davidson, "What Metaphors Mean," 45; White, *Structure of Metaphor*, 113–7.

75. White, *Structure*, 93. Complex metaphors may necessitate the use of "dummy variables." For example, in White's interpretation of a line from Shakespeare's *Othello* ("His unbookish Ielousie must construe poore Cassio's smiles, gestures and light behaviours quite in the wrong"), the first pass at a primary and a secondary sentence are formulated as "I. His x jealousy must construe poore Cassio's smiles, gestures, and light behaviours quite in the wrong" and "II. Unbookish x must construe y quite in the wrong." White suggests "uncultured" for the primary sentence and "schoolboy" and "the *Iliad*" for the secondary sentence. White's complete analysis of *Othello* IV.i.119ff. appears in chapter 4 of *Structure of Metaphor.*

76. George Berkeley, *Three Dialogues* (G. James, 1713), 141. For a gloss on this passage, see Kenneth P. Winkler's "Berkeley and the Doctrine of Signs," *Cambridge Companion to Berkeley* (Cambridge: Cambridge UP, 2005), 155–7.

77. *Death and Character: Further Reflections on Hume* (Cambridge, MA: Harvard UP, 2008), 138. Baier's felicitous term "figurative empiricism" is introduced above. Analogy serves for a warrant when we decide that "our ideas about the world derive from the experience of that same world," and "if we choose to think about 'the intellectual world,' we need metaphors from our 'impressions of sense,' from our experience of the ordinary world, in order to describe our ideas" (138).

78. Friedrich Nietzsche, "On Truth and Lie in an Extra-Moral Sense," in *The Portable Nietzsche*, ed. Walter Kaufman (1954; repr., New York: Penguin Books, 1976), 46–47.

79. Paul de Man, "The Epistemology of Metaphor," *Critical Inquiry* 5:1 (1978): 14.

80. Gregory Ulmer states the thesis even more compactly: metaphoricity, in Derrida, destroys univocity. See Leonard Lawlor, "A Little Daylight: A Reading of Derrida's 'White Mythology,'" *Man and World* 24 (1991): 285. Cf. Ricoeur's summary: "Metaphor is metaphorically stated." *Rule of Metaphor*, 287.

81. Jacques Derrida, "White Mythology: Metaphor in the Text of Philosophy," *New Literary History* 6:1 (1974), 5–74.

82. See also Richard Rorty's "Unfamiliar Noises: Hesse and Davidson on Metaphor," *Proceedings of the Aristotelian Society* 61 (1987), 283–311. Samuel C. Wheeler reads Davidson and de Man together in "Metaphor According to Davidson and de Man," *Redrawing the Boundaries*, ed. R. W. Dasenbrock (Minneapolis: U of Minnesota Press,

1989), 116–39. The best summary of and rejoinder to Derrida is available in Ricoeur, *Rule of Metaphor*, 284–9, 290–5.

83. Peter de Bolla likewise recommends taking rhetoric itself as matter for history so as to "uncover the specific systems of figuration and orders of tropes for any given period, culture, and society." "Disfiguring History," *Diacritics* 16:4 (Winter 1986): 56.

84. See Eric Hayot on the alternatives to standard critical practice proposed by Franco Moretti and Wai Chee Dimock that focus on "historicizable features of the aesthetic that are either smaller or larger than the particular work of art"; in "Against Periodization; or, On Institutional Time," *New Literary History* 42 (2011): 743.

85. For evidence that my main terms may be, once again, synonymous, see Susan Greenfield, "Soul, Brain, and Mind" in *From Soul to Self*, ed. M. James Crabbe (London and New York: Routledge, 1999), 108. On distinctions between and conflations of the terms "soul," "mind," and "spirit," see Raymond Martin and Cyril Barresi, *Naturalization of the Soul: Self and Personality in the Eighteenth Century* (London and New York: Routledge, 2000); and, on pneumatology, see 70–2. Martin and Barresi's history is, in both its scope and details, quite rewarding, but I find the main narrative of naturalization may exaggerate the speed and significance of the shift from soul to mind. See also Edward Reed, *From Soul to Mind: The Emergence of Psychology from Erasmus Darwin to William James* (New Haven: Yale UP, 1997).

86. "What transgresses the boundaries of all imagination, of all possible thought, is simply that alphabetical series (a, b, c, d) which links each of those categories to all the others." Michel Foucault, *The Order of Things: An Archaeology of the Human Sciences* (New York: Vintage, 1970), xvi.

87. *The Poetics of Aristotle: Translation and Commentary*, trans. Stephen Halliwell (Chapel Hill: U of North Carolina P, 1987), 55.

88. J. R. Firth, "A Synopsis of Linguistic Theory, 1930–1955," in *Studies in Linguistic Analysis* (Oxford: Blackwell, 1957), 11. On the limits of collocation and a call for "collocations of collocations on a much larger scale," see Matt Jockers, *Macroanalysis: Digital Methods and Literary History* (Urbana: U of Illinois P, 2013), 122.

89. Williams, *Keywords*, 15.

90. Martin Jay, *Cultural Semantics: Keywords of Our Time* (Amherst: U of Massachusetts P, 1998), 3.

91. Ricoeur, *Rule of Metaphor*, 44.

92. Marianne Moore, *Complete Poems* (New York: Penguin, 1994), 267.

93. See Michael J. Reddy, "The Conduit Metaphor: A Case of Frame Conflict in Our Language about Language," in Ortony, *Metaphor and Thought*, 164–201. Other widespread metaphors that I have collected only haphazardly include the figuration of impassioned feelings as fire and other temperatures of emotion, the mental metaphorics of pain, and the motions of thought.

94. See the third part of *The Children of Thespis* (J. Strahan, 1788), 23. I have, as yet, found only one other eighteenth-century snowball-mind. See also Bounderby in

Charles Dickens's *Hard Times* thinking on Mrs. Sparsit's presumption, turning it "over and over in his mind, until it accumulated with turning like a great snowball."

95. Matthew Wickman, "Moretti and the Picturesque, or Reading for the Middle Distance," American Society for Eighteenth-Century Studies Annual Meeting, Cleveland, April 6, 2013.

96. Moretti, "Critical Response. II. 'Relatively Blunt'" *Critical Inquiry* 36:1 (Autumn 2009): 173–4.

97. Nathan Bailey, George Gordon, and Philip Miller, *Dictionarium Britannicum* (1730; repr., Hildesheim: G. Olms, 1969); Samuel Johnson, *A Dictionary of the English Language*, 2 vols. (Strahan, 1755; repr., New York: AMS, 1967).

98. I read my philosophers' modern editions, search them in digital editions, and source my quotations from seventeenth- or eighteenth-century editions. I rely especially on my copies of John Locke's *An Essay Concerning Human Understanding*, ed. Peter H. Nidditch (Oxford: Oxford UP, 1975); and David Hume's *A Treatise of Human Nature*, ed. David Fate Norton and Mary J. Norton (Oxford: Oxford UP, 2000).

99. For the *Spectator* and *Tatler* I provide volume and page numbers in Donald F. Bond's editions: *The Spectator*, ed. D. F. Bond, 5 vols. (Oxford: Clarendon, 1965); and *The Tatler*, ed. D. F. Bond, 3 vols. (Oxford: Clarendon, 1987).

100. Perry Miller, *The New England Mind* (Cambridge: Harvard UP, 1954), ix.

Animals

1. The distribution of animal metaphors does not indicate an overall trend or an obviously shifting metaphorics. That said, the literature of the eighteenth century teems with animal metaphors and a more thorough census of metaphors employing a larger corpus might well return a different result. As explained in the text below, the hunt for animal metaphors has not been exhaustive because a thorough accounting of the species would require the exercise of a new keyword for each species of animal: I did not search for rhinoceroses nor for ocelots, but I did encounter animals I was not looking for. As frequencies of the total number of metaphors discovered in each decade, animal metaphors average around 4.6%. A relative increase of animal metaphors in the drama of the 1720s involves clusters in tragedies by Edward Young and Elijah Fenton. Edward Young's *Night Thoughts*, published in the 1740s, contributes the largest cluster of animal metaphors of mind.

2. The example is also cited in my introduction. Roger M. White enlists this metaphor in an explanation of his differences with Monroe Beardsley in *The Structure of Metaphor: How the Language of Metaphor Works* (Oxford: Blackwell, 1996), 93–6. I return to White's theory of metaphor in this entry.

3. *Zoonomia* (J. Johnson, 1796), 1:137. On the increasingly hostile response to Darwin's dangerous ideas, see Norman Garfinkle, "Science and Religion in England, 1790–1800," *Journal of the History of Ideas* 16:3 (1955): 376–88. See also Deborah Boyle, "Hume on Animal Reason," *Hume Studies* 29:1 (April 2003): 3–28.

4. The list originates in Borges. See Michel Foucault, *The Order of Things: An Archaeology of the Human Sciences* (New York: Vintage Books, 1970), xv.

5. "The Rape of the Locke. An Heroi-Comical Poem," in *Miscellaneous Poems and Translations* (Lintott, 1712), 366.

6. See A. O. Lovejoy, *The Great Chain of Being: A Story of the History of an Idea* (1936; repr., Cambridge, MA: Harvard UP, 2001), 195–8. See also Laura Brown on Lovejoy in *Fables of Modernity: Literature and Culture in the English Eighteenth Century* (Ithaca, NY: Cornell UP, 2001), 228. My analysis in this entry is indebted to Brown's, but where Brown collects instances in which the animal is a figure of alterity, I am keen to treat those animals that are enlisted in the metaphorics of identity. See also Laura Brown's book-length survey of the period and of animal studies as a field in *Homeless Dogs and Melancholy Apes: Humans and Other Animals in the Modern Literary Imagination* (Ithaca, NY: Cornell UP, 2010).

7. Mary Wollstonecraft, *A Vindication of the Rights of Woman* (J. Johnson, 1792), 93.

8. John Gregory, *Comparative View of the State and Faculties of Man, with those of the Animal World* (J. Dodsley, 1765), 8.

9. Thomas Willis's *The Anatomy of the Brain and Nerves*, trans. Samuel Pordage, ed. William Feindel, vol. 2 (Montreal: McGill UP, 1965), 52. On comparative anatomy and feral children, see Richard Nash's *Wild Enlightenment: The Borders of Human Identity in the Eighteenth Century* (Charlottesville: U of Virginia P, 2003). A treatment of Aesop in England is available in Jayne Lewis's *The English Fable: Aesop and Literary Culture, 1651–1740* (Cambridge: Cambridge UP, 1996). On the metaphorics of breeding see Jenny Davidson's *Breeding: A Partial History of the Eighteenth Century* (New York: Columbia UP, 2009), 58–97. On the ambivalent status of pets, Brown, *Homeless Dogs*, and Lynn Festa, "Person, Animal, Thing: The 1796 Dog Tax and the Right to Superfluous Things," *Eighteenth-Century Life* 33:2 (Spring 2009): 1–44.

10. Compare Gilbert Ryle on the Humean "Problem of Self," in which the philosopher fails to "catch more than the flying coat-tails of that which he was pursuing." Ryle notes simply, "His quarry was the hunter." *The Concept of Mind* (Chicago: U of Chicago P, 1949), 198.

11. The formula *homo homine lupus* proves complicated in both the literary contexts. Hobbes, in fact, balances aphorisms in *De Cive*: "To speak impartially, both sayings are very true; *That Man to Man is a kind of God*; *And that Man to Man is an arrant Wolfe*." *Philosophicall Rudiments Concerning Government and Society* (J. and R. Royston, 1651), Epistle Dedicatory, [A4]. God and beast will be a recurring doublet in this entry. See also Jacques Derrida, *The Beast and the Sovereign*, trans. Geoffrey Bennington (Chicago: U of Chicago P, 2009), 1:11.

12. Mary Midgley, *Beast and Man: The Roots of Human Nature* (Ithaca, NY: Cornell UP, 1978), 44.

13. See the *OED*; Paul S. MacDonald, *History of the Concept of Mind* (Aldershot, Hants: Ashgate, 2003), 80–7; and R. B. Onians, *The Origins of European Thought about*

the Body, the Mind, the Soul, the World, Time, and Fate. (Cambridge: Cambridge UP, 1951), 168–73. Robert Whytt discusses the distinction in his *Essay on the Vital and Other Involuntary Motions of Animals* (Edinburgh: Hamilton, 1751), 278–85.

14. Edward Young, *The Complaint: or, Night Thoughts* (R. Dodsley, 1742), 6. On Young, see Lovejoy, *Chain of Being*, 190. Earl R. Wasserman notes that "In the Great Chain of Being man is the transition point from sense to intelligence, and therefore in him these two faculties are fused." "The Inherent Values of Eighteenth-Century Personification," *PMLA* 65:4 (1950): 450.

15. *King Lear* III.iv.106; Laurie Shannon, "Poor, Bare, Forked: Animal Sovereignty, Human Negative Exceptionalism, and the Natural History of *King Lear*," *Shakespeare Quarterly* 60:2 (2009): 170; *Memoirs of the Extraordinary Life, Works, and Discoveries of Martinus Scriblerus* (Dublin: George Faulkner, 1741), 89.

16. Versions of Locke's sortal thought problems date to early journal entries: see *An Early Draft of Locke's Essay*, ed. R. I. Aron and Jocelyn Gibb (New York: Clarendon, 1936), 99.

17. For complicating examples of interspeciation, including the offspring of women and drills, see *Essay*, III.vi.23. But see also Locke's decisive sorting: "this is a Man, that a Drill: And in this, I think, consists the whole business of *Genus* and *Species*" (III.vi.36). At issue is Locke's position on nominal and real essences or "the Workmanship of the Understanding," a topic about which much has been written in the Locke scholarship.

18. See Brown, *Homeless Dogs*, 28–58; Nash, *Wild Enlightenment*, 15–41.

19. Alexander Pope, *An Essay on Man* (Lawton Gilliver, 1734), 18; John Dryden, *Absalom and Achitophel* (Jacob Tonson, 1681), 6; Edward Young, *Night the Third. Narcissa* [*Night Thoughts*] (R. Dodsley, 1742), 29.

20. The phrase is borrowed by Jonathan Lamb from J. M. Coetzee's character Elizabeth Costello. See "Sympathy with Animals and Salvation of the Soul," *Eighteenth Century* 52:1 (Spring 2011): 69–85, at 74. Lamb's essay sharpened my own readings in this entry. See also Lamb's *The Things Things Say* (Princeton, NJ: Princeton UP, 2011), xxiii.

21. Ted Cohen, "Notes on Metaphor," *Journal of Aesthetics and Art Criticism* 34 (1976): 249–59, 253. See also Verena Haser's discussion of the "man is a wolf" metaphor and the category of animal in *Metaphor, Metonymy, and Experientialist Philosophy: Challenging Cognitive Semantics* (Berlin: Mouton de Gruyter, 2005), 19–20, 29–30.

22. Ludwig Wittgenstein, *Philosophical Investigations*, 3rd ed., trans. Elizabeth Anscombe (Oxford: Blackwell, 2002), II.xi.165–6. See also White, *Structure of Metaphor*, 113–7. The duck-rabbit serves as mascot in other discussions of metaphor by Hester and Davidson, among others.

23. *Historia Animalium*, trans. A. L. Peck (Cambridge, MA: Harvard UP, 1965), vol. 1, I.xv, 494a, p. 55. See C. A. Patrides, "Renaissance Ideas on Man's Upright Form," *Journal of the History of Ideas* 19:2 (April 1958): 256–8.

24. I quote from *The Tatler*, ed. Donald F. Bond (1987), 2:195.

25. Londa Schiebinger, *The Mind Has No Sex? Women in the Origins of Modern Science* (Cambridge, MA: Harvard UP, 1991), 160ff.

26. *Summa Theologiae* (I, Q76 A8, Obj 3). Aquinas refers to Aristotle's *De Anima* 412b17-25. I quote from *Aquinas: Basic Works*, ed. Jeffrey Hause and Robert Pasnau (Indianapolis: Hackett, 2014), 195.

27. On animal metaphors see Keith Thomas, *Man and the Natural World: A History of the Modern Sensibility* (New York: Pantheon Books, 1983), 40, 41–3, 99, 113, 148–9.

28. Edith Hamilton and Huntington Cairns, eds., *The Collected Dialogues of Plato, Including the Letters* (1961; repr., Princeton, NJ: Princeton UP, 1978).

29. John Donne, *Poems* (John Marriot, 1633), 82. See J. B. Bamborough, *The Little World of Man* (London: Longmans, Green, 1952), 15–6.

30. Jonathan Swift, *A Tale of a Tub*, 2nd ed., corr. (John Nutt, 1704), 304.

31. See Hans Peter Reill, *Vitalizing Enlightenment* (Berkeley: U of California P, 2005), 133.

32. *Rameau's Nephew and D'Alembert's Dream*, trans. L. Tancock (New York: Penguin Books, 1966), 170. On Diderot's metaphors, see Herbert Dieckmann, "The Metaphoric Structure of the *Rêve de D'Alembert*," *Diderot Studies* 17 (1973): 15–24. See also Geoffrey Cantor, "Figures of the Unthinkable: Diderot's Materialist Metaphors," in *The Figural and the Literal: Problems of Language in the History of Science and Philosophy, 1630–1800*, ed. A. E. Benjamin et al. (Manchester: Manchester UP, 1987).

33. Laurence Sterne, *Tristram Shandy* (R. and J. Dodsley, 1760), 1:166. James Boswell recycles the image in his *Hypochondriack* papers (no. 6, March 1778): "It would truly be very pretty and amusing if our bodies were transparent, so that we could see one anothers sentiments and passions working as we see bees in a glass-hive." See Ann Jessie Van Sant, *Eighteenth-Century Sensibility and the Novel: The Senses in Social Context* (Cambridge: Cambridge UP, 1993), 60.

34. Ephraim Chambers, *Cyclopaedia*, 2 vols. (James and John Knapton, 1728), 1:102.

35. Thomas Willis, *Two Discourses Concerning the Souls of Brutes*, trans. Samuel Pordage, ed. Solomon Diamond (1683; facs., Gainesville, FL: Scholars' Facsimiles and Reprints, 1971). On the perdurance of Willis's metaphors, which survive in contemporary textbooks, see Hansruedi Isler, *Thomas Willis, 1621–1675* (New York: Hafner, 1968), 118.

36. G. S. Rousseau, "'Sowing the Wind and Reaping the Whirlwind': Aspects of Change in Eighteenth-Century Medicine," in *Studies in Change and Revolution: Aspects of English Intellectual History, 1640–1800*, ed. Paul J. Korshin (Menston, Yorkshire: Scolar, 1972), 151.

37. John W. Yolton, *John Locke and the Way of Ideas* (London: Oxford University Press, 1956), 175.

38. George Cheyne, *The English Malady* (G. Strahan, 1733), 78.

39. Ibid., 69. Cheyne's metaphor appears in his earlier *Essay of Health and Long Life* (George Strahan, 1724), 144. In a short essay on metaphor and paradigms,

Joseph Musser provides a similar reading of Willis and Cheyne. See his "The Perils of Relying on Thomas Kuhn," *Eighteenth-Century Studies* 18:2 (1984–5): 221–2.

40. For a summary of the debate concerning nervous fluids and fibers, see John Dussinger's *The Discourse of the Mind in Eighteenth-Century Fiction* (The Hague: Mouton, 1974), 28–9. See also Theodore M. Brown, "From Mechanism to Vitalism in Eighteenth-Century Physiology," *Journal of the History of Biology* 7 (Fall 1974): 179–216.

41. Thomas Reid, *An Inquiry into the Human Mind on the Principles of Common Sense* (London: A. Millar, and Edinburgh: A. Kincaid and J. Bell, 1764), 396. The philosopher and his menagerie may be borrowed from a famous passage in Locke, *Essay*, II.xiii.19. See also the "INDIAN philosopher and his elephant" in Hume's *Dialogues Concerning Natural Religion* (s.n., 1779), 52–3.

42. Associated with sapience, the elephant remains a kind of marvelous if not mythical beast throughout the period. See Christopher Plumb, "'Strange and Wonderful': Encountering the Elephant in Britain, 1675–1830," *Journal for Eighteenth-Century Studies* 33:4 (December 2010): 530.

43. John Wesley, *A Survey of the Wisdom of God in the Creation: Or a Compendium of Natural Philosophy*, 2 vols. (Bristol: William Pine, 1763), 1:21; John Aikin, *A Sketch of the Animal Economy* (Warrington: William Eyres, 1781), 23–4.

44. David Hume, *A Treatise of Human Nature* (John Noon, 1739), 1:112.

45. Samuel Garth, *The Dispensary* (John Nutt, 1699), 23; Richard Savage, *Miscellaneous Poems and Translations* (Samuel Chapman, 1726), 129.

46. Richard Blackmore, *The Nature of Man. A Poem* (Sam. Buckley, 1711), 7–8.

47. *A Description of Three Hundred Animals* (J. F. and C. Rivington, B. Law, G. G. J. and J. Robinson, T. Carnan, R. Baldwin, and E. Newbery, 1786), 5–6.

48. *Enquiry Concerning the Principles of Morals* (A. Millar, 1751), 176–7.

49. Hobbes, *Leviathan* (Andrew Crooke, 1651), 10.

50. Sarah Fielding, *The History of the Countess of Dellwyn* (A. Millar, 1759), 1:93.

51. Hester Chapone, *Miscellanies in Prose and Verse* (E. and C. Dilly, 1775), 171; John Hopkins, *Amasia* (Tho. Warren, 1700), 58; Edward Young, *Night the Sixth* (R. Dodsley, 1744), 11–12; S. T. Coleridge, *Biographia Literaria*, ed. James Engell and W. Jackson Bate (Princeton, NJ: Princeton UP, 1983), 124.

52. "Remarks on the Profession of a Player," *London Magazine, or Gentleman's Monthly Intelligencer* 39 (1770): 470.

53. *Homeless Dogs*, 70, 72.

54. On figurative dogginess as a key to the relation between man and animal, see William Empson's *The Structure of Complex Words* (London: Chatto and Windus, 1964), 163–74.

55. *The Works of Alexander Pope* (R. Dodsley, 1739), 2:162.

56. Hamilton and Cairns, *Dialogues of Plato*, 904; William James, "On Some Omissions of Introspective Psychology," *Mind* 9:33 (January 1884): 2. Surveying examples from Egyptian drawings to the poetry of Yeats, Rosalie Osmond suggests that birds

may provide the "most common analogy for the soul." *Imagining the Soul: A History* (Phoenix Mill: Sutton, 2003), 137.

57. John and Charles Wesley, *Hymns and Sacred Poems* (Bristol: Felix Farley, 1742), 109, see also 40, 290; John Cennick, *Sacred Hymns for the Children of God, in the Days of Their Pilgrimage* (B. Miles, 1741), 75.

58. The "simile of a bird new-caught" appears in Samuel Richardson, *Clarissa*, 7 vols. (S. Richardson, 1748), 3:348. The second quoted phrase appears in an addenda to the first edition. See *Letters and Passages Restored from the Original Manuscripts of the History of Clarissa* (S. Richardson, 1751), 74. On Richardson's mixing of fable and natural history, see Robert James Merrett, "Natural History and the Eighteenth-Century Novel," in *Eighteenth-Century Studies* 25:2 (Winter 1991–2): 145–70, at 161–4.

59. Peter Pindar, *Lyric Odes to the Royal Academicians*, 5th ed. (Kearsley, 1787), 12.

60. In R. Lonsdale, ed., *Eighteenth-Century Women Poets* (Oxford: Oxford UP, 1989), 325, ll. 5–6. I imagine four and twenty learned ladies baked in More's humble pies.

61. Pope asks in his *Essay on Man*, "What modes of Sight betwixt each wide extreme, / The Mole's dim curtain, and the Lynx's beam?" (17).

62. See also Lord Monboddo, *Origin and Progress of Language*, 2nd ed. (Edinburgh: J. Balfour, 1774), 1:182–3.

63. *Pamela: or, Virtue Rewarded*, vol. 4 (S. Richardson, 1742), 335. Dryden's *All for Love* is the most Shakespearean of his plays, and Dryden's mole metaphor may work by indirect allusion to the famous lines from *Hamlet*: "Well said, old mole! Canst work I' th' earth so fast? / A worthy pioneer!" (I.v.162–3). Richardson uses the mole—or rather molehill—metaphor again in *Clarissa*. The burrowing creature surfaces in that text from out of a similar subterranean intertext when Belford transcribes lines from Nathaniel Lee's *Oedipus*: "Each mole-hill thought swells to a huge Olympus; / While we, fantastic dreamers, heave and puff, / And sweat with our imagination's weight" (7:10).

64. The mole that flees the light is then a mascot of both Enlightenment and counter-Enlightenment. As dramatized in the *Dunciad*, scholarship burrows through footnotes; the poet Leonard Welsted is compared to a didapper, an eel, and then at more length, a mole. Welsted is instructed to mark the mole in his "dirty hole" who keeps a "mighty stir" below only to raise a molehill. *The Dunciad Variorum* (Lawton Gilliver, 1735), V, p. 148, l. 199, n. 3. The mole is an explicit figure for the philosopher in Samuel Boyse's philosophical poem *Deity* and for the more grave than wise natural philosopher of fossils who appears in John Gay's epistle "To a Lady on Her Passion for Old China." Boyse's philosopher is a "sceptic mole"; Gay's "digs for knowledge, like a Mole." See *Deity* (J. Roberts, 1739), 33; and *To a Lady* (Dublin: 1725), 2. In Henry Brooke's novel *The Fool of Quality* (Dublin: Dillon Chamberlaine, 1765–70), one Mr. Mole appears. He is an atheistic philosopher who prefers "Justification by Charity" to "Sanctification by Faith" and scuffles with the devout protagonist (4:270). In Brooke's Methodist novel, Mr. Mole is a villain.

65. Oliver Goldsmith, *The Vicar of Wakefield* (Salisbury: B. Collins, 1766), 1:54–5. A similar whatever-is-is-right sentiment is available in Samuel Jackson Pratt's *Sympathy*, where the poet observes "A due proportion to all creatures given, / From the mole's mansion to the seraph's heav'n." In *Miscellanies*, 4 vols. (Printed for T. Becket, 1785), 1:23.

66. Samuel Bishop, *The Poetical Works* (A. Strahan, 1796), 83.

67. "An Inquiry Concerning Virtue of Merit." I quote the more vivid variant text from *Characteristicks* (J. Darby, 1714), 2:130. The original 1699 publication differs slightly: "the Spirits unconsum'd help to consume the Body, and Nature as it were preys upon it self." (140).

68. *Boswell's London Journal, 1762–1763*, ed. Frederick Pottle (New York: McGraw-Hill, 1950), 202, emphasis added.

69. *Vertue Rewarded* (R. Bentley, 1693), 71–2. The allusion is to *Lycurgus*, xviii.1. Henry Fielding uses a similar figure in *Tom Jones*, 6 vols. (A. Millar, 1749), 2:161.

70. From the preface to Butler's *Fifteen Sermons*, 2nd ed. (W. Botham, 1729), xiii; Fielding, *Tom Jones*, 2:40.

71. Published piratically in 1716. I quote from John Butt's one-volume edition of *The Poems of Alexander Pope* (New Haven: Yale UP, 1963), 298–9.

72. *Charlotte: A Tale of Truth* (Minerva, 1791), 22. "On the Death of Mr Clark, Organist at St Pauls. Who Lately Shot Himself. An Ode," from *The Diverting Muse, or, The Universal Medly* (B. Bragge, 1707), 214.

73. Foucault connects animals and madmen: "at the beginning of the Renaissance, the [medieval] relations with animality are reversed; the beast is set free. . . . And by an astonishing reversal, it is now the animal that will stalk man, capture him, and reveal him to his own truth." *Madness and Civilization: A History of Insanity in the Age of Reason* (New York: Vintage Books, 1988), 21; see also 73–8.

74. See Donna Landry, *Noble Brutes: How Eastern Horses Transformed English Culture* (Baltimore: John Hopkins UP, 2009), 68.

75. Ibid., 31. See also essays collected in *The Culture of the Horse: Status, Discipline, and Identity in the Early Modern World*, ed. Karen Raber and Treva J. Tucker (New York: Palgrave Macmillan, 20005), especially Elizabeth Leguin's "Man and Horse in Harmony."

76. *Theron and Aspasio*, 3 vols. (John and James Rivington, 1755), 2:189.

77. John Wolcot, *A Rowland for an Oliver* (G. Kearsley, 1790), 42. Spelled "martingal" in the original. *The Genuine Remains in Verse and Prose of Mr. Samuel Butler* (J. and R. Tonson, 1759), 1:266.

78. A. D. Nuttall, "Gulliver among the Horses," *Yearbook of English Studies* 18 (1988): 51–67, at 58–60. See also Howard Erskine-Hill, ed., *Gulliver's Travels* (Cambridge: Cambridge UP, 1993), 65–6. David Kunzle, "The World Turned Upside Down: The Iconography of a European Broadsheet Type," in *The Reversible World*, ed. Barbara Babcock (Ithaca, NY: Cornell UP), 39–94.

79. Laurence Sterne, *Tristram Shandy*, 2nd ed. (R. and J. Dodsley, 1760), 2:29.

80. Margaret Cavendish, *Poems and Phancies* (printed by William Wilson, 1664), 261.

81. *Poems and Songs by Thomas Flatman* (Benjamin Took and Jonathan Edwin, 1674), n.p.

82. Alexander Gerard, *An Essay on Genius* (W. Strahan, T. Cadell, and W. Creech, 1774), 71.

83. Butler, *Genuine Remains*, 225; Edward Gibbon, "Memoirs of My Life and Writings," in *Miscellaneous Works*, 2 vols. (A. Strahan and T. Cadell, 1796), 1:67.

84. Alexander Pope, *An Essay on Criticism* (W. Lewis, 1711), 7.

85. The scene reads as an allegory of poetic production and significantly features a mare and a stallion. Lintot is, of course, the publisher of Pope's poem titled *Windsor-Forest*, the setting in which Pope is overtaken, and of Pope's translation of the *Iliad*. Pope is mounted on a mare borrowed from the Earl of Burlington, a well-known patron of the arts and recipient of the letter in which the story is related as well as the addressee of Pope's Horatian *Epistle to Burlington*. Lintot's borrowed "stonehorse" belonged to the poet Oldmixon but was sold to Lintot's publisher for a debt. The two discuss the business of translation—the "method of *managing*" translators (emphasis added)—while the printer's devil rides behind. The whole is related in *Letters of Mr. Alexander Pope* (J. Wright, 1737), 210–4.

86. See Plato's *Phaedrus*, trans. R. Hackforth (Cambridge: Cambridge UP, 1989), 246a and following.

87. John Byrom, *Miscellaneous Poems*, 2 vols. (Manchester: J. Harrop, 1773), 1:98–9; Alexander Pope, *The Rape of the Lock* (Bernard Lintott, 1714), 7.

88. Isaac Bickerstaff, *Love in the City; a Comic Opera* (W. Griffin, 1767), 51.

89. Bamborough, *The Little World of Man*, 17.

90. In the accounts of great ape shows in London discussed by Laura Brown, I am struck by how often the animal is advertised as "taking a Glass of Ale in his hand like a Christian" or drinking "a glass of Ale, like any reasonable Creature." *Fables*, 229–30.

91. Henry Payne, *The Morning Ramble* (Dring, 1673), 2.

92. From Blair's lecture on metaphor, *Lectures on Rhetoric and Belle Lettres* (Dublin: Messrs. Whitestone, Colles [etc.], 1783), 371.

93. *The Journal of John Wesley: A Selection*, ed. Elisabeth Jay (Oxford: Oxford UP, 1987), xiv.

94. *The Journal of the Reverend John Wesley*, 2 vols. (New York: Carlton and Philips, 1856), 2:325–6.

95. Anita Guerrini describes the chamber horse as "an eighteenth-century 'Nordic Track'." "The Hungry Soul: George Cheyne and the Construction of Femininity," *Eighteenth-Century Studies* 32:3 (1999): 284.

96. Fuller builds upon insights from Sydenham, who recommended fresh air and exercise in the treatment of consumption and hypochondriasis. *Gymnastica* went through nine editions by 1777.

97. Cheyne to Richardson, April 20, 1740, in *Letters of Doctor George Cheyne to Samuel Richardson*, ed. Charles F. Mullett (Columbia: U of Missouri P, 1943), 59–60.

98. John Wesley, *Primitive Physick: or, An Easy and Natural Method* (Thomas Trye, 1747), xxi. On Wesley's medical writings, see James G. Donat, "John Wesley on the Estimation and Cure of Nervous Disorders," in *Brain, Mind, and Medicine: Essays in Eighteenth-Century Neuroscience*, ed. C. U. M. Smith, H. Whitaker, and S. Finger (New York: Springer, 2007), 285–99. See also Carol Houlihan Flynn's important essay, "Running out of Matter: The Body Exercised in Eighteenth-Century Fiction," in *The Languages of Psyche*. G. S. Rousseau, ed. (Berkeley, CA: Univ. of California Press, 1990), 158–9.

99. The "hunting ground" of "civilized man" is "the unified cosmos, in which nothing exists but prey." Max Horkheimer and Theodor W. Adorno, *Dialectic of Enlightenment* (1972; repr., Stanford, CA: Stanford UP, 2002), 6.

100. Jacques Derrida, "The Animal That Therefore I Am (More to Follow)," *Critical Inquiry* 28:2 (2002): 369–418, at 409.

101. Paul de Man, "The Epistemology of Metaphor," *Critical Inquiry* 5:1 (1978): 18.

102. E. M. W. Tillyard, *The Elizabethan World Picture* (London: Chatto and Windus, 1943), 61.

103. Howard D. Weinbrot, *Eighteenth-Century Satire: Essays on Text and Context from Dryden to Peter Pindar* (Cambridge: Cambridge UP, 1988), 4. In an early modern frontispiece pointed out by Weinbrot, a satyr is depicted riding on a donkey, lashing it with a whip. See *Menippean Satire Reconsidered: From Antiquity to the Eighteenth Century* (Baltimore: Johns Hopkins UP, 2005), 324n.

104. John Wilmot, Earl of Rochester, *A Satyr Against Mankind* (s.n., 1675), 3. See *Selected Works* (New York: Penguin, 2004), 49.

105. *Anatomy of Criticism* (Princeton, NJ: Princeton UP, 1957), 225.

106. Jonathan Swift, *Travels into Several Remote Nations of the World. In Four Parts. By Lemuel Gulliver*, 2nd ed., 2 vols. (Benj. Motte, 1726), 2:123.

Coinage

1. As in the previous entry, the distribution of metaphors does not indicate an obvious shift in metaphorics. And the sample, 123 metaphors in total, is even smaller, with coinage metaphors amounting to only 1% of all metaphors collected between 1700 and 1799. The largest clusters of metaphors appear in the poetry of the 1740s (the bulk originating in the poetry of Edward Young) and the prose of the 1790s (Edgeworth, Boswell, Burke, and more).

2. C. B. Macpherson, *The Political Theory of Possessive Individualism: Hobbes to Locke* (Oxford: Oxford UP, 1962), 37–40. Objections to Macpherson's arguments are cited below.

3. William Walker discovers continuity between Locke's *Essay Concerning Human Understanding* and his *Two Treatises of Government* in just these terms: the *Essay*

is an "allegory of mind" informed by the literal account of labor provided in the *Treatises*. See *Locke, Literary Criticism, and Philosophy* (Cambridge: Cambridge UP, 1994), 50–1. A similar, but more ambitious claim by John O'Brien is quoted in the text below.

4. Jacques Derrida, "White Mythology: Metaphor in the Text of Philosophy," *New Literary History* 6:1 (1974): 14.

5. Metaphor theorists have noticed that reversing metaphors and similes typically results in incongruity. See Robert Fogelin on Monroe Beardsley in *Figuratively Speaking* (New Haven, CT: Yale UP, 1986), 61–5.

6. I follow James Thompson, who makes the same point about bills of exchange: "Paper money is not government-issued, not anonymous, and not impersonal in this period, but it is something which can be literally 'told' and narrated." *Models of Value: Eighteenth-Century Political Economy and the Novel* (Durham, NC: Duke UP, 1996), 137. Thompson's monograph, along with Peter de Bolla, *The Discourse of the Sublime: History, Aesthetics, and the Subject* (Oxford: Blackwell, 1989); Colin Nicholson, *Writing and the Rise of Finance: Capital Satires of the Early Eighteenth Century* (Cambridge: Cambridge UP, 1994); and Deidre Lynch, *The Economy of Character: Novels , Market Culture, and the Business of Inner Meaning* (Chicago: U of Chicago P, 1998), informs much of the analysis in this entry.

7. Marc Shell, *The Economy of Literature* (Baltimore: Johns Hopkins UP, 1978), 62. See also George Thomson, *The First Philosophers* (London: Lawrence and Wishart, 1955), 341.

8. Hobbes, *Leviathan* (Andrew Crooke, 1651), 15–6.

9. Maria Edgeworth, *Practical Education* (J. Johnson, 1798), 1:64.

10. Elizabeth Carter, trans., *Works of Epictetus* (Richardson, 1758), 383.

11. Lynch, *Economy of Character*, 35. See also Lynch's "Personal Effects and Sentimental Fictions," *Eighteenth-Century Fiction* 12:2 (2000): 354.

12. See Joseph Addison's *Tatler* no. 249 (1710) and Charles Johnstone's *Chrysal; or the Adventures of a Guinea* (1760). Deidre Lynch discusses these and two more money-centered narratives in *Economy of Character*, 95–9.

13. Lynch contrasts coins and banknotes, claiming that coins, "unlike bank-notes with their personal history," are imprinted with the king's head when they are struck, "but after leaving the mint, they would be imprinted no more." *Economy of Character*, 97. However, coins may be countermarked, and worn coins may be withdrawn and reminted at a different standard. During the French wars of the later eighteenth century, the Bank of England counterstamped colonial coins from the Spanish American colonies; when the price of silver continued to rise, the bank called in silver coinage and "overstruck" it at Matthew Boulton's Birmingham foundry. See C. R. Josset, *Money in Great Britain and Ireland* (Devon: David and Charles Newton Abbot, 1971), 166.

14. See Rice Vaughan, *A Discourse of Coin and Coinage*, ed. W. E. Minchton (New York: Johnson Reprint Corporation, 1970), 5; John Locke, *Two Treatises of Govern-*

ment, ed. Peter Laslett (Cambridge: Cambridge UP, 1988), 302; and Adam Smith, *An Inquiry into the Nature and Causes of the Wealth of Nations* (W. Strahan and T. Cadell, 1776), 1:28–30.

15. *The Works of Augustus Toplady* (W. Row, 1794), 4:291.

16. Shaftesbury, *Soliloquy, or Advice to an Author* (John Morphew, 1710), 320; Mandeville, *Fable of the Bees. Part II* (J. Roberts, 1729), 294.

17. Oliver Goldsmith, *Retaliation*, (G. Kearsley, 1774), 8.

18. *Poems by William Cowper* (J. Johnson, 1782), 69. I. A. Richards's and William Empson's discussions of mutual metaphor and mutual comparison are treated in the conclusion of this book.

19. On Mandeville's debts to and borrowings from Shaftesbury, see Irwin Primer, "Mandeville and Shaftesbury: Some Facts and Problems," in *Mandeville Studies* (The Hague: Kluwer, 1975), 126–41.

20. This process is detailed in *The Royal Mint: An Outline History* (London: Her Majesty's Stationery Office, 1977), 10.

21. The motto is from Virgil's *Aeneid*, V, 262. The inscription may refer to the image of the king stamped on the coin or may be more self-referential. See Josset, *Money*, 133. See also Joseph Addison, *Dialogues Upon the Usefulness of Ancient Medals*, in *The Works of Joseph Addison*, ed. George Washington Greene (Philadelphia: J. B. Lippincott, 1888), 2:121.

22. *An Epistle from Mr. Pope to Dr. Arbuthnot* (J. Wright, 1734), 2. On the mint, see Nigel Stirk, "Arresting Ambiguity: The Shifting Geographies of a London Debtors' Sanctuary in the Eighteenth Century," *Social History* 25:3 (October 2000): 316–29.

23. See Charles Oman, *The Coinage of England* (Oxford: Clarendon, 1931), 337.

24. Thompson notes that Locke, arguing against the devaluing of the coinage, "insisted again and again that 'silver is silver,' whatever form it takes." *Models of Value*, 18.

25. Montagu found himself positioned against Robert Harley (1661–1724), first Earl of Oxford, and Mortimer. Harley represented the country gentleman, arguing that new coins should be issued at the weight to which the currency had been reduced. A fictionalized eighteenth-century account of the debates is available in *The Works and Life of the Right Honourable Charles, Late Earl of Halifax* (printed for E. Curll, J. Pemberton, and J. Hooke, 1715), 30–3. The larger pamphlet war is admirably sampled and summarized in Joyce Oldham Appleby, *Economic Thought and Ideology in Seventeenth-Century England* (Princeton, NJ: Princeton UP, 1978), 210–52. Appleby emphasizes that the decision in favor of a "balance of trade" subordinated merchant interests to manufacturing ones (261). See also Andreas Andreades, *History of the Bank of England, 1640–1903* (New York: Augustus M. Kelley, 1966), 98–102.

26. In *Memoirs of the life of Charles Montagu, late Earl of Halifax*, mercantilist arguments are assigned to Montagu: "*That there was no way possible to keep our Money at Home, but by out-trading our Neighbours, and sending them more Commodities, or of greater Value than we received from them.*" *Works and Life*, 33.

27. Halifax, *Works and Life*, p. 12, ll. 33–4; pp. 16–7, ll. 114–23.

28. There is further inflationary ambiguity here: "raised" might be used in two different ways. Montagu's opponent, Robert Harley, argued that the standard should be raised so as to "prevent the Exportation of our Coin, and the melting it down, which of late Years had been much practis'd, to the great Prejudice of the Kingdom; and that it would encourage People to bring in their Plate and Bullion into the Mint." Halifax, *Works and Life*, 33. Montagu argued that the light silver should be recoined at (raised to) the old standard.

29. The mercantilist economist will often invoke a different cluster of metaphors by comparing this circulation of money with the circulation of blood. See Foucault's remark, following a citation of Bernardo Davanzati: "We meet once more with the old metaphor of a coinage that is to society what blood is to the body." *The Order of Things: An Archaeology of the Human Sciences* (New York: Vintage Books, 1970), 179.

30. Karl Marx, *Grundrisse: Foundations of the Critique of Political Economy*, trans. Martin Nicolaus (New York: Vintage, 1973), 157. See also Geoffrey Pilling, *Marx's Capital: Philosophy and Political Economy* (London: Routledge and Kegan Paul, 1980), 177.

31. Samuel Cobb, *A Pindarique Ode* (John Whitlock, 1694), 6; John Dryden, *The Medall* (Edinburgh: s.n., 1682), 1.

32. *Poems on Several Occasions* (Dublin: George Faulkner, 1735), 114.

33. Horace Walpole, *Walpoliana*, 2 vols. (R. Phillips, 1799), 1:7.

34. Oman, *Coinage of England*, 335.

35. John Wolcot, *The Lousiad. An Heroi-Comic Poem. Canto II.* 2nd ed. (G. Kearsley, 1787), 28–29.

36. Dryden dubs Tories "Anti-Brominghams" (or true Protestants) in the preface to *Absalom and Achitophel.* See also Dryden's preface to *The Spanish Friar.*

37. See John Styles, "'Our Traitorous Money Makers: The Yorkshire Coiners," in *An Ungovernable People: The English and Their Law in the Seventeenth and Eighteenth Centuries*, ed. John Brewer and John Styles (New Brunswick, NJ: Rutgers UP, 1980).

38. A silver (rather than gold) standard prevailed in most of the world until the middle of the nineteenth century; see William F. Hixson, *Triumph of the Bankers: Money and Banking in the Eighteenth and Nineteenth Centuries* (Westport, CT: Praeger, 1993), 27. See also Thompson, *Models of Value*, 69–70.

39. Oman, *Coinage of England*, 6. On Samuel Pepys's preference for gold, see Thompson, *Models of Value*, 49. In fact, much gold is drawn into circulation by the shortage of silver in England. Eighteenth-century Britain effectively worked on a gold standard.

40. Andreades reports, "During the months of May, June, and July, 1695, 572 bags of silver coin, of £100 each, were brought into the exchequer. They should have weighed 18,451 lbs.; they did, in fact, weigh 9,480 lbs., that is, there was a difference of nearly 50 per cent." *Bank*, 93. See also Josset, *Money*, 141, 168–9; Hixson, *Triumph of the Bankers*, 4, 11; and Thompson, *Models of Value*, 52.

41. See, for example, Lynch, *Economy of Character*, 114–7; see also her "Personal Effects," 362–3.

42. *A Sentimental Journey* (T. Becket and P. A. De Hondt, 1768), 87–8.

43. The coins can be dated more precisely to the time of recoinage when Yorick describes the them as "jingling and rubbing one against another for seventy years together in one body's pocket or another's" (ibid., 87). Sterne's *Journey* was written in 1767.

44. *The Life and Poetical Works of James Woodhouse*, ed. R. I. Woodhouse, 2 vols. (London: Leadenhall, 1896), 1:114.

45. *Characteristicks* (London: J. Darby, 1714), 3:64.

46. Cited in Albert O. Hirschman, *The Passions and the Interests* (Princeton, NJ: Princeton UP, 1977), 60–1.

47. Mark Akenside, *The Pleasures of Imagination* (R. Dodsley, 1744), 54.

48. Joseph Addison, *Dialogues Upon the Usefulness of Ancient Medals* (s.n., 1726), 24.

49. *The Order of Things*, 183.

50. *Tristram Shandy* (T. Becket and P. A. Dehondt, 1767), vol. 9, dedication, n.p.

51. The asterisks are so many marks of distinction separating Mr. *** (Pit[t]) from Lord ******* (Chatham). I thank my anonymous reviewer for John Hopkins University Press for marking Sterne's use of the plural form of "honor" in the citation and underlining its connotations.

52. From the 1754 edition (R. and J. Dodsley), 123.

53. Fordyce's picture of the mind's mint looks to be an anticipation of Kant's location of the imagination between reason and sensation. Fordyce was a "celebrated" author in Germany; see the introduction to *Elements of Moral Philosophy*, ed. Thomas Kennedy (Indianapolis: Liberty Fund, 2003), x.

54. The more "modern" political economists make the case that a country's money supply must increase with its production of goods and services. Hixson notes statements found in Locke, John Law, William Petty, and David Hume but credits Adam Smith with giving the issue prominence in later economic debates. See *Triumph of the Bankers*, 4.

55. David Alvarez argues that Addison treats ancient medals and modern coinage as aesthetic and political remedies to the dangers of a public sphere threatened by noise, pedantry, and enthusiasm. See his "Poetical Cash: Joseph Addison, Antiquarianism, and Aesthetic Value," *Eighteenth-Century Studies* 38:3 (2005): 509–31.

56. Henry Fielding, *Amelia*, 4 vols. (A. Millar, 1752), 3:259.

57. Nicholson, *Writing and the Rise of Finance*, xii.

58. For a list of similar terms, see Susan C. Greenfield, "Money or Mind? *Cecilia*, the Novel, and the Real Madness of Selfhood," *Studies in Eighteenth-Century Culture* 33 (2004): 53.

59. "John Locke, Desire, and the Epistemology of Money," *British Journal for the History of Philosophy* 15:4 (2007): 687.

60. *Shakespeare's Comedies, Histories, & Tragedies* (Isaac Iaggard and Ed. Blount, 1623), 271.

61. The *Discourse* is "prefix'd" to Dryden's translations of Juvenal and Persius. See *The Satires* (Jacob Tonson, 1697), viii.

62. John Dryden, *The Works of Virgil Containing His Pastorals, Georgics and Aeneis* (Jacob Tonson, 1697), Dedication [n.p.]. See T. R. Steiner, *English Translation Theory, 1650–1800* (Assen, Netherlands: Koninkilje Van Gorcum, 1975), 73.

63. The commercial couplet is quoted in William K. Wimsatt and Cleanth Brooks's multivolume history of literary criticism and explicated thus: "Let Congreve, Southerne, Wycherley, and especially Dryden, be melted down and coined into new, sound wit (good sense) and a safe national balance be deposited in a new Bank of Wit." Wimsatt's and Brooks's allusion to the historical context of the 1690s is, at best, opaque. See *Literary Criticism: A Short History* (Chicago: U of Chicago P, 1957), 1:241.

64. Richard Ames, *The Folly of Love*, 2nd ed. (E. Hawkins, 1693), 2. William Mason, *Elfrida*, 3rd ed. (J. and P. Knapton, 1752), 68; William Walsh, *Letters and Poems, Amorous and Gallant* (Jacob Tonson, 1692), 81.

65. G. N. Cantor, "Two Letters Relating to Berkeley's Social Circle," *Berkeley Newsletter* 4 (1980): 3.

66. Philip Rawlings, "Dodd, William (1729–1777)" *Oxford Dictionary of National Biography*, www.oxforddnb.com/view/article/7744, accessed May 26, 2009.

67. Samuel Johnson's attempts to intercede on Dodd's behalf are recorded in James Boswell's *The Life of Samuel Johnson* (Henry Baldwin, 1791), 2:134–40.

68. Forgery remained a capital offense until 1832. Josset describes the significant increase in forged notes from 1797 to 1817. See *Money*, 171. See also Derrick Byatt, *Promises to Pay: The First Three Hundred Years of Bank of England* (London: Spink, 1994), 33–42.

69. William Dodd, *Thoughts in Prison* (Edward and Charles Dilly and G. Kearsly, 1777), 58, 97–8. Note the pun on "tempering" in Dodd's choice of the phrase "distempered fancy." See **Metal**.

70. See Dodd's *The Beauties of Shakespeare*, 3rd ed. (G. Kearsley, 1784), 303.

71. Kames, *Elements of Criticism*, 3 vols. (Edinburgh: A. Millar, 1762), III.xix, 42.

72. On originality, authority, and copyright, see Mark Rose, *Authors and Owners: The Invention of Copyright* (Cambridge, MA: Harvard UP, 1993). See also Christina Lupton's chapter on Dodd's handwriting and authorship/forgery in *Knowing Books: The Consciousness of Mediation in Eighteenth-Century Britain* (Philadelphia: U of Pennsylvania P, 2012), 95–121.

73. Young, *Conjectures on Original Composition* (A. Millar, 1759), 14.

74. Wordsworth, *Lyrical Ballads, with Other Poems*, 2nd ed., 2 vols. (T. N. Longman and O. Rees, 1800), 1:xiv–xv; Wordsworth, *Lyrical Ballads, with Pastoral and Other Poems*, 2nd ed., 2 vols. (T. N. Longman and O. Rees, 1802) 2:245–7.

75. Thompson analyzes a passage from Adam Smith's *The Wealth of Nations* on wealth and purchasing power in order to illuminate what it might mean to be, like

Jane Austen's Darcy, a man of £10,000 a year. See *Models of Value*, 150–1. Information on the pricing of slaves can be found in Trevor Burnard and Kenneth Morgan, "The Dynamics of the Slave Market and Slave Purchasing Patterns in Jamaica, 1655–1788," *William and Mary Quarterly*, 3rd ser., 58:1 (2001): 217; and Richard B. Sheridan's *Sugar and Slavery: An Economic History of the British West Indies, 1623–1775* (Kingstown, Jamaica: Caribbean UP, 2000), 252. See also J. R. Ward, *British West Indian Slavery, 1750–1834: The Process of Amelioration* (Oxford: Oxford UP, 1988), 210. In his poem "The Negro's Complaint," William Cowper writes, "Minds are never to be Sold." The poem originally appeared in 1788; I quote from Cowper's *Poems* (J. Johnson, 1798), 1:331.

76. Thomas Piketty, *Capital in the Twenty-First Century*, trans. Arthur Goldhammer (Cambridge, MA: Harvard UP, 2014), 105–6, 411, 414. Compare Alex Woloch, *The One vs. the Many: Minor Characters and the Space of the Protagonist in the Novel* (Princeton, NJ: Princeton UP, 2003), 61–2, 119–20.

77. Hobbes, *Leviathan*, 42. Quoted in Macpherson, *Individualism*, 37. Against Macpherson, see Keith Thomas, "The Social Origins of Hobbes' Political Thought," in *Hobbes Studies*, ed. Keith C. Brown (Oxford: Blackwell, 1965), 185–236. D. D. Raphael suggests that Hobbes is satirical here, in *Hobbes: Morals and Politics* (London: Allen and Unwin, 1977), 93.

78. See Hume and Blackstone, who both discuss *weregeld* and are cited in the *OED*. On the boom, see Geoffrey W. Clark, *Betting on Lives: The Culture of Life Insurance in England, 1696–1775* (Manchester: Manchester UP), 91–2; the actuarial figures are from p. 105. On flipping coins, playing cards, and the "new" metaphor of life as a lottery, see Jesse Molesworth, *Chance and the Eighteenth-Century Novel: Realism, Probability, Chance* (Cambridge: Cambridge UP, 2010), 61–81.

79. On the root metaphor, see G. A. Cohen, *Self-Ownership, Freedom, and Equality* (Cambridge: Cambridge UP, 1995), 67ff. On possessive individualism, I am thinking of Cambridge School responses to Macpherson. A critical defense of Macpherson and a survey of his critics is available in Jules Townshend, *C. B. Macpherson and the Problem of Liberal Democracy* (Edinburgh: Edinburgh UP, 2000). See also James Tully, "The Possessive Individualism Thesis in Democracy and Possessive Individualism," in *Democracy and Possessive Individualism: The Intellectual Legacy of C. B. Macpherson*, ed. Joseph H. Carens (Albany: SUNY P, 1993), 19–44.

80. See Keith Thomas, *The Ends of Life: Roads to Fulfilment in Early Modern England* (Oxford: Oxford UP, 2009), 176–7, 182.

81. "Advice to a Young Tradesman," in *The Political Thought of Benjamin Franklin*, ed. Ralph Ketcham (Indianapolis: Hackett, 2003), 52, cited in Max Weber, *The Protestant Ethic and the Spirit of Capitalism*, trans. Talcott Parsons (London: Routledge, 1992), 49. On money as a model for self, see Matthew Garrett, "Money and the Circulation of Social Success after Franklin," *Journal of Cultural Economy* 4:3 (August 2011): 315–28.

82. Compare *Essays and Treatises* (T. Cadell, 1770), 4:64, and the same essay as originally published in *Political Discourses* (Edinburgh: R. Fleming, 1752), 63. Hume drops

the appeal to convention and raises the adverb "merely" to "chiefly." With Hume in mind, J. G. A. Pocock connects coin, credit, and personality in the eighteenth century: "Once property was seen to have a symbolic value, expressed in coin or credit, the foundations of personality themselves appeared imaginary or at best consensual: the individual could exist, even in his own sight, only at the fluctuating value imposed on him by his fellows." *The Machiavellian Moment: Florentine Thought and the Atlantic Republican Tradition* (Princeton, NJ: Princeton UP, 2003), 464. Pocock's nuanced syntax balances imagination and consensus, as marked in Hume's revision.

83. Lady Mary Lee Chudleigh, *Poems on Several Occasions* (Bernard Lintott, 1703), 56.

84. Oliver Goldsmith, *The Vicar of Wakefield* (Salisbury: B. Collins, 1766), 2:116.

85. Kant, *Practical Philosophy*, ed. and trans. Mary J. Gregor (Cambridge: Cambridge UP, 1996), 50.

86. Some neo-Kantians, like Christine Korsgaard, argue that intrinsic value is "conferred" by persons and that the language of means and ends should be kept distinct from the terminology of "intrinsic" and "extrinsic." See Korsgaard's "Kant's Formula of Humanity," in *Kant-Studien* 77:2 (1986): 183–203.

87. Thomas Gray, *An Elegy Wrote in a Country Church Yard* (R. Dodsley, 1751), 8.

88. Ceri Sullivan observes, appositely, "A miser's cash is not a metaphor for something else; it does not stand in the place of an opportunity to purchase goods in the future." *The Rhetoric of Credit: Merchants in Early Modern Writing* (Cranbury, NJ: Associated UPs, 2002), 85.

Court

1. I have collected 182 metaphors for this entry, just under 2% of the total number of metaphors collected between 1700 and 1799. A cluster from prose works of the 1750s and 1760s is discussed in the text. Although "judgment" is surely an eighteenth-century keyword, it does not number among the terms in my set list (mind, heart, soul, idea, thought, imagination, fancy, reason, passion, head, breast, bosom, brain). Looking for lively metaphors, I have only searched collocations of "judgment" and my set list of keywords, along with the other collocated terms listed at the top of the entry. That this sorting of metaphors from more commonplace talk of "the judgment" called for interpretive judgment in every instance is thematized in the entry.

2. Quotations from *The Making of the English Working Class* (New York: Pantheon Books, 1964), 80; see also Thompson, *Whigs and Hunters: The Origins of the Black Act* (New York: Pantheon Books, 1975), 263. On the centrality of the law in Thompson's research, see Daniel H. Cole, "'An Unqualified Human Good': E. P. Thompson and the Rule of Law," *Journal of Law and Society* 28:2 (June 2001): 177–203.

3. See Howard Nenner, "The Later Stuart Age," in *The Varieties of British Political Thought, 1500–1800*, ed. J. G. A. Pocock (Cambridge: Cambridge UP, 1996), 204.

4. See J. H. Langbein on "Blackstone's polite doctrinal fig leaf" and the distance between legal theory and legal reality in the eighteenth century in "Blackstone on Judging," in *Blackstone and His Commentaries: Biography, Law, History*, ed. Wilfrid Prest (Oxford: Hart, 2009), 68. This entry is informed by Langbein's essays, as well as his *The Origins of Adversary Criminal Trial* (Oxford: Oxford UP, 2003). I have also profited from J. H. Baker's *An Introduction to English Legal History*, 4th ed. (London: Butterworths, 2002), and resources at the Old Bailey Online. Steven L. Winter's *A Clearing in the Forest: Law, Life, and Mind* (Chicago: U of Chicago P, 2001) is an interesting and readable treatment of legal metaphors that brings cognitivist theory to the law.

5. See *The Gray's-Inn Journal: In Two Volumes* (W. Faden, 1756), 2:263. I quote from issue no. 94 (August 3, 1754).

6. *Commentaries on the Laws of England*, 4 vols. (1765–9; facs., Chicago: U of Chicago P, 1979).

7. Elliott Visconsi, *Lines of Equity: Literature and the Origins of Law in Later Stuart England* (Ithaca, NY: Cornell UP, 2008), 82–3. See also Quentin Skinner, "Classical Liberty and the Coming of the English Civil War," in *Republicanism: A Shared European Heritage*, ed. Martin van Gelderen and Quentin Skinner (Cambridge: Cambridge UP, 2002), 22, 25.

8. *The Table Talk of John Selden*, ed. S. H. Reynolds (Oxford: Clarendon, 1892), 61. I thank Paul Halliday for bringing the aphorism to my attention and am indebted to him for reading an early draft of these pages.

9. *Of the Lawes of Ecclesiasticall Politie*, 2nd ed. (Iohn Windet, 1604), I.i.xvi, p. 94. Cf. pp. 49, 51, 52.

10. See Blackstone, *Commentaries*, 1:39–46. In Hobbes's *Dialogue between a Philosopher and a Student of the Common Laws of England*, the student, seemingly proud to have mastered the diversity of law, reports on the "extraordinary great number of courts in England," rattling them off by name. *The English Works of Thomas Hobbes of Malmesbury*, ed. Sir W. Molesworth, 7 vols. (London: John Bohn, 1839–45), 6:38.

11. *Redemption: A Divine Poem, in Six Books* (A. Bettesworth, 1722), 301, but see also 262, where the "reason's bar" metaphor also appears.

12. Blackmore follows Richard Hooker: see *Ecclesiasticall Politie*, III.viii, pp. 140ff. On revelation and Anglican rationalism, see also Philip Harth, *Swift and Anglican Rationalism: The Religious Background of "A Tale of a Tub"* (Chicago: U of Chicago P, 1961), 23–9.

13. Quentin Skinner, *The Foundations of Modern Political Thought* (Cambridge: Cambridge UP, 1978), 1:205.

14. "No man (out of his own private Reason) ought to be wiser than the Law, which is the Perfection of Reason." I quote from an eighteenth-century edition of *Coke upon Lyttleton*: see *The First Part of the Institutes of the Laws of England* (Savoy: Edward Sayer, 1719), §138, fol. p. 97. See also Blackstone's *Commentaries*, 1:70.

15. The distinction between written and unwritten law descends from Aristotle's *Rhetoric*: see James B. Murphy, "Habit and Convention at the Foundation of Custom," in *The Nature of Customary Law: Legal, Historical, and Philosophical Perspectives*, ed. Amanda Perreau-Saussine and James B. Murphy (Cambridge: Cambridge UP, 2009), 64. See Blackstone's *Commentaries*, vol. 1, §3, 63ff. J. G. A. Pocock figures written and unwritten law as Achilles and tortoise in his reissued edition of *The Ancient Constitution and Feudal Law* (Cambridge: Cambridge UP, 1987), 261. Thomas C. Grey discusses backgrounds and the early American context in "Origins of the Unwritten Constitution: Fundamental Law in American Revolutionary Thought," *Stanford Law Review* 30 (1977–8): 843–93.

16. Blackstone writes, "An equitable light must not be indulged too far, lest thereby we destroy all law, and leave the decision of every question entirely in the breast of the judge." *Commentaries*, 1:62.

17. Chrysippus equates law and reason, *koinos nomos* and *orthos logos*. See Paul A. Vander Waerdt, "Zeno's *Republic* and the Origins of Natural Law," in *The Socratic Movement*, ed. Waerdt (Ithaca, NY: Cornell UP, 1994), 272–6. See also Louis I. Bredvold, *The Intellectual Milieu of John Dryden: Studies in Some Aspects of Seventeenth-Century Thought* (Ann Arbor: U of Michigan P, 1956).

18. *Fifteen Sermons Preached at Rolls Chapel* (James and John Knapton, 1726), sermon 2 (see also Montesquieu's claim that "in a free state every man will be his own legislator." *Spirit of the Laws*, LIV.ix.6); Churchill, *Night, an Epistle to Robert Lloyd* (1761), 3.

19. Allen W. Wood, *Kantian Ethics* (Cambridge: Cambridge UP, 2007), 184.

20. James Thomson, *A Poem to the Memory of the Right Honourable the Lord Talbot* (Edinburgh: A. Millar, 1737), 13. The expression "sole perfect judge" also appears in Mark Akenside's ode "On Love of Praise," in *The Poems of Mark Akenside* (W. Bowyer and J. Nichols, 1772), 327.

21. The legal theorist Peter Goodrich provocatively describes "an absorption of the ecclesiastical into the secular, of canon law into common law" in the period. "The New Casuistry," *Critical Inquiry* 33:4 (Summer 2007): 686.

22. Gilbert Ryle, *The Concept of Mind* (Chicago: U of Chicago P, 1949), 315. On Hobbes's metaphorical conception of conscience, see Karen Feldman, "Conscience and the Concealments of Metaphor in Hobbes' *Leviathan*," *Philosophy and Rhetoric* 34:1 (2001): 21–37.

23. *Concept of Mind*, 155.

24. *Leviathan*, 31. A proverb I find also in Shakespeare's *Richard III* (V.v.147): "My Conscience hath a thousand seuerall Tongues." *Shakespeare's Comedies, Histories, & Tragedies* (Isaac Iaggard and Ed. Blount, 1623), 202.

25. James Q. Whitman, *The Origins of Reasonable Doubt: Theological Roots of the Criminal Trial* (New Haven, CT: Yale UP, 2008), 106.

26. Victoria Kahn, *Wayward Contracts: The Crisis of Political Obligation in England, 1640–1674* (Princeton, NJ: Princeton UP, 2004), 43. Compare Peter Goodrich's read-

ing of legal history in which the ecclesiastical is absorbed into the secular and canon law into common law in "The New Casuistry," 686.

27. Reinhart Koselleck, *Critique and Crisis: Enlightenment and the Pathogenesis of Modern Society* (Cambridge, MA: MIT P, 1988), 39.

28. J. Paul Hunter, *Before Novels: The Cultural Contexts of Eighteenth-Century Fiction* (New York: Norton, 1990), 290–2. See also G. A. Starr, "From Casuistry to Fiction: The Importance of the Athenian Mercury," *Journal of the History of Ideas* 28:1 (1967): 17–32.

29. *Prompter* no. 105 (November 11, 1735). See W. W. Appleton et al., *The Prompter: A Theatrical Paper (1734–1736)* (New York: Benjamin Blom, 1966), 122.

30. *Spectator* no. 1, in *The Spectator*, ed. D. F. Bond, 5 vols. (Oxford: Clarendon, 1965), 1:2.

31. See Baker, *English Legal History*, 99–108, on Chancery and equity.

32. Cardinal Wolsey observed the court of chancery "hath commonly been called the court of conscience." Quoted in J. W. Tubbs, *The Common Law Mind: Medieval and Early Modern Conceptions* (Baltimore: Johns Hopkins UP, 2000), 97. See Lowell Gallagher, *Medusa's Gaze: Casuistry and Conscience in the Renaissance* (Stanford, CA: Stanford UP, 1991), 144ff. See also Dennis R. Klinck, "Lord Nottingham and the Conscience of Equity," *Journal of the History of Ideas* 67:1 (2006): 123.

33. Diana Woodhouse, *The Office of the Lord Chancellor* (Oxford: Hart, 2001), 2–3.

34. Charles Macklin, "Commonplace Book [Manuscript], 1778–1790," in Folger Shakespeare Library, Washington, DC.

35. Keith Thomas, "Cases of Conscience in Seventeenth-Century England," in *Public Duty and Private Conscience in Seventeenth-Century England*, ed. J. S. Morill, Paul Slack, and D. R. Woolf (Oxford: Clarendon, 1993), 29. See also Klinck, "Nottingham," 123n2.

36. See D. E. C. Yale, ed., *Lord Nottingham's Chancery Cases*, 2 vols. (London: Selden Society, 1961), 2:639. See also Francis Bacon's distinction between "private conscience" and "the general conscience of the realm which is Chancery." Bacon is cited in Klinck, "Nottingham," 125–6.

37. Yale, *Nottingham's Chancery Cases*, 2:639.

38. Charles Macklin, *The Man of the World: A Comedy* (Dublin: s.n., 1785), 55. Matthew J. Kinservik calls the Wilkite satire, which was continually suppressed in the 1770s, "the most heavily censored play of the eighteenth century." See his "New Light on the Censorship of Macklin's *The Man of the World*," *Huntington Quarterly* 62:1–2 (1999): 43.

39. Klinck cites examples from John Hughes and Immanuel Bourne. "Nottingham," 126n18.

40. *Tom Jones*, 6 vols. (A. Millar, 1749), II.iv.6. As I pursue metaphors through literary history, the limits of the monograph form will not allow me to follow each metaphor through contemporary literary criticism as well. This long note is included as a case in point. Here I provide a compressed review of the critical literature. John

Preston identifies this passage as "the hub of the book's meaning" and connects the image of the lord high chancellor with "the high ideal which, in Butler's sermons, is called conscience." "*Tom Jones* and the 'Pursuit of True Judgment,'" *English Literary History* 33:3 (1966): 324. Mary Poovey reads the figure of the lord high chancellor as an image of "an innate faculty of judgment and guidance" identified with conscience. "Journeys from This World to the Next: The Providential Promise in *Clarissa* and *Tom Jones*," *English Literary History* 43:3 (1976): 311. Frederick G. Ribble pulls a different thread from this passage and discusses the literary critical figure of the Trunk-maker instead, emphasizing aesthetics and moral sense theory. "Aristotle and the 'Prudence' Theme of *Tom Jones*," *Eighteenth-Century Studies* 15:1 (1981): 41–2. John P. Zomchick works harder to place the figure in juridical (and gender) history: "Like the Lord Chancellor, Tom's conscience bridges the gap between knowledge and corruption because it is endowed with a peculiarly masculine power to penetrate while at the same time remaining free from penetration" and argues this "essentialist, naturalist position" is echoed in at least one "eighteenth-century treatise writer's definition of equity." "A Penetration Which Nothing Can Deceive: Gender and Juridical Discourse in Some Eighteenth-Century Narratives," *Studies in English Literature, 1500–1900* 29:3 (1989): 537.

41. When Fielding published *Tom Jones* in 1749, Philip Yorke, the first Earl of Hardwicke was lord chancellor (in office 1737–56). Hardwicke's conduct of the treason trials after Culloden, the final battle of the 1745 Jacobite rebellion, was considered severe: hundreds of prisoners of war were executed, transported, or banished. See Martin C. Battestin and Ruthe R. Battestin, *Henry Fielding: A Life* (London: Routledge, 1989), 397–9, 402–3, 510–1. See also Martin C. Battestin, *A Henry Fielding Companion* (Westport, CT: Greenwood, 2000), 71–2.

42. Peter D. G. Thomas, "Yorke, Philip, First Earl of Hardwicke (1690–1764)," *Oxford Dictionary of National Biography*, ed. H. C. G. Matthew and Brian Harrison (Oxford: Oxford UP, 2004), October 2005 online edition, ed. Lawrence Goldman.

43. *Fifteen Sermons*, 35–6.

44. Woodhouse, *Office of the Lord Chancellor*, 5.

45. The complications of head and heart are dramatized in Launcelot's description of his conscience "hanging about the neck of my heart," in the *Merchant of Venice*, II.ii, l. 13.

46. *Letters of the Late Ignatius Sancho, An African*, 2 vols. (J. Nichols, 1782), 2:89.

47. See Wood, *Kantian Ethics*, 182. See also Stephen Darwall, who writes, "The principle of reflection is, for Butler, a *principle* of action in the early-eighteenth-century sense—namely, a *motivational* source of conduct, like the principles of calm self-love or benevolence." *The British Moralists and the Internal "Ought," 1640–1740* (Cambridge: Cambridge UP, 1995), 247.

48. I agree here with Preston, "Pursuit," 324. After Preston all of the critics cited above in note 40 equate the "Somewhat" with Tom's conscience. Preston alone makes an explicit argument for identifying the Somewhat with conscience. See also Clif-

ford Johnson, "Joseph Butler: Laodicean Rationalist?," *Modern Language Studies* 4:2 (1974): 78, 83.

49. See J. H. Langbein, "Bifurcation and the Bench: The Influence of the Jury on English Conceptions of the Judiciary," in *Judges and Judging in the History of the Common Law and Civil Law*, ed. Paul Brand and Joshua Getzler (Cambridge: Cambridge UP, 2012), 67–8, 82. I also draw here from John Bender, *Imagining the Penitentiary: Fiction and the Architecture of Mind in Eighteenth-Century England* (Chicago: U of Chicago P, 1987), 144–5, 167–70. See also Gerald Newman, ed., *Britain in the Hanoverian Age, 1714–1837* (New York: Garland, 1997), 382.

50. See Langbein, *Origins*, 14, 51–3; and Bender, *Imagining the Penitentiary*, 175.

51. See Knud Haakonssen, "The Character and Obligation of Natural Law According to Cumberland," in *English Philosophy in the Age of Locke*, ed. M. A. Stewart (Oxford: Clarendon, 2000).

52. *Soliloquy, or Advice to an Author* (John Morphew, 1710), 186.

53. Francis Hutcheson, *An Essay on the Nature and Conduct of the Passions and Affections* (John Smith and William Bruce, 1728), 192.

54. The contemporary philosopher Harry Frankfurt sounds a similar note by locating the terms "caring" and "importance" at the center of the vocabulary of moral philosophy. See the title essay in *The Importance of What We Care About: Philosophical Essays* (Cambridge: Cambridge UP, 1988), 80–94.

55. Whitman, *Doubt*, 105.

56. Quoted in Tubbs, *Common Law*, 97. Conscience is to be grounded in law; Nottingham echoes St. Germain: in "suits in equity the Lord Chancellor must order his conscience after the rules and grounds of the laws of this realm." Quoted in Klinck, "Nottingham," 134.

57. Zomchick describes the masculine principle of conscience as ostensibly "unimpeachable," but the office of lord chancellor is not beyond impeachment: Bacon was famously impeached in 1621; and in 1725, at Walpole's instigation, the Earl of Macclesfield was investigated by a committee of the privy council and impeached for accepting bribes and selling offices of masters of chancery. See A. A. Hanham, "Parker, Thomas, First Earl of Macclesfield (1667–1732)," *Oxford Dictionary of National Biography*. *Tom Jones* was published twenty-four years after Chancellor Macclesfield's very public impeachment. Because Macclesfield was the Earl of Hardwicke's patron, Hardwicke was excused from the impeachment proceedings.

58. On the improvement in case reporting after 1750, see Baker, *English Legal History*, 184. The study of "pre-Romantic" shifts in literary theory and practice is large and contentious, but see Marshall Brown's important *Preromanticism* (Stanford, CA: Stanford UP, 1991) and Heinz Joachim Müllenbrock's "The Middle Ages in Eighteenth-Century England: A Guide to Periodization?," in *The Living Middle Ages*, ed. Uwe Böker, Manfred Markus, and Rainer Schöwerling (Stuttgart: Belser, 1989), 197–209.

59. Addison and Steele's character Isaac Bickerstaff seems first to seat himself as the "Censor of *Great-Britain*" in *Tatler* no. 103 (see his threats to do so in no. 89 and

his censorial exertions in the numbers preceding this installation), only formally assuming the title in no. 144. In several papers, Bickerstaff hears cases or entertains petitioners in his apartment, with the most famous case being the "trial of the petticoat" in no. 116. Fielding's court first meets in no. 5 of the *Covent-Garden Journal.* (The court trope is also found in Fielding's *Champion* no. 11 and his *Jacobite's Journal* no. 43.) Lance Bertelsen observes the interpenetration of law and literature in *The Covent-Garden Journal*: "Law was providing the metaphor for judging literary and journalistic practice, while literary and journalistic practice was providing the vehicle for profitably exploiting official legal judgments." See "Committed by Justice Fielding: Judicial and Journalistic Representation in the Bow Street Magistrate's Office January 3–November 24, 1752," *Eighteenth-Century Studies* 30:4 (1997): 337–63, quote on 351. On the figure of the censor, see also Iona Italia, *The Rise of Literary Journalism in the Eighteenth Century: Anxious Employment* (New York: Routledge, 2005), 23–6.

60. *The Art of Rhetoric, With a Discourse of the Laws of England* (William Crooke, 1681), 57.

61. On the allegory of the court embedded in the sermon, see Arthur A. Cash, "The Sermon in *Tristram Shandy*," *English Literary History* 31:4 (1964): 395–417. Cash claims, sweepingly, "The court of conscience is ever present in the fiction of Laurence Sterne" (411).

62. The law also takes the form of writing as formal records of the court and in written reports.

63. See Thomas Keymer, *Sterne, the Moderns, and the Novel* (Oxford: Oxford UP, 2002). See also Christina Lupton, *Knowing Books: The Consciousness of Meditation in Eighteenth-Century Britain* (Philadelphia: U of Pennsylvania P, 2012).

64. Edith Hamilton and Huntington Cairns, eds., *The Collected Dialogues of Plato, Including the Letters* (1961; repr., Princeton, NJ: Princeton UP, 1978). See J. G. A. Pocock, *The Machiavellian Moment: Florentine Thought and the Atlantic Republican Tradition* (Princeton, NJ: Princeton UP, 2003), 20–1.

65. *Case of Prohibitions del Roy* (1608), 12 Co. Rep. 63. See also *Co. Inst.*, vol. IV, p. 97 (both cited in Baker, *English Legal History*, 98), cited in Christopher Hill, *Intellectual Origins of the English Revolution, Revisited* (Oxford: Oxford UP, 1997), 218–20.

66. Hobbes, *Dialogue*, 50. In chapter 3 of *De Cive* Hobbes gives "*that no man is judge in his own cause*" as the sixteenth Law of Nature. *Works*, 61. See also Hobbes, *Leviathan* (Andrew Crooke, 1651), 125.

67. *The Theory of Moral Sentiments*, 2nd ed. (A. Millar, 1761), 202. In Kant's lectures on ethics the inner judicial proceedings of the conscience demands a self divided into three persons: an accuser, an advocate, and a judge. See *Vorlesungen über Ethik, Kants Schriften* (Cambridge: Cambridge UP, 1996), 27:354. Cited in Wood, *Kantian Ethics*, 184.

68. Charles Griswold, *Adam Smith and the Virtues of Enlightenment* (Cambridge: Cambridge UP, 1999), 188–9.

69. In Smith's first edition, 269. Compare Smith and Kant, who diverge over the court metaphor. Allen Wood argues that in Kant's ethics we are often meant to take the conscience-as-court metaphor *literally*. Kant divides us "quite literally" into "distinct moral persons whose interaction, in Kant's view, typically follows a pattern similar to that of the prosecutor, the defense attorney, and the judge in an external court." I quote from Allen Wood's "Kant on Conscience," forthcoming in *Kantovskii Sbornik*, trans. Leonard Kalinnikov.

70. *Tristram Shandy*, 2nd ed. (R. and J. Dodsley, 1760).

71. On the assizes, see Melvyn New, "Reading the Occasion: Understanding Sterne's Sermons," in *Divine Rhetoric: Essays on the Sermons of Laurence Sterne* (Newark: U of Delaware P, 2010), 106–7. See also Arthur Cash, "Sterne as a Judge in the Spiritual Courts," in *English Writers of the Eighteenth Century*, ed. John H. Middendorf (New York: Columbia UP, 1971), 17–36.

72. J. Paul Hunter pursues a related line of argument. See his "Response as Reformation: *Tristram Shandy* and the Art of Interruption," *Novel: A Forum on Fiction* 4:2 (Winter 1971): 132–46. Compare Lupton, *Knowing Books*, 116–7.

73. *The Ghost: Book IV* (J. Coote et al., 1763), 133.

74. *The Apology* (W. Flexney, 1761), 20; *Independence* (J. Almon, 1764), 9.

75. Wallace Cable Brown, *Charles Churchill: Poet, Rake, and Rebel* (1953; repr., New York: Greenwood, 1968), 99–100.

76. Context for these lines is provided in *Charles Churchill: Selected Poetry*, ed. Adam Rounce (Nottingham: Trent Editions, 2003). See also Morris Golden, "Sterility and Eminence in the Poetry of Charles Churchill," *Journal of English and Germanic Philology* 66:3 (1967): 333–46. It is a recognized tactic of Wilkite bourgeois radicalism to draw parallels between the 1760s and the radical movements of the seventeenth century. See Kathleen Wilson, *The Sense of the People: Politics, Culture, and Imperialism in England, 1715–1785* (Cambridge: Cambridge UP, 1998), 215.

77. *The Ghost. By C. Churchill. Book III*, 2nd ed. (W. Flexney, 1763), p. 89, ll. 725–6. Churchill is particularly upset about *judge-made law*. *The Ghost: Book IV*, 161, 193.

78. *The Ghost: Book IV*, 133–4.

79. See John Brewer, "The Wilkites and the Law, 1763–74," in *An Ungovernable People: The English and Their Law in the Seventeenth and Eighteenth Centuries*, ed. John Brewer and John Styles (New Brunswick, NJ: Rutgers UP, 1980), 143.

80. See E. P. Thompson, *The Making of the English Working Class* (1963; repr., New York: Vintage Books, 1966), 80.

81. E. P. Thompson boggles at the imbrications of the law within modes of production, its presence in the philosophy of Locke, its ideological disguises: "It danced a cotillion with religion, moralizing over the theatre at Tyburn; it was an arm of politics and politics was one of its arms . . . above all, it afforded an arena for class struggle." *The Poverty of Theory & Other Essays* (New York: Monthly Review Press, 1978), 96.

82. The variant appears at least as early as 1772, in a Dublin edition of Akenside's *Poems*. See also *The Poetical Works of Mark Akenside* (Edinburg: Martins, 1781), 176. The line reads "the native honours of the human soul" in earlier printings. Again, as with Smith and Sterne, I would have noted a possible correlation of inward judgment and revision, but in this case it seems unlikely that the variant has Akenside's authority.

83. In the *Critique of Pure Reason* Kant writes: "We can, however, trace all actions of the understanding back to judgments, so that the **understanding** in general can be represented as a **faculty for judging**" (205). Reason and understanding are reconciled in the operations of imagination. In an earlier work titled *False Subtlety*, however, Kant argues that these are not fundamentally different faculties. See Allen Wood's introduction to the *Critique of Pure Reason*, ed. P. Guyer and A. W. Wood (Cambridge: Cambridge UP, 1998), 29.

84. *The Libertine: A Tragedy* (printed by T.N. for Henry Herringman, 1676), 40.

85. On earlier suspensions of the Habeas Corpus Act and the context of the 1790s, see Paul Halliday, *Habeas Corpus: From England to Empire* (Cambridge, MA: Harvard University Press, 2010), 247–56.

86. On metaphor as a duck-rabbit, see Roger White, *Structure of Metaphor: How the Language of Metaphor Works* (Oxford: Blackwell, 1996), 115. See also Donald Davidson, "What Metaphors Mean," in *On Metaphor*, ed. Sheldon Sacks (Chicago: U of Chicago P, 1979), 45.

87. James T. Mitchell, *The Unequalled Collection of Engraved Portraits Belonging to Hon. James T. Mitchell*, compiled by Stan V. Henkels (Philadelphia: W. F. Fell, 1908), 40.

88. Alexander Murdoch, "Wedderburn, Alexander, first earl of Rosslyn (1733–1805)," in *Oxford Dictionary of National Biography* (Oxford: Oxford UP, 2004), online edition, January 2008, www.oxforddnb.com/view/article/28954, accessed February 23, 2010.

89. The difficulty goes to the root: Hannah Arendt discusses the etymology of *kategoria* (a key concept in the treatment of metaphor as "category mistake") as borrowed, in its earliest philosophical usage, by Aristotle from court procedures in which "an indictment (*katagoreuein ti tinos*) hands something down (*kata*) to a defendant that he is charged with, hence that belongs to him." *The Life of the Mind* (San Diego: Harcourt, 1978), 105.

Empire

1. I count metaphors in this entry from two categories in the database: Government and War (metaphors are here counted if they belong to one or the other category). These **Empire** metaphors compose more than 18% of all the metaphors collected, 1700–1799. Of interest is the distribution: metaphors of rule and conquest fall off after the 1770s, as if responding to the American War of Independence and the loss of colonies. The historical shift, one of the few confidently marked in this study, is visualized and considered in the main text of the entry.

2. Compare Michael Hardt and Antonio Negri, *Empire* (Cambridge, MA: Harvard UP, 2000), 222–9.

3. *The History of Miss Betsy Thoughtless*, 4 vols. (T. Gardner, 1751), 4:230.

4. *The History of the Decline and Fall of the Roman Empire* (W. Strahan and T. Cadell, 1776), 1:125.

5. In the 1766 wordbook *The Difference Between Words Esteemed Synonymous* (J. Dodsley, 1766), John Trusler writes, "It appears to me, that the word, *empire*, conveys an idea of a vast territory, composed of various people; whereas, that of *kingdom*, implies, one more bounded; and, intimates the unity of that nation, of which it is formed" (2:15). These distinguishing characteristics are treated in some detail by James Sheehan in "States and Empires: The Problem of Legitimate Violence," Vienna Conference on Imperium, 2005 (unpublished). I draw from Sheehan in this paragraph and the next. See also Hannah Arendt on heterogeneity of empire and homogeneity of the nation-state in *Imperialism* (1968; repr., New York: Harcourt Brace, 1976), 5.

6. J. G. A. Pocock frames the "terminological problem" of empire in "Political Thought in the English-Speaking Atlantic, 1760–1790: Part 1: The Imperial Crisis," in *The Varieties of British Political Thought, 1500–1800*, ed. J. G. A. Pocock, G. J. Schochet, and Lois G. Schwoerer (Cambridge: Cambridge UP, 1993), 257. See also Anthony Pagden, *Lords of All the World: Ideologies of Empire in Spain, Britain and France c. 1500–c. 1800* (New Haven, CT: Yale UP, 1995), 12. On the ambiguity of the term in Marxist theory, see Giovanni Arrighi, *The Geometry of Imperialism: The Limits of Hobson's Paradigm*, trans. Patrick Camiller (London: NLB, 1978), 9–17.

7. To historians surveying competing political claims about trade on the world's seas, the application of uniformity in Ireland, the plantations in America, and the administration of common law in India, the period itself "seems to have . . . no real concept of a single British empire of rule over land and peoples throughout the world until the end of the Seven Years War." P. J. Marshall, "Burke and Empire," in *Hanoverian Britain and Empire*, ed. Stephen Taylor, Richard Connors, and Clyve Jones (Woodbridge, Suffolk: Boydell, 1998), 289.

8. Johnson quotes from Temple's "Essay Upon the Original and Nature of Government," written in 1672 and collected in his *Miscellanea*.

9. William C. Dowling summarizes the problem of translation in *The Cambridge History of English Literature, 1660–1780*, ed. John Richetti (Cambridge: Cambridge UP, 2005), 512.

10. While collecting empire metaphors, I read Arendt, Arrighi, Hardt and Negri, Pocock, and Kathleen Wilson. As a literary historian, I benefited in particular from reading Suvir Kaul's *Poems of Nation, Anthems of Empire* (Charlottesville: U of Virginia P, 2000) and Lynn Festa's *Sentimental Figures of Empire in Eighteenth-Century Britain and France* (Baltimore: Johns Hopkins UP, 2006).

11. Max Horkheimer and Theodor W. Adorno, *Dialectic of Enlightenment* (1972; repr., Stanford, CA: Stanford UP, 2002), 70.

12. On tropicalization (a portmanteau of "tropical" and "tropological"), see Srinivas Aravamudan, *Tropicopolitans: Colonialism and Agency, 1688–1804* (Durham, NC: Duke UP, 1999). On the tropes and figures of empire fashioned by sentimental fiction, see Festa, *Sentimental Figures*, 8.

13. See Kaul, *Poems of Nation*, 1–43.

14. Mary Louise Pratt writes, "The frontier is only a frontier with respect to Europe." *Imperial Eyes: Travel Writing and Transculturation* (London: Routledge, 1992), 7.

15. John Home, *Douglas: A Tragedy* (Edinburgh: G. Hamilton, 1757), 11, 55.

16. Edward Gibbon, *The History of the Decline and Fall of the Roman Empire*, 6 vols. (W. Strahan and T. Cadell, 1776–83), 1:63; *The Writings and Speeches of Edmund Burke*, ed. Paul Langford, vol. 7, *India: The Hastings Trial, 1789–1794*, ed. P. J. Marshall (Oxford: Oxford UP, 2000), 568.

17. Quoted in Gibbon, *Decline and Fall*, 1:57.

18. The translation is from Marcus Manilius's *Astronomicon*: see *Medulla Poetarum Romanorum*, 2 vols. (D. Midwinter [et al.], 1737), 2:295.

19. That the ruling part of the self is so gendered in eighteenth-century literature is remarkable, as women, over and over, are designated as unreasonable creatures in this same discursive field. Perhaps the late eighteenth century may better balance its metaphors and misogyny: the historian Londa Schiebinger observes a decline in the feminine iconography epitomized by Cesare Ripa's and Francis Quarles's emblems and argues for a disappearance of gendered personifications in last-decade eighteenth-century philosophy and science. Wollstonecraft's description of patriarchal usurpations of reason's—of *its*—throne is studied in its gendering of weak tyrannical power but not reason itself, participating in and illustrating the historical change Schiebinger describes. See Schiebinger, *The Mind Has No Sex? Women in the Origins of Modern Science* (Cambridge, MA: Harvard UP, 1989), 121–59. Schiebinger's reading of Descartes and her claim that "modern philosophy eventually did away with personification" (148) overstate the case. As I argue in **Inhabitants**, personifications thrive in empiricist philosophy.

20. Crabbe, *Tales* (London: J. Hatchard, 1812), 192; Haywood, *The Injur'd Husband* (D. Brown, 1723), 89; Mary Barber, *Poems on Several Occasions* (C. Rivington, 1734), 15.

21. *Miscellany Poems, on Several Occasions* (printed for J. B., 1713), 166.

22. Edward T. Corp, *A Court in Exile: The Stuarts in France, 1689–1718* (Cambridge: Cambridge UP, 2004), 171–2. See also Edward Gregg, "Monarchs without a Crown," in *Royal and Republican Sovereignty in Early Modern Europe*, ed. Ragnhild Marie Hatton et al. (Cambridge: Cambridge UP, 1997), 382–422.

23. *A Treatise of Human Nature* (John Noon, 1739), 1:326–7. See Kevin Hart on divine right and its *archè* or first principles in *The Trespass of the Sign: Destruction, Theology, and Philosophy* (Cambridge: Cambridge UP, 1989), 133.

24. Adams argued, "We must have a seat for him. *In England*, it is called a *throne*." See William Maclay, *Sketches of Debate in the First Senate of the United States, in 1789–90/91*, ed. George W. Harris (Harrisburg, PA: Lane S. Hart, 1880), 35.

25. Ephraim Chambers, *Cyclopaedia*, 2 vols. (James and John Knapton, 1728), 2:56.

26. Quotation from Descartes's *Treatise of Man*, in *The Philosophical Writings of Descartes*, trans. J. Cottingham et al. (Cambridge: Cambridge UP, 1985), 1:106. See also Descartes's *The Passions of the Soul*, ibid., 1:340. In Chambers, Descartes is said to make the gland the "seat of the reasonable soul" (2:815). See Gert-Jan Lokhorst, "Descartes and the Pineal Gland," *Stanford Encyclopedia of Philosophy* (Summer 2011), ed. Edward N. Zalta, http://plato.stanford.edu/archives/sum2011/entries/pineal-gland/.

27. See John Vanbrugh, *Aesop. A Comedy* (Thomas Bennet, 1697), 11. William Sherlock, for one, however, claims "the Soul is the seat of Personality." Quoted in Udo Thiel, *The Early Modern Subject: Self-Consciousness and Personal Identity from Descartes to Hume* (Oxford: Oxford UP, 2011), 58.

28. Alexander Pope and John Arbuthnot, *Memoirs of the Extraordinary Life, Works, and Discoveries of Martinus Scriblerus* (Dublin: George Faulkner, 1741), 90–1.

29. See Christopher Fox, *Locke and the Scriblerians: Identity and Consciousness in Early Eighteenth-Century Britain* (Berkeley: U of California P, 1988), 101–3. See also Raymond Martin and Cyril Barresi, *Naturalization of the Soul: Self and Personality in the Eighteenth Century* (London: Routledge, 2000), 38–9.

30. See Locke's *Essay*, II.iii.1. See also Michael McKeon, *The Secret History of Domesticity: Public, Private, and the Division of Knowledge* (Baltimore: Johns Hopkins UP, 2005), 223.

31. *Eliza: An Epick Poem* (Awnsham and John Churchill, 1705), 105.

32. The picture may originate in Zeno's description of the soul as corporeal, a vital pneuma that circulates in the body and communicates sense impressions to a central "Hegemonikon."

33. See Maynard Mack, *Alexander Pope: A Life* (New York: Norton, 1985), 237.

34. *The History of Sir Charles Grandison* (S. Richardson, 1754), 1:294.

35. *Elegiac Sonnets*, 6th ed. (R. Noble, 1792), 51.

36. In the "heart-religion" of Methodism, thrones found in the hearts of the faithful belong to the Lord. Typical of Wesleyan verses is the hymn "After the Sacrament," wherein "Jesus makes our hearts His throne, / There He lives, and reigns alone." See *Hymns and Sacred Poems* (William Strahan, 1739), 191. Because the evangelical preaching of John Wesley stresses conversion, God's throne may be "sealed," "fixed," or "erected" in a heart or soul that has not yet experienced God's grace. In many of the hymns, the hymner invites the Lord to "Come, and erect Thy throne / Eternal in my heart."

37. *Poems upon Several Occasions* (H. Clements, 1713), 19.

38. From *Medulla Poetarum Romanorum*, 2:199 (the translation is from Creech, altered by Baker), and from *The Works of the Most Celebrated Minor Poets* (F. Cogan,

1749), 2:52–3 (the translation, George Stepney's, was collected in the first part of Tonson's miscellany as early as 1684).

39. One might take up Pope's *The First Epistle of the Second Book of Horace, Imitated* (T. Cooper, 1737) as an example, although as a symbolic figure in the eighteenth-century imagination Caesar Augustus is an ambiguous one: both polite ruler and debased tyrant. Dryden compares Charles II and Augustus in the dedication of his play *The Assignation: or, Love in a Nunnery* (Henry Herringman, 1673). Opponents to Hanoverian rule depict George I and George II as a despotic Caesars. For a brief summary of the literature on Augustus, see Frank Stack, *Pope and Horace: Studies in Imitation* (Cambridge: Cambridge UP, 1985), 152. On the valences of "Augustan," see Howard D. Weinbrot, *Augustus Caesar in "Augustan" England: The Decline of a Cultural Norm* (Princeton, NJ: Princeton UP, 1978).

40. *Naucratia*, 2nd ed. (W. Bulmer, 1798), 35.

41. Howard D. Weinbrot, *Britannia's Issue: The Rise of British Literature from Dryden to Ossian* (Cambridge: Cambridge UP, 1993), 237–75. Pye's poem, an uneasy mixture of martial and commercial themes, celebrates Rodney's victory with citations from Propertius and Horace. See Pye's *Naucratia*, 50n; compare Weinbrot, *Britannia's Issue*, 488n.

42. I quote Lynn Festa, *Sentimental Figures*, 64. On commerce and conquest, see David Hume's essay "Of the Jealousy of Trade," in *Essays Moral, Political, and Literary* (Indianapolis: Liberty Fund, 1987), 327–31, cited in Pagden, *Lords of All the World*, 182. Festa cites Julie Ellison on the "connivance" of commerce and conquest.

43. See Linda Colley, *Britons: Forging the Nation, 1707–1837* (New Haven, CT: Yale UP, 1992). See also her "Britishness and Otherness: An Argument," *Journal of British Studies* 31:4 (October 1992): 309–29.

44. A throne is often used a metonym for empire—thus the congruence.

45. See, for example, Robert Nugent's "Ode to Mankind," which is inscribed to the prince, or Leonard Welsted's *An Epistle to Mr. Steele, on the King's Accession to the Crown* (Tim. Childe, 1714). See also Aaron Hill's poem "Writ on a Blank Leaf of Alzira," which was given to the Prince of Wales. *The Works of the Late Aaron Hill*, 4 vols. (London, 1753). An empire fixed in subjects' hearts is suggestive of mid-sixteenth-century meanings of the word "empire," in which "empire" is synonymous with "sovereign state."

46. "D'ailleurs ce Roi est un grand Magicien: il exerce son Empire sur l'esprit même de ses Sujets; il les fait penser comme il veut." *Lettres persane* (Cologne: Pierre Marteau, 1721), 1:53.

47. Blackmore, *The Nature of Man* (Sam. Buckley, 1711), 47; Chapone, *Letters on the Improvement of the Mind*, 2 vols. (H. Hughs, 1773), 2:194.

48. Edmund Burke, *A Third Letter to a Member of the Present Parliament* (F. and C. Rivington, 1797), 78.

49. *The Dunciad, in Four Books* (M. Cooper, 1743), 208.

50. *An Essay on History*, 2nd ed. (J. Dodsley, 1781), 44, ll. 364–7.

51. "To Mr. Garrick," item 23 in "Collection of Poems and Letters by David Garrick's Admirers and Members of His Circle," manuscript, Folger Shakespeare Library, n.p., ll. 2, 37.

52. The phrase is from Bridget Orr's *Empire on the British Stage, 1660–1714* (Cambridge: Cambridge UP, 2001), 27.

53. On the "retreat" of drama from the direct expression of colonial desire, see Kaul, *Poems of Nation*, 12–6. See also Kaul's chapter "Theatres of Empire" in *Eighteenth-Century British Literature and Postcolonial Studies* (Edinburgh: Edinburgh UP, 2009), 35–60.

54. *A Poem to the Memory of Mrs. Oldfield* (George Faulkner, 1731), 6; *The Poetical Works of Anna Seward* (Edinburgh: James Ballantyne, 1810), 3:383.

55. *Miscellanies, By Mr. Pratt*, 4 vols. (T. Becket, 1785), 1:274.

56. *The Brothers* (W. Griffin, 1770), vii. See also the epilogue to *The Welch Heiress* (1795), in which an actress pleads with the empowered audience on behalf of the company to commend their wit, "stamp the coin," and decide their fate: "Like Britain's Monarch, act your generous parts,/And fix your empire, in our greatful hearts." In Edward Jerningham, *The Welch Heiress* (Richard White, 1795). Note the **Coinage** metaphor doubling the **Empire** metaphor.

57. *An Essay on Acting* (W. Bickerton, 1744), 5; Seward, *Works*, 1:168.

58. See *The Political Theory of Possessive Individualism: Hobbes to Locke* (Oxford: Oxford UP, 1962). Jonathan Lamb departs from and would improve upon Macpherson in *Preserving the Self in the South Seas, 1680–1840* (Chicago: U of Chicago P, 2001), 26, 134–6.

59. "Adventitious" is Locke's adjective. A main insight in Adela Pinch's *Strange Fits of Passion: Epistemologies of Emotion, Hume to Austen* (Stanford, CA: Stanford UP, 1996) is that "feelings may be impersonal; that one's feelings may really be someone's else's" (7).

60. *Elements of Criticism*, 3 vols. (Edinburgh: A. Millar, 1762), 1:4–5.

61. See Adam Smith, *Wealth of Nations* (W. Strahan and T. Cadell, 1776), 2:233. In contrast to the example of Rome, Smith argues that the English Parliament could absorb fifty or sixty American representatives without upsetting the balance of the constitution; he even admits, sanguinely, that should the produce of America eventually exceed British taxation, the "seat of empire would then naturally remove itself to that part of the empire which contributed most to the general defence and support of the whole" (2:235).

62. Macpherson, sensitive to this sense of "invasion," cites Overton's *Arrow Against all Tyrants*: "To every Individuall in nature is given an individual property by nature, not to be invaded or usurped by any: for every one as he is himselfe, so he hath a selfe propriety." See *Possessive Individualism*, 140.

63. Compare William Walker's emphasis on Locke's active metaphors of labor in his connection of the *Essay* and the *Second Treatise* in *Locke, Literary Criticism, and Philosophy* (Cambridge: Cambridge UP, 1994), 49–52.

64. *Posthumous Works of John Locke* (printed by W.B. for A. and J. Churchill, 1706), 116.

65. Typically Locke prefers container metaphors to metaphors of command and territorialization: for example, the "yet empty cabinet" (I.ii.15), in which the gentleman virtuoso collects specimens from new-discovered, rude, uncultivated, far-flung habitats, ordering a world in miniature, in self-definition, or the "Store-house" (II.x.2) of the memory, in which ideas, figured as material objects are stored and stocked (see **Rooms**). The point is emphasized in Walker, *Locke, Literary Criticism, and Philosophy*, 31–54.

66. "Ode to Amyntas," *London Magazine* (May 1758), 253.

67. *The Pleasures of Imagination* (R. Dodsley, 1744), 93.

68. *An Essay on the Nature and Immutability of Truth* (Edinburgh: A Kincaid and J. Bell, 1770), 161.

69. Blackmore, *King Arthur* (Awnsham, John Churchil, and Jacob Tonson, 1697), 185–6. In one miscellany of commonplaces, the lines appear under the heading "KILL'D" (the next heading is "KINDNESS"). See *The British Parnassus* (J. Nutt, 1714), 1:457.

70. *Soliloquy, or Advice to an Author* (John Morphew, 1710), 187.

71. *Treatise*, 5.

72. Hume, *Philosophical Essays Concerning Human Understanding* (A. Millar, 1748), 251.

73. Tristan Marshall locates early distinctions between inward *imperium* and outward empire in sixteenth and seventeenth-century political and literary history in *Theatre and Empire: Great Britain on the London Stage under James VI and I* (Manchester: Manchester UP, 2000); see especially 11–23.

74. Henry More, *The Immortality of the Soul* (J. Flesher, 1659), 411; Ralph Cudworth, *The True Intellectual System of the Universe* (Royston, 1678), 844.

75. John Williams, *A Postscript to the New Bath Guide* (J. Strahan, 1790), 84.

76. Francis Hutcheson, *A Short Introduction to Moral Philosophy* (Glasgow: Robert Foulis, 1747), 47; Hume, *Abstract* (C. Borbet, 1740), 31; Smith, *The Theory of Moral Sentiments*, 2nd ed. (A. Millar, 1761), 170; Godwin, *Memoirs of the Author of A Vindication of the Rights of Woman*, 2nd ed. (J. Johnson, 1798), 200–1.

77. Benjamin Martin, *The Young Gentleman and Lady's Philosophy* (W. Owen, 1782), 13.

78. See J. G. A. Pocock, *The Machiavellian Moment: Florentine Thought and the Atlantic Republican Tradition* (Princeton, NJ: Princeton UP, 2003), 510.

79. Joseph Addison, *Spectator* no. 411, in *The Spectator*, ed. D. F. Bond (Oxford: Clarendon, 1965), 3:538. Erin Mackie describes the spectator's "imaginative consumption" as "grasping imperialism" in *Market à la Mode: Fashion, Commodity, and Gender in "The Tatler" and "The Spectator"* (Baltimore: Johns Hopkins UP, 1997), 84. See also Carole Fabricant, "The Aesthetics and Politics of Landscape in the Eighteenth Century," in *Studies in Eighteenth-Century British Art and Aesthetics*, ed. Ralph Cohen (Berkeley: U of California P, 1985), 56. William Walker offers a Cambridge school rejoinder to Mackie's and Fabricant's Marxist readings in "Ideology and Ad-

dison's Essays on the Pleasures of the Imagination," *Eighteenth-Century Life* 24:2 (Spring 2000): 65–84.

80. *Spectator* no. 69, 1:296.

81. Smith, *Wealth of Nations*, 2:221.

82. On the ambivalence of credit, see Pocock's *Machiavellian Moment*, 423–505, and *Virtue, Commerce, and History: Essays on Political Thought and History, Chiefly in the Eighteenth Century* (Cambridge: Cambridge UP, 1985).

83. The line, from the closing lines of the *Deserted Village* is, in fact, authored by Samuel Johnson. See Kaul's interesting reading of Goldsmith's poetry through the metaphor of depopulation in *Poems of Nation*, 112–21.

84. Roger Lonsdale quotes from Goldsmith's journalism, which repeats and extends the simile: "A kingdom may be compared to a single individual in this respect, and when no arts are encouraged but the art of luxury, every mind will set upon trifles, the inhabitants must necessarily degenerate, till all at last, like the modern Italians, they seem castrated at a single blow. . . . Their passion for finery is in general in a reciprocal proportion." *The Poems of Thomas Gray, William Collins, Oliver Goldsmith* (New York: Longman and Norton, 1969), 640n. The verses are quoted from the same (640–1).

85. Linda Colley cites a British peer: "The riches of Asia have been poured in upon us, and have brought with them not only Asiatic luxury, but I fear Asiatic principles of government." *Britons*, 102–3.

86. Quoted in John Richetti, "*Robinson Crusoe*: The Self as Master," in *Modern Essays on Eighteenth-Century Literature*, ed. Leopold Damrosch (Oxford: Oxford UP, 1988), 223.

87. "Lectures on Law," part 2, chapter 11, in *Collected Works of James Wilson*, 2 vols., ed. Kermit L. Hall and Mark David Hall (Indianapolis: Liberty Fund, 2007), 2:1048. Quoted in Pagden, *Lords of All the World*, 23.

88. Daniel Defoe, *True-Born Englishman* (s.n., 1701), 5, 6; *Spectator* no. 69, 1:294. See chapter 2 of Wolfram Schmidgen's *Exquisite Mixture: The Virtues of Impurity* (Philadelphia: U of Pennsylvania P, 2013) and his orienting reading of Defoe (6–9).

89. John Brown, *Estimate of the Manners and Principles of the Time* (London, 1757), 1:58–9. Kathleen Wilson cites Brown's example as influential; see the discussion of effeminacy in her *Sense of the People: Politics, Culture, and Imperialism in England, 1715–1785* (Cambridge: Cambridge UP, 1998), 185–90. See also Caroline Robbins, *The Eighteenth-Century Commonwealthman* (1959; repr., New York: Atheneum, 1968), 308–10.

90. *Alfred* (W. Botham, 1723), 191.

91. Charles Taylor has recently drawn a distinction between "porous" and "buffered" selves, associating the latter with modernity and secularization. But I find that **Empire** metaphors complicate the distinction at just the moment Taylor would see it beginning to take hold. See his *A Secular Age* (Cambridge, MA: Harvard UP, 2007), 35–41.

92. To be inserted in I.iii.14; but see the appendix, p. 299 in the first edition. I take the second thought to be an example of "authority" exerted.

93. Julie Ellison, *Cato's Tears and the Making of Anglo-American Emotion* (Chicago: U of Chicago P, 1999), 97.

94. Ibid. See also Aravamudan, *Tropicopolitans*, 103–35. Aravamudan reads Addison's *Cato* as a synthesis of neostoicism and mercantilism.

95. Marcus Aurelius, *Meditations* (Glasgow: Robert Foulis, 1742). In-text parenthetical citations give book and paragraph numbers.

96. Joseph Addison, *Cato* (J. Johnson, 1713).

97. Mandeville, *The Fable of the Bees* (J. Roberts, 1714), 118. On the appeal to stoicism in "commonsense" writings by Shaftesbury, Hutcheson, and Reid, see Lois Peters Agnew, *Outward, Visible Propriety: Stoic Philosophy and Eighteenth-Century British Rhetorics* (Columbia: U of South Carolina P, 2008).

98. Peter Burke, "Tacitism, Scepticism, and Reason of State," in *The Cambridge History of Political Thought, 1450–1700*, ed. J. H. Burns and Mark Goldie (Cambridge: Cambridge UP, 1991), 492.

99. On Ross's poetry and its relation to the court see Christopher Bond, "The Phoenix and the Prince: The Poetry of Thomas Ross and Literary Culture in the Court of Charles II," *Review of English Studies* 60:246 (2009): 588–604.

100. Thomas Ross, *The Second Punick War Betwwen Hannibal, and the Romanes* (Tho. Roycroft, 1661), 6.

101. A "vivid metaphor" that Edward Said associates with Antonio Gramsci in *Culture and Imperialism* (New York: Vintage, 1994), 195. See also "Orientalism Reconsidered," in Said, *Reflections on Exile and Other Essays* (Cambridge, MA: Harvard UP, 2000), 215. Said seems to have §138 of Gramsci's sixth notebook in mind: see the *Prison Notebooks*, trans. J. A. Buttigieg (New York: Columbia UP, 2007), 109.

102. *Poems* (J. Johnson, 1798), 1:333; Hannah More, *Slavery: A Poem* (T. Cadell, 1788), 6.

103. Dryden, *Don Sebastian* (Jo. Hindmarsh, 1690), 12; Blackmore, *Alfred*, 168; Godwin, *Political Justice* (G. G. J. and J. Robinson, 1793), 2:865.

104. *Clarissa* (S. Richardson, 1748), 7:393. Early in the novel, Lovelace writes to Belford that he would take a new motto (from Virgil): *debellare superbos* (to pull down the proud). The Roman should impose peace, sparing the underdog and taming the arrogant. The motto, of course, cuts both ways. See Weinbrot, *Britannia's Issue*, 239n.

105. Fielding, *Miscellanies* (A. Millar: 1743): 3:197; *The Morality of Shakespeare's Drama Illustrated: By Mrs. Griffith* (T. Cadell, 1775), 444.

106. Festa, *Sentimental Figures*, 45.

107. First published in *Bath Journal* (1752). Text from Roger Lonsdale's *Eighteenth-Century Women Poets* (Oxford: Oxford UP, 1989), 231.

108. Eliza Haywood, in *Secret Histories, Novels, and Poems*, 4 vols., 2nd ed. (Dan Browne, Jun., and S. Chapman, 1725), 3:25.

109. On the metaphor of warfare and its use as political allegory in Restoration drama, see J. Douglas Canfield, "Tupping Your Rival's Women: Cit-Cuckolding as Class Warfare in Restoration Comedy," in *Broken Boundaries: Women & Feminism in Restoration Drama*, ed. Katherine Quinsey (Lexington: UP of Kentucky, 1996), 113–28.

110. The erotics of conquest may be illustrated in the maps used to represent foreign territories. Felicity Nussbaum notes that the four corners of the earth are represented iconographically with female figures. America and Africa are typically naked, Asia placed in the context of a harem, and Europe surrounded with "signs of military victory." See Felicity A. Nussbaum, ed., *The Global Eighteenth Century* (Baltimore: Johns Hopkins UP, 2003), 2.

111. Pamela Cheek, *Sexual Antipodes: Enlightenment Globalization and the Placing of Sex* (Stanford, CA: Stanford UP, 2003), 41.

112. Sarah Fielding, *History of Countess of Dellwyn*, 2 vols. (A. Millar, 1759), preface.

113. Haywood, *Secret Histories*, 1:103.

114. *Pamela: or, Virtue Rewarded*, vol. 3 (S. Richardson, 1742), 212.

115. Fielding, *Tom Jones*, 6 vols. (A. Millar, 1749), 3:342, 3:351.

116. On the unpleasantness of eighteenth-century jest books and rape jokes, see chapter 5 of Simon Dickie's *Cruelty and Laughter: Forgotten Comic Literature and the Unsentimental Eighteenth Century* (Chicago: U of Chicago P, 2011). Dickie's work with archival materials disturbs traditional ideas of eighteenth-century sentimentalism and gives shape to my comments on Fielding and Richardson.

117. "Imperial" becomes a keyword in *Clarissa*'s contest of wills. Martin Green characterizes Clarissa as "anti-imperialist" in *Dreams of Adventure, Deeds of Empire* (London: Routledge and Kegan Paul, 1980), 64. See M. John Cardwell on military metaphors in Richardson: "The Rake as Military Strategist: *Clarissa* and Eighteenth-Century Warfare," *Eighteenth Century Fiction* 19:1–2 (2006): 153–80. See also Said, *Culture and Imperialism*, 70.

118. Julie Park makes a related claim in *The Self and It: Novel Objects in Eighteenth-Century England* (Stanford, CA: Stanford UP, 2010), 130–1.

119. Quoted in Mary Wollstonecraft, *A Vindication of the Rights of Woman* (J. Johnson, 1792), 113n. Anna Letitia Barbauld responds in her unpublished "The Rights of Woman," a poem in which the true rights of woman are a "native empire o'er the breast." See Anne K. Mellor, "The *Rights of Woman* and the Women Writers of Wollstonecraft's Day," in *Cambridge Companion to Mary Wollstonecraft*, ed. Claudia L. Johnson (Cambridge: Cambridge UP, 2002), 153. See also William McCarthy's reading of Barbauld's poem's imperial allusions and military metaphors in *Anna Letitia Barbauld: Voice of the Enlightenment* (Baltimore: Johns Hopkins UP, 2008), 352–3.

120. See Saree Makdisi's discussion of Jacobins who authorize a modern Western sense of self against "an Oriental culture supposedly incompatible with and hostile to all those values" in *William Blake and the Impossible History of the 1790s* (Chicago:

U of Chicago P, 2003), 4. See also his *Romantic Imperialism: Universal Empire and the Culture of Modernity* (Cambridge: Cambridge UP, 1998).

Fetters

1. I consider a group of 329 metaphors in this entry, about 3.3% of the total number of metaphors collected in the database between 1700 and 1799. Chain and fetter metaphors may be clustering at the end of the period in the late 1780s and 1790s, especially in poetry. The most visible shift in metaphorics is in drama, in the 1790s. In the text of the entry, abolition, the obvious historical context, is explored.

2. David Brion Davis, *The Problem of Slavery in Western Culture* (1966; repr., Oxford: Oxford UP, 1988), 63. Davis surveys a variety of related parallel dualisms rooted in distinctions personal and commercial, physical and spiritual, the law of nature and laws of nations; I am interested more narrowly in mind-body dualism. I rely on Davis and Robin Blackburn's *The Making of New World Slavery: From the Baroque to the Modern, 1492–1800* (London: Verso, 2010) throughout. Blackburn's *Overthrow of Colonial Slavery, 1776–1848* (London: Verso, 1988) and Ian Baucom's *Specters of the Atlantic: Finance, Capital, Slavery, and the Philosophy of History* (Durham, NC: Duke UP, 2005) were also essential reading. I am impressed by Marcus Wood's analyses in *Blind Memory: Visual Representations of Slavery in England and America* (Manchester: Manchester UP, 2000), *Slavery, Empathy, and Pornography* (Oxford: Oxford UP, 2002), and *The Horrible Gift of Freedom: Atlantic Slavery and the Representation of Emancipation* (Athens: U of Georgia P, 2010). As in the previous entry, **Empire**, I am indebted to Lynn Festa's analysis of "reversible figures" in *Sentimental Figures of Empire in Eighteenth-Century Britain and France* (Baltimore: Johns Hopkins UP, 2006). My discussion also draws on Simon Gikandi's recent work with the metaphors and paradoxes of slavery in *Slavery and the Culture of Taste* (Princeton, NJ: Princeton UP, 2011). Finally, my conversations with Dorothy Couchman have greatly informed the literary-critical line of argument pursued here. Couchman read this entry in draft and made many improvements to the text and its exposition.

3. Peter Garnsey, *Ideas of Slavery from Aristotle to Augustine* (Cambridge: Cambridge UP, 1996), 16. See also Eric Slauter, "Neoclassical Culture in a Society with Slaves: Race and Rights in the Age of Wheatley," *Early American Studies* 2:1 (Spring 2004): 81–122, especially his comments on enslaved blacks applying "the metaphor of political slavery to themselves" (82).

4. Edward Long, *Candid Reflections Upon the Judgement Lately Awarded by the Court of King's Bench* (printed for T. Lowndes, 1772), 4. Long repeatedly likens "Negroes" to commodities, "*goods*," or "articles of *merchandize*." See *Candid Reflections*, 33, 39, 42.

5. Davis, *The Problem of Slavery in Western Culture*, 35. See also Davis, *The Problem of Slavery in the Age of Revolution, 1770–1823* (Oxford: Oxford UP, 1999), 42, 82. I find the first volume of Davis's study of the "problem" of slavery especially useful as it delivers a panoramic intellectual history that attends to dualities and dichotomies.

6. Long cites the 1732 revision of bankruptcy law: 5 Geo. II, c. 30.

7. See Gikandi on the "double paradox of having slavery in the midst of a culture of freedom," in *Slavery*, 88.

8. *Hegel's Logic, Being Part I of the Encyclopoedia of the Philosophical Sciences*, trans. William Wallace (Oxford: Clarendon, 1975), §38, p. 64. See G. A. Cohen's discussion in *If You're an Egalitarian, How Come You're So Rich* (Cambridge, MA: Harvard UP, 2000), 89.

9. See Dale B. Martin, *Slavery as Salvation: The Metaphor of Slavery in Pauline Christianity* (New Haven, CT: Yale UP, 1990). Marx writes of Luther that he "liberated the body from its chains because he fettered the heart with chains." "Contribution to the Critique of Hegel's Philosophy of Right," in *The Marx-Engels Reader* (New York: Norton, 1978), 60.

10. Consider the depictions of Crispus Attucks after the Boston Massacre or the "faithful Negro" often misidentified as Peter Salem in John Trumbull's painting of Bunker Hill. Karsten Fitz, "Commemorating Crispus Attucks: Visual Memory and the Representations of the Boston Massacre, 1770–1857," *Amerikastudien/American Studies* 50:3 (2005): 463–84. See also Wood, *Blind Memory*, 254ff.

11. *Politics*, I.iv, 1254b, p. 10. See also Plato, *Laws*, 777b, cited in Garnsey, *Ideas of Slavery*, 16. Garnsey emphasizes that slave theory in antiquity neither begins nor ends with Aristotle (13–5).

12. *Aristotle in 23 Volumes*, trans. H. Rackham (Cambridge, MA: Harvard UP; London, William Heinemann, 1981), 20. From the *Eudemian Ethics*, 1241b18-24.

13. Descriptions of living and dead chained together recurs in several reports on the horrors of the Middle Passage. The image of abjection works through grotesquerie (the dead bodies may be described in a state of putrefaction) and through evangelical associations of living souls and dead bodies. See Alan Liu's close reading of a section from the *Parliamentary Papers* that links a report by Captain Hayes, which describes "*living men . . . confined to dead bodies*," to Edmund Burke's figuration of tradition as a chain that links the living and the generations of the dead. *Local Transcendence: Essays in Postmodern Historicism and the Database* (Chicago: U of Chicago P, 2008), 244–9.

14. I quote Seneca in an early modern translation: "The bodies are bred and subiect to their Masters, but the minde is priuiledged in it selfe. . . . This bought he, this selleth he: that interior part cannot be bought or sold, or suffer seruitude." *The Workes of Lucius Annaeus Seneca* (William Stansby, 1614), 52. The sentiment is to be found throughout antiquity: see Theodoret, *On Divine Providence*, 677b–680b (cited in Garnsey, *Ideas of Slavery*, 51).

15. *The Poems of William Cowper* (J. Johnson, 1798), 1:331.

16. Newton, *Thoughts Upon the African Slave Trade* (J. Buckland, 1788), 3. Marcus Wood likewise describes Newton's appropriation of the metaphor of bondage: "He talks about slavery from the position of being the slave of his memory of slavery." *Slavery, Empathy, and Pornography*, 48.

17. *The Law of Freedom* (London, 1652), 18. See Christopher Hill, "The Religion of Gerrard Winstanley," supplement, *Past and Present* 5 (1978): 28–9, 33–6, 43, 45–7.

18. William Everard et al., *The True Levellers Standard Advanced* (1649), 15; John Lilburne, *Englands New Chains Discovered* (1649).

19. Marvell, *Miscellaneous Poems* (Robert Boulter, 1681), 12–3. Marvell rewrites conventional soul-body dialogues, reworking imagery in Hermann Hugo's *Pia Desideria* (Antwerp, 1624). The verses cited are unusually ambiguous: are the Soul's chains the same as the Body's bonds? On the poem's context, see Christopher Hill, *Puritanism and Revolution* (London: Panther, 1958), 337–66.

20. See, for example, the castigation of West Indian slavers in *Tyranipocrit, Discovered* (Rotterdam, 1649), 23; and Richard Baxter, *A Christian Directory* (1655).

21. Henry Noel Brailsford, *The Levellers and the English Revolution*, ed. Christopher Hill (Stanford, CA: Stanford UP, 1961), 333–4. Seventy Royalists shipped to Barbados to "slave" in the sugar plantations were the focus of a parliamentary debate in 1659. See Godfrey Davies, *The Restoration of Charles II, 1658–1660* (Oxford: Oxford UP, 1955), 66–7; and Hilary Beckles, *White Servitude and Black Slavery in Barbados, 1627–1715* (Knoxville: U of Tennessee P, 1989), 52–4. See also Blackburn, *Making*, 248. Ruth Paley observes, "In the seventeenth century the term 'slave' was applied to those accused of rebellious/treasonous activities who were consequently deported to the colonies as indentured labourers." "Imperial Politics and English Law: The Many Contexts of *Somerset*," *Law and History Review* 24:3 (Fall 2006): 660.

22. Quoted in Beckles, *White Servitude and Black Slavery*, 53. See also an example of white indentured servants termed "goods" (60) and discussions of white "chattels" and "proto-slavery" (71–8, 115–39).

23. Kitty Scoular Datta traces the imagery of the cage to Origen and translates lines from Hugo's *Pia Desideria*: "Feet fetters, hands manacles, nerves chains, bones a cage for showing off a slave in a market." See her "New Light on Marvell's 'A Dialogue between the Soul and Body,'" *Renaissance Quarterly* 22:3 (Autumn 1969): 242n, 243. Max Weber famously identifies the iron cage with modernity. *The Protestant Ethic and the Spirit of Capitalism*, trans. Talcott Parsons (London: Routledge, 1992), 181.

24. James Walvin, *Black Ivory: A History of British Slavery* (Washington, DC: Howard UP, 1994).

25. *The Poetry and Prose of William Blake*, ed. D. V. Erdman (Garden City, NY: Doubleday, 1965), 27. On Blake and metaphors of slavery, see Anne K. Mellor, "Sex, Violence, and Slavery: Blake and Wollstonecraft," and David Bindman, "Blake's Vision of Slavery Revisited," in *William Blake: Images and Texts* (San Marino, CA: Huntington Library, 1997), 69–94, 97–106. Mellor and Bindman respond to David Erdman's "Blake's Vision of Slavery," *Journal of the Warburg and Courtauld Institutes* 15:3–4 (1952): 242–52.

26. Elsa Goveia's reading of the case in *West Indian Slave Law of the 18th Century* (Barbados: Caribbean Universities Press, 1970), 20, is cited in Gikandi, *Slavery*, 91.

On the reception of the decision in British journalism, see Jerome Nadelhaft, "The Somersett Case and Slavery: Myth, Reality, and Repercussions," *Journal of Negro History* 51:3 (July 1966): 193–208, esp. 193–201.

27. Thomas Bellamy, *The Friends; Or, the Benevolent Planters* (J. Debrett, 1789), 13. The only detailed treatment of the play I have encountered is in Jenna Marie Gibb's dissertation, "Performing the Temple of Liberty" (UCLA, 2008), 156–61.

28. Charles Lamb, *The Essays of Elia: Including the Last Essays of Elia*, ed. Malcolm Elwin (London: Macdonald, 1952).

29. Wesley, *Thoughts on Slavery*, 4th ed. (Dublin: W. Whitestone, 1775), 3. See also Francis Hargrave, *An Argument in the Case of James Sommersett, a Negro* (London; repr., Boston: E. Russell, 1774), 9.

30. *Encyclopedia Britannica*, 3rd ed. (Edinburgh: A. Bell and C. MacFarquhar, 1797), 17:522.

31. *The Digest of Justinian*, I.v.4.1, trans. Alan Watson (Philadelphia: U of Pennsylvania P, 1998), 15. See Hargrave, *Argument*, 9. See also Quentin Skinner, "Classical Liberty and the Coming of the English Civil War," in *Republicanism: A Shared European Heritage*, ed. M. van Gelderen and Q. Skinner (Cambridge: Cambridge UP, 2002), 9.

32. See Orlando Patterson's discussion of the Roman law's peculiarly human thing, the slave, and its "contradictory" historical status, in *Slavery and Social Death: A Comparative Study* (Cambridge, MA: Harvard UP, 1982), ix, 29–32, 71–5, 296, 340–2.

33. Is the imperative to remember addressed to Christians, to Negroes, or both? For Wheatley, of course, "Christian" and "Negro" overlap. See James A. Levernier on the ironies of Wheatley's verses and the ambiguity color-coded in *Cain/sugarcane*: "Phillis Wheatley (ca. 1753–1784)," *Legacy* 13:1 (1996): 65–75, at 69–70.

34. Samuel Jackson Pratt, *Humanity* (T. Cadell, 1788), 86, 87. Pratt's inverted world illustrates the Christian-savage, Anglo-African dialectics analyzed at length by Moira Ferguson in *Subject to Others: British Women Writers and Colonial Slavery, 1670–1834* (New York: Routledge, 1992).

35. *Plain Truth; Addressed to the Inhabitants of America* (Philadelphia: R. Bell, 1776), 74. On slavery metaphors in revolutionary America, see Davis, *Age of Revolution*, 255–84. See also Peter Dorsey, "To 'Corroborate Our Own Claims': Public Positioning and the Slavery Metaphor in Revolutionary America," *American Quarterly* 55:3 (September 2003): 353–86. See also his book-length study, *Common Bondage: Slavery as Metaphor in Revolutionary America* (Knoxville: U of Tennessee P, 2009).

36. Patterson, *Slavery and Social Death*, 338–42. Patterson reworks Hegelian master-slave antitheses. On the interdependence of slavery and freedom, see also Edmund Morgan, "Conflict and Consensus," in *The Challenge of the American Revolution* (New York: Norton, 1976), 175–95.

37. Johnson, *Taxation No Tyranny* (T. Cadell, 1775), 89. Quoted in Boswell, *The Life of Samuel Johnson* (Henry Baldwin, 1791), 2:174.

38. Skinner, "Classical Liberty," 9–28.

39. Aristotle *Nicomachean Ethics*, 4.3, 1123a–1125a. *Introduction to Aristotle*, ed. and trans. Richard McKeon (Chicago: U of Chicago P, 1973). Cicero, *De Officiis*, trans. Walter Miller (London: William Heinemann, 1913), 62–73.

40. Hume, *An Enquiry Concerning the Principles of Morals* (A. Millar, 1751), 146.

41. Compare Felicity Nussbaum on Oroonoko (and Friday) in "Being a Man: Olaudah Equiano and Ignatius Sancho," in *Genius in Bondage: Literature of the Early Black Atlantic*, ed. Vincent Carretta and Philip Gould (Lexington: UP of Kentucky, 2001), 54–5. See also Wylie Sypher, *Guinea's Captive Kings: British Anti-slavery Literature of the XVIIIth Century* (New York: Octagon Books, 1969).

42. Asserted under the headings SLAVERY and PHILOLOGY in *Encyclopaedia Britannica*, 3rd ed. (Edinburgh: A. Bell, 1797), 17:522, 14:565. The contranymic etymology was perpetuated in Brewer's *Dictionary of Phrase and Fable*, 17th ed. (Cassell, 1885), 829.

43. *The Order of Things: An Archaeology of the Human Sciences* (New York: Vintage Books, 1970), 312.

44. Edward Young, *Night the Sixth* (R. Dodsley, 1744), 61; Alexander Pope, *An Essay on Man* (Lawton Gilliver, 1734), 30.

45. Cotton, *Visions in Verse* (J. Dodsley, 1790), 77.

46. Quoted in Marcus Wood, *The Poetry of Slavery: An Anglo-American Anthology, 1764–1865* (Oxford: Oxford UP, 2003), 193. Wood claims the phrase "slave of love" peaks with the Cavalier poets. But I find the phrase and variations on it seem particularly popular in the late eighteenth century, especially in the 1760s and 1790s. See *The Poetry of Slavery* 184–5.

47. On similarities in Hume and Pope's figuration and the question of influence, see Christopher Fox, "Defining Eighteenth-Century Psychology: Some Problems and Perspectives," in *Psychology and Literature in the Eighteenth Century*, ed. Fox (New York: AMS, 1987), 11.

48. Richard Cumberland, *The West Indian* (W. Griffin, 1771), 8.

49. Battestin traces the metaphor through Locke, Clarke, Berkeley, and Hume and surveys the homiletic tradition of Hoadly, South, and Jackson in "The Problem of *Amelia*: Hume, Barrow, and the Conversion of Captain Booth," *English Literary History* 41:4 (1974): 613–48, at 631–2.

50. Tillotson, *Several Discourses of Repentance* (Printed for Ri. Chiswell, 1700), 228.

51. Garnsey, *Ideas of Slavery*, 206–19.

52. Augustine, *Homilies on the Gospel of John. Homilies on the First Epistle of John*, trans. J. Gibb, vol. 7 of *The Nicene and Post-Nicene Fathers* (Edinburgh: T. Clark, 1873–4), xli.4.

53. Cotton Mather, *The Negro Christianized* (Boston: B. Green, 1706), 37–8.

54. Blackburn, *Making*, 259–60, 417.

55. See Bob Tennant, "Sentiment, Politics, and Empire: A Study of Beilby Porteus's Anti-Slavery Sermon," in *Discourses of Slavery and Abolition: Britain and Its Colo-*

nies, 1760–1838, ed. Brycchan Carey, Markman Ellis, and Sara Salih (New York: Palgrave Macmillan, 2004), 158–74.

56. See *A Narrative of the Lord's Wonderful Dealings with John Marrant* (1785), in *Unchained Voices: An Anthology of Black Authors in the English-Speaking World of the Eighteenth Century*, expanded ed., ed. Vincent Carretta (UP of Kentucky, 2004), 112.

57. Jean-Jacques Rousseau, *On the Social Contract*, ed. Roger D. Masters and Judith R. Masters (New York: St. Martin's, 1978), 46.

58. For a useful literary consideration of Hobbes's and Locke's statements on free will, see Jonathan Kramnick, *Actions and Objects from Hobbes to Richardson* (Stanford, CA: Stanford UP), 4–6, 161–2.

59. Of "Democraticall writers," Hobbes complains "that the Subjects in a Popular Common-wealth enjoy Liberty, but that in a Monarchy they are all Slaves." Thomas Hobbes, *Leviathan* (Andrew Crooke, 1651), 171. An analysis of "Liberty" is given in chapter 21 of *Leviathan*, 107–15.

60. Patterson, *Slavery and Social Death*, 340.

61. See, as a contemporary contribution, Eddy Nahmias et al., "Is Incompatibilism Intuitive?," *Philosophy and Phenomenological Research* 73:1 (July 2006): 28–53.

62. The famous phrase, associated with Thomas Jefferson's draft of the Declaration of Independence, finds its way from Locke's *Essay* (where it appears four times), through variations in Hutcheson, Goldsmith, Sterne, Blackstone, Johnson (in *Rasselas*, his *Dictionary*, and in other writing), George Mason, and others. See Garry Wills's discussion in *Inventing America: Jefferson's Declaration of Independence* (1978; repr., New York: Mariner Books, 2002), 240–7.

63. Berkeley, *Three Dialogues* (G. James, 1713), 124; Blackmore, *Alfred* (London: W. Botham, 1723), 98.

64. Cowper, *Poems* (J. Johnson, 1782), 188.

65. *The Pleasures of Memory*, 5th ed. (T. Cadell, 1793), 20. G. J. Barker-Benfield, finding these lines used as an epigraph in Radcliffe's *Udolpho*, mistakenly attributes them to Akenside. See *The Culture of Sensibility: Sex and Society in Eighteenth-Century Britain* (Chicago: U of Chicago P, 1992), 18.

66. Pope, *The Dunciad, in Four Books* (M. Cooper, 1743), 157–8, 167–8.

67. Sarah Fielding, *The History of the Countess of Dellwyn* (A. Millar, 1759), 2:155–6.

68. Johnson, *Prefaces, Biographical and Critical* (J. Nichols, 1781), 9:9.

69. Hume, *An Abstract of a Book Lately Published* (C. Corbett, 1740), 32.

70. David Hume, *A Treatise of Human Nature* (John Noon, 1739), 2:233.

71. Christopher Hibbert, *The Road to Tyburn: The Story of Jack Sheppard and the Eighteenth-Century Underworld* (Cleveland: World, 1957).

72. *The Malefactor's Register; or, The Newgate and Tyburn Calendar*, 5 vols. (Alexander Hogg, 1779), 1:410.

73. *A Letter on the Abolition of the Slave Trade* (London: Luke Hansard, 1807), 100.

74. John Gay, *The Beggar's Opera* (John Watts, 1728), 28.

75. *The Rape of the Lock* (Bernard Lintott, 1714), 11; *An Essay on Man* (Lawton Gilliver, 1734), 38; *The History of Emily Montague* (J. Dodsley, 1769), 2:195.

76. *Declaring Independence: Jefferson, Natural Language, and The Culture of Performance*, (Stanford: Stanford UP, 1993), 35–62.

77. Akenside, *The Pleasures of Imagination* (R. Dodsley, 1744), 76; Wheatley, *Poems on Various Subjects* (A. Bell, 1773), 36.

78. Burney, *Camilla* (T. Payne, 1796), 4:65; Wollstonecraft (J. Johnson, 1788), 65.

79. On softness and slavishness in Wollstonecraft, see Helen Thompson, *Ingenuous Subjection: Compliance and Power in the Eighteenth-Century Domestic Novel* (Philadelphia: U of Pennsylvania P, 2005), 200–2.

80. Thomas Gisborne, *An Enquiry into the Duties of the Female Sex* (1797), cited in Julie Park, *The Self and It: Novel Objects in Eighteenth-Century England* (Stanford, CA: Stanford UP, 2009), 129. Park, surveying metaphors for the debutante (a vessel, a slave, a movable good, an actress, etc.), cleverly figures woman *as* metaphor.

81. Wollstonecraft, *A Vindication of the Rights of Woman* (J. Johnson, 1792), 227.

82. Mitchell, *Poems on Several Occasions*, 2 vols. (Harmen Noorthouck, 1732), 1:66.

83. Soame Jenyns, *Disquisitions on Several Subjects*, 2nd ed. (1782; repr., London: Charles Baldwyn, 1822), 21.

84. I quote from Richardson's *Collection of the Moral and Instructive Sentiments* (S. Richardson, 1755), 69. Compare the sentiment as versified in Richardson's first novel: "*Nor let the* Rich *the* lowest Slave *disdain*; / *He's* equally *a* Link of Nature's Chain." *Pamela: or, Virtue Rewarded*, vol. 2 (C. Rivington and J. Osborn, 1741), 55. The lines reappear in the third volume (1742), 360. Cited in A. O. Lovejoy, *Chain of Being: A Story of the History of an Idea* (1936; repr., Cambridge, MA: Harvard UP, 2001), 207; and Davis, *Western Culture*, 369. See also Davis, *Age of Revolution*, 384; and Winthrop D. Jordan *White over Black: American Attitudes toward the Negro, 1550–1812* (Chapel Hill: U of North Carolina P, 1968), chapter 13, on "the Negro bound by the chain of being."

85. Gilbert Francklyn, *An Answer to the Rev. Mr. Clarkson's Essay on the Slavery and Commerce of the Human Species, Particularly the African* (J. Walter, C. Stalker, and W. Richardson, 1789), 204, cited in Dorsey, *Common Bondage*, 33.

86. Pratt, *Cottage-Pictures; or, The Poor*, 3rd ed. (J. N. Longman and O. Rees, 1803), 34–5.

87. *Seneca's Morals by Way of Abstract*, 11th ed. (Jacob Tonson, 1718), 133.

88. Henry Higden, *The Wary Widdow* (Abell Roper, 1693), 44; George Lillo, *Silvia; or, the Country Burial* (J. Watts, 1731), 46.

89. See, for example, Hannah Cowley, *A Day in Turkey, or, The Russian Slaves* (G. G. J. and J. Robinson, 1792); August von Kotzebue, *Negro Slaves* (T. Cadell and J. Edwards, 1796); and Prince Hoare, *Chains of the Heart* (Barker, 1802).

90. See Gikandi, *Slavery*, 180–7. On "Coromantee" uprisings in Jamaica, see Michael Craton, *Testing the Chains: Resistance to Slavery in the British West Indies* (Ithaca, NY: Cornell UP, 2009), 75–80, 139.

91. Festa, *Sentimental Figures*, 178–87.

92. Stedman, *Narrative of a Five Years' Expedition* (J. Johnson, 1796), 1:325.

93. *The Speech of William Wilberforce, Esq., Representative for the County of York, on Wednesday the 13th of May, 1789, on the Question of the Abolition of the Slave Trade* (Logographic, 1789), 47–8. Compare Equiano's question "Does not slavery depress the mind?" in *The Interesting Narrative of the Life of Olaudah Equiano* (printed for the author, 1789), 1:43.

94. Compare Eric Williams: "Slavery was not born of racism: rather, racism was the consequence of slavery." *Capitalism and Slavery* (1944; repr., New York: Perigee Books, 1980), 7.

95. *The Debate on a Motion for the Abolition of the Slave-Trade: in the House of Commons on Monday the second of April, 1792* (Woodfall, 1792), 135. On the debates, see Festa, *Sentimental Figures*, 187–92, 202–4. See also Srividhya Swaminathan, *Debating the Slave Trade, 1759–1815: Rhetoric of British National Identity* (Burlington, VT: Ashgate, 2009), esp. chapter 5.

96. See Anne K. Mellor, "Blake and Wollstonecraft," 88, on literal and figurative slaveries.

97. *Slavery, a Poem* (London: T. Cadell, 1788), 8.

98. Sterne, "The Prisoner," in *A Sentimental Journey* (T. Becket and P. A. De Hondt, 1768). Sterne likely alludes to the translation in the *Book of Common Prayer* (21st day, morning prayer): "Whose feet they hurt in stocks: the iron entered into his soul." As noted by the King James translators, and often recorded in eighteenth-century bibles, the Hebrew translates (literally?), "his soul came into iron."

99. *Monthly Review* 78 (March 1788): 247.

Impressions

1. Impression metaphors make up 7.5% of all metaphors collected in the database (1700–1799). But, as in my first entry, **Animals**, I am not confident that I was able to collect a representative sample of these metaphors. I have not numbered isolated mentions of "impressions," and I despaired of exhausting philosophical texts of their collocations.

2. Boswell, *The Life of Samuel Johnson* (Henry Baldwin, 1791), 1:257.

3. See H. F. Hallett, "Dr. Johnson's Refutation of Bishop Berkeley," *Mind* 56:222 (April 1947): 132–47.

4. Boswell, *Life of Johnson*, 1:471–2, 1:465.

5. Like Bailey and Philips, the editors of the *OED* do not mark the sense of the term "impression" as figurative when the word is defined as "the effect produced by external force or influence on the senses or mind."

6. Locke locates sensation in the body without fully detailing the relationship between an impression made "in some part of the body" with a "perception in the understanding." Later in the *Essay* Locke acknowledges, "How any thought should produce

a motion in Body is as remote from the nature of our *Ideas*, as how any Body should produce any Thought in the Mind" (IV.iii.28).

7. On the ordering of word senses, William Wimsatt observes, Johnson conceives "an over-all drift of metaphor from physical to spiritual" and "makes the philosophic or physical meaning the primitive or natural, the psychological meaning secondary." *Philosophic Words: A Study of Style and Meaning in the Rambler and Dictionary of Samuel Johnson* (Hamden, CT: Archon Books, 1968), 46.

8. The string "impression" appears 497 times in the Restoration and Eighteenth-Century Poetry collections, 887 times in the Eighteenth-Century Prose collection, and 144 times in the Restoration and Eighteenth-Century Prose Drama collection. In the Pastmasters collection of "British Philosophy, 1600–1900," the term appears more than 500 times. In ECCO, a search for "impression" produces over 350,000 volumes. I have not minutely considered these search hits in collecting figurative instances. Instead, I focused on collocations of "impression" with other search terms—those listed at the head of this entry and the set of keywords I've employed in every other entry ("mind," "heart," "soul," "idea," "thought," "imagination," "fancy," "reason," "passion," "head," "breast," "bosom"). On the possibility and promise of automated metaphor collection, see Brad Pasanek and D. Sculley, "Mining Millions of Metaphors," in *Literary and Linguistic Computing* 23:3 (2008): 345–60. On the perils, see, by the same authors, "Meaning and Mining: The Impact of Implicit Assumptions in Data-Mining for the Humanities," in *Literary and Linguistic Computing* 23:4 (2008): 409–24.

9. John Cleland, *Memoirs of a Woman of Pleasure* (G. Fenton, 1749): 2:239. And yet the *imprint* is false: Thomas Parker printed the pornographic work for Ralph Griffiths, using the assumed name of his brother Fenton.

10. *Poems on Several Occasions* (printed for the Author, 1736), 133.

11. Henry Mackenzie, *Julia de Roubigné*, 2 vols. (W. Strahan, T. Cadell, W. Creech, 1777), 1:124–5.

12. Shenstone, "The Scholar's Relapse," in *The Vocal Medley Part the Second* (York: John Jackson, [1755?]), 58. Dodsley describes Shenstone, though a bachelor, "no stranger to the tenderest impressions" and traces an example of his poetry to one such impression "received in his youth" that was only "with difficulty surmounted." In William Shenstone, *The Works, in Verse and Prose*, 2 vols. (Dodsley, 1764), 1:iv.

13. The first quotation is from Locke's *Essay*, II.x.4; the second, from Sterne's sermon on Job 14:1–2 in *The Sermons of Mr. Yorick* (R. and J. Dodsley, 1760) 2:90. The passage from Sterne is cited in Jonathan Lamb, *Sterne's Fiction and the Double Principle* (Cambridge: Cambridge UP, 1989), 21.

14. This is a tendentious way to put the question. From Hegel to Austin, Wilfrid Sellars, and Rorty, philosophers have argued against perceptual immediacy of sense data. For a discussion of eighteenth-century perceptual acquaintance that treats sense perception in the light of these later discussions of sense data, see John W. Yolton,

"As in a Looking-Glass: Perceptual Acquaintance in Eighteenth-Century Britain," *Journal of the History of Ideas* 40:2 (1979): 207–34.

15. Berkeley would leave undisturbed the "vulgar sense" of a word like *substance*, but he notes that "It is indeed an opinion strangely prevailing amongst Men, that Houses, Mountains, Rivers, and in a word all sensible Objects have an Existence Natural or Real, distinct from being perceived." See *A Treatise Concerning the Principles of Human Knowledge* (Dublin: Rhames, 1710), I.4, p. 44. Berkeley would have us "*Think with the Learned, and Speak with the Vulgar*" (I.51, p. 93). Hume observes, "philosophy informs us, that every thing, which appears to the mind, is nothing but a perception, and is interrupted, and dependent on the mind; whereas the vulgar confound perceptions and objects, and attribute a distinct and continued existence to the very things they feel or see" (*Treatise* I.iv.2).

16. Locke also mentions a "third sort" of qualities "which are allowed to be barely Powers though they are as much real Qualities" (*Essay* II.viii.10).

17. Stamp taxes date from 1670. See H. Dagnall, *The Taxation of Paper in Great Britain, 1643–1861: A History and Documentation* (Edgware: published by the author in collaboration with The British Association of Paper Historians, 1998). *Spectator* no. 445, July 31, 1712, predicts the effect of the law (which took effect on the next day): "A Sheet of Blank Paper that must have this new Imprimatur clapt upon it, before it is Qualified to Communicate any thing to the Publick, will make its Way in the World but very heavily." See *The Spectator*, ed. D. F. Bond (Oxford: Clarendon, 1965), 4:63. A later number (no. 488) jokes about price increases and likens the red-stamped papers to cherries "sold single" for the delight of those readers who could afford the increased price and bought the numbers as they came out. *Spectator* 4:231.

18. Howard Robinson notes, "The inconvenience of the tax to publishers was very great, for each sheet of paper had to be stamped before it was put through the press." *The British Post Office: A History* (Princeton, NJ: Princeton UP, 1948), 245.

19. I quote from Fielding's discussion of Horace's theory of character. See *Tom Jones*, 6 vols. (A. Millar, 1749), 3:150. On character as a kind of stamp, see Deidre Lynch, *The Economy of Character: Novels, Market Culture, and the Business of Inner Meaning* (Chicago: U of Chicago P, 1998).

20. *The Elements of Moral Philosophy* (R. and J. Dodsley, 1754), 28.

21. *Dialogues Concerning Education*, 2 vols. (s.n., 1745), 1:57, 1:58, 1:114–5.

22. See Dror Wahrman's parallel discussion of this passage in *The Making of the Modern Self: Identity and Culture in Eighteenth-Century England* (New Haven, CT: Yale UP), 282–3.

23. On horticulture, see Jenny Davidson, *Breeding: A Partial History of the Eighteenth Century* (New York: Columbia UP, 2009), 46, 59–63.

24. See also Hume's *Philosophical Essays Concerning Human Understanding* (A. Millar, 1748), 22–4. Thomas Reid associates the metaphor, alternately, with Hume and Aristotle. See his *Inquiry into the Human Mind* (Edinburgh: A. Millar, A. Kincaid

and J. Bell, 1764), 159; and his *Essays on the Intellectual Powers of Man* (Edinburgh and London: Printed for John Bell and G. G. J. and J. Robinson, 1785), 22–33.

25. Our ideas of the mind, thinking, space, and so forth are likewise difficult to trace to their impression sources. See Annette Baier's magnificent discussion, "Hume's Impressions and His Other Metaphors," in *Death and Character: Further Reflections on Hume* (Cambridge, MA: Harvard UP, 2008), 114–44, esp. 122–7.

26. With resemblance structuring the relations of impressions and ideas, the resemblance of perceptions and objects is not primarily at issue. See David Fate Norton, "An Introduction to Hume's Thought," in *The Cambridge Companion to Hume*, ed. Norton (Cambridge: Cambridge UP, 1993), 7–8.

27. Lamb, *Sterne's Fiction*, 73.

28. Hume, *Philosophical Essays Concerning Human Understanding*, 23.

29. Baier is unsure from what Hume takes the copy metaphor but notices his first ostensive definition appeals to words on a page. *Death and Character*, 120, 122. Christina Lupton cleverly observes that "IMPRESSIONS" appears with small-caps emphasis on its first mention in the *Treatise*. See *Knowing Books: The Consciousness of Meditation in Eighteenth-Century Britain* (Philadelphia: U of Pennsylvania P, 2012), 74–5. Jerome Christensen seems to me overconfident that the metaphor derives from print culture: "The printing press makes possible the metaphor of impression and the associated 'copy theory of knowledge.'" *Practicing Enlightenment: Hume and the Formation of a Literary Career* (Madison: U of Wisconsin P, 1987), 136.

30. In Chambers, "IMPRESSION, a Term in Philosophy" is dispatched in a paragraph, which is followed by the information that "IMPRESSION is also frequently used in speaking of the Editions of a Book." *Cyclopaedia*, 2:378.

31. See John W. Yolton, *Thinking Matter: Materialism in Eighteenth-Century Britain* (Minneapolis: U of Minnesota P, 1983).

32. See G. J. Barker-Benfield on impressions, spirits, vapors, and vibrations in *Culture of Sensibility: Sex and Society in Eighteenth-Century Britain* (Chicago: U of Chicago P, 1992), 17–23.

33. See Lamb, *Sterne's Fiction*, 60–2.

34. See Nancy L. Maull, "Berkeley on the Limits of Mechanistic Explanation," *Berkeley: Critical and Interpretive Essays*, ed. Colin Turbayne (Minneapolis: U of Minnesota P, 1982), 103–4.

35. See Toulmin's chapter "The Politics of Certainty" in *Cosmopolis: The Hidden Agenda of Modernity* (Chicago: U of Chicago P, 1990), 69–80.

36. Hume's copy theory requires that simple ideas be "correspondent" to and "exactly represent" the simple impressions from which they derive (*Treatise* I.i.1). Again, see Baier's analytic contortions on Hume's behalf in *Death and Character*, 124–34.

37. *Dissertations Moral and Critical* (Strahan, Cadell, and Creech, 1783), 8.

38. On one reading the *pia mater*, a meningeal membrane, is personified (the Latin is "tender mother"). Housewife and the mother meet—or are one and the same?

39. The phrase "something it is like to be" is associated with Thomas Nagel. See his "What Is It Like to Be a Bat?," *Philosophical Review* 83:4 (October 1974): 435–50. See also David Chalmers, *The Conscious Mind: In Search of a Fundamental Theory* (Oxford: Oxford UP, 1995), 4ff.

40. Puttenham, *The Arte of English Poesie* (Richard Field, 1589), 149; Ricoeur, *Rule of Metaphor: Multi-disciplinary Studies of the Creation of Meaning in Language*, trans. Robert Czerny (Toronto: U of Toronto P, 1977), 17. Puttenham's observation is a commonplace in poststructuralist accounts of metaphor. See, for example, Patricia Parker, "The Metaphorical Plot," in *Metaphor: Problems and Perspectives*, ed. David S. Miall (Sussex: Harvester, 1982): 133–57.

41. Nietzsche describes the transfer of nerve stimulus to mental representation as "first metaphor," to be followed by the imitation of image in sound (a "second" metaphor). See "On Truth and Lie in an Extra-Moral Sense," in *The Portable Nietzsche*, ed. Walter Kaufmann (1954; repr., New York: Penguin Books, 1988), 46.

42. The language is borrowed from J. L. Austin, *Sense and Sensibilia* (Oxford: Oxford UP, 1962), 4, 9, 142.

43. A point made by Plato in the *Theaetetus*, in which the metaphor is rejected. See Chris Westbury and Daniel Dennett, "Mining the Past to Construct the Future: Memory and Belief as Forms of Knowledge," in *Memory, Brain, and Belief*, ed. Daniel L. Schacter and Elaine Scarry (Cambridge, MA: Harvard UP, 1999) 14–9.

44. Richard Rorty, *Philosophy and the Mirror of Nature* (Princeton, NJ: Princeton UP, 1979), 143–4.

45. Written in Latin around 1628, the work was not published in Descartes's lifetime. A Dutch translation was published in 1684; the first Latin edition, in 1701. Its print history and reception are further detailed in René Descartes, *The Philosophical Writings of Descartes*, trans. J. Cottingham et al. (Cambridge: Cambridge UP, 1985), 1:7.

46. On the way wax figures in the passage and in the *Meditations*, see Margreta de Grazia, "Imprints: Shakespeare, Gutenberg, and Descartes," in *Printing and Parenting in Early Modern England* (Aldershot: Ashgate, 2005), 29–58. Neil Hertz also remarks on Cartesian figuration in his powerfully associative "Dr. Johnson's Forgetfulness, Descartes' Piece of Wax," *Eighteenth-Century Life* 16:3 (1992): 167–81. I discovered de Grazia's brilliant essay rather late in revising this work; to my chagrin, I found she had taken up many of my metaphors—wax, coins, and writing—and made much of them. In polishing these pages, I have taken her and Hertz as exemplars.

47. De Grazia's reading is close to my own: "What was literally true in relation to the senses is in relation to the mind no more than a figure of speech." "Imprints," 31.

See also Rorty, *Philosophy and the Mirror of Nature*, 146, on philosophical notions of an "immaterial tablet.".

48. See Peter Walmsley, *The Rhetoric of Berkeley's Philosophy* (Cambridge: Cambridge UP, 1990). On Berkeley's Wittgensteinian remarks on language, see Anthony Flew, "Was Berkeley a Precursor to Wittgenstein?," in *Alciphron; or, The Minute Philosopher: In Focus*, ed. David Berman (London: Routledge, 1993): 214–26.

49. Berkeley, *Three Dialogues* (G. James, 1713), 141. Walmsley reads Berkeley exploding materialist metaphor and, alternately, appealing to traditional and scriptural metaphors. *Rhetoric*, 13, 49–56. See also John Richetti, *Philosophical Writing: Locke, Berkeley, Hume* (Cambridge, MA: Harvard UP, 1983), 141–63; and Colin Murray Turbayne, "Berkeley's Two Concepts of Mind," *Philosophy and Phenomenological Research* 20:1 (1959): 85–92.

50. Edith Hamilton and Huntington Cairns, eds., *The Collected Dialogues of Plato, Including the Letters* (1961; repr., Princeton, NJ: Princeton UP, 1978), 191d–e.

51. *Introduction to Aristotle*, ed. and trans. Richard McKeon (Chicago: U of Chicago P, 1973).

52. I quote from Elizabeth Carter's translation of the *Discourses*, in the *Works of Epictetus* (S. Richardson, 1758), 272.

53. *Enchiridion*, in *Works of Epictetus*, trans. E. Carter, 452; but compare an earlier, conflicting assertion in the same: "REMEMBER that you are an Actor in a Drama . . . act well the Character assigned to you: to chuse it, is another's" (443). The Greek term *kharakter* relates contrasting ideas: "while the term presupposed the malleability of the object stamped, it also implied the stability of the stamp on the object; while it referred to outward appearance, it might also refer to an underlying pattern." Lawrence E. Klein, *Shaftesbury and the Culture of Politeness: Moral Discourse and Cultural Politics in Early Eighteenth-Century England* (Cambridge: Cambridge UP, 1994), 91. Deidre Lynch also remarks that the Greek root of "character" denotes "brand" or "stamp." *Economy of Character*, 30–1.

54. *Fables Ancient and Modern* (Jacob Tonson, 1700), 512.

55. The lines from Dryden are quoted in *Spectator* no. 211. For more context, see Chi-Ming Yang, "Gross Metempsychosis and Eastern Soul," in *Humans and Other Animals in Eighteenth-Century British Culture: Representation, Hybridity, Ethics*, ed. Frank Palmeri (Aldershot: Ashgate, 2006), 13–30, esp. 21.

56. "These imprints being distinct and well spaced are quickly assigned to their several stamps—the 'real things' as they are called." Hamilton and Cairns, *Collected Dialogues of Plato*, 191b–d.

57. See Fulke Greville's *Treatise on Monarchy*, where "some water-like, easie . . . take impression / And like it leave not any print behind." *The Remains of Fulk Grevill Lord Brooke* (printed by T. N. for Henry Herringman, 1670), 33. A mind or heart may too easily take and keep an impression, as in the epilogue to Richard Cumberland's *False Impressions* (C. Dilly, 1797), 74.

58. This recalls Locke's complaint that the thoughts of the soul that are not remembered are as useful as "Characters drawn on Dust, that the first breath of wind effaces" (*Essay* II.i.15). See my discussion of this passage in **Writing**.

59. On liquid ladies, see Terry Castle, *The Female Thermometer: Eighteenth-Century Culture and the Invention of the Uncanny* (New York: Oxford UP, 1995), 21–43. The female thermometer featured in Castle's title is filled with the "wax of virgin-bees" (21).

60. *Lucrece* (printed by Richard Field, for Iohn Harrison, 1594).

61. "Part the Second" of *Love in Excess* (W. Chetwood, [1719?]), 36.

62. *Clarissa* (S. Richardson, 1748), 3:111, 7:176.

63. John Locke, *Some Thoughts Concerning Education* (A. and J. Churchill, 1693), 261; John Dryden, *Eleonora: A Panegyrical Poem* (Jacob Tonson, 1692), 15.

64. *Miscellanies in Prose and Verse* (John Morphew, 1711), 258.

65. *Pamela: or, Virtue Rewarded*, vol. 4 (S. Richardson, 1742), 358.

66. Samuel Wesley, *Poems on Several Occasions* (Edward Say, 1736), 94.

67. William Cowper, *Poems* (J. Johnson, 1782), 59; Ann Yearsley, *Poems, on Several Occasions*, 2nd ed. (T. Cadell, 1785), 50.

68. *The Works of John Sheffield* (The Hague: John Barber, 1726), 1:236.

69. *Hymns on the Lord's Supper* (Bristol: Felix Farley, 1745), 26. Jean-Pierre van Noppen describes how the Wesleys select "*clay* . . . an infrequent Biblical image (Job 10:9, Isa 64:8)" and invest it with new values and meanings. Humans are figured as "'breathing clods' of earth shaped by the Potter/Creator: 'My Potter stamp on me thy clay, Thy only stamp of love!'" See *Transforming Words: The Early Methodist Revival from a Discourse Perspective* (Bern: Peter Lang, 1999), 121.

70. Isaac Watts, *Reliquiae Juveniles* (Richard Ford and Richard Hett, 1734), 274.

71. *Hymns and Sacred Poems*, 2 vols. (Bristol: Felix Farley, 1749), 1:20.

72. Charles Wesley, *Short Hymns on Select Passages of the Holy Scriptures*, 2 vols. (Bristol: E. Farley, 1762), 1:241.

73. The servants of God are "sealed in their foreheads" (Revelation 7:3).

74. Isaac Watts, *Horae Lyricae* (John Lawrence, 1706), 26.

75. Statistically, 74 of 112 entries (or about 66% of the entries); more than half of the *Seal* entries belong to the Wesleys. It is this Methodist hymning, for example, that contributes to a marked increase in the frequency of *Stamp* and *Seal* metaphors in the 1760s. Other metaphors are the produce of Samuel Boyse, Moses Browne, William Cowper, George Jeffreys, Benjamin Keach, Thomas Parnell, Alexander Pennecuik, Samuel Pordage, Isaac Watts, and Samuel Woodford.

76. *An Inquiry into the Human Mind*, 159. See also Chambers's entry on "IMPRESSION" in the *Cyclopaedia*.

77. For some of the earlier history in England and its literary implications, see Joseph Loewenstein's readings of Shakespeare in the context of sigillography: "Forms in Wax: Shakespeare and the Personality of the Seal," in *Ornamentalism:*

The Art of Renaissance Accessories, ed. Bella Mirabella (Ann Arbor: U of Michigan P, 2011), 202–20. Loewenstein summarizes practices of authentication and privacy: "By means of the seal, a person represents him- or herself within a consequential network of commercial and legal practices, and by such authenticating representation formally binds him- or herself into a formal structure of obligations" (206).

78. J. Harvey Bloom, *English Seals* (London: Methuen, 1906), 176. Bloom notes, with antiquarian disdain, that many seventeenth-century seals are typically affixed without much care: "Perhaps it mattered little, the law was fast losing sense of individuality, and was beginning to consider the impersonal wax and not the honourable device 'the very act and deed' of the signatory" (8).

79. Letters were stamped with the date so that a letter's progress from posthouse to posthouse could be measured: "A stamp is invented that is putt upon every letter showing the day of the moneth that every letter comes to the office, so that no Letter Carrier may dare detayne a letter from post to post, which before was usual." Robinson, *The British Post Office*, 58. Letters were stamped with the date and the initials of the person in charge of the receiving office.

80. William Dockwra is to be credited with the creation of an efficient system of postmarks. Letters were stamped in sorting offices with a mark that showed where it was originally received. The triangular mark certified the letter as "Penny Post Paid." In the center of the triangle was a capital letter that indicated which district the letter was to be delivered to. The letter was also marked with a heart-shaped stamp, indicating the hour when the letter was marked for delivery. "Af. 3" indicated a letter was delivered at 3:00 in the afternoon; "Mor 8" that it was sent at eight in the morning. Stamped hearts in letters would suggest the stamped hearts I discuss above, but when the government took over Dockwra's post service in 1682, the new official Penny Post modified the postmarks. The triangular postmarks were maintained, with the spelling altered to "Peny Post Payd." These postmarks remained in use until 1794. In the center of the triangle were placed the initials for the post office and the day of the week. Dockwra's heart-shaped stamp was replaced with a circular stamp, although a new heart-shaped stamp was used to indicate the transfer of a letter from the General Post to the Penny Post. Robinson, *The British Post Office*, 72–3, 75. I thank Paul Skinner, head curator of the Philatelic Collections at the British Library, for showing me two examples (e-mail message, September 15, 2014): a Dockwra handstamp at shelf mark Add MSS. 29558, vol. 9, fol. 3777, and a postmark from the Philatelic Collections: Fletcher Collection, vol. 140, item 140024.

81. See Robinson's discussion of the opening of private letters by government officials in *The British Post Office*, 119–25. During King William's reign a "secret man" was installed at the post office, but after 1711, letters were only to be opened if a warrant was issued by a secretary of the state.

82. Franking was taken advantage of by Johnson, who had Boswell sign his letters, and Shelley, who forged his father's signature. Other famous writers who took

advantage of the post included Horace Walpole and Hester Thrale. See Robinson, *The British Post Office*, 118, 56–7.

83. Wolcot, *Brother Peter to Brother Tom* (G. Kearsley, 1788), 27.

84. John Lewis, *A Dissertation on the Antiquity and Use of Seals in England* (William Mount and Thomas Page, 1740), 31.

85. Lamb, *The Things Things Say* (Princeton, NJ: Princeton UP, 2011), 98.

Inhabitants

1. Inward peoplings bulk large in my database, making up nearly 8% of the total number of eighteenth-century metaphors. I note a high mark in the second decade of the century, with concentrations found in poetry. Blackmore, Pope, and Prior contribute a great many personifications in the 1710s; Akenside and Young contribute more in the 1740s. But I have undercounted, I fear: as discussed in this entry, personifications can be very hard to number, and I have not always been consistent in collecting examples for the database. Many **Empire** metaphors, for example, might have been counted under this heading but were not. With almost any proper noun available for personification in eighteenth-century verse, the figuration can be hard to locate.

2. Paul S. MacDonald reads Shakespeare's *Richard II* in *History of the Concept of Mind* (Aldershot: Ashgate, 2003), 268.

3. Like Steven Knapp, I am interested in how allegorical personifications erase distinctions between literal and figurative agency by endowing "metaphors with the agency of literal persons." See *Personification and the Sublime: Milton to Coleridge* (Cambridge, MA: Harvard UP, 1985), 2.

4. See *The Party of Humanity: Writing Moral Psychology in Eighteenth-Century Britain* (Baltimore: Johns Hopkins UP, 2000), 2. For all I (or Vermeule) know, personifications outnumber metaphors in the eighteenth century. Writers imagine striving wigs and sword knots, talking snuffboxes, purses, and lapdogs; a rupee has a picaresque adventure. Eighteenth-century poetic diction distributes agency and intention through much it describes. Even those person-like Greek gods come out of semiretirement to pose as mock mascots in mock epics and reanimate some of the more obscure corners of clockwork nature. See Earl R. Wasserman, "The Inherent Values of Eighteenth-Century Personification," *PMLA* 65:4 (1950): 435–63.

5. See Frances Ferguson, *Wordsworth: Language as Counter-Spirit* (New Haven, CT: Yale UP, 1977), 27–8. See also Heather Keenleyside, "Personification for the People: On James Thomson's *The Seasons*," *English Literary History* 76:2 (2009): 447–72. Kames is aware of the related difficulties in his remarks on personification in the *Elements of Criticism*, 3 vols. (Edinburgh: A. Millar, 1762), II.xx.542–3, and preserves the distinction between persons and things by drawing a new distinction between personifications and so-called "figures of speech."

6. See Locke's discussion of personal identity in the *Essay* (II.xxvii).

7. On metaphoric personification generally, see W. Bloomfield Morton, "Personification-Metaphors," *Chaucer Review* 14:4 (1980): 287–97.

8. *Death and Character: Further Reflections on Hume* (Cambridge, MA: Harvard UP, 2008), 119.

9. An argument made in Kames, *Elements of Criticism*, II.xx.540.

10. Robert Lowth describes the personification of persons in a discussion of Job. See James Engell, *The Committed Word: Literature and Public Values* (University Park: Pennsylvania State UP, 1999), 133.

11. Richard Rorty emphasizes that "the Sellarsian notion that the inside of people and quasi-people is to be explained by what goes on outside (and, in particular, by their place in the community." *Philosophy and the Mirror of Nature*, (Princeton, NJ: Princeton UP, 1979), 191. Sellarsians may be vindicated by the personification I observe in this entry.

12. Portions of this entry were presented on a panel titled "The Strange Eighteenth Century" at the 2006 American Society for Eighteenth-Century Studies conference in Montreal. I credit Jesse Molesworth for prompting me to think more deeply about "being surrounded at all times by complete strangers."

13. *Strange Fits of Passion: Epistemologies of Emotion, Hume to Austen* (Stanford, CA: Stanford UP, 1996), 23.

14. By emphasizing the personification of mental contents in the age of empirical philosophy, I mean to temper the assumptions of critics who hold that "empiricism and especially associational philosophy had weakened personification in the eighteenth century by emphasizing the evocative power of the particular." Wasserman, "Personification," 437. In Wasserman's survey of eighteenth-century rhetoric and criticism, personification appears to be most strongly allied with passionate and sublime moments in literature (with "vehement feeling and imagination flying to the farthest reaches its sensory nature will allow"), especially in allegory, dream vision, and ode (446). I add that personification also pervades introspective moments in prose works as well.

15. See J. B. Bamborough, *Little World of Man* (London: Longmans, Green, 1952), 22–3; and Joseph R. Roach, *The Player's Passion: Studies in the Science of Acting* (Newark: U of Delaware P, 1985), 40.

16. Jones, *Merit. A Poem* (R. and J. Dodsley, 1753), 6.

17. Darwin, *Zoonomia*, 2 vols. (J. Johnson, 1794); Savage, *The Wanderer* (J. Walthoe, 1729), 67. The doublet "trains or tribes" appears throughout *Zoonomia*.

18. Thomas Hobbes, *The Elements of Law Natural and Politic*, 2nd ed., ed. Ferdinand Tönnies (London: Frank Cass, 1969).

19. *Fifteen Sermons* (James and John Knapton, 1726), 4. Compare chapter 16, "Of Persons, Authors, and Things Personated," in Thomas Hobbes, *Leviathan* (Andrew Crooke, 1651).

20. The metaphor of the soul as a commonwealth, republic, or system of government is of ancient vintage. Hobbes and Butler would both have been familiar with those passages in Plato's *Republic*, in which the just soul is analogized to the just republic.

21. Annette Baier suggests Locke's and Hobbes's rougher personifications are civilized somewhat in Hume's more sociable philosophy. *Death and Character*, 119. See also Baier's *A Progress of Sentiments: Reflections on Hume's Treatise* (Cambridge, MA: Harvard UP, 1991), 29–30.

22. *Pleasures of the Imagination* (R. Dodsley, 1744), III, ll. 319–22.

23. *Conjectures on Original Composition* (A. Millar, 1759), 56.

24. Katherine Philips, *Poems* (H. Herringman, 1667), 114.

25. Isaac Watts, *Reliquiae Juveniles* (Richard Ford and Richard Hett, 1734), 156.

26. Anna Letitia Barbauld, *Poems* (Joseph Johnson, 1773), 134; William Godwin, *Thoughts on Man* (London, 1831), 10. While revising, I read Robert Miles's essay "Romanticism, Enlightenment, and Mediation: The Case of the Inner Stranger," in *This Is Enlightenment* (Chicago: U of Chicago P, 2010). Miles uses Young and Barbauld to mount a reading of "Frost at Midnight." Miles's reading I do not dispute, but some of his more ambitious ideas about periodization seem premised on a claim that "the trope of the inner stranger is comparatively rare," a generalization this entry should discredit.

27. *Conjectures on Original Composition* (A. Millar and J. Dodsley, 1759), 53.

28. *The Complaint: or, Night-Thoughts on Life, Death, and Immortality* (R. Dodsley, 1742), 6.

29. The lines quoted from Martial are actually "Non conuiuere, nec uidere saltem, / non audire licet, nec urbe tota / quisquam est tam prope tam proculque nobis" (86, ll. 8–10). Robert Miles notes that as "a Calvinist, Young overturns the customary meaning of the Latin tag." "Inner Stranger," 176.

30. M. H. Abrams sees in these and other lines "adumbrated, however scatteredly, the essential attributes of the romantic genius as . . . characterized by Fichte, Jean Paul, and Carlyle." *The Mirror and the Lamp: Romantic Theory and the Critical Tradition* (New York: Oxford UP, 1953), 200. D. W. Odell reads Young's metaphors through a theological lens in "The Argument of Young's Conjectures on Original Composition," *Studies in Philology* 78 (1981): 87–106. Robert L. Chibka advances the narcissistic reading. See Chibka's characterization of Odell in "The Stranger within Young's Conjectures," *English Literary History* 53:3 (1984), 564n. Miles brings in Charles Taylor on the shift from a "porous" to a "buffered" self in the period in "Inner Stranger."

31. Abrams mentions Shaftesbury in his discussion of Young's organicism but is busy drawing distinctions between the prescient but neoclassical Shaftesbury and the preromantic Young. See *Mirror and Lamp*, 200–1.

32. Shaftesbury, *Soliloquy: or, Advice to an Author* (Morphew, 1710), 18. Butler, so often in dialogue with Shaftesbury, puts his own spin on this "ancient precept": "the very Constitution of our Nature requires, that we bring our whole Conduct before this superior Faculty [the principle of reflection or conscience]; wait its Determination; enforce upon ourselves its Authority, and make it the Business of our Lives . . . to conform ourselves to it. This is the true meaning of that ancient

Precept, *Reverence thy Self.*" *Fifteen Sermons*, 2nd ed., corr. (James and John Knapton, 1729), xvi–xvii.

33. In an interesting essay Udo Thiel locates Locke in the context of trinitarian controversies. See "The Trinity and Human Personal Identity," in *English Philosophy in the Age of Locke*, ed. M. A. Stewart, (Oxford: Oxford UP, 2000), 217–44.

34. Raymond Martin and Cyril Barresi survey examples of eighteenth-century fission in *Naturalization of the Soul: Self and Personality in the Eighteenth Century* (London: Routledge, 2000), 30–48. See especially their sampling of Abraham Tucker's rhetoric, 44–7.

35. *The Light of Nature Pursued* (T. Jones, 1768), 3:71–2.

36. Hume takes back the metaphor almost as soon as he deploys it: "The comparison of the theatre must not mislead us. They are successive perceptions only, that constitute the mind; nor have we the most distant notion of the place, where these scenes are represented, or of the materials, of which it is composed" (I.iv.6).

37. This is Locke's contribution to the philosophy of personal identity. Ian Watt discusses the "problem of defining the individual person" in the opening pages of *The Rise of the Novel: Studies in Defoe, Richardson, and Fielding* (Berkeley: U of California P, 1957), 18.

38. Nicholas Billingsley, *Kosmobrephia or the Infancy of the World* (Robert Crofts, 1658), 50; John Dryden, *The Mistaken Husband* (J. Magnes and R. Bentley, 1675), 22; Daniel Defoe, *An Essay on the History and Reality of Apparitions* (J. Roberts, 1727), 100; *Memoirs of Mrs. Laetitia Pilkington* (Dublin: R. Griffiths and G. Woodfall, 1748), 138; Ralph Cudworth, *A Treatise Concerning Eternal and Immutable Morality* (James and John Knapton, 1731), 140.

39. Charles Johnson, *The Country Lasses* (J. Tonson, 1715), 48; Samuel Richardson, *Pamela: or, Virtue Rewarded*, vol. 4 (S. Richardson, 1742), 11.

40. See Blackmore's *Prince Arthur* (Awnsham and John Churchil, 1695), *The Nature of Man* (Sam Buckley, 1711), *Creation* (S. Buckley and J. Tonson, 1712), and *Alfred* (James Knapton, 1723).

41. *Strange Fits of Passion*, 18.

42. Johnson, *The Vanity of Human Wishes* (R. Dodsley, 1749); Gray, *An Elegy Wrote in a Country Church Yard* (R. Dodsley, 1751).

43. John Moore, *A View of Society and Manners in Italy* (W. Strahan and T. Cadell, 1781).

44. Frances Burney, *Evelina, or, a Young Lady's Entrance into the World*, 3 vols. (T. Lowndes, 1778), 1:30.

45. Roy Porter, *London: A Social History* (London: Hamish Hamilton, 1994), 131.

46. Tobias Smollett, *The History and Adventures of an Atom*, 2 vols. (Robinson and Roberts, 1769), 1:172.

47. The verse line, adapted above for a section heading, is from *Paradise Lost*, IX.445.

48. *The Complete Essays of Michel de Montaigne*, trans. D. M. Frame (Stanford, CA: Stanford UP, 1976), 176.

49. I cite Montaigne's metaphor of the back shop under the heading **Rooms** and observe that Montaigne—and this is true of Descartes and Defoe—put an urban or mercantile twist to the *beatus ille* tradition. In his essay on self-presentation in Restoration and early eighteenth-century England, Michael G. Ketcham locates a shift in the imagery of social space: the apartness of retirement and withdrawal is brought "into the social world" in figures like Addison and Steele's Spectator, who is both in the crowd but also separate from the crowd. See "Setting and Self-Presentation in the Restoration and Early Eighteenth Century," *Studies in English Literature, 1500–1900* 23:3 (1983): 409. Michael McKeon uses Boswell to illustrate the "paradox" of the crowd in *The Secret History of Domesticity: Public, Private, and the Division of Knowledge* (Baltimore: Johns Hopkins UP, 2005), 165–6.

50. *A Patch-Work Screen for the Ladies* (E. Curll and T. Payne, 1723), 64.

51. Defoe, *Robinson Crusoe* (W. Taylor, 1719), 232.

52. John Richetti finds that "Crusoe defines himself in implicit dialogue with absent interlocutors, with God of course, but also with unknown others, fellow Europeans (Hobbesian rivals in this state of nature) who do not materialize for many years, and of course with unknown savage others, the cannibals and cannibal culture as he comes to imagine and evoke it" (66–7). Richetti cites Taylor's *Sources of the Self*: "one cannot be a self on one's own. I am a self only in relation to certain interlocutors" (quoted on 67). See "Secular Crusoe: *The Reluctant Pilgrim* Re-Visited," in *Eighteenth-Century Genre and Culture: Serious Reflections on Occasional Forms, Essays in Honor of J. Paul Hunter*, ed. Dennis Todd and Cynthia Wall (Newark: U of Delaware P, 2001).

53. Defoe, *Serious Reflections* (W. Taylor, 1720), 2.

54. In *The Philosophical Writings of Descartes*, trans. J. Cottingham et al. (Cambridge: Cambridge UP, 1985).

55. After this admission, and in the next section of the *Discourse*, Descartes shares an abridged account of his famous meditations. Descartes's description of Holland's crowds stages, as it were, the lonely meditations in an urban scene, albeit one that soon fades away in the moment of hyperbolical doubt. In the *Meditations* Descartes sets his thinking in a *poêle*, or small, stove-heated room (see **Rooms**).

56. Blair, *Lectures on Rhetoric and Belles Lettres* (Dublin: Messrs. Whitestone, Colles [etc.], 1783), 176.

57. *Dissertations Moral and Critical* (Strahan, Cadell, and Creech, 1783), 78–9.

58. See Maximillian E. Novak, *Realism, Myth, and History in Defoe's Fiction* (Lincoln: U of Nebraska P, 1983), 24–46.

59. I take Crusoe's motto to be "I made double" (69), a variant of Shaftesbury's "*Be* TWO": two fences, two tents, two ways in and out of his cave—the duplications of his fortification epitomize historical and allegorical doublings in the narrative at

large. See also his double-entry ledger of evil and good: Defoe criticism continually struggles to reconcile *Homo economicus* and *Homo puritannicus*.

60. Of course, much of the novel is consumed with representing the busy goings-on in Crusoe's head.

61. Henry Mackenzie, *Julia de Roubigné*, 2 vols. (W. Strahan, T. Cadell, W. Creech, 1777), 2:64.

62. Pope, *Essay on Man* (John Wright, 1734), 28.

63. Goldsmith, *Deserted Village* (W. Griffin, 1770), 17–8.

64. Glanvill quoted in Louis Bredvold, *The Intellectual Milieu of John Dryden* (Ann Arbor: U of Michigan P, 1962), 63; Collins, *Odes on Several Descriptive and Allegoric Subjects* (A. Millar 1747), 17. Nancy Armstrong and Leonard Tennenhouse read Locke's blank slate as a "*terra nullius*" to be populated by the aggregate of individual ideas given in experience. "A Mind for Passion: Locke and Hutcheson on Desire," in *Politics and Passion, 1500–1850*, ed. Victoria Kahn, Neil Saccamano, and Daniela Coli (Princeton, NJ: Princeton UP, 2006), 131–50.

65. From the Second Meditation, *The Philosophical Writings of Descartes*, 2:21.

66. *Poems on Several Occasions* (Edward Say, 1736), 8.

67. Published in *Miscellaneous Poems and Translations* (Bernard Lintott, 1712), 10.

68. *The Female Thermometer: Eighteenth-Century Culture and the Invention of the Uncanny* (New York: Oxford UP, 1995), 142–3.

69. Ferguson, *Solitude and the Sublime: Romanticism and the Aesthetics of Individuation* (New York: Routledge, 1992), 98.

70. *Treatise*, IV.i.5–6. On the influence of Cudworth and other Cambridge Platonists on Sterne, see Geoff Newton, "The Sermons of Laurence Sterne, Neoplatonism, and Two Short Works," in *Divine Rhetoric: Essays on the Sermons of Laurence Sterne* (Newark: U of Delaware P, 2010), 149–63. For classical commonplaces on the spermatic faculty, see *Plutarch's Morals: Translated from the Greek by Several Hands*, 5th ed., 5 vols. (London: William Taylor, 1718), 3:206–7.

71. Ronald De Sousa considers the "metaphor of multiplicity" in the essay "Rational Homunculi," in *The Identity of Persons*, ed. A. O. Rorty (Berkeley: U of California P, 1976), 231. Other writers, including those cited in the following note, take multiplicity to be something more than metaphor.

72. See Fred Attneave, "In Defense of Homunculi," in *Sensory Communication: Contributions to the Symposium on Principles of Sensory Communication, July 19–August 1, 1959, Edicott House, M.I.T.*, ed. Walter A. Rosenblith (Cambridge, MA: MIT P; New York: John Wiley, 1961), 777–82; Marvin Minsky, *The Society of Mind* (New York: Simon and Schuster, 1986); and Francis Crick and Christoph Koch, "The Unconscious Homunculus," in *Neural Correlates of Consciousness: Empirical and Conceptual Questions*, ed. Thomas Metzinger (Cambridge, MA: MIT P, 2000), 103–10. See also Daniel Dennett's description of consciousness as like "fame in the brain" in *Sweet Dreams: Philosophical Obstacles to a Science of Consciousness* (Cambridge, MA: MIT P, 2005).

Metal

1. All told, mineralogical metaphors (metal, dross, dirt, and more) make up nearly 7% of all metaphors collected in the period 1700–1799. The increasing number of iron and steel metaphors is a focus of this entry.

2. See the *OED*'s etymology of "mettle." The differentiation of *mettle* in figurative senses is first recognized in the sixth edition of Phillips's *New World of Words*, published in 1706. In Bailey's *Dictionarium Britannicum* "mettle" is also marked as figurative. Samuel Johnson gives "Courage; spirit" for the second sense of "METAL" and observes that "In this sense it is more frequently written *mettle*."

3. Timon digs in the earth and apostrophizes it: "O thou! Whose self-same *mettle*, / Whereof thy proud child, arrogant man, is puft, / Engenders the black toad, and adder blue." See Johnson, *Dictionary* "METTLE." Johnson takes his example from *Timon of Athens*, IV.iii.

4. An additional example of orthographical ambiguity may be found in Fielding's *Jonathan Wild*: "Now in *Wild*, every thing was truly GREAT, almost without Alloy, as his Imperfections (for surely some small ones he had) were only such as served to denominate him a human Creature, of which kind none ever arrived at consummate Excellence: But surely his whole Behaviour to his Friend *Heartfree* is a convincing Proof, that the true Iron or Steel Greatness of his Heart was not debased by any softer Mettle." *Jonathan Wild* from Fielding's *Miscellanies*, 3 vols. (printed for the author, 1743), 3:416–7.

5. Samuel Butler, *Hudibras* (s.n., 1663), 38. Johnson adduces these lines from *Hudibras*, prefacing his selection with the explanation "Upon this [metaphorical] signification the following ambiguity is founded." See Johnson, *Dictionary*, "METAL." The lines read in full: "Both kinds of *metal* he prepar'd, / Either to give blows or to ward; / Courage and steel both of great force / Prepar'd for better or for worse" (ll. 83–6).

6. *Amelia* (A. Millar, 1752), 3:153.

7. In the eighteenth century lead was more valuable than copper and tin combined and until 1750 had a value broadly equivalent with iron. See Lynn Willies, "Lead: Ore Preparation and Smelting," in *The Industrial Revolution in Metals*, ed. Joan Day and R. F. Tylecote (London: Institute of Metals, 1991), 84–130.

8. Quoting John Gilles, *Aristotle's Ethics and Politics*, 2 vols. (A. Strahan and T. Cadell, 1797), 2:85. Compare 414e–c in *The Republic*. Translations and summaries of myth of the metals circulate in the eighteenth century, many based on an early 1701 abridgment translated (see following note), with its commentaries, from André Dacier's *Les Oeuvres de Platon*.

9. *The Works of Plato Abridg'd*, 2 vols. (A. Bell, 1701), 1:84. Compare Plato 414b. See also Jenny Davidson, *Breeding: A Partial History of the Eighteenth Century* (New York: Columbia UP, 2009), 78–9, on Swift's use of Plato's fables of inequality in the Houyhnhnmland episode of *Gulliver's Travels*.

10. *A Defence of the Constitutions of Government of the United States of America* (C. Dilly, 1787), 153, 190, 192.

11. See Michael McKeon, *The Origins of the English Novel, 1600–1740* (Baltimore: Johns Hopkins UP, 1987), 152.

12. Pope, *Essay on Man* (John Wright, 1734), 31.

13. William Langhorne, *Job. A Poem* (R. Griffiths, 1760), 61.

14. Elizabeth Tollet, *Poems on Several Occasions* (John Clarke, 1724), 62; Lady Mary Chudleigh, *Essays Upon Several Subjects in Prose and Verse* (T.H., 1710), 35.

15. Frederick Pilon, *He Would Be a Soldier* (G. G. J. and J. Robinson, 1786), 26.

16. The brain itself appears fissured, folded, and wrinkled. The appearance may be responsible for images of the mind's veins and fissures.

17. Thomas Burnet, *Third Remarks Upon an Essay Concerning Humane Understanding* (M. Wotton, 1699), 7; G. W. Leibniz, *New Essays on Human Understanding*, ed. Peter Remnant and Jonathan Bennett (Cambridge: Cambridge UP, 1996), 86. See Barbara Maria Stafford's reading of Leibniz's image in the context of marbled papers in *Body Criticism: Imaging the Unseen in Enlightenment Art and Medicine* (Cambridge, MA: MIT P, 1993), 203–4.

18. As stressed throughout this study, most every metaphor is available to all who would use it. Addison, a follower of Locke, sees in a block of quarried marble a substance that "shews none of its inherent Beauties, till the Skill of the Polisher fetches out the Colours, makes the Surface shine." *Spectator* no. 215, in *The Spectator*, ed. D. F. Bond (Oxford: Clarendon, 1965), 2:338. Addison, unaware of Leibniz's metaphorics, uses the marble metaphor to make a broadly Lockean case for education, even as the German philosopher will use it to upset Locke's dismissal of innate or intrinsic qualities. The marbled and veined self is invoked by any number of eighteenth-century writers, most of whom do not follow Leibniz in using the image to make a case for innate knowledge. Of interest is Addison's contention that the soul of philosophers, saints, and heroes often "lie concealed in a Plebeian" until "disinterred" by "proper Education" (ibid.).

19. This is Addison's verb. See previous note.

20. *An Elegy Wrote in a Country Church Yard* (R. Dodsley, 1751), 8.

21. Bowden, *Poems on Various Subjects* (Bath: T. Boddely, 1754), 55.

22. Jonathan Swift calls him a "*brazen* Minister of State" in a poetic epistle to John Gay, in *Miscellanies* (Charles Davis, 1735), 5:123.

23. *Pamela: or, Virtue Rewarded*, 2 vols. (C. Rivington and J. Osborn, 1741), 2:59.

24. Fielding recycles the Richardson's terms of abuse in *Shamela*: "I stood still, and my Master cryed out, Hussy, Slut, Sauce-box, Boldface, come hither." When Shamela is dismissed and allowed to go free, she resolves to "brazen it out" and tells Mrs. Jewkes she leaves with pleasure a place where her "Vartue" (a portmanteau of value and virtue) was in continual danger. See Henry Fielding, *An Apology for the Life of Mrs. Shamela Andrews* (A. Dodd, 1741), 13, 36.

25. *The Works of Hesiod*, 2 vols. (N. Blandford, 1728), 1:81–2.

26. *A Collection of All the Dialogues Written by Mr. Thomas Brown* (John Nutt, 1704), 380.

27. *The Theory of Moral Sentiments*, 6th ed., 2 vols. (A. Strahan and A. Cadell, 1790), 2:241.

28. J. G. Holman, *The Votary of Wealth*, 2nd ed. (T. N. Longman and O. Rees, 1799), 28. *OED* defines "Gentoo" as "a non-Muslim inhabitant of Hindustan." Sharp-set may be echoing Berowne in *Love's Labour's Lost*: "Can any face of brass hold out longer?" (V.ii.395).

29. W. C. Oulton, *The Beauties of Modern Dramatists*, 2 vols. (West and Hughes, 1800), 1:155.

30. *Shakespeare's Comedies, Histories, & Tragedies* (Isaac Iaggard, and Ed. Blount, 1623), 83.

31. See especially "Prometheus: On *Wood* the Patentee's *Irish Half-Pence*," in *Miscellanies* (B. Motte, 1727), 219–23, and "Will. Wood's Petition to the People of *Ireland*," in *Works* (Dublin: George Faulkner, 1746), 8:315–7. Swift uses a brass-pass rhyme to close couplets in both these poems.

32. Frances Burney, *Evelina, or, a Young Lady's Entrance into the World*, 3 vols. (T. Lowndes, 1778), 1:126.

33. *Some Familiar Letters Between Mr. Locke, and Several of His Friends* (A. and J. Churchill, 1708), 107–8.

34. See Johnson's definition of "AQUA REGIA." Gold is the "King of metals" in Thomas Amory's *The Life of John Buncle, Esq.* (J. Noon, 1756), 2:357.

35. *Short Hymns on Select Passages of the Holy Scriptures*, 2 vols. (Bristol: E. Farley, 1762), 1:241.

36. *Fables Ancient and Modern* (Jacob Tonson, 1700), 37. The softness of rich and precious metals is characteristic of connotations of the metal in Dryden's works. Johnson cites Dryden in his first definition of "STAMP *n.s.*": "'Tis gold so pure, It cannot bear the stamp without allay." Dryden is cited again under "DUCTILE": "Gold, as it is the purest, so it is the softest and most ductile of all metals." Dryden is also cited in Pope's translation of the *Odyssey*: "*Each gentle mind the soft infection felt, / For richest metals are most apt to melt.*"

37. *Theory of Moral Sentiments* (A. Millar, 1759), 55.

38. *The Works of William Cowper* (London: Baldwin and Cradock, 1835–7), 8:26–7.

39. Alexander Pope and John Arbuthnot, *Memoirs of the Extraordinary Life, Works, and Discoveries of Martinus Scriblerus* (Dublin: George Faulkner, 1741), 4.

40. Amory, *The Life of John Buncle, Esq.*, 2:361.

41. See J. Gwyn Griffith's discussion of Hesiod's ordering in "Archaeology and Hesiod's Five Ages," *Journal of the History of Ideas* 17:1 (January 1956): 110. Griffith proposes an "archaeological" explanation of Hesiod's hierarchy.

42. *Fruits of Retirement* (T. Sowle, 1702), 100.

43. *Cyclopaedia; or, an Universal Dictionary of Arts and Sciences*, 2 vols. (James and John Knapton, 1728).

44. See Lynn Willies, "Lead: Ore Preparation and Smelting," 119.

45. *The Works of the Rev. John Wesley* (London: Thomas Cordeux, 1810), 5:287.

46. Laurence Sterne, *The Sermons of Mr. Yorick*, 4 vols. (printed for T. Becket and P. A. De Hondt, 1766), 3:131–2.

47. *An Inquiry Into the Nature and Causes of the Wealth of Nations*, 2 vols. (W. Strahan; and T. Cadell, 1776), 1:6.

48. R. F. Tylecote, "Iron in the Industrial Revolution," in Day and Tylecote, *The Industrial Revolution in Metals*, 259.

49. Mandeville, however, uses iron to figure ductility: "As Iron is to be hammer'd whilst it is hot and ductile, so Children are to be taught when they are young." *Fable of the Bees. Part II* (J. Roberts, 1729), 184.

50. In a famous analogy from *Tatler* no. 107, Steele matches the coquette to a soldier; see Addison and Steele, *The Tatler*, ed. Donald Bond (Oxford: Oxford UP, 1965), 1:151.

51. Steel is, in fact, "iron alloyed with from 0.5 per cent to 1.5 per cent carbon, so distinguishing it from wrought iron, which has much less carbon, and from cast iron, which has more carbon." K. C. Barraclough, "Steel in the Industrial Revolution," in Day and Tylecote, *The Industrial Revolution in Metals*, 261. Not until the end of the eighteenth century was the role played by carbon in the production of steel properly understood.

52. *The Rape of the Lock* (Bernard Lintott, 1714), 26.

53. Barraclough, "Steel," 261.

54. *The Dunciad, in Four Books* (M. Cooper, 1743), 122.

55. But see also *The Theory of Moral Sentiments* (A. Millar, 1759), 421–2, where Smith uses the word to translate (the platonic ideal) *sophrosyne*.

56. *The Theory of Moral Sentiments*, 6th ed., 2 vols. (A. Strahan; and A. Cadell, 1790), 2:142, 2:130.

57. Smith's metaphor of the "harmony of minds" demands discussion under a new rubric in an as yet unwritten entry. *Theory of Moral Sentiments* (A. Millar, 1759), 541. Bach's *Well-Tempered Clavier* is one of the better-known pieces of eighteenth-century music. A readable introduction to the history of temperament is Stuart Isacoff, *Temperament: The Idea That Solved Music's Greatest Riddle* (New York: Alfred A. Knopf, 2001).

58. On the production of iron harpsichord wires, see Tylecote, "Iron in the Industrial Revolution," 203. It should be noted that Smith denies that music will *literally* soften the heart or mend the morals. In his *Wealth of Nations* Smith controverts the authority of Plato, Aristotle, and Polybius when he observes that even though "there was nothing that corresponded to the musical education of the Greeks" among

the Romans, the Romans' morals were a good deal superior to those of the Greeks. See Smith, *Wealth of Nations*, 1:359. On the same page Smith alludes to a passage from the *Esprit des lois* in which Montesquieu "endeavours to support that authority." In Montesquieu, then, we find a possible source for Smith's metaphors of music, metal, and tempering: the quotation from Montesquieu shows Smith, at least, to be familiar with the connotations he enlists in his selection of the term "temper."

59. *Shakespeare's Comedies, Histories, & Tragedies*, 91, 267.

60. William Harvey replaced the metaphor of the heart as a furnace with a Copernican metaphor in his *Exercitatio Anatomica de Motu Cordis et Sanguinis in Animalibus* (Frankfurt: William Fitzer, 1628). The new metaphor suits Harvey's identification of the heart as a pump. In *L'Homme* Descartes figures the heart as both furnace and sun. In this instance, as elsewhere, we see two opposed writers deploy the same metaphor (of the sun) in different ways. On Descartes's rejection of Harvey's metaphorics, see Stephen Gaukroger, *Descartes' System of Natural Philosophy* (Cambridge: Cambridge UP, 2001), 22. See also Robert A. Erickson, *The Language of the Heart, 1600–1750* (Philadelphia: U of Pennsylvania P, 1997).

61. *Pneumatologia* (Francis Tyton, 1685), 325.

62. See also J. J. Timaeus's translation of a Schiller tragedy, *Cabal and Love* (1795), in which a character warns that the "anvil of gnawing conscience is never cool."

63. "On Mrs. Montague's Feather Hangings," in *Poems*, new ed. (J. Johnson, 1798), 2:342

64. The "heart of steel" is a site of sympathy because it is able to temper and modulate passions so that others can enter into them. See especially Smith on "temper," in the first edition of *Theory of Moral Sentiments* (A. Millar, 1759), 34–40

65. The "Hearts of Steel" or "Steelboys" were a secret agrarian organization that agitated in Northern Ireland in the 1770s for lower tithes and rents. See Gerald Newman et al., eds., *Britain in the Hanoverian Age, 1714–1837: An Encyclopedia* (New York: Garland, 1997), 324.

66. G. J. Barker-Benfield, *The Culture of Sensibility: Sex and Society in Eighteenth-Century Britain* (Chicago: U of Chicago P, 1992), 395.

67. Tylecote, "Iron in the Industrial Revolution," 226; Barraclough, "Steel in the Industrial Revolution," 278.

68. Compare Caterina Albano's claim: "Generally, the model used to describe the brain, and consequently, to conceptualize the mind matches the most recent technical achievements." "Seeing the Mind: Considerations on Visual Metaphors of the Mind in Western Thought (16th–18th Centuries)," *Developmental Medicine & Child Neurology* 47:12 (2005): 843. Albano gives blank sheets, labyrinths, clockwork, looms, and network systems as examples. While I undertook my project with the intention of substantiating commonsense claims like Albano's, I have found that **Metal** metaphors prove one of the few examples where technology and metaphorics can be correlated directly and straightforwardly.

69. Nietzsche, "On Truth and Lie in An Extra-Moral Sense," in *The Portable Nietzsche*, ed. Walter Kaufman (1954; repr., New York: Penguin Books, 1976), 47.

Mirror

1. Optical metaphors (that make the mind out as a mirror, a lens, or the like) make up nearly 2.4% of all metaphors collected in the period. Light metaphors, more numerous but less consistently collected, make up 6.1%. Neither indicates a shifting trend in usage. I find, on average, twenty-one mirror metaphors per decade (with the metaphors appearing more frequently in the last two decades).

2. On mirror metaphors as constitutive of literary theory, see *The Mirror and the Lamp: Romantic Theory and the Critical Tradition* (Oxford: Oxford UP, 1953), 30–46. Abrams sees his metaphors as belonging to "submerged conceptual models" or "archetypal analogies" (31). In stated contrast, my effort, throughout this dictionary, is to show that models of mind are neither submerged nor superficial; metaphors are both rampant and multivarious. A metaphor may belong to ancient tradition of use and still be repurposed in an encounter with a new material fact. A metaphor may be put to conflicting uses, and a poet's practice—as Abrams observes of Shelley—may be owing to contradicting metaphors (126–7).

3. Abrams varies and broadens the formulation later in the book in claiming that "implicit semantic shifts" in word use "reflect the changes in [a writer's] underlying theory" (313). A close reader of Abrams will note he repeatedly employs the language of reflection in his criticism: a passage in a Dryden preface reflects Dryden's personal interests; likewise "Lamia" reflects Keats's anxiety that poetry is vulnerable to scientific disenchantment (307–8). For Abrams, a literary product *reflects* the faculties of its producer (228).

4. Paul de Man's "The Rhetoric of Temporality" ranks among the best-known full-dress responses to Abrams's claims for metaphor. My own thinking about mirror metaphors and periodization was influenced by Rayna Kalas's *Frame, Glass, Verse: The Technology of Poetic Invention in the English Renaissance* (Ithaca, NY: Cornell UP, 2007); Herbert Grabes's now-classic survey of mirror metaphors, *The Mutable Glass: Mirror-Imagery in Titles and Texts of the Middle Ages and the English Renaissance*, trans. Gordon Collier (Cambridge: Cambridge UP, 1982); and Katherine Jewett's translation of Sabine Melchior-Bonnet's *Histoire du miroir* (The Mirror: A History) (1994; trans., New York: Routledge, 2001). Michael McKeon collects eighteenth-century mirror metaphors in his *Secret History of Domesticity: Public, Private, and the Division of Knowledge* (Baltimore: Johns Hopkins UP, 2005), 621–3.

5. Laurence Sterne, *Tristram Shandy* (R. and J. Dodsley, 1761), 3:81–2. Sterne may recall the meat-roasting jack used to explain consciousness and personal identity in *Memoirs of the Extraordinary Life, Works, and Discoveries of Martinus Scriblerus* (Dublin: George Faulkner, 1741), 94–95.

6. Melchior-Bonnet, *Histoire du miroir*, 70–2. See also 81.

7. Grabes names the four-hundred-year span *before* the eighteenth century the "Age of the Mirror." *Mutable Glass*, 71.

8. On the persistence and complexity of Romantic mirror metaphors, see Frederick Burwick, "Reflections in the Mirror: Wordsworth and Coleridge," in *Reflecting Senses: Perception and Appearance in Literature, Culture, and the Arts*, ed. Walter Paper and Frederick Burwick (New York: De Gruyter, 1994); and Burwick, *Mimesis and Its Romantic Reflections* (University Park: Pennsylvania State UP, 2001). Seamus Perry, in a retrospective account of Abrams's continuing influence, notes that mirror and lamp are both "metaphors for an art that comes recognizably from the 'human world' and speaks for it." See "The Mirror and the Lamp," *Essays in Criticism* 54:3 (2004): 276. Although he does not cite Wordsworth's mirror metaphor, Perry notes both mirror and lamp are useful in characterizing Wordsworthian practice (276).

9. Curtius cites Cassiodorus as an early instance of "speculum mentis" metaphor. *European Literature and the Latin Middle Ages* (Princeton, NJ: Princeton UP, 1990), 336n. Grabes surveys scholarship on "metaphor of the soul or spirit as a mirror" in antiquity before asserting that "the mind-mirror began to be put to a wide variety of uses by English writers from around 1590." *Mutable Glass*, 88–9. See also Marjorie Nicholson, *Newton Demands the Muse: Newton's Opticks and the Eighteenth Century Poets* (Princeton, NJ: Princeton UP, 1946), esp. 107–64.

10. *The Concept of Mind* (Chicago: U of Chicago P, 1949), 194–5.

11. Letter to Edward Blount, 1725, from *Letters* (J. Wright, 1737), 171, 172. It should be emphasized that the cavernous interior also had a fountain in it: a splashing spring that filled the space with the continuous murmur of running water. In 1739, Pope, newly interested in geology, converted the space to a kind of mine, decorated with flints and ore, pointing us back, again, to the metaphorics of **Metal**. See Pope's "Verses on a Grotto by the River," first published in *The Gentleman's Magazine* 11 (December 1741), 660, for the conflation of mirror, cave, lamp, fountain, and metal metaphors. For a description of Pope's grotto, architectural plans and sketches, and an account of the renovations that supplemented mirrored fragments with glittering iron ores, see Anthony Beckles Wilson, "Alexander Pope's Grotto at Twickenham," *Garden History* 26:1 (Summer 1998): 31–59.

12. It would be unfair, I recognize, to reduce Abrams to this paraphrased thesis and then further reduce him to his warrant for that thesis. *The Mirror and the Lamp* is not single-minded but everywhere complicates its periodizing thesis as it puts it forward. Its title is even, as René Wellek observed, "something of a misnomer," failing to advertise a concern with musical and organic metaphorics and heterocosmic aesthetics. See "*The Mirror and the Lamp: Romantic Theory and Critical Tradition* by M. H. Abrams," *Comparative Literature*, 6: 2 (Spring 1954): 179. And in the reply printed at the end of the festschrift *High Romantic Argument*, ed. Lawrence Lipking (London: Cornell UP, 1981), Abrams repeats that displaced metaphors continue to recur. But I would follow Jerome McGann in illuminating the workings of Romantic

ideology in Abrams's study: Abrams requires the eighteenth century to serve as a foil to the nineteenth.

13. Abrams knows that "only in his poetry, not in his criticism, does Wordsworth, make the transition from the eighteenth-century view of man and nature to the concept that the mind is creative in perception, and an integral part of an organically inter-related universe." *Mirror and Lamp*, 104–5. I am hardly the first to notice the irony: see Murray Krieger, *A Window to Criticism* (Princeton, NJ: Princeton UP, 1964). I am likewise aware that my argument risks converting my counts and frequencies to a new kind of reflected image of the age.

14. Which is not to say new images of the age won't serve by way of reflex: I do not claim Abrams is *wrong* about Wordsworth's metaphorics: to quote Terry Eagleton, "Bourgeois ideas do indeed accurately mirror the state of things in bourgeois society; but it is the very state of affairs which is somehow twisted out of true." *Ideology: An Introduction*, 2nd ed. (London: Verso, 2007), 104.

15. William Ivins, *On the Rationalization of Sight* (New York: Da Capo, 1973); Erwin Panofsky, *Perspective as Symbolic Form* (New York: Zone Books, 1991).

16. *Mutable Glass*, 12. Grabes decides on the late seventeenth century as his terminus, as it "coincides with a marked decrease in literary applications of the metaphor" (ibid.). Grabes and Abrams are my bookends. That the mirror metaphor is believed to be on the wane in both the late seventeenth and in the late eighteenth century suggests to me that we had better think harder, as literary critics, about what we mean by "frequency."

17. Rorty, *Philosophy and the Mirror of Nature* (Princeton, NJ: Princeton UP, 1979), 12.

18. Dan Edelstein, *The Enlightenment: A Genealogy* (Chicago: U of Chicago P, 2010), 36. See also Marjorie Nicholson, *Newton Demands.*

19. Abrams starts with Plato. On Chinese mirror-heart metaphors, see Erin M. Cline, "Mirrors, Minds, and Metaphors," *Philosophy East and West* 58:3 (2008): 337–57.

20. *The Relapse* (Samuel Briscoe, 1697), 28–9.

21. *The Hypochondriack* no. 7 (April 1778), from *The London Magazine, or Gentleman's Monthly Intelligencer.* Compare Martin Jay, who follows Jean Starobinski and Derrida in readings of Rousseau, whose politicized antitheatricality conflates spectator with spectacle. *Downcast Eyes: The Denigration of Sight* (Berkeley: U of California P, 1993), 90–5.

22. *Spectator* no. 275, in *The Spectator*, ed. D. F. Bond (Oxford: Clarendon, 1965), 2:571.

23. Boswell, *The Life of Samuel Johnson* (Henry Baldwin, 1791), 2:189.

24. Erik Bond, *Reading London: Urban Speculation and Imaginative Government in Eighteenth-Century Literature* (Columbus: Ohio State UP, 2007), 153.

25. *Spectator* no. 159, 2:121–6; Steele, *Conscious Lovers* (J. Tonson, 1723), 13. John O'Brien pointed out the passage to me.

26. Atterbury, *A Discourse Occasion'd by the Death of the Right Honourable the Lady Cutts* (Tho. Bennet, 1698), 14.

27. Goldsmith, *The Citizen of the World* (printed for the author, 1762), 1:195.

28. Jürgen Habermas claims, perhaps controversially, that in the *Spectator*, and in similar periodicals, "the public held up a mirror to itself." *The Structural Transformation of the Public Sphere: An Inquiry into a Category of Bourgeois Society*, trans. Thomas Burger (Cambridge, MA: MIT P, 1999), 43. Erin Mackie complicates the claim in *Market à la Mode: Fashion, Commodity, and Gender in "The Tatler" and "The Spectator"* (Baltimore: Johns Hopkins UP, 1997), 182–3, 187.

29. Goldsmith, *Citizen*, 1:200; *Mirror* (February 20, 1779).

30. *Man a Machine* (W. Owen, 1749), 33.

31. *Soliloquy, or Advice to an Author* (John Morphew, 1710), 47. See McKeon, *Domesticity*, 103–4.

32. *The Theory of Moral Sentiments* (A. Millar, 1759), 254–5.

33. Jonathan Miller, *On Reflection* (London: National Gallery, 1998), 175.

34. Hagstrum, *The Sister Arts: The Tradition of Literary Pictorialism and English Poetry from Dryden to Gray* (Chicago: U of Chicago P, 1958), 136–7, 141. On ambiguity of reflection in empiricism, see 135–40. See also W. J. T. Mitchell, *Iconology: Image, Text, Ideology* (Chicago: U of Chicago P, 1986), 12, 116–50.

35. Rorty, *Mirror of Nature*, 43.

36. Cited in Jonathan Lamb, "Sympathy with Animals and Salvation of the Soul," *The Eighteenth Century: Theory and Interpretation* 52:1 (Spring 2011): 69–85, 75.

37. *A Treatise Concerning Eternal and Immutable Morality* (James and John Knapton, 1731), 130.

38. *Essays Moral and Philosophical* (J. Osborn and T. Longman, 1734), 88.

39. See Mark Blackwell, *British It-Narratives, 1750–1830* (London: Pickering and Chatto, 2012), 4:166, 167, 169.

40. Locke's critic Henry Lee believes ideas are literally visible representations; writing in his *Anti-Scepticism*—a work that mirrors Locke essay chapter by chapter—Lee redefines Locke's keyword: "Thus a man's Face in the Glass is properly the *Idea* of that Face." *Anti-Scepticism* (R. Clavel and C. Harper, 1702), 2, quoted in John Yolton, "As in a Looking-Glass: Perceptual Acquaintance in Eighteenth-Century Britain," *Journal of the History of Ideas* 40:2 (1979): 214.

41. See Peter de Bolla, *The Discourse of the Sublime: Readings in History, Aesthetics, and the Subject* (New York: Basil Blackwell, 1989), 201–8.

42. *Locke's Essay and the Rhetoric of Science* (Cranbury, NJ: Associated UPs, 2003), 82.

43. Picciotto, *Labors of Innocence in Early Modern England* (Cambridge, MA: Harvard UP, 2010), 14, 323–6. See also Abrams on Young, who sees in Locke's quality dualism an opportunity for a "metaphoric substitution" that converts sensationalism into its epistemological opposite. *Mirror and Lamp*, 63.

44. Hume, *Philosophical Essays Concerning Human Understanding* (A. Millar, 1748), 22. The phrase "faded and dead" reads "faint and dull" in revised editions.

45. I quote from the English translation, *Of the Advancement and Proficience of Learning* (Oxford: Robert Young and Edward Forrest, 1640), 249. On Bacon's ambivalent mirror metaphors (and the materiality of metaphorics), see Kalas, *Frame, Glass, Verse*, 148–51.

46. *A Collection of English Proverbs* (Cambridge: W. Morden, 1678), 280.

47. *An Essay on Human Life* (George Faulkner, 1741), 5.

48. Pope, *Essay on Man* (John Wright, 1734). W. K. Wimsatt finds compressed in the line "classical tradition of the mirror joined with the new rationalism and scientific standards of observation," the result is a surprising Augustan "unreality." *Hateful Contraries: Studies in Literature and Criticism* (Lexington: U of Kentucky P, 1965), 155, 158.

49. *An Essay on Criticism* (W. Lewis, 1711), 16.

50. Warton, "Ode on Approach of Summer," in *The Union: or, Select Scots and English Poems* (R. Baldwin, 1759), 88; Jones, *Merit. A Poem* (R. and J. Dodsley, 1753), 19.

51. Somervile, *The Chace. A Poem*, 4th ed. (1735), 5; Maria and Harriet Falconar, *Poems on Slavery* (Messrs. Egertons, Mr. Murray, and J. Johnson, 1788), 20; Headley, *An Invocation of Melancholy* (Oxford: s.n., 1785), 12. On fancy's glass and the "inversions" of ideology in Shaftesbury, see Picciotto, *Labors of Innocence*, 269, 272.

52. *Poems on Several Subjects By E. Rack* (Richardson and Urquhart, and T. Letchworth, 1775), 107–8; William Hayley, *The Triumphs of Temper* (J. Dodsley, 1781), 42.

53. Laurence Sterne, *Tristram Shandy* (R. and J. Dodsley, 1761), 3:327; Henry Mackenzie, *The Man of Feeling* (T. Cadell, 1771), 44.

54. Abrams cites the German, not the English translation. *Mirror and Lamp*, 44.

55. Radcliffe, *A Sicilian Romance* (T. Hookham, 1790), 215.

56. Radcliffe, *The Italian* (T. Cadell, 1797), 3:172.

57. Both essays are collected in Terry Castle, *The Female Thermometer* (Oxford and New York: Oxford UP, 1995), 120–39, 140–67.

58. Louis Althusser famously complicates the metaphor of ideology as an inverted or "mirror" image: "It is not their real conditions of existence, their real world, that 'men' 'represent to themselves' in ideology, but above all it is their relation to those conditions of existence which are represented to them there." "Ideology and Ideological State Apparatuses," in *Lenin and Philosophy*, trans. Ben Brester (New York: Monthly Review Press, 1971), 164.

59. Castle ingeniously describes the Gothic as the "first 'postmodern' experiment" in English literary history." *Boss Ladies Watch Out: Essays on Women, Sex, and Writing* (New York: Routledge, 2002), 78.

60. Antoine-Louis-Claude Destutt de Tracy, *Traité de la volonté et de ses effets* (Geneva: Slatkine Reprints, 1984), 342. The term "ideology" appears in English in *Monthly Magazine* 3 (1797): 285. On Tracy's metaphor, see Emmet Kennedy, *A Philos-*

ophe in the Age of Revolution: Destutt de Tracy and the Origins of "Ideology" (Philadelphia: American Philosophical Society, 1978), 206. See also W. J. T. Mitchell, *Iconology: Image, Text, Ideology*, 165–8.

61. *Reflections on the Revolution in France* (J. Dodsley, 1790), 113.

62. Not more than two hundred "mirrors," mirrours," "looking-glasses" and the like. I do not claim to have exhausted the mirror metaphors in online archives; I only emphasize that this is a fraction of the more than ten thousand metaphors delivered into my database by my search protocols. I have collected far more metaphors under other headings.

Rooms

1. Architectural metaphors are 5.6% of the total number of metaphors collected in the period, although they make up a much higher percentage of the metaphors dated to the 1710s (8.6%). There may also be a slight falling away of architectural metaphors as such at the century's end, although the metaphorics of interiority as indexed strictly by the keywords listed at the head of this entry seems more persistent. As in other entries, I find a cluster of metaphors in the poetry of Pope, Prior, and Blackmore in the second decade that unsettles the distribution.

2. *The Concept of Mind* (Chicago: U of Chicago P, 1949), 27.

3. On the imaginative reconception of space, see Cynthia Wall's study, *The Literary and Cultural Spaces of Restoration London* (Cambridge: Cambridge UP, 1998). In this entry I have relied much on her final chapter, which treats narratives of private spaces. My investigation also looks to Michael McKeon's *The Secret History of Domesticity: Public, Private, and the Division of Knowledge* (Baltimore: Johns Hopkins UP, 2005). I was influenced early by John Bender's study of "the architecture of mind" in *Imagining the Penitentiary: Fiction and the Architecture of Mind in Eighteenth-Century England* (Chicago: U of Chicago P, 1987).

4. John Lukács, "The Bourgeois Interior," *American Scholar* 39:1 (Winter 1969–70): 626–30; Witold Rybczynski, *Home: A Short History of an Idea* (New York: Viking Books, 1986), 35–6. See also Kathy Mezei and Chiara Briganti, "Reading the House: A Literary Perspective," *Signs* 27:3 (2002): 839. On the metaphor of interiority, see also Julia Prewitt Brown, *The Bourgeois Interior* (Charlottesville: U of Virginia P, 2008), 10.

5. Catherine Belsey, *The Subject of Tragedy: Identity and Difference in Renaissance Drama* (New York: Methuen, 1985), 48, 7, 33ff. See also Francis Barker on the "bourgeois subjectivity" and the "metaphysic of interiority" in *The Tremulous Private Body: Essays on Subjection* (New York: Methuen, 1984), 58, 39, 52. Katherine Eisaman Maus surveys the scholarship on early modern interiority and offers a nuanced explanation of inwardness in the period in her *Inwardness and Theater in the English Renaissance* (Chicago: U of Chicago P, 1995).

6. Dror Wahrman builds on the criticism of Deirdre Lynch and Catherine Gallagher in his argument for the postponement of "interiority." *The Making of the*

Modern Self: Identity and Culture in Eighteenth-Century England (New Haven, CT: Yale UP), 182–9. Sandra Macpherson takes issue with Wahrman (and with a comparable argument by Wolfram Schmidgen) in *Harm's Way: Tragic Responsibility and the Novel Form* (Baltimore: Johns Hopkins UP, 2010), 32–3. See also Diana Fuss, *The Sense of an Interior: Four Writers and the Rooms That Shaped Them* (London: Routledge, 2004). Fuss argues for the emergence of a "notion of interiority" in the nineteenth century (8).

7. Stephen Toulmin makes a valuable distinction between interiority and inwardness in "The Inwardness of Mental Life," *Critical Inquiry* 6:1 (1976): 1–16. Ryle provides a compact analysis of interiority in his *Concept of Mind* (38–9). Derek Melser has updated behaviorist analysis in his *Act of Thinking* (Cambridge, MA: MIT P, 2004): "notions of 'abbreviation' and 'inhibition' are useful only up to the point where the behavior is no longer occurring. Interiorization is a metaphor" (49).

8. As Ludwig Wittgenstein observes, "An 'inner process' stands in need of outward criteria." See *Philosophical Investigations*, 3rd ed., trans. G. E. M. Anscombe (New York: Blackwell, 2001), §580. See also §290, on the differences between describing a room and describing a state of mind.

9. John Norris, *An Essay towards the Theory of the Ideal or Intelligible World* (S. Manship and W. Hawes, 1701), 391.

10. The Augustinian formula should read, "Noli foras ire, in teipsum redi, in interiore homine habitat veritas." On the phrase "in interiore homine," see Charles Taylor, *Sources of the Self: The Making of the Modern Identity* (Cambridge, MA: Harvard UP, 1989), 127–42. On the seemingly paradoxical relation of interiority and objectivity in Augustine, see Charles T. Matthewes, "Augustinian Anthropology: Interior intimo meo," *Journal of Religious Ethics* 27:2 (1999): 195–221.

11. Jean-Marie Goulemot, "Literary Practices: Publicizing the Private," in *The History of Private Life*, vol. 3, *Passions of the Renaissance*, ed. Roger Chartier and Arthur Goldhammer (Cambridge, MA: Harvard UP), 384. See also Wall, *Spaces*, 212–8.

12. Georg Lukács, *The Theory of the Novel: A Historico-philosophical Essay on the Forms of Great Epic Literature*, trans. Anna Bostock (Harvard, MA: MIT P, 1971), 89.

13. Philippa Tristram writes, "From the beginning the house and the novel are interconnected, for the eighteenth century, which saw the rise of the novel, was also the great age of the English house." *Living Space in Fact and Fiction* (London: Routledge, 1989), 2. See also Kathy Mezei and Chiara Briganti, "Reading the House," 838.

14. Christina Marsden Gillis, *The Paradox of Privacy: Epistolary Form in Clarissa* (Gainesville: U Ps of Florida, 1984), 22; Simon Varey, *Space and the Eighteenth-Century English Novel* (Cambridge: Cambridge UP, 1990), 186.

15. See Mark Girouard on *cabinets* and the Palladian "formal plan" in *Life in the English Country House: A Social and Architectural History* (New Haven, CT: Yale UP, 1978), 128–9. Philippa Tristram marks 1715, a year that saw the publication of *Vitruvius Britannicus* and a translation of Palladio's *Quattro Libri*, as an important date in

the establishment of the Palladian style as dominant. *Living Space in Fact and Fiction*, 5. See also Wall, *Spaces*, 214–5.

16. See Ruth Perry's interpretations of the figure of the writing desk in *Women, Letters, and the Novel* (New York: AMS Press, 1980), 134.

17. The titles and the practices of private devotion are discussed in Foucauldian terms in chapter 3 of Richard Rambuss, *Closet Devotions* (Durham, NC: Duke UP, 1998). See also Alan Stewart, "The Early Modern Closet Discovered," *Representations* 50 (Spring 1995), 76–101. Michael McKeon discusses Matthew 6:6 in *Domesticity*, 40–3.

18. Although architectural developments do "trickle down." On this process see McKeon, *Domesticity*, 252–9.

19. Toulmin, "Inwardness." See also Anthony Kenny's rehearsal of a similar line of argument in chapter 2 of *The Metaphysics of Mind* (Oxford: Oxford UP, 1992).

20. See Toulmin, "Inwardness," 4. Toulmin revisits the sensorium metaphor in *Cosmopolis: The Hidden Agenda of Modernity* (Chicago: U of Chicago P, 1990), where he writes of the architecture of the pineal gland: "Fifty years on" Descartes's conjecture that the pineal gland was the site of body-soul interaction, had become "general doctrine" (108). "To Newton, it was evident that mental experience and activity take place within an Inner Theatre (or *sensorium commune*) to which the sensory nerves bring 'ideas' from the peripheral receptors and from which, in turn, motor nerves carry the 'commands' of the will back to the muscles" (108–9). See **Inhabitants** and **Empire**.

21. *Spectator* no. 275, in *The Spectator*, ed. D. F. Bond (Oxford: Clarendon, 1965), 2:570–3. Swift writes, "Yesterday I ordered the Carcass of a *Beau* to be stript in my Presence; when we were all amazed to find so many unsuspected Faults under one Suit of Cloaths: Then I laid open his *Brain*, his *Heart*, and his *Spleen*; But I plainly perceived at ever Operation, that the farther we proceeded, we found the Defects encrease upon us in Number and Bulk." *A Tale of a Tub* (John Nutt, 1704), 174–5.

22. See Perry, *Women*. The seat-of-the-soul metaphor is further treated in **Empire** and **Inhabitants**.

23. The *Tatler*, as it were, moves almost completely into Bickerstaff's apartment one-third of the way into its run; the *Spectator* abandons this convention entirely. Stuart Sherman associates Bickerstaff's private apartment with the author's mind in *Telling Time: Clocks, Diaries, and English Diurnal Form, 1660–1785* (Chicago: U of Chicago. P, 1996), 129–30.

24. See Taylor, *Sources of the Self*, 143.

25. *The Philosophical Writings*, trans. J. Cottingham et al. (Cambridge: Cambridge UP, 1999), 47.

26. Mollineux, *Fruits of Retirement* (T. Sowle, 1702), 120; Duck, *Poems on Several Occasions* (printed for the author, 1736), 216.

27. *The Complete Essays of Michel de Montaigne*, trans. D. M. Frame (Stanford, CA: Stanford UP, 1976), 177.

28. See Horace's *Epode* II.

29. See Michael G. Ketcham, "Setting and Self-Presentation in the Restoration and Early Eighteenth Century," *Studies in English Literature, 1500–1900* 23:3 (1983): 402–3. Ketcham juxtaposes a reading of the *beatus ille* tradition and J. G. A. Pocock's analysis of property and credit in the republican tradition.

30. Wollstonecraft, *A Vindication of the Rights of Woman* (J. Johnson, 1792), 306.

31. McKeon sees a hiving or subdividing of space at work in the eighteenth century, a process that involves both a model of linear hierarchy (represented in the French scheme of the *appartement*) and one of separation and difference (represented in the segregation of public from private spaces, servants from tenants, and business from leisure) in the architecture of the home (*Domesticity*, 212–68). The changes in architecture are later mapped onto changes in the domestic novel: "Developments in the way architectural inside spaces get hived and subdivided bear a loose but fruitful analogy to developments in narrative form" (710).

32. The "mind's Presence-room" is often cited from Locke's *Essay*, II.iii.1. The metaphor appears in Helkiah Crooke, *ΜΙΚΡΟΚΟΣΜΟΓΡΑΦΙΑ: A Description of the Body of Man* (William Iaggard, 1615), 5. See also Thomas Shipman, among the epigraphs to this entry. On Locke and the "presence-chamber," see McKeon, *Domesticity*, 223.

33. Perhaps, like Norbert Elias, we should picture the rising class developing within themselves structures modeled on the superior royal or aristocratic household. See *The Civilizing Process*, rev. ed. (London: Blackwell, 2000), 430–3. And again, see McKeon, *Domesticity*, 252–9.

34. Fielding, *Tom Jones* (A. Millar, 1749), 2:14–5. See Ian Watt, *The Rise of the Novel: Studies in Defoe, Richardson, and Fielding* (Berkeley: U of California P, 1957), 273. See also Dorrit Cohn, *Transparent Minds: Narrative Modes for Presenting Consciousness in Fiction* (Princeton, NJ: Princeton UP, 1978), 22, 22n3, 22n4.

35. The sonnet was published in the first volume of the third edition of *Clarissa* (1751). Edward is likely borrowing Richardson's own vocabulary as exercised in "The Editor to the Reader," from the second part of *Clarissa*: epistolary fiction, in its recording of the impressions that "*Things present*" make on the characters, "leads us farther into the recesses of the Human Mind, than the colder more general reflections suited to a continued and more contracted Narrative" (4:v).

36. In the paragraphs that follow the comic peripety or discovery of Square, Fielding admits he has done some "prying" in the closets of philosophers: "certain Books and Pictures find their way into the most private Recesses of [the philosopher's] Study, and a certain liquorish Part of natural Philosophy is often the principal Subject of their Conversation" (2:148). The closet is a convenient place to hide (and converse with) pornography. A good part of the comedy in the scene results from placing Square, a seeker after "conversation," in the closet of another, or rather a "little Hole" in which he is ranked among Molly's other "female Utensils" (2:144–5). As is usual in Fielding's comedy of penetration, interiors, not interiorities, are pried open and looked into.

37. Although when Boswell repeats a sentence overheard in Minorca—"a man's mind grows narrow in a narrow place,"—with pointed pedantry, Johnson takes the opportunity to revise the assertion: "A man's mind grows narrow in a narrow place, whose mind is enlarged only because he has lived in a large place: but what is got by books and thinking is preserved in a narrow place as well as in a large place." James Boswell, *The Life of Samuel Johnson* (Henry Baldwin, 1791), 2:200.

38. *The Guardian* (J. Tonson, 1714), 1:155. Peter Walmsley identifies this freethinker as Anthony Collins in "Guardian #39: Berkeley's Allegory of Mind," in *Enlightening Allegory: Theory, Practice, and Contexts of Allegory in the Late Seventeenth and Eighteenth Centuries*, ed. Kevin L. Cope (New York: AMS, 1993), 373–88.

39. Shenstone, *Works* (R. and J. Dodsley, 1764), 1:261.

40. *A Pindarick Ode* (E.W., 1696), 17.

41. In Hume's *Treatise*, animal spirits "rummage" cells in the brain for ideas (I. ii.5). See also *Tristram Shandy*, (R. and J. Dodsley, 1761), where Sterne surveys the "veral receptacles, cells, cellules, domiciles, dormitories, refectories, and spare places of our brains" (3:88).

42. "Cell" is a preferred term among natural philosophers and anatomists. Johnson defines "CELL" as "1. A small cavity or hollow place, 2. The cave or habitation of a religious person, 3. A small close apartment in a prison, 4. Any small place of residence." Two of the illustrations (for sense 1 and sense 4) involve metaphors of mind. For the first sense Prior is cited: "The brain contains ten thousand *cells*, / In each some active fancy dwells"; and for the fourth sense, Milton, "Mine eyes he clos'd, but open left the *cell* / Of fancy, my internal sight."

43. *The Works of Mr. Henry Needler* (J. Watts, 1724), 18. I cite Terry Castle on the spectralization or "ghostifying" of the mental spaces in **Inhabitants** and **Mirror**.

44. Lennox, *Female Quixote* (A Millar, 1752), 2:3.

45. *Rise of the Novel*, 175.

46. See John W. Yolton, *John Locke and the Way of Ideas* (London: Oxford UP, 1956).

47. "Homunculus," "Cartesian Theater," and "Cartesian Spectator" are terms of art exercised in the philosophy of Daniel Dennett, from whom I draw in the present paragraph. On using homunculi in psychology, see Daniel C. Dennett, *Brainstorms: Philosophical Essays on Mind and Psychology* (Cambridge, MA: MIT P, 1978), 122. Dennett discusses homunculi in several of his works. The foregoing citation places them in the context of British empiricism and what Dennett calls "Hume's Problem."

48. In the sixth meditation Descartes writes, "Nature also teaches me, by these sensations or pain, hunger, thirst and so on, that I am not merely present in my body as a sailor is present in a ship, but that I am very closely joined and, as it were, intermingled with it." *Philosophical Writings*, 1:56. The picture follows so naturally that Descartes takes pains to deny it.

49. On Locke's "architectural and spatial vocabulary," see Varey, *Space*, 58–9.

50. S. H. Clark identifies the "*dark Room*" as the single most famous image in the *Essay*. Clark characterizes the "domesticity of Locke's images of constriction" as

making the image particularly effective and explores long eighteenth-century resonances in Blake's "Five windows" that "light the cavern'd Man," Plato's cave, and the "dark closet" in which Newton performed his optical experiments. See S. H. Clark, "'The Whole Internal World His Own': Locke and Metaphor Reconsidered," *Journal of the History of Ideas* 59:2 (1998): 246–7.

51. This clever suggestion is S. H. Clark's. See "Locke and Metaphor," 247n25. In the footnote Clark points us specifically to Newton's *Opticks* (London, 1704), III.ii, 18, but the "dark chamber" or "dark Room" is named in any number of experiments, for example, I.ii ("dark Chamber") and III.i ("dark Room").

52. *The Grand Impostor Discovered* (B. Harris, 1675), 209.

53. *All for Love* (H. Herringman, 1692), 38.

54. *Pamela: or, Virtue Rewarded*, vol. 4 (S. Richardson, 1742), 335.

55. Pamela's explication of the lines centers on Dryden's sentiment "Men are but Children of a larger Growth" (*Pamela*, 4:335). She has nothing to say about the dark room or the inhabiting mole, although Miss Goodwin's dairy house may be seen as a kind of opposite: the school of the breast, or the self's room abroad. In something like a parody or demonstration of Lockean associationism, Pamela rambles without "Method" or "Connexion" and pictures her struggles—by extension all essays of female knowledge—as a babe much in need of swaddling. The passage is rich with ambiguity; Pamela's comments read as both patent misogyny and something more suggestive.

56. See *Essays on the Law of Nature* (Oxford: Oxford UP, 2002), 139. Cited in Clark, "Locke and Metaphor," 247.

57. Swift, *A Tale of a Tub*, 160–1; Fielding, *Tom Jones*, 2:224.

58. Soame Jenyns, *Poems* (R. Dodsley, 1752), 176.

59. See, for example, Daniel L. Sepper's *Newton's Optical Writings: A Guided Study* (New Brunswick, NJ: Rutgers UP, 1994), book I, part ii, experiment 1.

60. Where William Walker would separate a picture of interiority out from one of writing, I believe that the two need not be incompatible. See Walker, *Locke, Literary Criticism, and Philosophy* (Cambridge: Cambridge UP, 1994), 34. See also my discussion of the "white Paper" metaphor in **Writing**. Walker argues that Locke prefers container metaphors to paper metaphors. I am not sure that they are easily separated in the imagination of the period. Another critic who has commented on Locke's use of writing and room metaphors as "mutually exclusive analogues" is Michael S. Kearns: "How could the mind be like both white paper and a monarch? How could it both possess a presence-room and be a closet?" Kearns poses his rhetorical questions in the context of Sir William Hamilton's complaints about Locke's "figurative, ambiguous, vacillating, various, and even contradictory" philosophy. See *Metaphors of Mind in Fiction and Psychology* (Lexington: UP of Kentucky, 1987), 48–9. I hope that I have filled in Locke's picture of the mind both here and in **Writing** so that it is clear that interiors may well include paper surfaces and, more often than not, an occupant.

61. The French materialist Julien Offray de la Mettrie was also sensitive to these figures and literalized them in *Man, a Machine*, in which he described the process by which ideas are engraved on the "*medullar canvas*" of the brain. See Julien Offray de la Mettrie, *Man, a Machine, and Man, a Plant*, ed. Justin Leiber (Indianapolis: Hackett, 1994), 43. As in Jenyns's poem, metaphors of optics, writing, and interiority are brought together in La Mettrie's figures.

62. William Gilpin, *Three Essays* (R. Blamire, 1792), 52.

63. In the patristic tradition, the figure follows from Origen's reading of the wall and latticed window in his commentary on the Canticles. See Ruth H. Cline, "Heart and Eyes," *Romance Philology* 25:3 (February 1972): 286–7.

64. On the origin of the conceit and the ambivalence between "window" and "mirror," see M. B. Ogle, "The Classical Origin and Tradition of Literary Conceits," *American Journal of Philology* 34:2 (1913): 135n, 136–7.

65. *Letters of Mr Pope, and Several Eminent Persons* (T. Cooper, 1735), 1:152. On the metaphor and the related heart language of recesses, see Ann Jessie Van Sant, *Sensibility and the Novel: The Senses in Social Context* (Cambridge: Cambridge UP, 1993), 60–4.

66. John Wilson, *Belphegor: or, The Marriage of the Devil* (J. Leake, 1691), 50. *An Extract of the Rev. Mr. John Wesley's Journal, From Sep. 2, 1770, to Sep. 12, 1773* (R. Hawes, 1777), 42.

67. Toulmin's essay on inwardness and interiority departs from Sterne's conceit. See Toulmin, "Inwardness," 1. So does Judith Frank's essay on characterization, "'A Man Who Laughs Is Never Dangerous': Character and Class in Sterne's *A Sentimental Journey*," *English Literary History* 56:1 (1989). Dorrit Cohn opens her study on narrative modes for presenting consciousness with the passage from Sterne placed in contrast with a passage from Hoffman (*Minds* 3).

68. Mandeville, *Fable of the Bees. Part II* (J. Roberts, 1729), 191–2; Burney, *Cecilia*, ed. Peter Sabor and Margaret Doody (Oxford: Oxford UP, 1999), 945.

69. C. S. Lewis, *Studies in Words*, 2nd ed. (Cambridge: Cambridge UP, 1967), 15.

70. Mandeville, *The Fable of the Bees* (J. Roberts, 1714), 120.

71. On the changes in interior decoration, see Cynthia Wall, *The Prose of Things: Transformations of Description in the Eighteenth Century* (Chicago: U of Chicago P, 2006), 177–200; and Tristram, *Space*, 5.

72. Pope, *The Rape of the Lock* (Bernard Lintott, 1714), 7.

73. In Roger Lonsdale, ed., *Eighteenth-Century Women Poets* (Oxford: Oxford UP, 1989), 346, l. 14.

74. Holcroft, *The Deserted Daughter* (G. G. and J. Robinson, 1795), 20.

75. *Clarissa* (S. Richardson, 1748), 6:261. Richardson is pleased enough with the metaphor that it appears twice in his novels. Its first appearance is in *Pamela*, a novel in which the character's shop signs are much easier to make out: "For, as I have heard you, my best Tutor, often observe, the Peculiarities of Habit, where a Person aims at something fantastick, or out of Character, are an undoubted Sign of a wrong Head:

For such an one is so kind, as always to hang out on his Sign, what sort of Furniture he has in his Shop, to save you the Trouble of asking Questions about him; so that one may know what he *is*, as much as one can know a Widow by her Weeds." *Pamela*, 4:338.

76. "Verses Written at Sixteen," in *The Works of John Hookham Frere in Verse and Prose* (London: Pickering, 1872): 1:34.

77. See, for example, my discussion of the "court of conscience" in **Court**, "mettle" in **Metal**, or my discussions of the Stamp Acts and iron gall ink in **Writing**.

78. See also the opening pages of the *Treatise* (I.i.2), in which Hume shuts his eyes and thinks on his chamber: "the ideas I form are exact representations of the impressions I felt."

79. *A Treatise Concerning the Principles of Human Knowledge* (Dublin: Jeremy Pepyat, 1710), 85.

80. *Poetical Works*, ed. R. I. Woodhouse, 2 vols. (London: Leadenhall, 1896), 1:152.

81. *Pace* McKeon. I've found only one "cabinet of curiosities" in my searches, and it is not an eighteenth-century example. Charles Lamb writes, "Not that I affect ignorance—but my head has not many mansions, nor spacious; and I have been obliged to fill it with such cabinet curiosities as it can hold without aching." *The Essays of Elia*, ed. Malcolm Elwin (London: Macdonald, 1952).

82. Swift, *Travels into Several Remote Nations of the World. By Lemuel Gulliver*, 2nd ed., 2 vols. (Benj. Motte, 1726), 2:111.

83. Katherine Philips, *Poems* (H. Herringman, 1667), 48; Penelope Aubin, *The Strange Adventures of the Count De Vinevil and His Family* (E. Bell, J. Darby, A. Bettesworth, F. Fayram, J. Pemberton, J. Hooke, C. Rivington, F. Clay, J. Batley, and E. Symon, 1721), 12.

84. On the storehouse image, see Chris Westbury and Daniel C. Dennett, "Mining the Past to Construct the Future: Memory and Belief as Forms of Knowledge," in *Memory, Brain, and Belief*, ed. Daniel L. Schacter and Elaine Scarry (Cambridge, MA: Harvard UP, 2000), 16.

85. For example, Tom Telescope, *The Newtonian System of Philosophy Adapted to the Capacities of Young Gentlemen and Ladies* (John Newbery, 1761), 100.

86. Pope, *The Dunciad, in Four Books* (M. Cooper, 1743), 168.

87. First published in 1704–5. I quote from the slightly longer version in Prior's *Poems* (Jacob Tonson, 1708), 106, 108.

88. Danielle Bobker provided an impressive list of these in her "Printed Cabinets and Intimate Publics," a conference paper presented at the Thirty-Sixth Annual Meeting of American Society for Eighteenth-Century Studies, Las Vegas (2005). The surprising range of titles surveyed include cookbooks, dictionaries, religious tracts, poetry anthologies, secret correspondences, and pornographic collections. See also Ruth Perry, who observes that invasion is often signaled in the titles of epistolary novels: "The most unholy thing in these books is uninvited access to another's inner life,

and that is just what such novels offer, even in their titles: *A Lady's Packet of Letters Broke Open*; *The Post-Boy Rob'd of His Mail*; *The Cabinet Opened.*" Perry, *Women*, 131.

89. *Tristram Shandy*, 2nd ed. (T. Becket and P. A. Dehondt, 1767), 6:13–4. See Mark Loveridge, *Laurence Sterne and the Argument about Design* (London: Macmillan, 1982), 102–3. Loveridge discusses this passage in light of "a *man within*."

90. *Works*, 1:252, iii, l. 507

91. *Bacchanalia: or, A Description of a Drunken Club* (Robert Boulter, 1680), 11.

92. See Locke, *Essay*, IV.i.1. A. D. Nuttall analyzes eighteenth-century skepticism in the context of solipsism and metaphysical confinement in *A Common Sky: Philosophy and the Literary Imagination* (London: Chatto and Windus, 1974), 13–44. Ronald Paulson reads Locke's dark room as a prison and sees Hogarth, a habitual painter of interiors and confinements, as producing the "definitive image that dark room of the mind by which Locke's figured the process of perception." *The Art of Hogarth* (London: Phaidon, 1974), 14, quoted in John Bender, *Imagining the Penitentiary: Fiction and the Architecture of Mind in Eighteenth-Century England* (Chicago: U of Chicago P, 1987), 111. See also Paulson, *Emblem and Expression: Meaning in English Art of the Eighteenth Century* (Cambridge, MA: Harvard UP, 1975), 45.

93. See *Thoughts on Man* (London: 1831), 11.

94. Arwaker, *Pia Desideria*, 4th ed., corr. (R. and J. Bonwicke, 1712), 205; *The Odyssey of Homer*, 5 vols. (Bernard Lintot, 1725–26), 1:209.

95. Hay, *Deformity, An Essay*, 2nd ed. (R. and J. Dodsley, 1754), 71–2.

96. Toulmin, "Inwardness," 13.

97. *The Man of Feeling* (T. Cadell, 1771), 25.

98. Wollstonecraft, *A Vindication of the Rights of Woman* (J. Johnson, 1792), 90.

99. Fielding, *The Wedding-Day* (A. Millar, 1743), V.iv, 70.

100. Inchbald, *Every One Has His Fault* (G. G. J. and J. Robinson, 1793), 17.

101. Shaftesbury, *The Moralists* (John Wyat, 1709), 3; Addison, *Spectator*, no. 10, 1:44.

102. *An Enquiry Concerning Political Justice* (G. G. J. and J. Robinson, 1793), 2:388.

103. Boswell compares Johnson's mind to "the Colisaeum at Rome" in *Life of Johnson*, 1:329.

104. Daniel Dennett's object in *Consciousness Explained* is to replace a traditional model of conscious, a model he calls the "Cartesian Theater," with his own "Multiple Drafts" model of consciousness. See *Consciousness Explained* (Boston: Little, Brown, 1991), 17. Dennett swaps a **Room** metaphor for a **Writing** metaphor.

105. John O'Brien, *Harlequin Britain: Pantomime and Entertainment, 1690–1760* (Baltimore: Johns Hopkins UP, 2004), 76–85; Joseph R. Roach, *The Player's Passion: Studies in the Science of Acting* (Newark: U of Delaware P, 1985), 62–92.

106. John Loftis, "Richard Steele's Censorium," *Huntington Library Quarterly* 14:1 (1950): 43–66.

107. Johnstone, *Chrysal; or, The Adventures of a Guinea* (T. Becket, 1760), 8.

108. Ramsay, *An Essay on the Treatment and Conversion of African Slaves* (James Phillips, 1784), 214.

109. *The First Volume of Letters Writ by a Turkish Spy*, 2nd ed. (Henry Rhodes, 1691), 211.

110. Fielding, *The Temple Beau* (J. Watts, 1730), 3.

111. Davys, *The Reform'd Coquet* (H. Woodfall, 1724), 18.

112. *Alma: or, The Progress of the Mind* (J. Tonson and J. Barber, 1718), 321.

113. Ephesians 3:17 reads, "That Christ may dwell in your hearts by faith."

114. *The Poetical Works of Thomas Chatterton* (George Bell, 1875), 152.

115. In *A Tale of a Tub*, Swift's Hack claims *court* "in the Phoenician tongue is a word of great signification, importing if literally interpreted, *the place of sleep*" (26).

116. Goldsmith, *Vicar of Wakefield* (Salisbury: B. Collins, 1766), 2:85–6.

117. The prison is described in chapter 27, p. 153. On Goldsmith's anticipation of later eighteenth-century prison reforms, see John Bender, "Prison Reform and the Sentence of Narration in *The Vicar of Wakefield*," in *The New Eighteenth Century*, ed. Felicity Nussbaum and Laura Brown (New York: Methuen, 1987), 170–3.

118. The closet-parlor formulation is Philippa Tristram's; the public-private one is, of course, Jürgen Habermas's. See Tristram's *Space*, 12, 250. Habermas avails himself of architectural analogies: "The privatization of life can be observed in a change in architectural style." *The Structural Transformation of the Public Sphere: An Inquiry into a Category of Bourgeois Society*, trans. Thomas Burger (Cambridge, MA: MIT P, 1999), 44. Public and private, inner and outer are not facile distinctions: "Subjectivity, as the innermost core of the private, was always already oriented to an audience." The subjectivity, in Habermas's jargon, is "audience-oriented subjectivity." The private sphere is a place where private people come together as if in public, to practice publicity in a domestic setting. The public sphere is an "expansion" and "completion" of the private sphere: "Living room and *salon* were under the same roof" (49–50).

119. See also Anthony Kenny's claim, "If we say that he did the arithmetic 'in his head' this does not give a further localization which is more precise than the localization 'at his desk.'" *Metaphysics of Mind*, 27.

Writing

1. Writing metaphors make up 5.3% of all the eighteenth-century metaphors collected in the database. After the first two decades of the period, a reliable number of these metaphors are found in nonfiction prose and prose fiction, especially in epistolary fiction. I also mark a slight decline in frequency in the last decade of the century.

2. Paper and its inscription matter much in *Paper Machine*, a late collection of punning pieces in which Derrida looks back over a career in which he has "always written, and even spoken, *on* paper" and admits that he has "never had any other *subject*." *Paper Machine*, trans. Rachel Bowlby (Stanford, CA: Stanford UP, 2005), 41. In a chapter that has informed this entry's readings, Christina Lupton arraigns

deictic invocations of "this paper" by Hume and Beattie alongside those of de Man and Derrida. In "The Theory of Paper," in *Knowing Books: The Consciousness of Mediation in Eighteenth-Century Britain* (Philadelphia: U of Pennsylvania P, 2012). See also Christopher Flint, who follows a great number of critics in describing paper and ink as "primary symbols of a new form of subjectivity," with paper serving as a "metaphor" for "self-expressive identity." *The Appearance of Print in Eighteenth-Century Fiction* (Cambridge: Cambridge UP, 2011), 80, 96. I have benefited from Michael McKeon's dialectical presentation of publication and personality in the period: *The Secret History of Domesticity: Public, Private, and the Division of Knowledge* (Baltimore: Johns Hopkins UP, 2005), 83–88.

3. Frances Ferguson, "Rape and the Rise of the Novel," *Representations* 20 (Autumn 1987): 105.

4. On reading as master metaphor in the humanities and for bookish metaphors of mind more generally, see Leah Price's chapter "Reader's Block," in *How to Do Things with Books in Victorian Britain* (Princeton, NJ: Princeton UP, 2012).

5. See, for example, Nancy Armstrong's claim that "the history of the novel and the history of the modern subject are, quite literally, one and the same," in *How Novels Think: The Limits of Individualism from 1719–1900* (New York: Columbia UP, 2005), 3. "Quite literally"—one wonders what that means in this context.

6. Robert Adams Day's *Told in Letters: Epistolary Fiction before Richardson* (Ann Arbor: U of Michigan P, 1966) remains a useful introduction to the epistolary representation of interior motions and mental monologue. See pp. 97–8, 120–32. I also rely here on Elizabeth Heckendorn Cook's *Epistolary Bodies: Gender and Genre in the Eighteenth-Century Republic of Letters* (Stanford, CA: Stanford UP, 1992).

7. See Ludwig Wittgenstein, *Philosophical Investigations*, trans. G. E. M. Anscombe, 3rd ed. (New York: Blackwell, 2001), §422–4.

8. See Kenneth MacLean's observation that "the tabula rasa itself is to be found in the writings of Aristotle, and has reappeared in one form or another all through the ages." *John Locke and English Literature of the Eighteenth Century* (New York: Russell and Russell, 1962), 32. Richard Rorty contrasts Aristotle and Locke in *Philosophy and the Mirror of Nature* (Princeton, NJ: Princeton UP, 1979), 144. S. H. Clark emphasizes that Locke's originality "lies in his connecting [the image] with the continual temporal erosion of consciousness itself." "'The Whole Internal World His Own': Locke and Metaphor Reconsidered," *Journal of the History of Ideas* 59:2 (1998): 253.

9. *European Literature and the Latin Middle Ages*, Bollingen Series 36 (Princeton, NJ: Princeton UP, 1990), 304.

10. *Phaedrus*, 276a. A standard set piece of Derridean deconstruction analyzes the "paradoxical" overlay of literal and figurative claims for and against writing in the dialogue. See *Of Grammatology*, trans. Gayatri Chakravorty Spivak (Baltimore: Johns Hopkins UP, 1997), 15; and "Plato's Pharmacy," in *Dissemination*, trans. Barbara John-

son (Chicago: U of Chicago P, 1981). See also Hannah Arendt, *The Life of the Mind* (San Diego: Harcourt, 1978), 116; and Charles L. Griswold, *Self-Knowledge in Plato's "Phaedrus"* (New Haven, CT: Yale UP), 210–1.

11. Quoted in Frederick Kiefer, *Writing on the Renaissance Stage: Written Words, Printed Pages, Metaphoric Books* (Newark: University of Delaware Press, 1996), 120. The earliest paper metaphor I have collected is from Aetius (ca. 100 A.D.). See A. A. Long and D. N. Sedley, eds., *The Hellenistic Philosophers* (Cambridge: Cambridge UP, 1987), 1:238.

12. Stefano Guazzo, *The Art of Conversation* (J. Brett, 1738), 228. Compare *The Ciuile Conversation of Stephano Guazzo*, trans. George Pettie (Richard Watkins, 1581), 27.

13. Richard Hooker, *Of the Lavves of Ecclesiasticall Politie*, 2nd ed. (Iohn Windet, 1604), 56. Neal Wood observes that Hooker's is "perhaps the best known" early modern example. "Tabula Rasa, Social Environmentalism, and the 'English Paradigm,'" *Journal of the History of Ideas* 53:4 (1992): 652. See also Kiefer, *Writing on the Renaissance Stage*, 122.

14. Montaigne and Charron cited in Louis I. Bredvold, *The Intellectual Milieu of John Dryden: Studies in Some Aspects of Seventeenth-Century Thought* (Ann Arbor: U of Michigan P, 1956), 32, 35.

15. Hooker, *Of the Lavves of Ecclesiasticall Politie*, 56.

16. *Reason: A Poem* (J. Nutt, 1700), 8.

17. Kenneth MacLean cites John Earle's "A Childe," in which the infant soul is pictured as "a white paper vnscirbled with obseruations of the world, wherewith at length it becomes a blurr'd Note-booke." *Locke and English Literature of the Eighteenth Century* (1936; repr., New York: Russell and Russell, 1962), 33. Samuel Speed asserts that the infant soul "appears like Paper white, / That yet had scarce bore word aright." *Prison-Pietie* (printed by J.C. for S.S., 1677), 76, ll. 6–7.

18. See Wood, "Environmentalism," 658. See also David Johnson, *The Rhetoric of Leviathan: Thomas Hobbes and the Politics of Cultural Transformation* (Princeton, NJ: Princeton UP, 1986), 89.

19. Thomas Hobbes, *The Elements of Law, Natural & Politic*, ed. Ferdinand Tönnies (Cambridge: Cambridge UP, 1928), 39, 146; *Leviathan* (Andrew Crooke, 1651), 176.

20. For a recent example, see Steven Pinker, *The Blank Slate: The Modern Denial of Human Nature* (New York: Viking, 2002), 5. Jenny Davidson's is a sharp and welcome correction of Pinker's misinterpretations of Locke. See her *Breeding: A Partial History of the Eighteenth Century* (New York: Columbia UP, 2009), 39–45.

21. See Philip Vogt, "Seascape with Fog: Metaphor in Locke's *Essay*," *Journal of the History of Ideas* 54:1 (1993): 13. See also William Walker, *Locke, Literary Criticism, and Philosophy* (Cambridge: Cambridge UP, 1994), 31–2 (quoted in text); and Erling Eng, "Locke's Tabula Rasa and Freud's 'Mystic Writing Pad,'" *Journal of the History of Ideas* 41:1 (1980): 137. Locke does invoke the tabula rasa in early writing on the law of nature: "the newly born are just empty tablets." See John Locke, *Essays on the Law*

of Nature, ed. W. von Leyden (Oxford: Oxford UP, 1988), 137. In draft B of the *Essay* he writes, "at first [the soul] is perfectly rasa tabula, quite void but altogether capable of those characters notions of ideas which are proper objects of our understanding." See John W. Yolton, *A Locke Dictionary*, Blackwell Philosopher Dictionaries (Cambridge, MA: Blackwell, 1993), 288–9.

22. See, for example, John Napleton, *Advice to a Student in the University* (Oxford: Fletcher and Hanwell, 1795), 91. William Oldisworth remarks on the difference between the ancient and modern metaphor in the preface to *A Dialogue Between Timothy and Philatheus* (Bernard Lintot, 1709–11), iii [a].

23. Yolton, *A Locke Dictionary*, 100. Yolton also cites examples from William Sclater, Matthew Hale, Nathaniel Culverwell, and Samuel Parker. See also Brian Cummings, "Book as Symbol," in *The Book: A Global History*, ed. Michael F. Suarez and H. R. Woudhuysen (Oxford: Oxford UP, 2013), 94.

24. See G. A. J. Rogers, "Locke, Newton, and the Cambridge Platonists on Innate Ideas," *Journal of the History of Ideas* 40:2 (1979): 192.

25. Walker, *Locke, Literary Criticism, and Philosophy*, 34. See also Joanna Picciotto, *Labors of Innocence in Early Modern England* (Cambridge, MA: Harvard UP, 2010), 261.

26. Howard's play is cited in MacLean, *Locke and Literature*, 33.

27. "Third Remarks Upon an Essay Concerning Human Understanding," in *Remarks Upon an Essay Concerning Human Understanding: Five Tracts* (New York: Garland, 1984), 7.

28. The figure finds its way into *Critique of Pure Reason*, where in Kant's account of schematism, the schemata that ground pure sensible concepts are compared to monograms. See *Critique of Pure Reason*, trans. Paul Guyer and Allen W. Wood (Cambridge: Cambridge UP, 1998), A142/B181; see also Arendt, *Life of the Mind*, 101.

29. David Pearson, *Provenance Research in Book History: A Handbook* (New Castle, DE: Oak Knoll, 1994), 16–9, 119–22.

30. Compare Wood, "Environmentalism," 649.

31. Burnet, "Third Remarks," 4. See also Jeremiah 31:33 and Hebrews 8:10. Henry Brooke refers to the same passage as Burnet. See *The Fool of Quality* (Dublin: printed for the author by Dillon Chamberlaine, 1765), IV.i.96–7.

32. See also Pierre de la Primaudaye's *The French Académie*, which mixes metaphors of the law written and white paper. Cited in Kiefer, *Writing on the Renaissance Stage*, 118, 120. Hooker also pictures the soul as a "book, wherein nothing is writ" and the soul as containing the law of nature. Compare Wood, "Environmentalism," 653.

33. John Locke, *Two Treatises of Government* (Awnsham Churchill, 1690), 229.

34. *The Mirror and the Lamp: Romantic Theory and the Critical Tradition* (Oxford: Oxford UP, 1953), 57.

35. See the example cited by Christopher Flint in *The Appearance of Print*, 81. The text, quoted from a late eighteenth-century novel reads, "Our minds are like blank

paper, as a great philosopher has observed." Flint calls this an "explicit" Lockean reference. I am not so sure.

36. John Grose, *Ethics, Rational and Theological* (I. Moore, 1782), 431.

37. Ralph Cudworth, *A Treatise Concerning Eternal and Immutable Morality* (James and John Knapton, 1731), 287.

38. For a comparison of Cudworth's and Locke's use of the image, see Charles Taylor, *Sources of the Self: The Making of the Modern Identity* (Cambridge, MA: Harvard UP, 1989), 165.

39. Preface to *The First Volume of Letters Writ by a Turkish Spy, Who Lived Five and Forty Years, Undiscover'd at Paris*, 20th ed. (J. Rhodes, D. Brown, R. Sare, B. and S. Tooke, G. Strahan, W. Mears, S. Ballard, and F. Clay, 1723).

40. *The Dictionary Historical and Critical of Mr Peter Bayle*, 2nd ed., 5 vols. (D. Midwinter, J. Brotherton, A. Bettesworth, C. Hitch, and J. Hazard, 1734–8), 4:81.

41. Matthew Henry, *A Sermon Preach'd at the Ordination of Mr. Atkinson* (J. Lawrence, R. Robinson, N. Cliff, and D. Jackson, 1713), 20.

42. Robert South, *Twelve Sermons* (Thomas Bennett, 1692), 306.

43. William Sherlock, *A Discourse Concerning the Happiness of Good Men, and the Punishment of the Wicked, in the Next World* (W. Rogers, 1704), 138.

44. Bernard Mandeville, *Fable of the Bees. Part II* (J. Roberts, 1729), 168. Abel Evans, *Prae-Existence. A Poem, In Imitation of Milton* (John Clark, 1714), 113.

45. Philip Gaskell, *A New Introduction to Bibliography* (Oxford: Oxford UP, 1972), 65–6.

46. After 1814, John Bell widely advertises an edition of Locke's *Treatise* in a series titled British Constitutional Classics that is printed on "beautiful wove paper."

47. David Allan, *Commonplace Books and Reading in Georgian England* (Cambridge: Cambridge UP, 2010), 51–2, 64–7. Barbara Benedict claims that John Bell's commonplace book "attempts to shape his readers' subjectivity to fit print." *Making the Modern Reader: Cultural Mediation in Early Modern Literary Anthologies* (Princeton, NJ: Princeton UP, 1996), 60.

48. "Popular Works Just Published by John Walker," p. 2 of 4, inserted after *New Monthly Magazine* 10 (1818).

49. Eliza Haywood, *The British Recluse* (D. Brown, Jun., W. Chetwood, J. Woodman, and S. Chapman, 1722), 23.

50. Jürgen Habermas writes, "In the age of sentimentality letters were containers for the 'outpourings of the heart.' . . . In the jargon of the time . . . the letter was considered an 'imprint of the soul,' a 'visit of the soul'; letters were to be written in the heart's blood, they practically were wept." *The Structural Transformation of the Public Sphere: An Inquiry into a Category of Bourgeois Society*, trans. Thomas Burger (Cambridge: MIT P, 1999), 49.

51. Robert Lloyd, "The Cobler of Tissington's Letter to David Garrick, Esq. 1761," *St. James's Magazine* (W. Flexney, T. Davies, and J. Coote, 1764), 2:68.

52. Discussed in Ian Watt's *Rise of the Novel: Studies in Defoe, Richardson, and Fielding* (Berkeley: U of California P, 1957), 191. But see also Cook on Watt's failure to read Johnson's ironic citation of an "idée recue." *Epistolary Bodies*, 16, 86. See also Tom Keymer, *Richardson's "Clarissa" and the Eighteenth-Century Reader* (Cambridge: Cambridge UP, 1992), 1–15.

53. Jonathan Lamb has written insightfully on "tautologies" and "double principles." See, for example, Lamb on "writing on writing" in *The Rhetoric of Suffering: Reading the Book of Job in the Eighteenth Century* (Oxford: Oxford UP, 1995), 87–8. See also his *Sterne's Fiction and the Double Principle* (Cambridge: Cambridge UP, 1989).

54. Sarah Scott, *Millenium Hall* (J. Newbery, 1762), 1–2.

55. Frances Burney, *Evelina, or, a Young Lady's Entrance into the World*, 3 vols. (T. Lowndes, 1778), 3:261.

56. Anonymous, *Remarkable Trials and Interesting Memoirs*, 2 vols. (W. Nicoll, 1765), 1:v.

57. *A Collection of English Proverbs Digested into a Convenient Method for the Speedy Finding Any One upon Occasion: with Short Annotations* (Cambridge: W. Morden, 1678), 24. I quibble here with Dror Wahrman, who claims that, following Locke, there is a new eighteenth-century emphasis on a "child's susceptibility to the formative influences." *Modern Self*, 200. I do not find the shift in the metaphor's usage from devotional to pedagogical uses that Wahrman contends for.

58. John Locke, *Some Thoughts Concerning Education* (A. and J. Churchill, 1693), 261.

59. On Duck's education, see Joseph Spence, *A Full and Authentick Account of Stephen Duck* (J. Roberts, 1731); I quote from p. 10. Verses from *Hints to a Schoolmaster* (J. Roberts and R. Dodsley, 1741), 3.

60. Barry Gaines suggests that such "confusion of long *s* and *f* is common," even in the eighteenth century. "A Textual Emendation in *A Yorkshire Tragedy*: Confusion of *ſ* and *f*," *Library* 27:2 (June 1972): 143. David Vander Meulen brought the Gaines article to my attention and also pointed me to a *New York Times* letter to the editor (August 7, 1990) in which Gordon Messing corrects Hester Thrale's "misreporting" of Samuel Johnson's description of the "sutile work" of needlepoint as "futile work," another confusion of the *s* and *f*.

61. The same image is used in Swift's correspondence but with very different effect. Musing over improvements at Moor Park, Swift writes, "I have heard it is very much changed for the better, as well as the gardens. The tree on which I carved those words *factura nepotibus umbram*, is one of those elms that stand in the hollow ground . . . but I suppose the letters are widened and grown shapeless by time." See Melinda Alliker Rabb, "'Soft Figures' and 'a Pastes of Composition Rare': Pope, Swift, and Memory," in *Studies in Eighteenth-Century Culture* 19 (1989): 193.

62. Walter Harte, *An Essay on Reason*, 3rd ed. (Lawton Gilliver, 1735), 10.

63. For example, MacLean, *Locke and Literature*, 39; Clark, "Locke and Metaphor," 251–2.

64. Thomas Jefferson, *Notes on the State of Virginia* (John Stockdale, 1787), 258; William Godwin, *An Enquiry Concerning Political Justice* (G. G. J. and J. Robinson, 1793), 1:12–18. Pinker makes a point of citing Godwin: "Children are a sort of raw material put into our hands, [their minds] like a sheet of white paper." *Blank Slate*, 11.

65. *Memoirs of Emma Courtney*, 2 vols. (G. G. and J. Robinson, 1796), 1:35–6.

66. *A Vindication of the Rights of Woman* (J. Johnson, 1792), 427.

67. Samuel Whyte, *A Collection of Poems on Various Subjects* (Dublin: Robert Marchbank, 1792), 75.

68. See the second part of Charles Brockden Brown's *Arthur Mervyn* (New York: George F. Hopkins, 1800), 208: "The pen is a pacifyer. It checks the mind's career; it circumscribes her wanderings."

69. Delarivier Manley, *Memoirs of Europe* (John Morphew, 1710), 44; Charles Churchill, *An Epistle to William Hogarth* (J. Coote and by J. Gardiner, 1763), 647–8.

70. Alexander Pope, *The First Satire of the Second Book of Horace, Imitated* (Lawton Gilliver, 1733), 11, 7.

71. *Pamela: or, Virtue Rewarded*, vol. 4 (S. Richardson, 1742), 14.

72. I thank my anonymous reader for Johns Hopkins University Press for pointing out the double entendre to me. See also Janet E. Aikins on "blank" and "blot" in "Pamela's Use of Locke's Words," *Studies in Eighteenth-Century Culture* 25 (1996): 86–8.

73. *Spectator* no. 10, in *The Spectator*, ed. D. F. Bond, 5 vols. (Oxford: Clarendon, 1965), 1:46.

74. Elizabeth Griffith, *The Platonic Wife* (W. Johnston, J. Dodsley, and T. Davies, 1765), 37. Deidre Lynch connects social practice to the philosophy of Locke: describing how eighteenth-century readers "are invited to personalize the blank spaces of their consciousness in the same ways that they might use transcribed quotations to personalize the blank pages of their commonplace books." *The Economy of Character: Novels, Market Culture, and the Business of Inner Meaning* (Chicago: U of Chicago P, 1998), 34.

75. Edmund Arwaker, *Truth in Fiction* (J. Churchill, 1708), 114.

76. *Buffon's Natural History, Abridged* (C. and G. Kearsley, 1792), 1:76; Bancroft, *Experimental Researches Concerning the Philosophy of Permanent Colours* (T. Cadell, Jun and W. Davies, 1794), 45.

77. Compare Aravamudan, *Tropicopolitans*, 1–2.

78. *The Journal of Frederick Horneman's Travels*, quoted in Mary Louise Pratt, *Imperial Eyes: Travel Writing and Transculturation* (London: Routledge, 1992), 74.

79. See Davidson, "Blots on the Landscape," in *Breeding*, 149–88, especially her discussion of Jefferson's figuring of enslaved Africans as a "blot in our country."

80. Richard Brinsley Sheridan, *The Rivals* (John Wilkie, 1775), 11. I thank Seth Lerer for bringing this particular malapropism to my attention.

81. John Dussinger writes, "The eighteenth-century philosopher's radical analysis of self as momentary consciousness is rendered fictionally in the act of writ-

ing." *The Discourse of the Mind in Eighteenth-Century Fiction* (The Hague: Moton, 1974), 39.

82. Ralph Cudworth, *A Treatise Concerning Eternal and Immutable Morality* (James and John Knapton, 1731), 98.

83. Compare Sheryl O'Donnell, "Mr. Locke and the Ladies: The Indelible Words on the Tabula Rasa," in *Studies in Eighteenth-Century Culture*, 8 (1979): 153.

84. George Berkeley, *A Treatise Concerning the Principles of Human Knowledge* (Aaron Rhames, 1710), 85. Cited also in **Rooms**.

85. Again, see Christina Lupton on Hume's self-conscious references to paper and the wider context of print mediation, in *Knowing Books*, 70–94.

86. Laurence Sterne, *Tristram Shandy* (R. and J. Dodsley, 1761), 3:104.

87. See John Richetti on the "antimetaphoric," literalizing aspects of writing to the moment in *Philosophical Writing: Locke, Berkeley, Hume* (Cambridge, MA: Harvard UP, 1983), 112–3. See also his discussion of Berkeley's metaphorics, which fuse the imagery of language and vision by literalizing the governing metaphor of reading (146).

88. The increase in the frequency of writing metaphors in 1760s poetry is also partly owing to the large number of such metaphors in the Wesleys' hymns, but Richardson and his earliest imitators are, likewise, contributing to the counts in the 1740s and 1750s. Of interest is the continuing high number of writing metaphors in the prose of the 1760s: Richardson's metaphorics—which was not as widely employed in earlier eighteenth-century novels in letters—became *the* metaphorics for the next generation of novelists writing epistolary fiction.

89. In what follows, I cite Angus Ross's edition of *Clarissa* (New York: Penguin Books, 1985). I will be weaving many short snippets of Richardson's text into my own and so draw from my hand-annotated copy of the modern text.

90. Ruth Perry observes, "The epistolary structure dwells on responses to events rather than on the events themselves." *Women, Letters, and the Novel* (New York: AMS, 1980), 86.

91. Janet Gurkin Altman writes, "The Richardsonian writer creates a sense of immediacy, of tension about the events themselves." *Epistolarity: Approaches to a Form* (Columbus: Ohio State UP, 1982), 128. See also Joe Bray on critical doubts about closing the "the gap between 'the event and its transcription,' insisting on a delay, however tiny." *The Epistolary Novel: Representations of Consciousness* (London: Routledge, 2003), 59.

92. See Ferguson, "Rape and the Rise of the Novel," 105. See also Terry Eagleton, *The Rape of Clarissa: Writing, Sexuality, and Class Struggle in Samuel Richardson* (Minneapolis: U of Minnesota P, 1982), 44; and Terry Castle, *Clarissa's Ciphers: Meaning & Disruption in Richardson's "Clarissa"* (Ithaca, NY: Cornell UP, 1982), 154.

93. *Pamela*, 4:287; *The History of Sir Charles Grandison* (S. Richardson, 1754), 7:256.

94. Keymer, *Richardson's "Clarissa,"* 202. See also Elizabeth Heckendorn Cook on Lady Bradshaigh's annotated copy of *Clarissa* as an "emblem" of writing in *Epistolary*

Bodies: Gender and Genre in the Eighteenth-Century Republic of Letters (Stanford, CA: Stanford University Press, 1996), 3.

95. Letter to Sophia Westcomb, in *The Correspondence of Samuel Richardson*, 6 vols. (1804; repr., New York: AMS, 1966), 3:246, quoted in Linda Kauffman, *Discourses of Desire: Gender, Genre, and Epistolary Fictions* (Ithaca, NY: Cornell UP, 1986), 125. Kauffman cites John Carroll, "Epistolary Theory and Practice," in *The Selected Letters of Samuel Richardson* (London: Oxford UP, 1964), 31–5. See also Janet Altman, who observes, "Epistolary language, which is the language of absence, makes present by make-believe." *Epistolarity*, 140.

96. This "character" encodes Lovelace's "Roman style," which we are to imagine decoded, remediated, and made legible in the letter forms of the printed roman type face (1202). When he forges one of Anna's letters, the printed text representing his "additions and connexions" is given an "italic character" (811n). See Castle, *Clarissa's Ciphers*, 161–2. See also Keymer, *Richardson's "Clarissa,"*, 182.

97. See *Clarissa*, 567. Compare Michael McKeon's reading of such fictive minglings as having the "presentational and objective power of drama while escaping its vulnerability to disconfirmation." Tremblings and tears, self-reflexive references to the text, and fictional internal readers contribute reality effects so that "the epistemological status of *Pamela* is difficult to disentangle from Pamela." *The Origins of the English Novel, 1600–1740* (Baltimore: Johns Hopkins UP, 1987), 358.

Conclusion

1. Clark complains of anachronism, prolepsis, and false teleology in standard histories of "Enlightenment" England and argues, instead, for a static hierarchical system giving shape to the long eighteenth century. J. C. D. Clark, *English Society, 1660–1832: Religion, Ideology, and Politics during the Ancien Regime*, 2nd ed. (Cambridge: Cambridge UP, 2003).

2. Tradition weighs upon the present, and in "epochs of revolutionary crisis," the living "conjure up the spirits of the past to their service and borrow from the names, battle slogans, and costumes in order to present the new scene of world history in this time-honoured disguise and borrowed language." Karl Marx, "Eighteenth Brumaire of Louis Bonaparte," *The Marx-Engels Reader*, ed. Robert C. Tucker (New York: Norton, 1978), 595.

3. The historical study of "root" or "constitutive metaphors" informs major works by A. O. Lovejoy, M. H. Abrams, Hans Blumenberg, Richard Rorty, Jacques Derrida, Paul de Man—and other theorists cited in the preceding pages—as well as many recent cognitivist studies.

4. *Body Criticism: Imaging the Unseen in Enlightenment Art and Medicine* (Cambridge, MA: MIT P, 1993), 465. M. H. Abrams writes of a "change in popular epistemology" in the period and "a movement from eighteenth- to early nineteenth-century schemes of the mind" that is "indicated by a mutation of metaphors." *The Mirror and the Lamp: Romantic Theory and the Critical Tradition* (Oxford: Oxford UP, 1953), 57.

5. See C. M. Turbayne, "Berkeley's Two Concepts of Mind," *Philosophy and Phenomenological Research* 20:1 (September 1959): 85–92, at 89.

6. For Berkeley, the Anglican churchman, natural language is further informed by the "the Universal Language of Nature," which is authored by God. *Essay Towards a New Theory of Vision* (Dublin: Rhames, 1709), 172. In the 1733 edition, Berkeley introduces the "Author of Nature" to his discussion of artificial and natural languages. See also comments in on the "grammar" of understanding and the "rational Discourse" of nature in *Siris*, 2nd ed. (W. Innys, C. Hitch, and C. Davis, 1744), §252, §254.

7. I quote Locke on *comprehending* below. Bolingbroke claims that we apply the verbs *perceive*, *discern*, *abstract*, *compound*, and *compare* "figuratively to inward sensations"; perhaps surprisingly, he believes the terms *think* and *know* "signify immediately, and without any figure." *The Philosophical Works* (s.n., 1754), 1:130.

8. Philonous will not allow ideas to mean "Fictions, and Fancies of the Mind," defining them instead as the "immediate Objects of the Understanding." Berkeley, *Three Dialogues* (G. James, 1713), 143.

9. Berkeley, *A Treatise Concerning the Principles of Human Knowledge* (Dublin: Rhames, 1710), 93. Kenneth Winkler characterizes Berkeley's technical vocabulary as "literally true, though metaphorically clothed." "Berkeley and the Doctrine of Signs," in *The Cambridge Companion to Berkeley*, ed. by K. Winkler (Cambridge: Cambridge UP, 2005), 157.

10. The contrast between "Things" and "Objects" is Berkeley's. See *Three Dialogues*, 143. See also David Jules Law, *Rhetoric of Empiricism: Language and Perception from Locke to I. A. Richards* (Ithaca, NY: Cornell UP, 1993), 95.

11. The young philosopher wrote an urgent memorandum in his notebooks on the use of the word "mind" for the "Concrete of Will & understanding." In treating bundles and congeries of ideas, arguments are "Carefully to omit of defining Person." In *Philosophical Commentaries*, no. 713, in *The Works of George Berkeley*, eds. A. A. Luce and T. E. Jessop, 9 vols. (London: Nelson, 1948–57): 1:87. And because Berkeley's arguments against the existence of a material substratum are readily turned against a mental one, R. G. Muehlmann argues that he must not have truly held the position he occasionally forwards in the *Treatise*. See "The Substance of Berkeley's Philosophy," in *Berkeley's Metaphysics: Structural, Interpretive, and Critical Essays*, ed. R. G. Muehlmann (University Park: Pennsylvania State UP, 1995), 89–105.

12. *Treatise*, 48, 50, 135. See also the *Three Dialogues*, in which Philonous forces Hylas to admit that nothing is "like a sensation or idea but another sensation or idea" (41). As recent philosophical discussions have come to insist on point of view or subjective character as the hallmark of consciousness, the standard formulation is that there is something "it is like" to be conscious—*likeness*, but that is as far as it goes. See Jonathan Kramnick's discussion of the "hard problem" of consciousness in *Actions and Objects from Hobbes to Richardson* (Stanford, CA: Stanford UP, 2010), 65–71, 85.

13. Reid, *Essays on the Intellectual Powers of Man* (Edinburgh: John Bell, 1785), 54. Samuel Johnson writes, "The mind is impressed . . . with the resemblance of things

generally unlike, as unlike as intellect and body." Quoted in Alex Page, "Faculty Psychology and Metaphor in Eighteenth-Century Criticism," *Modern Philology* 66:3 (1969): 238.

14. Also termed "indirect empiricism." Baier, *Death and Character: Further Reflections on Hume* (Cambridge, MA: Harvard UP, 2008), 138.

15. G. A. Cohen, *Karl Marx's Theory of History: A Defence* (Princeton, NJ: Princeton UP, 2000), 18.

16. Or, perhaps, what Jerome McGann calls in his article so titled, "Philology in a New Key," *Critical Inquiry* 39:2 (2013). For J. L. Austin, who coins the term "linguistic phenomenology," one uses a "sharpened awareness of words" to sharpen a perception of phenomena. *Philosophical Papers* (Oxford: Oxford UP, 1961), 182. For McGann, the philological effort may return to consciousness the trace of memories preserved in the archive. At one limit, Austin is not doing philosophy at all but literary criticism; at another, McGann's critical impulse carries him past bibliographical description to eschatology.

17. Gilbert Ryle, *The Concept of Mind* (Chicago: U of Chicago P, 1984), 16.

18. Theodor Adorno, *Negative Dialectics* (New York: Continuum, 1973), especially 146–58.

19. I cite Peter de Bolla's *The Architecture of Concepts: The Historical Formulation of Human Rights* (New York: Fordham UP, 2013) as a model of this sort of investigation in the introduction and here find his (metaphorical) descriptions of conceptual structures in terms of geometry and architecture a helpful characterization of the general analogy of language: he writes, "The network of connections . . . can be visualized as stretching across a planar surface, each concept marking its similarity and difference from every other concept on the plane" (42).

20. John Sitter, "About Wit: Locke, Addison, Prior and the Order of Things," *Rhetorics of Order/Ordering Rhetorics in English Neoclassical Literature*, ed. J. Douglas Canfield and J. Paul Hunter (London: Associated UPs, 1989), 145; W. B. Gallie, "Essentially Contested Concepts," *Proceedings of the Aristotelian Society* 56 (1955–6): 167–98.

21. But see Derek Melser's ingeniously argued chapters on mind and metaphor in *The Act of Thinking* (Cambridge, MA: MIT P, 2004).

22. Wilfrid Sellars, *Empiricism and the Philosophy of Mind* (Cambridge, MA: Harvard UP, 1997), 18.

23. "You have discovered these traits together ten times, but have you also counted the times you have not found them together?" So Georg Christoph Lichtenberg demands, in *The Waste Books*, trans. R. J. Hollingdale (New York: New York Review Books, 2000), 102.

24. In the *OED*, stubbornly metaphorical uses of terms are labeled "*fig.*" for "figurative."

25. While I favor the linguistic analysis of Davidson and White, Ricoeur admirably describes the interplay of conceptual and metaphorical orders and gives, I think, one of the best accounts of the historicity of metaphor. Aiming at Derridean para-

doxes of metaphoricity, Ricoeur neatly counters and dismisses "the false enigma of worn-out metaphor." See Paul Ricoeur, *The Rule of Metaphor: Multi-disciplinary Studies of the Creation of Meaning in Language* (Toronto: U of Toronto P, 1977), 290–3, 298–303, quotation at 290.

26. "The concrete is the concrete because it is the concentration of many determinations." Karl Marx, *Grundrisse: Foundations of the Critique of Political Economy*, trans. Martin Nicolaus (New York: Vintage, 1973), 101.

27. Samuel Johnson, *The Plan of a Dictionary of the English Language* (J. and P. Knapton, T. Longman, T. Shewell, C. Hitch, A. Millar, and R. Dodsley, 1747), 23–26.

28. William K. Wimsatt, *Philosophic Words: A Study of Style and Meaning in the Rambler and Dictionary of Samuel Johnson* (1948; repr., Hamden, CT: Archon Books, 1968), 46. See also Donald J. Greene, "'Pictures of the Mind': Johnson and Imagery," in *Johnson, Boswell, and Their Circle* (Oxford: Clarendon, 1965).

29. Hans Aarsleff, *The Study of Language in England, 1780–1860* (1967; repr., Minneapolis: U of Minnesota P; London: Athlone, 1983), 19–22. See also Murray Cohen, *Sensible Words: Linguistic Practice in England, 1640–1785* (Baltimore: Johns Hopkins UP, 1977), 123, 125–7. David Law's discussion in *The Rhetoric of Empiricism*, 38–50, neatly juxtaposes Richetti's and de Man's interpretations of Locke.

30. See Roger M. White, "Literal Meaning and 'Figurative Meaning,'" *Theoria* 6:71 (2001): 34.

31. See also William Empson's assertion that "the words for mental processes are all derived from older words for physical processes," in *The Structure of Complex Words* (Cambridge, MA: Harvard UP, 1989), 331. The insight is reprised in George Lakoff and Mark Johnson, *Metaphors We Live By* (Chicago: U of Chicago P, 1980), 177; and in Stuart Hampshire, *Justice Is Conflict* (Princeton, NJ: Princeton UP, 2000), 10. Derrida draws on a cognate passage from Hegel's *Philosophy of Fine Arts* in his "White Mythology." See Ricoeur's clarifying discussion of Derrida and Hegel in *Rule of Metaphor*, 286.

32. Donald Davidson, "What Metaphors Mean," in *On Metaphor*, ed. Sheldon Sacks (Chicago: U of Chicago P, 1979), 32.

33. Hans Aarsleff claims that III.i.5 became one of the most cited sections of the *Essay*. See "Locke's Influence," in *The Cambridge Companion to Locke*, ed. Vere Chappell (Cambridge: Cambridge UP, 1994), 273. On the ambiguity of "idea" in this linguistic context, see Walter R. Ott, *Locke's Philosophy of Language* (Cambridge: Cambridge UP, 2004), 3–4.

34. Meillasoux, *After Finitude: An Essay on the Necessity of Contingency* (London: Continuum, 2009), 5, 8.

35. Ibid., 3. See also Ray Brassier, *Nihil Unbound: Enlightenment and Extinction* (Basingstoke: Palgrave Macmillan, 2007), chapters 1 and 3.

36. Kant, *Critique of Pure Reason*, trans. Paul Guyer and Allen W. Wood (Cambridge: Cambridge UP, 1998), A255-7/B310-12. Hannah Arendt, reading the same in Kant, appeals to metaphor to bridge "the abyss between inward and invisible mental

activities and the world of appearances." *The Life of the Mind* (San Diego: Harcourt, 1978), 105. The problem she recognizes is that "there is no analogy," and yet it is by analogy that speculative reason is made manifest as metaphor and transcends the boundary in a seemingly impossible "transition from one existential state, that of thinking, to another, that of being an appearance among appearances" (103).

37. And as Derrida suggests as well. See "Deconstruction and the Other," in *States of Mind: Dialogues with Contemporary Thinkers*, ed. Richard Kearney (Manchester: Manchester UP, 1995), 123.

38. Richards, *The Philosophy of Rhetoric* (London: Oxford UP, 1936). I am here reading Richards's readings. I agree with Roger M. White that Richards's analyses are illuminating but do not constitute a theory of metaphor. See White, *The Structure of Metaphor: The Way the Language of Metaphor Works* (Oxford: Blackwell, 1996), 161–2.

39. Denham, *Coopers Hill* (Humphrey Moseley, 1655), 10.

40. Empson revises Richards and rereads these lines in terms of a "mutual comparison" of river and poem. See *Structure of Complex Words*, 345–6.

41. Rita Felski, "'Context Stinks!,'" *New Literary History* 42:4 (2011): 573–91, at 585–6.

42. As when Alexander Pope takes the Thames as motif in his *Windsor-Forest* (a poem that makes conscious allusion to Denham) and imagines its tide stemmed by the "Feather'd People" of the New World coming to make peaceful contact with the Old (see **Empire**). *Windsor-Forest* (Bernard Lintott, 1713), 17. New and old, ancient and modern, center and periphery: Pope's couplets join and divide. The dialectic inheres even in Pope's individual terms: because nominations of a "feathered race" or "feathered tribe" are periphrases for "birds" in the eighteenth-century poetic diction, Pope's figure of substitution reads uncomfortably against the descriptions of partridge hunting earlier in the poem. The mutual comparisons give back an image of genocide. On the violence of Pope's poem—the "circular and obsessive return to the theme of violence"—see Laura Brown, *Alexander Pope* (Oxford: Blackwell, 1985), 39–40. *Circular, obsessive*: with this endnote offered as my last reading of an eighteenth-century text, the circuit of cross-references may be traced again by the reader who starts over from **Animals**.

43. Empson, *Structure of Complex Words*, 349, 347.

44. See Braudel's "History and the Social Sciences: The *Longue Durée*," in *On History*, trans. Sarah Matthews (Chicago: U of Chicago P, 1980).

45. Johnson, *Prefaces, Biographical and Critical, to the Works of the English Poets* (C. Bathurst et al., 1779), 4:18–9. Johnson invokes Addison's test of translation for wit; see *Spectator* no. 61, in *The Spectator*, ed. D. F. Bond, 5 vols. (Oxford: Clarendon, 1965), 1:263.

46. Hagstrum's reading is in *Samuel Johnson's Literary Criticism* (Minneapolis: U of Minnesota P, 1952), 121–2. Important statements about the difficulty of Johnson's reading are available in Allen Tate, "Johnson on the Metaphysicals," *Kenyon Review*

11:3 (Summer 1949): 379–94; and William Edinger, "Johnson on Conceit: The Limits of Particularity," *English Literary History* (December 1972): 597–619.

Epilogue

1. The database is searchable by means of an inverted index, so-called (in fact, a Solr index) because it substitutes a keyword-structured organization of data for a page-centric one. As a humanist, I remain keenly aware of the inversions: I originally keyword-searched full-text files to create a database, which has been indexed for new searches. Of course, what computer sciences call an "inverted index," humanists call simply an "index" or "concordance." More information about Apache Solr, an open-source Java search server, is available at http://lucene.apache.org/solr/.

2. Geof Bowker credits Jonathan Eisen with coining the term (personal communication). For an example of an empty paper (the abstract reads "Here we present" instead of "Here we argue"), see M. I. Dunitz, P. M. James, G. Jospin, J. A. Eisen, D. A. Coil, and J. A. Chandler, "Draft Genome Sequence of *Tatumella* sp. Strain UCD-D_*suzukii* (Phylum *Proteobacteria*) Isolated from *Drosophila suzukii* Larvae," *GenomeA* 2:2 (2014): doi:10.1128/genomeA.00349-14.

Index